JLA SALVATION RUN

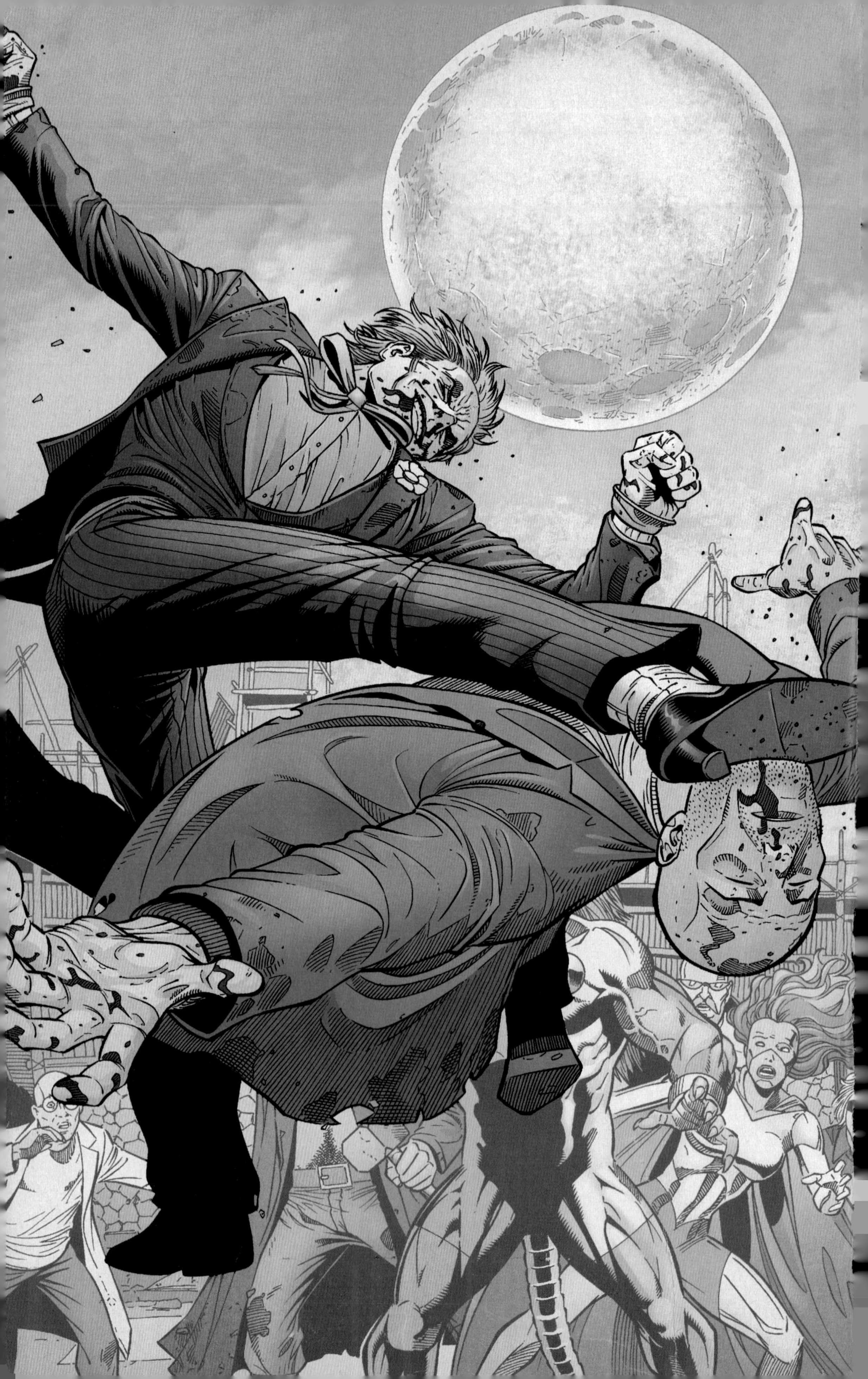

JLA SALVATION RUN

Matthew Sturges
Bill Willingham
Writers

Sean Chen
Joe Bennett
Pencillers

Walden Wong
Belardino Brabo
Wayne Faucher
Inkers

John Kalisz
Tom Chu
Colorists

Steve Wands
Letterer

Sean Chen & Walden Wong, with John Kalisz
Original Covers

Cover art by Joe Corroney

JLA: SALVATION RUN

DC Comics, 1700 Broadway, New York, NY 10019

A Warner Bros. Entertainment Company

Printed in Canada. First Printing.

ISBN: 978-1-4012-1930-7

A PERMANENT SOLUTION WAS NEEDED.

The super-villain problem was getting out of control.

With Black Adam's rampage bringing on World War III, the murder of The Flash by his Rogues Gallery, the Amazon's attack on the United States, and many other recent events causing death and destruction everywhere, it was time to put away the bad guys for good.

Normal prison cells were no longer a viable option. Criminals would be captured, and contained, again and again — but they would inevitably break free, to steal, destroy, and kill again.

Enough was enough.

Enter: Salvation — a once-peaceful planet, now turned into a deadly training ground by unseen forces. For some time, the black ops government strike team known as the Suicide Squad has been doing the dirty work of gathering the world's criminals together, with the intent to use "Boom Tube" technology to send them to Salvation to fend for themselves.

And that time...is now.

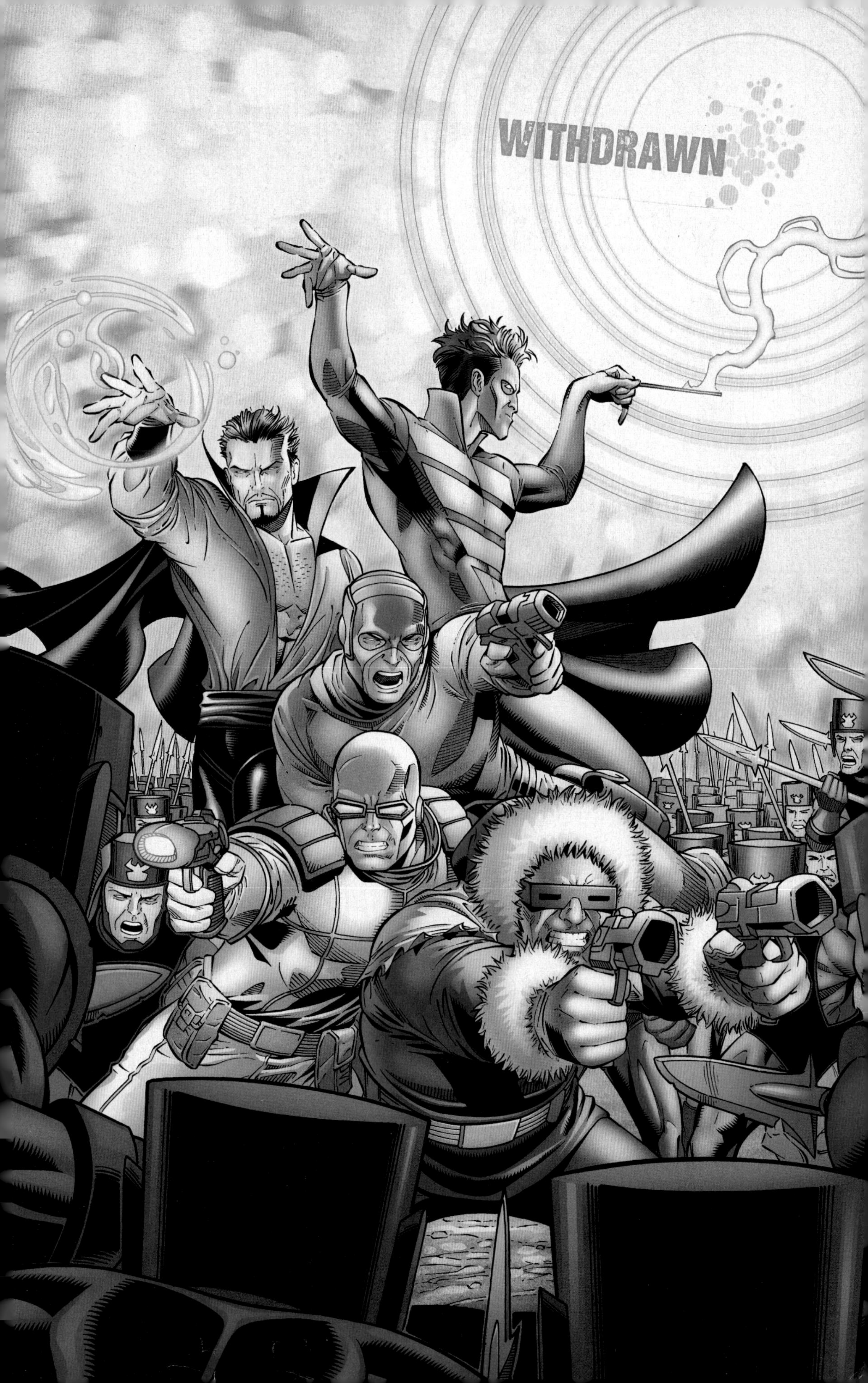

Bill Willingham
Writer

Sean Chen
Penciller

Walden Wong
Inker

John Kalisz
Colorist

Steve Wands
Letterer

CHAPTER ONE

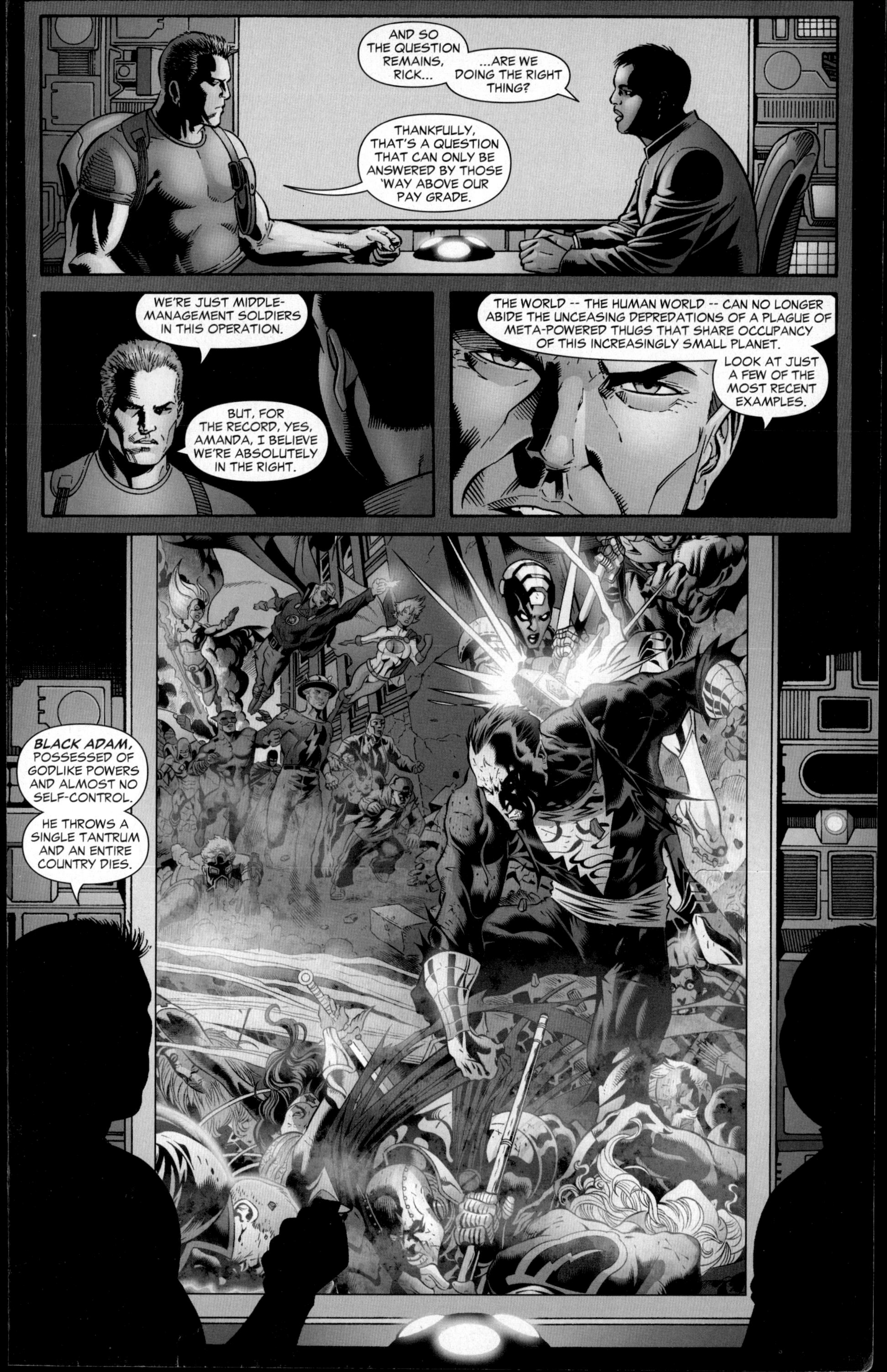
AND SO THE QUESTION REMAINS, RICK...
...ARE WE DOING THE RIGHT THING?
THANKFULLY, THAT'S A QUESTION THAT CAN ONLY BE ANSWERED BY THOSE 'WAY ABOVE OUR PAY GRADE.
WE'RE JUST MIDDLE-MANAGEMENT SOLDIERS IN THIS OPERATION.
BUT, FOR THE RECORD, YES, AMANDA, I BELIEVE WE'RE ABSOLUTELY IN THE RIGHT.
THE WORLD -- THE HUMAN WORLD -- CAN NO LONGER ABIDE THE UNCEASING DEPREDATIONS OF A PLAGUE OF META-POWERED THUGS THAT SHARE OCCUPANCY OF THIS INCREASINGLY SMALL PLANET.
LOOK AT JUST A FEW OF THE MOST RECENT EXAMPLES.
BLACK ADAM, POSSESSED OF GODLIKE POWERS AND ALMOST NO SELF-CONTROL.
HE THROWS A SINGLE TANTRUM AND AN ENTIRE COUNTRY DIES.

"AN ARMY OF AMAZONS ATTACKS THE FREE WORLD IN A FIT OF COLLECTIVE PIQUE OVER OUR PATRIARCHAL AUDACITY IN ACTUALLY IMPRISONING A SUSPECTED MURDERESS.

"AND SUDDENLY WE'RE FIGHTING FOR OUR VERY EXISTENCE.

"ANY TIME SOME OVERPOWERED META GETS HIS NOSE OUT OF JOINT, NORMAL HUMANS PAY THE BLOOD PRICE.

"OR EVEN OUR MOST REVERED HEROES DIE."

SO, YEAH, I THINK IT'S COMPLETELY REASONABLE AS A SPECIES TO DECIDE WE'VE QUITE SIMPLY HAD ENOUGH OF HOMICIDAL METAHUMAN PSYCHOPATHS.

IF I HAD MY WAY, WE'D DUMP THEM IN EMPTY SPACE, SO WE'RE BEING MORE THAN COMPASSIONATE IN GIVING THEM A WORLD OF THEIR OWN TO RUIN.

AND WHO KNOWS? MAYBE THEY'LL SURPRISE THEMSELVES BY FINALLY GROWING UP AND MAKING A LIVABLE SOCIETY OUT OF THEIR NEW HOME.

DO YOU HONESTLY BELIEVE THERE'S A CHANCE IN HELL THEY'LL DO THAT?

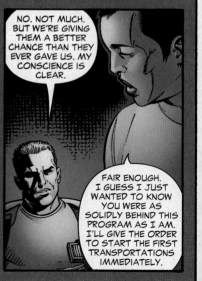

NO. NOT MUCH. BUT WE'RE GIVING THEM A BETTER CHANCE THAN THEY EVER GAVE US. MY CONSCIENCE IS CLEAR.

FAIR ENOUGH. I GUESS I JUST WANTED TO KNOW YOU WERE AS SOLIDLY BEHIND THIS PROGRAM AS I AM. I'LL GIVE THE ORDER TO START THE FIRST TRANSPORTATIONS IMMEDIATELY.

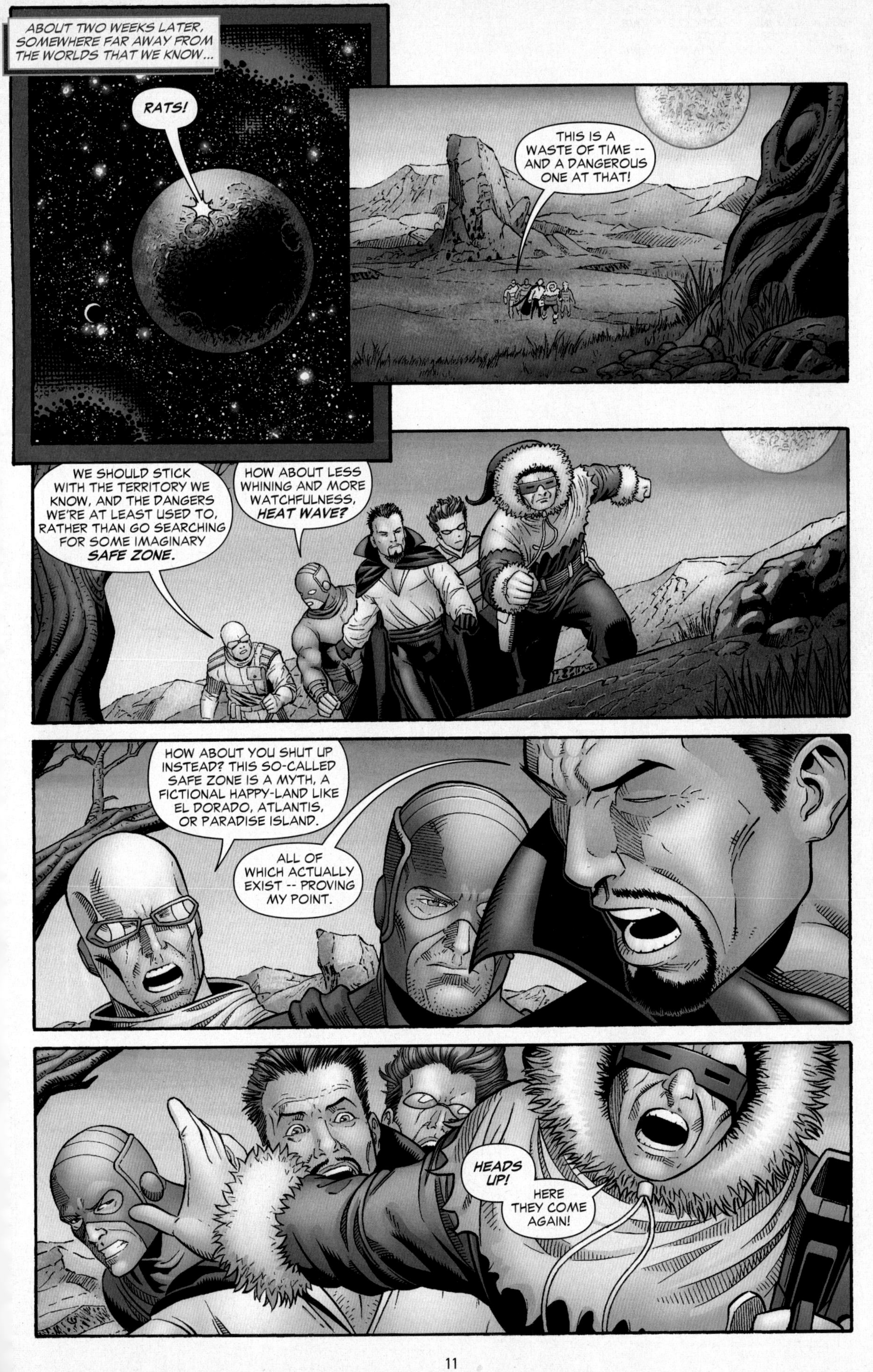
ABOUT TWO WEEKS LATER, SOMEWHERE FAR AWAY FROM THE WORLDS THAT WE KNOW...
RATS!
THIS IS A WASTE OF TIME -- AND A DANGEROUS ONE AT THAT!
WE SHOULD STICK WITH THE TERRITORY WE KNOW, AND THE DANGERS WE'RE AT LEAST USED TO, RATHER THAN GO SEARCHING FOR SOME IMAGINARY SAFE ZONE.
HOW ABOUT LESS WHINING AND MORE WATCHFULNESS, HEAT WAVE?
HOW ABOUT YOU SHUT UP INSTEAD? THIS SO-CALLED SAFE ZONE IS A MYTH, A FICTIONAL HAPPY-LAND LIKE EL DORADO, ATLANTIS, OR PARADISE ISLAND.
ALL OF WHICH ACTUALLY EXIST -- PROVING MY POINT.
HEADS UP!
HERE THEY COME AGAIN!

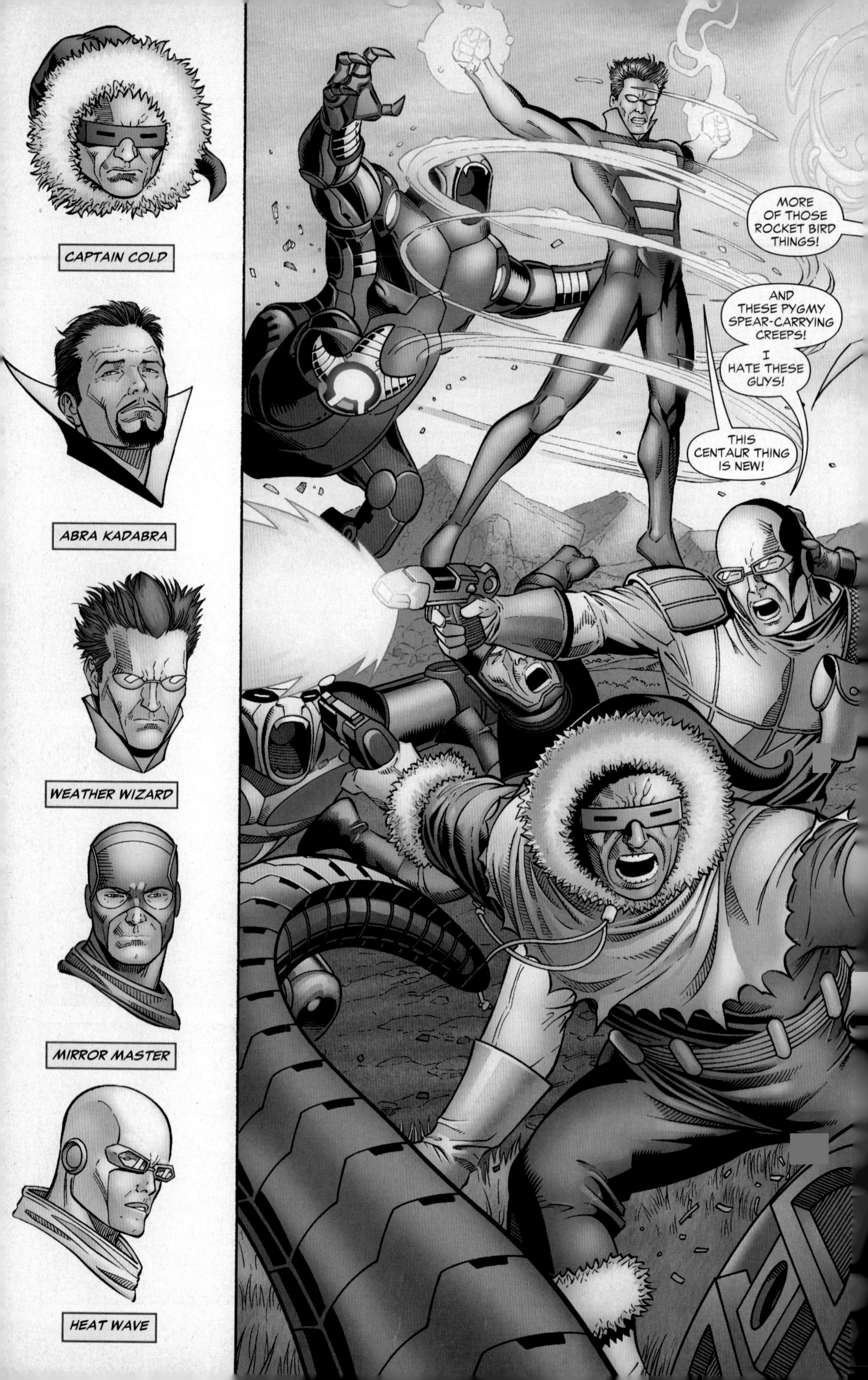
CAPTAIN COLD
ABRA KADABRA
WEATHER WIZARD
MIRROR MASTER
HEAT WAVE
MORE OF THOSE ROCKET BIRD THINGS!
AND THESE PYGMY SPEAR-CARRYING CREEPS!
I HATE THESE GUYS!
THIS CENTAUR THING IS NEW!

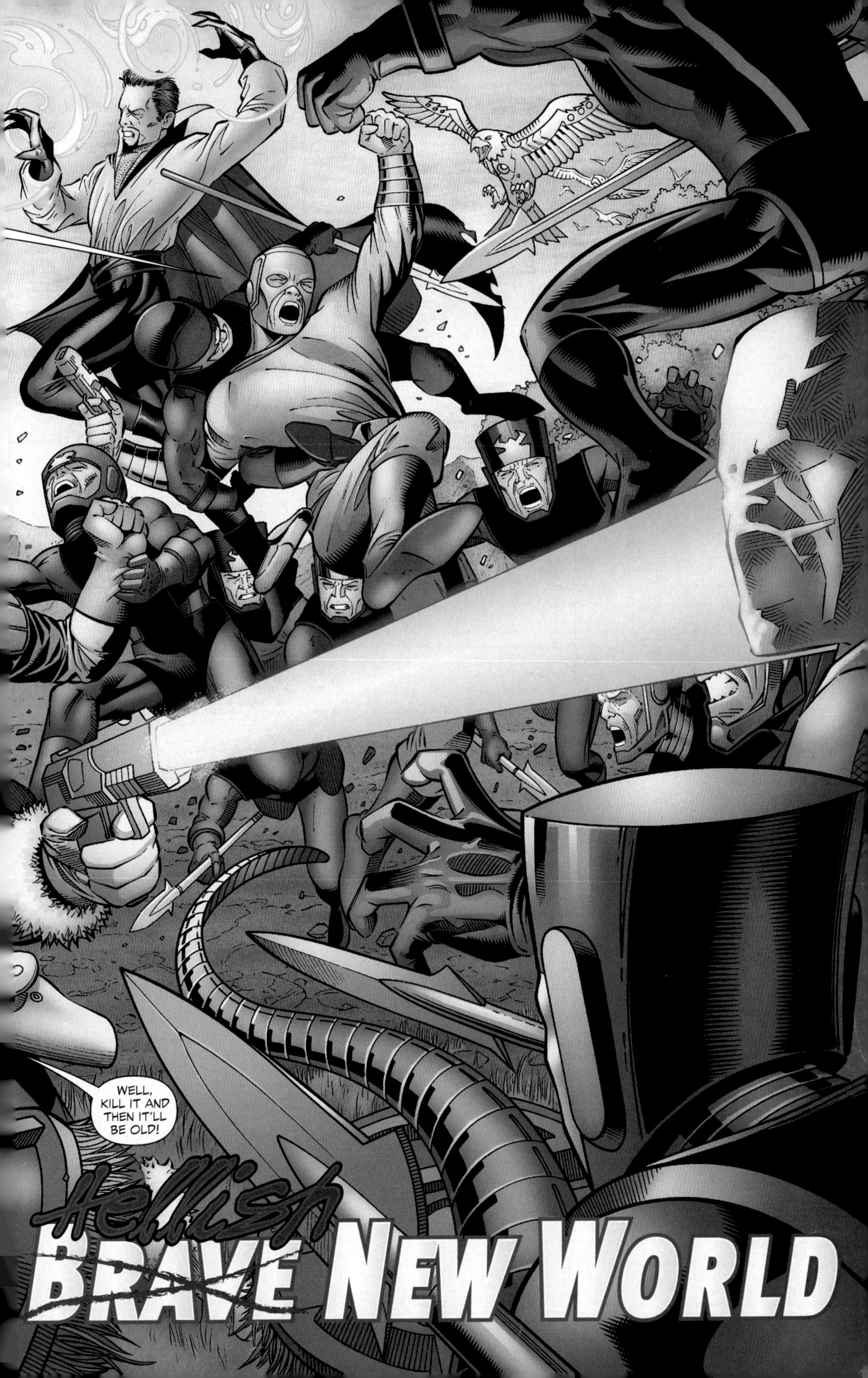

WELL, KILL IT AND THEN IT'LL BE OLD!
Hellish
BRAVE NEW WORLD

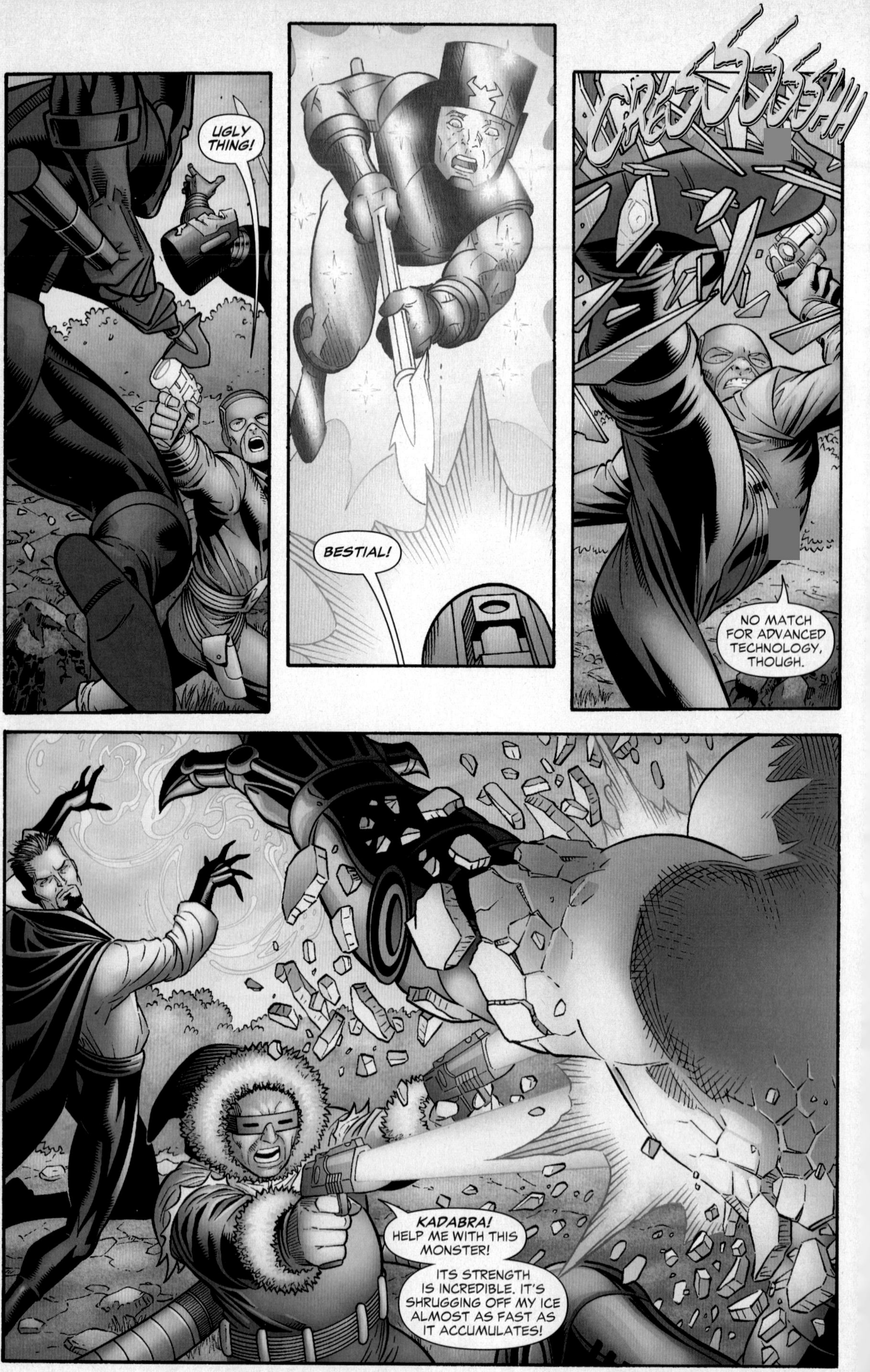
UGLY THING!
BESTIAL!
NO MATCH FOR ADVANCED TECHNOLOGY, THOUGH.
KADABRA! HELP ME WITH THIS MONSTER!
ITS STRENGTH IS INCREDIBLE. IT'S SHRUGGING OFF MY ICE ALMOST AS FAST AS IT ACCUMULATES!

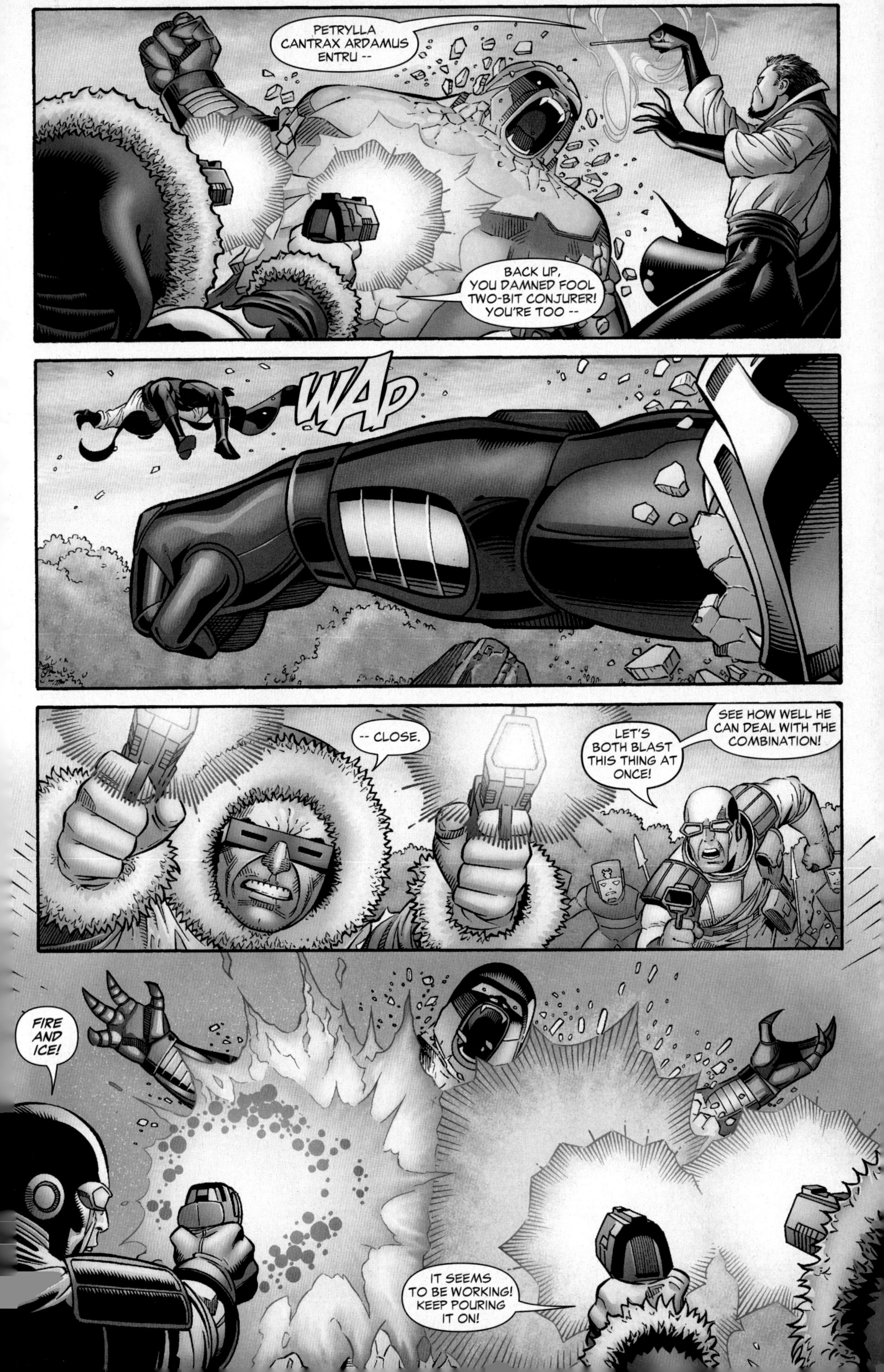
PETRYLLA CANTRAX ARDAMUS ENTRU --
BACK UP, YOU DAMNED FOOL TWO-BIT CONJURER! YOU'RE TOO --
WAP
-- CLOSE.
LET'S BOTH BLAST THIS THING AT ONCE!
SEE HOW WELL HE CAN DEAL WITH THE COMBINATION!
FIRE AND ICE!
IT SEEMS TO BE WORKING! KEEP POURING IT ON!

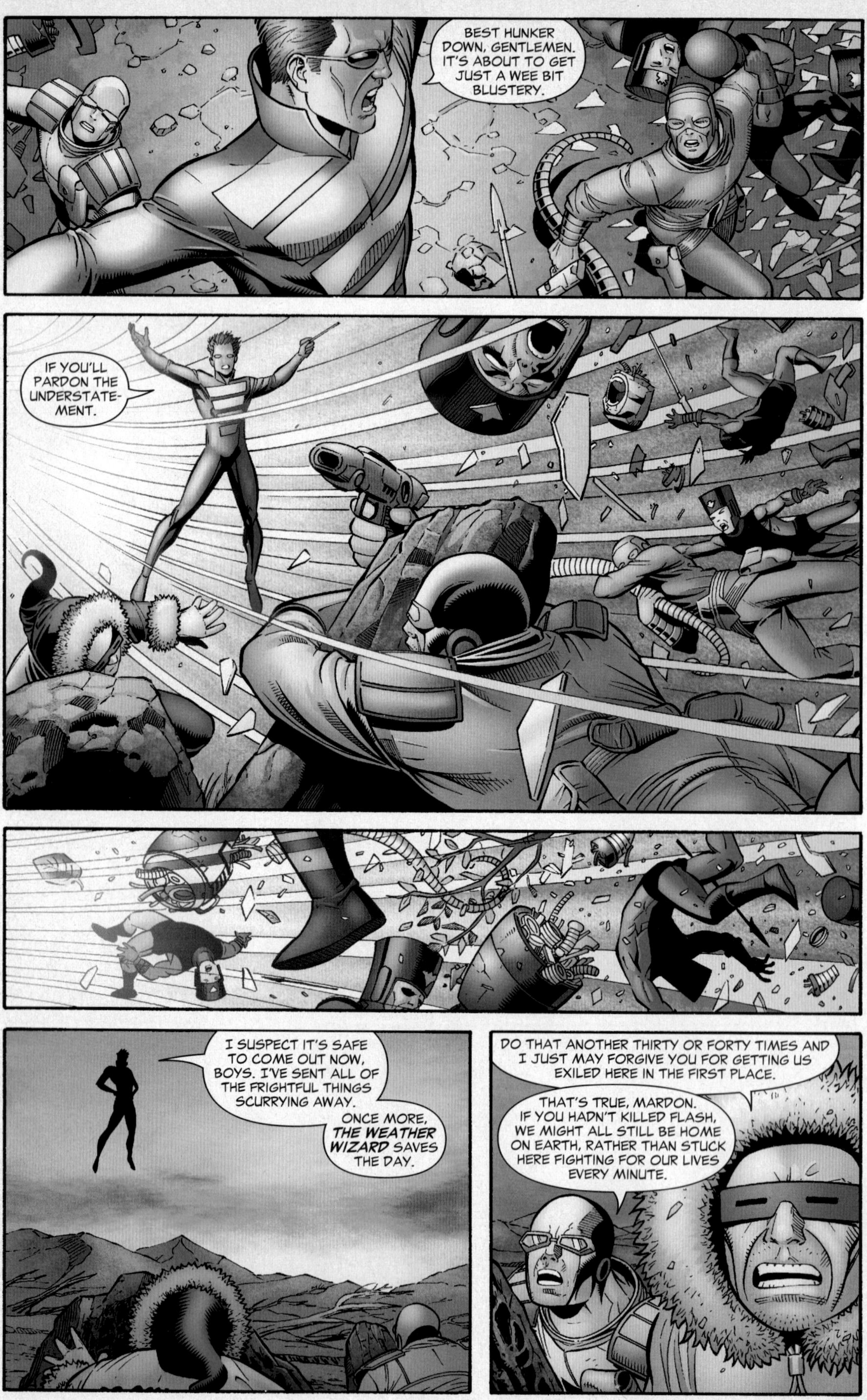
BEST HUNKER DOWN, GENTLEMEN. IT'S ABOUT TO GET JUST A WEE BIT BLUSTERY.
IF YOU'LL PARDON THE UNDERSTATEMENT.
I SUSPECT IT'S SAFE TO COME OUT NOW, BOYS. I'VE SENT ALL OF THE FRIGHTFUL THINGS SCURRYING AWAY.
ONCE MORE, **THE WEATHER WIZARD** SAVES THE DAY.
DO THAT ANOTHER THIRTY OR FORTY TIMES AND I JUST MAY FORGIVE YOU FOR GETTING US EXILED HERE IN THE FIRST PLACE.
THAT'S TRUE, MARDON. IF YOU HADN'T KILLED FLASH, WE MIGHT ALL STILL BE HOME ON EARTH, RATHER THAN STUCK HERE FIGHTING FOR OUR LIVES EVERY MINUTE.

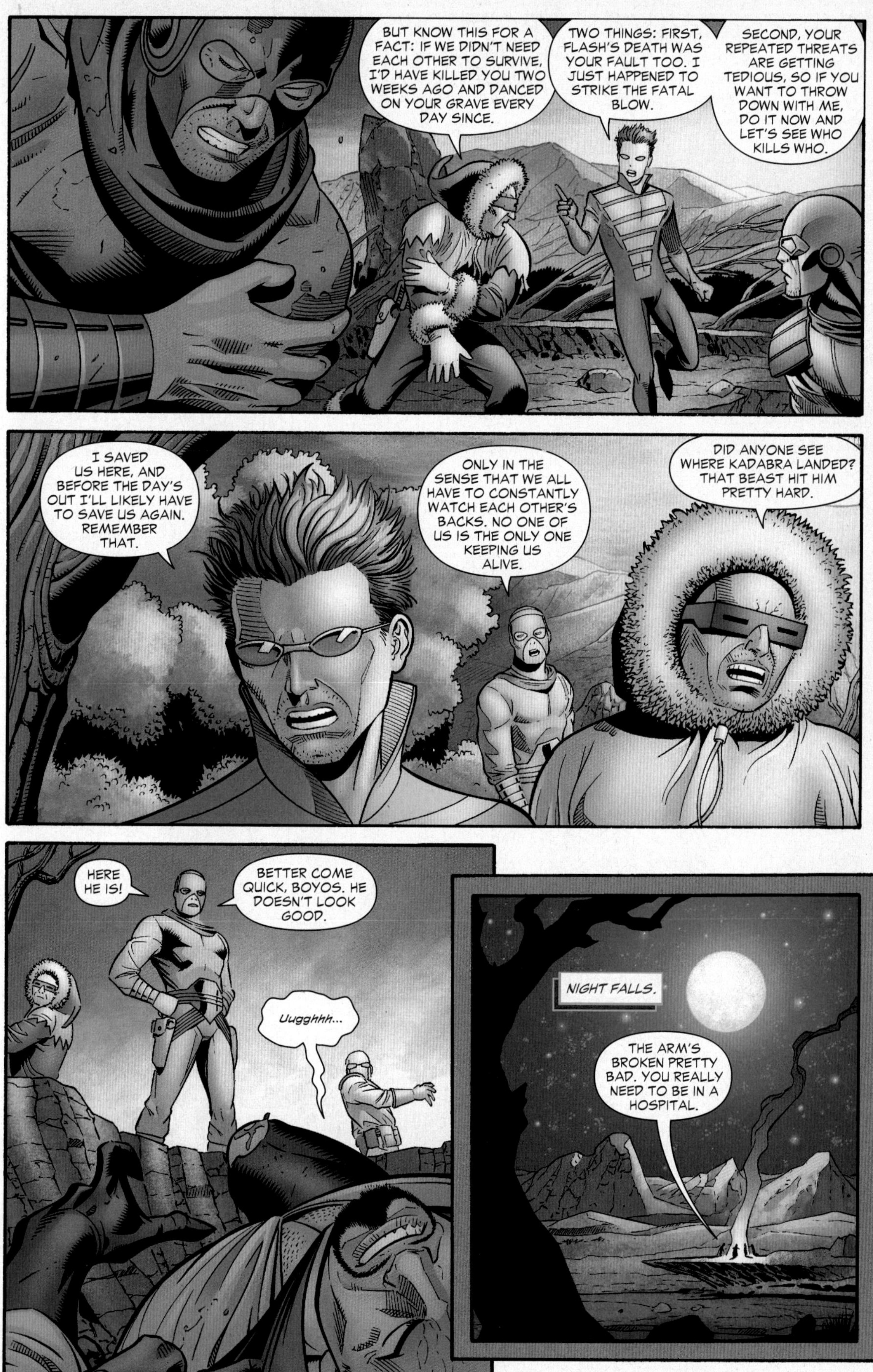
BUT KNOW THIS FOR A FACT: IF WE DIDN'T NEED EACH OTHER TO SURVIVE, I'D HAVE KILLED YOU TWO WEEKS AGO AND DANCED ON YOUR GRAVE EVERY DAY SINCE.
TWO THINGS: FIRST, FLASH'S DEATH WAS YOUR FAULT TOO. I JUST HAPPENED TO STRIKE THE FATAL BLOW.
SECOND, YOUR REPEATED THREATS ARE GETTING TEDIOUS, SO IF YOU WANT TO THROW DOWN WITH ME, DO IT NOW AND LET'S SEE WHO KILLS WHO.
I SAVED US HERE, AND BEFORE THE DAY'S OUT I'LL LIKELY HAVE TO SAVE US AGAIN. REMEMBER THAT.
ONLY IN THE SENSE THAT WE ALL HAVE TO CONSTANTLY WATCH EACH OTHER'S BACKS. NO ONE OF US IS THE ONLY ONE KEEPING US ALIVE.
DID ANYONE SEE WHERE KADABRA LANDED? THAT BEAST HIT HIM PRETTY HARD.
HERE HE IS!
BETTER COME QUICK, BOYOS. HE DOESN'T LOOK GOOD.
Uugghhh...
NIGHT FALLS.
THE ARM'S BROKEN PRETTY BAD. YOU REALLY NEED TO BE IN A HOSPITAL.

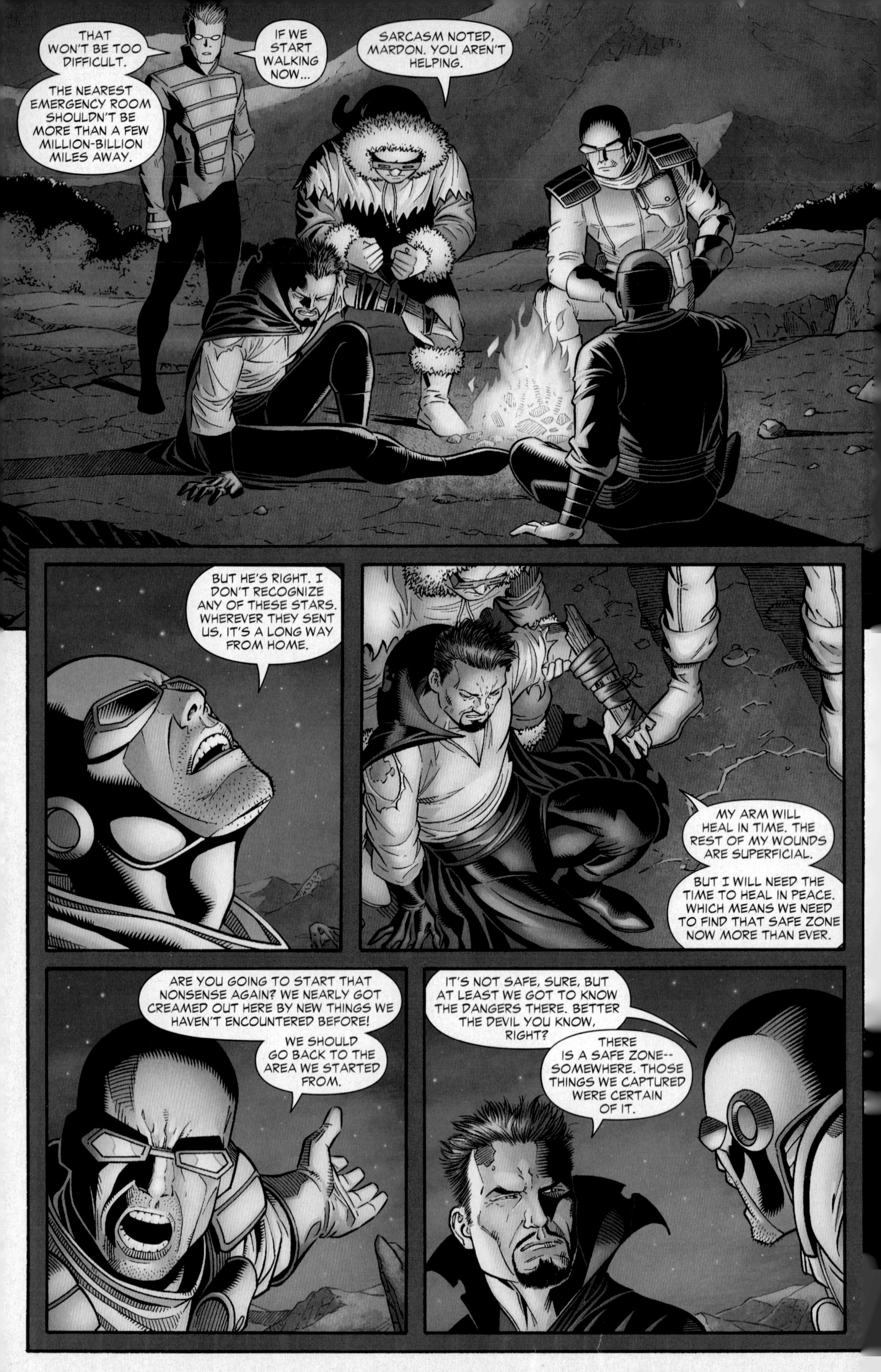
THAT WON'T BE TOO DIFFICULT.
THE NEAREST EMERGENCY ROOM SHOULDN'T BE MORE THAN A FEW MILLION-BILLION MILES AWAY.
IF WE START WALKING NOW...
SARCASM NOTED, MARDON. YOU AREN'T HELPING.
BUT HE'S RIGHT. I DON'T RECOGNIZE ANY OF THESE STARS. WHEREVER THEY SENT US, IT'S A LONG WAY FROM HOME.
MY ARM WILL HEAL IN TIME. THE REST OF MY WOUNDS ARE SUPERFICIAL.
BUT I WILL NEED THE TIME TO HEAL IN PEACE. WHICH MEANS WE NEED TO FIND THAT SAFE ZONE NOW MORE THAN EVER.
ARE YOU GOING TO START THAT NONSENSE AGAIN? WE NEARLY GOT CREAMED OUT HERE BY NEW THINGS WE HAVEN'T ENCOUNTERED BEFORE!
WE SHOULD GO BACK TO THE AREA WE STARTED FROM.
IT'S NOT SAFE, SURE, BUT AT LEAST WE GOT TO KNOW THE DANGERS THERE. BETTER THE DEVIL YOU KNOW, RIGHT?
THERE IS A SAFE ZONE-- SOMEWHERE. THOSE THINGS WE CAPTURED WERE CERTAIN OF IT.

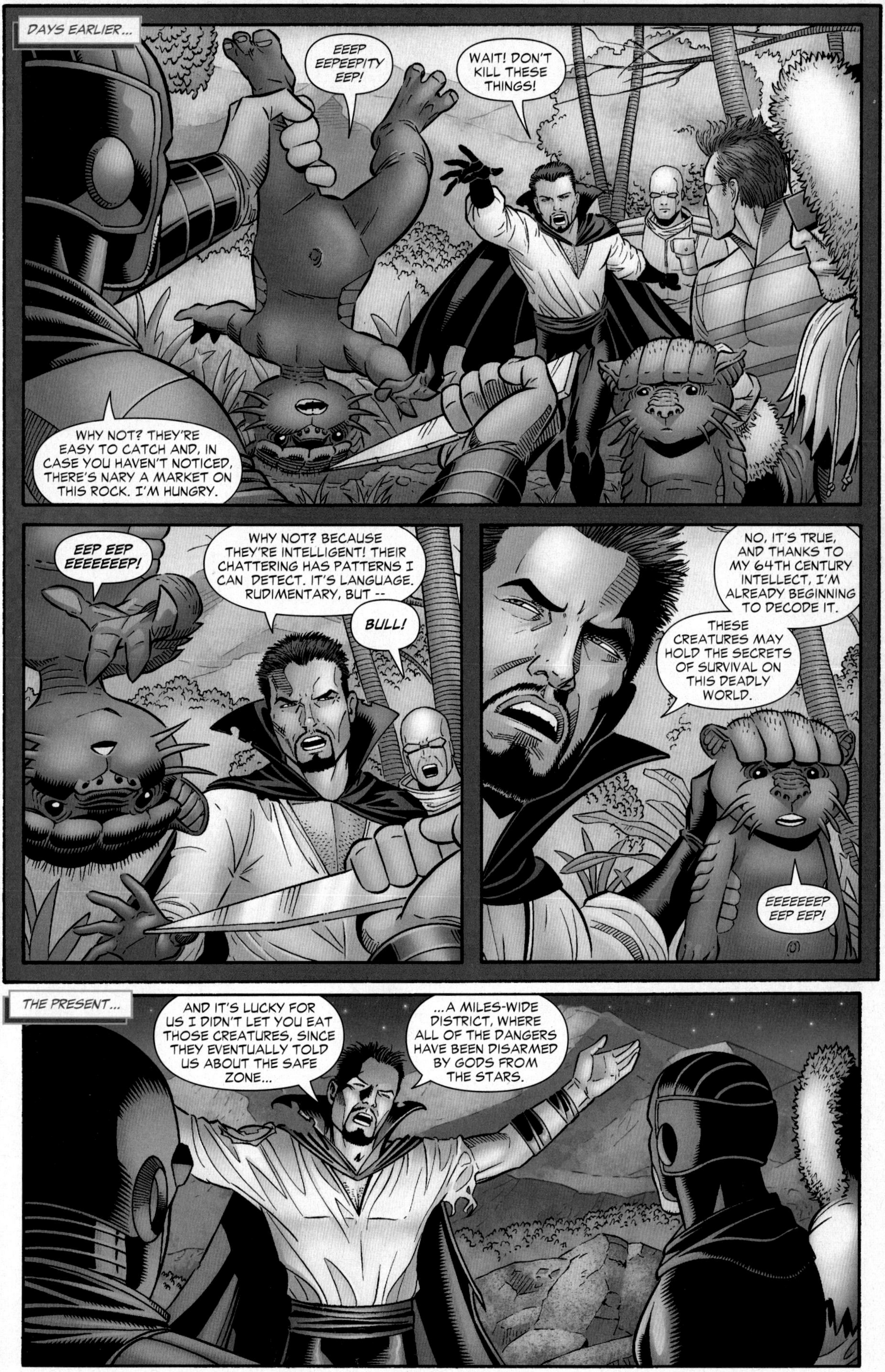
DAYS EARLIER...
EEEP EEPEEPITY EEP!
WAIT! DON'T KILL THESE THINGS!
WHY NOT? THEY'RE EASY TO CATCH AND, IN CASE YOU HAVEN'T NOTICED, THERE'S NARY A MARKET ON THIS ROCK. I'M HUNGRY.
EEP EEP EEEEEEEP!
WHY NOT? BECAUSE THEY'RE INTELLIGENT! THEIR CHATTERING HAS PATTERNS I CAN DETECT. IT'S LANGUAGE. RUDIMENTARY, BUT --
BULL!
NO, IT'S TRUE, AND THANKS TO MY 64TH CENTURY INTELLECT, I'M ALREADY BEGINNING TO DECODE IT.
THESE CREATURES MAY HOLD THE SECRETS OF SURVIVAL ON THIS DEADLY WORLD.
EEEEEEEP EEP EEP!
THE PRESENT...
AND IT'S LUCKY FOR US I DIDN'T LET YOU EAT THOSE CREATURES, SINCE THEY EVENTUALLY TOLD US ABOUT THE SAFE ZONE...
...A MILES-WIDE DISTRICT, WHERE ALL OF THE DANGERS HAVE BEEN DISARMED BY GODS FROM THE STARS.

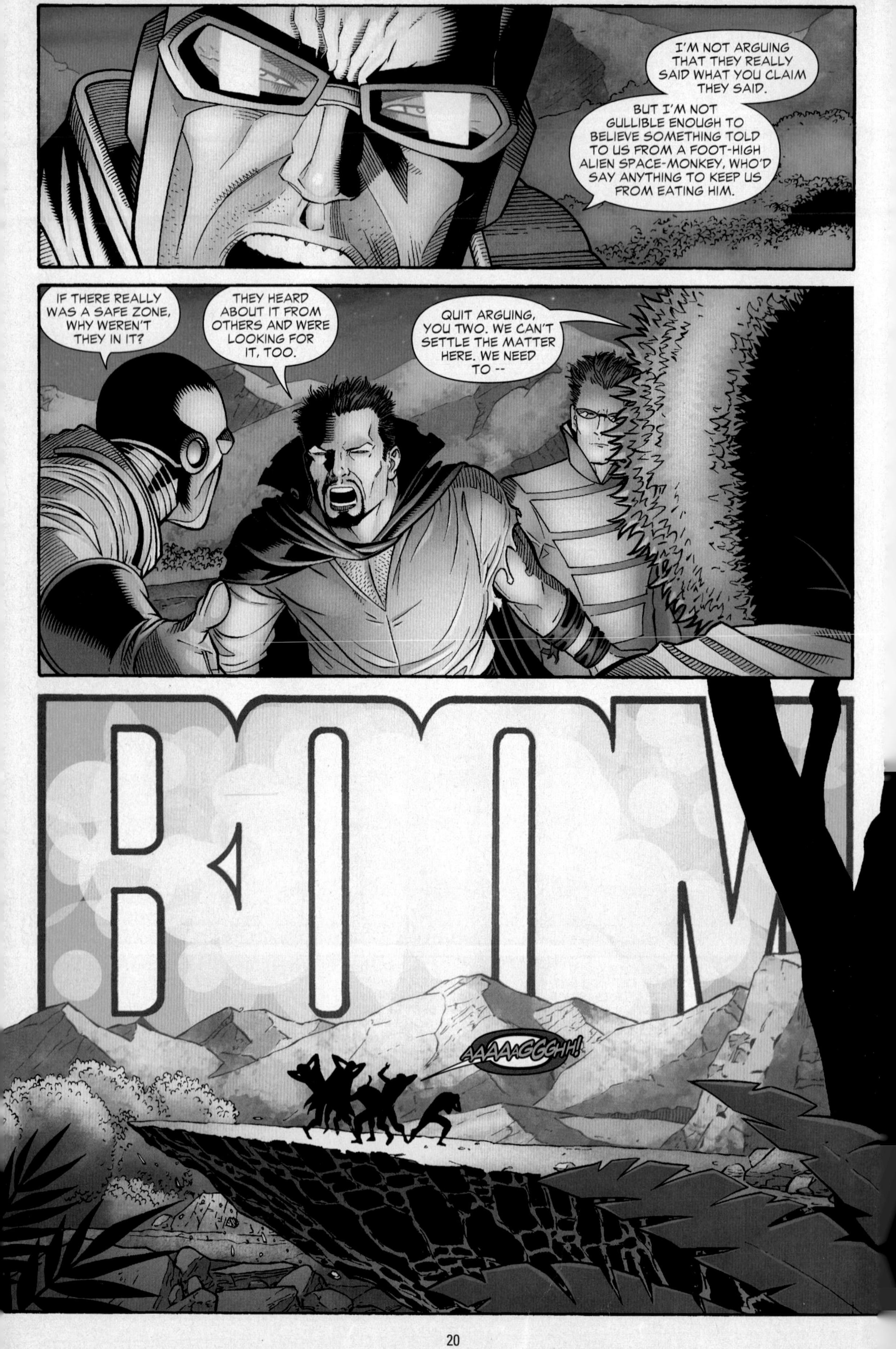
I'M NOT ARGUING THAT THEY REALLY SAID WHAT YOU CLAIM THEY SAID.
BUT I'M NOT GULLIBLE ENOUGH TO BELIEVE SOMETHING TOLD TO US FROM A FOOT-HIGH ALIEN SPACE-MONKEY, WHO'D SAY ANYTHING TO KEEP US FROM EATING HIM.
IF THERE REALLY WAS A SAFE ZONE, WHY WEREN'T THEY IN IT?
THEY HEARD ABOUT IT FROM OTHERS AND WERE LOOKING FOR IT, TOO.
QUIT ARGUING, YOU TWO. WE CAN'T SETTLE THE MATTER HERE. WE NEED TO --
BOOM
AAAAAGGGHH!

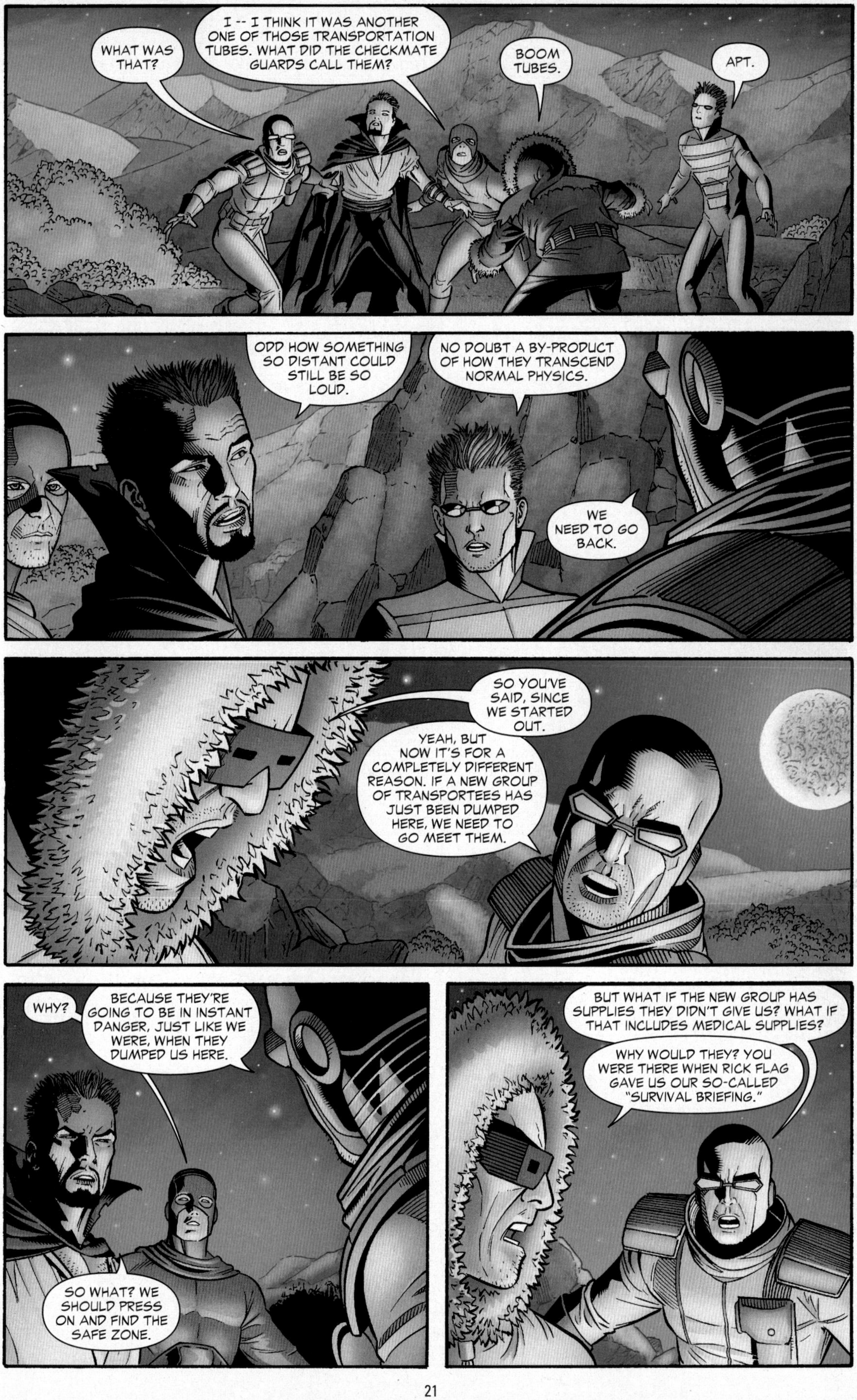
WHAT WAS THAT?
I -- I THINK IT WAS ANOTHER ONE OF THOSE TRANSPORTATION TUBES. WHAT DID THE CHECKMATE GUARDS CALL THEM?
BOOM TUBES.
APT.
ODD HOW SOMETHING SO DISTANT COULD STILL BE SO LOUD.
NO DOUBT A BY-PRODUCT OF HOW THEY TRANSCEND NORMAL PHYSICS.
WE NEED TO GO BACK.
SO YOU'VE SAID, SINCE WE STARTED OUT.
YEAH, BUT NOW IT'S FOR A COMPLETELY DIFFERENT REASON. IF A NEW GROUP OF TRANSPORTEES HAS JUST BEEN DUMPED HERE, WE NEED TO GO MEET THEM.
WHY?
BECAUSE THEY'RE GOING TO BE IN INSTANT DANGER, JUST LIKE WE WERE, WHEN THEY DUMPED US HERE.
SO WHAT? WE SHOULD PRESS ON AND FIND THE SAFE ZONE.
BUT WHAT IF THE NEW GROUP HAS SUPPLIES THEY DIDN'T GIVE US? WHAT IF THAT INCLUDES MEDICAL SUPPLIES?
WHY WOULD THEY? YOU WERE THERE WHEN RICK FLAG GAVE US OUR SO-CALLED "SURVIVAL BRIEFING."

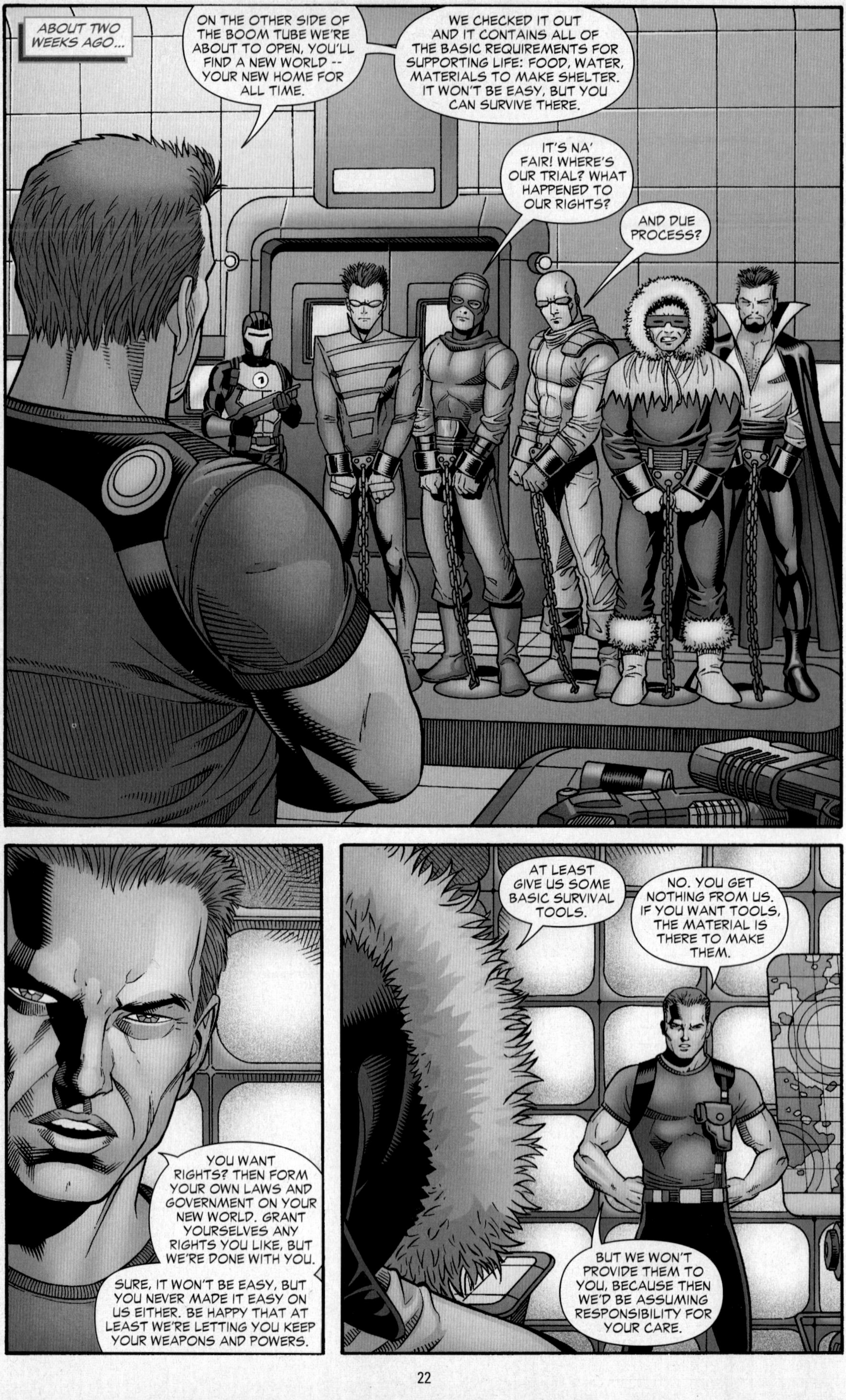

ABOUT TWO WEEKS AGO...
ON THE OTHER SIDE OF THE BOOM TUBE WE'RE ABOUT TO OPEN, YOU'LL FIND A NEW WORLD -- YOUR NEW HOME FOR ALL TIME.
WE CHECKED IT OUT AND IT CONTAINS ALL OF THE BASIC REQUIREMENTS FOR SUPPORTING LIFE: FOOD, WATER, MATERIALS TO MAKE SHELTER. IT WON'T BE EASY, BUT YOU CAN SURVIVE THERE.
IT'S NA' FAIR! WHERE'S OUR TRIAL? WHAT HAPPENED TO OUR RIGHTS?
AND DUE PROCESS?
YOU WANT RIGHTS? THEN FORM YOUR OWN LAWS AND GOVERNMENT ON YOUR NEW WORLD. GRANT YOURSELVES ANY RIGHTS YOU LIKE, BUT WE'RE DONE WITH YOU.
SURE, IT WON'T BE EASY, BUT YOU NEVER MADE IT EASY ON US EITHER. BE HAPPY THAT AT LEAST WE'RE LETTING YOU KEEP YOUR WEAPONS AND POWERS.
AT LEAST GIVE US SOME BASIC SURVIVAL TOOLS.
NO. YOU GET NOTHING FROM US. IF YOU WANT TOOLS, THE MATERIAL IS THERE TO MAKE THEM.
BUT WE WON'T PROVIDE THEM TO YOU, BECAUSE THEN WE'D BE ASSUMING RESPONSIBILITY FOR YOUR CARE.

AND YOU AREN'T OUR RESPONSIBILITY ANY LONGER. FOR THE FIRST TIME IN YOUR WRETCHED LIVES, YOU HAVE TO ASSUME SOLE ACCOUNTABILITY FOR YOURSELVES.

UNDERSTAND THAT THIS ISN'T A PUNISHMENT. IF YOU CAN PROSPER THERE, MORE POWER TO YOU. BUT THIS WORLD IS BONE WEARY OF YOU AND YOUR ILK.

SO WE'VE DECIDED TO WASH OUR HANDS OF YOU, ONCE AND FOREVER. YOU'VE EACH TRIED TO CONQUER THE WORLD BEFORE, NOW WE'RE GRANTING YOUR WISH.

A WORLD OF YOUR OWN TO CONQUER.

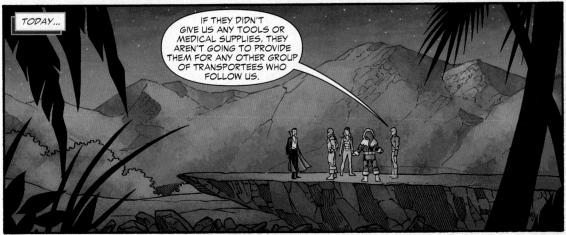

TODAY...

IF THEY DIDN'T GIVE US ANY TOOLS OR MEDICAL SUPPLIES, THEY AREN'T GOING TO PROVIDE THEM FOR ANY OTHER GROUP OF TRANSPORTEES WHO FOLLOW US.

FAIR ENOUGH, BUT THERE'S ONE OTHER REASON WE SHOULD CHECK TO SEE WHO ELSE HAS ARRIVED.

WHAT WOULD THAT BE?

WOMEN.

WHAT IF THERE'RE SOME FEMALES IN THIS NEW GROUP?

I DO BELIEVE *HEAT WAVE* HAS JUST MADE SENSE FOR THE FIRST TIME TODAY.

WORRY ABOUT THAT LATER!

23

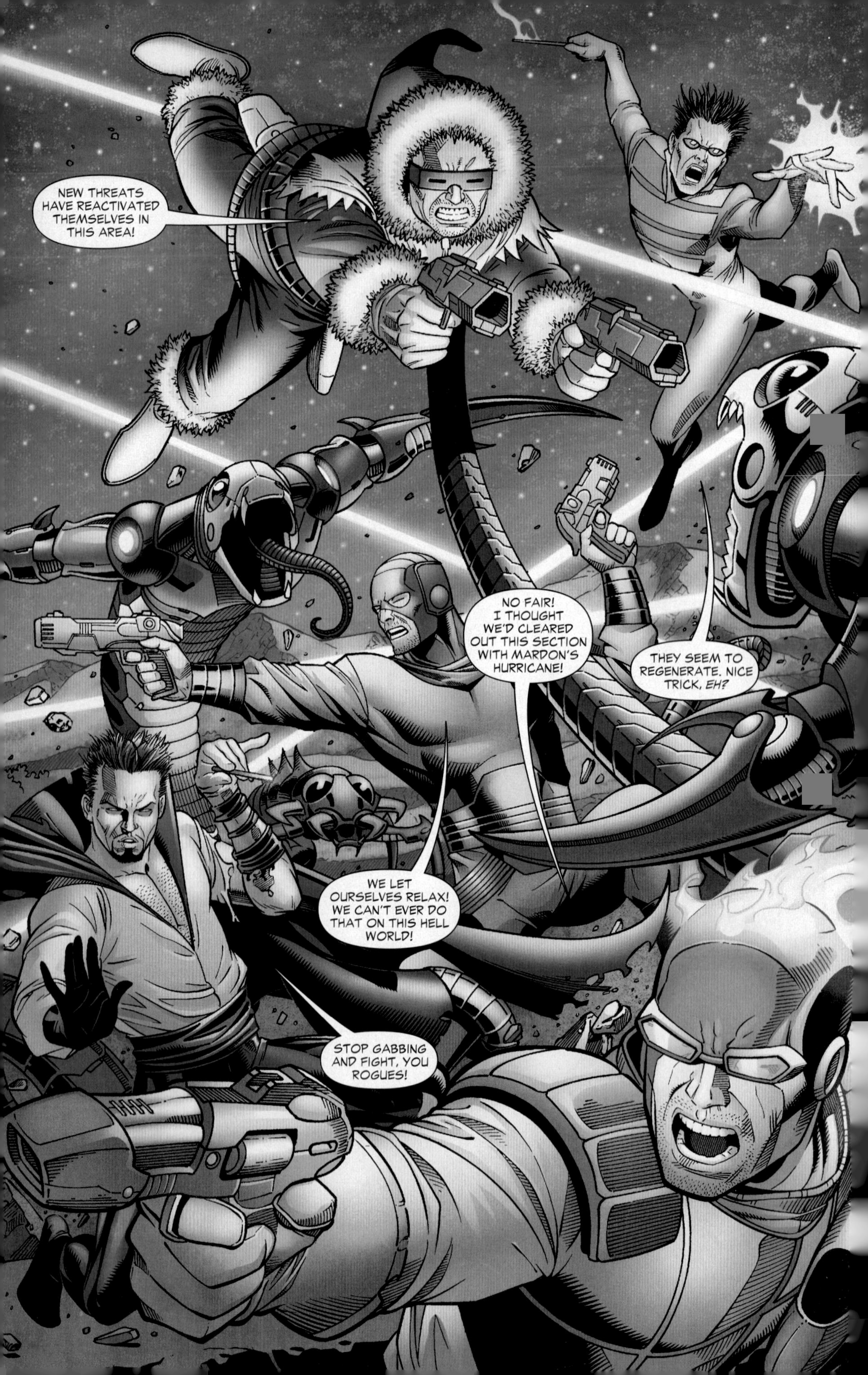
NEW THREATS HAVE REACTIVATED THEMSELVES IN THIS AREA!
NO FAIR! I THOUGHT WE'D CLEARED OUT THIS SECTION WITH MARDON'S HURRICANE!
THEY SEEM TO REGENERATE. NICE TRICK, EH?
WE LET OURSELVES RELAX! WE CAN'T EVER DO THAT ON THIS HELL WORLD!
STOP GABBING AND FIGHT, YOU ROGUES!

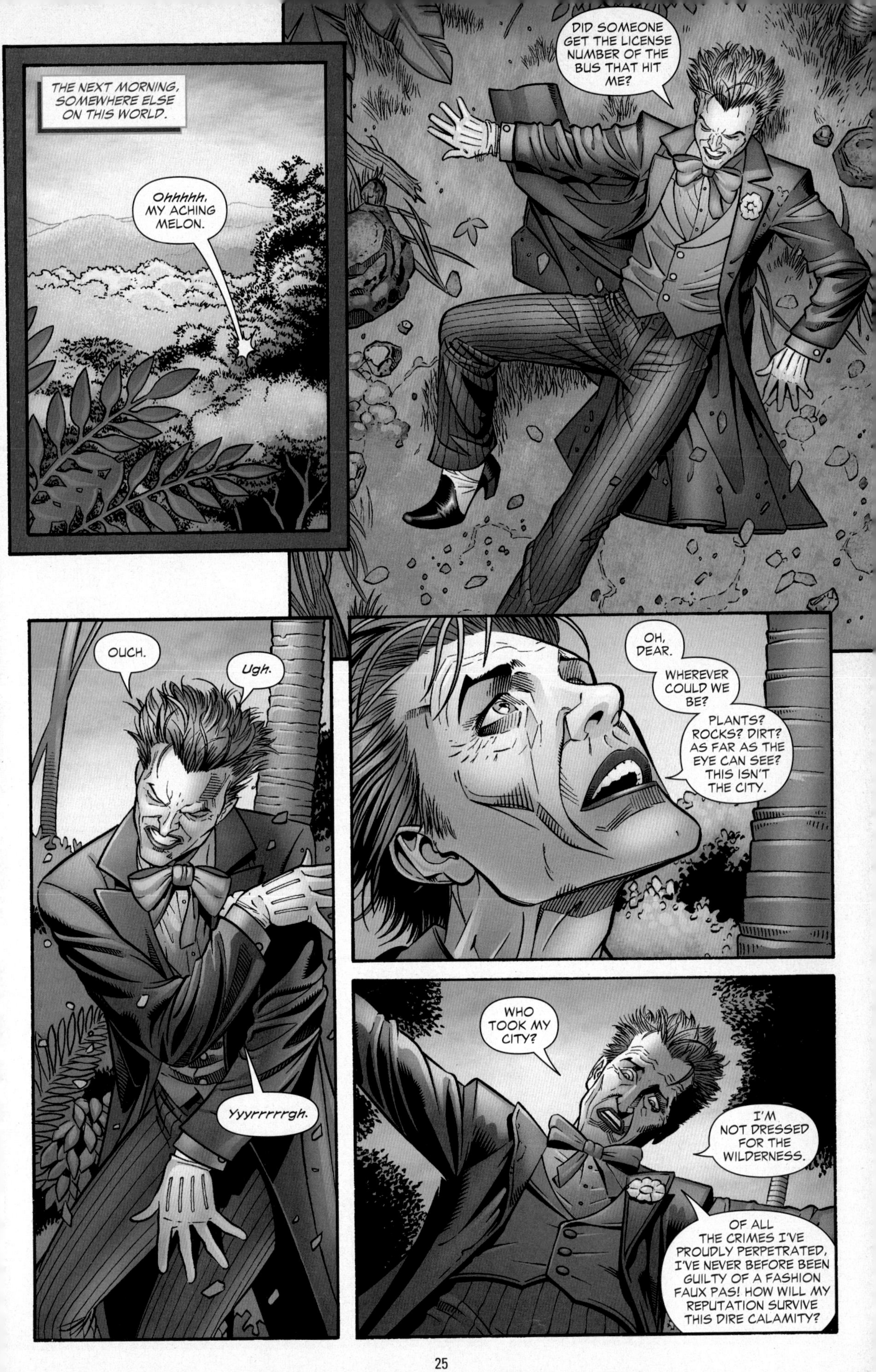

THE NEXT MORNING, SOMEWHERE ELSE ON THIS WORLD.
Ohhhhh. MY ACHING MELON.
DID SOMEONE GET THE LICENSE NUMBER OF THE BUS THAT HIT ME?
OUCH.
Ugh.
Yyyrrrrrgh.
OH, DEAR.
WHEREVER COULD WE BE?
PLANTS? ROCKS? DIRT? AS FAR AS THE EYE CAN SEE? THIS ISN'T THE CITY.
WHO TOOK MY CITY?
I'M NOT DRESSED FOR THE WILDERNESS.
OF ALL THE CRIMES I'VE PROUDLY PERPETRATED, I'VE NEVER BEFORE BEEN GUILTY OF A FASHION FAUX PAS! HOW WILL MY REPUTATION SURVIVE THIS DIRE CALAMITY?

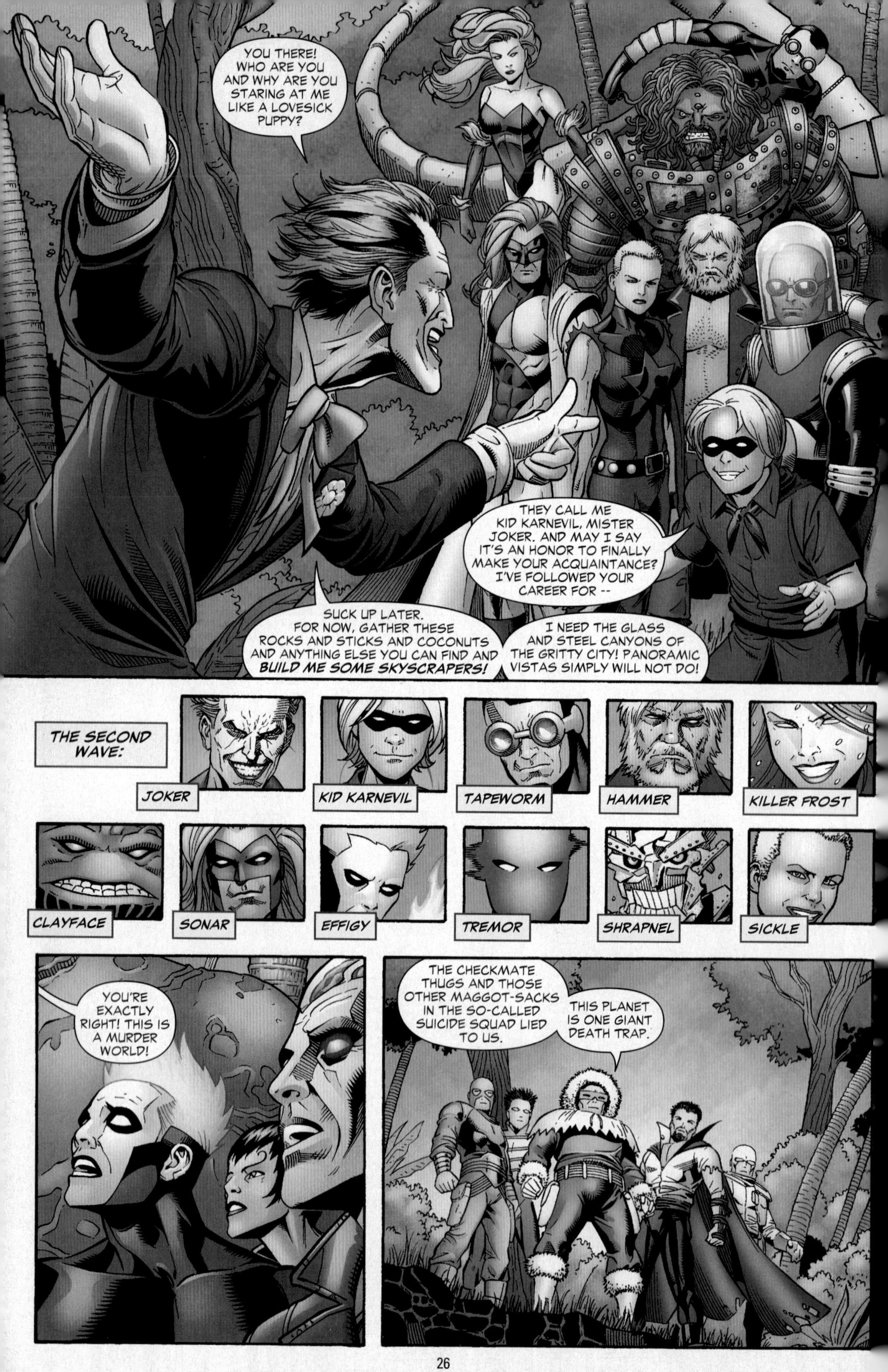
YOU THERE! WHO ARE YOU AND WHY ARE YOU STARING AT ME LIKE A LOVESICK PUPPY?
THEY CALL ME KID KARNEVIL, MISTER JOKER. AND MAY I SAY IT'S AN HONOR TO FINALLY MAKE YOUR ACQUAINTANCE? I'VE FOLLOWED YOUR CAREER FOR --
SUCK UP LATER. FOR NOW, GATHER THESE ROCKS AND STICKS AND COCONUTS AND ANYTHING ELSE YOU CAN FIND AND BUILD ME SOME SKYSCRAPERS!
I NEED THE GLASS AND STEEL CANYONS OF THE GRITTY CITY! PANORAMIC VISTAS SIMPLY WILL NOT DO!
THE SECOND WAVE:
JOKER
KID KARNEVIL
TAPEWORM
HAMMER
KILLER FROST
CLAYFACE
SONAR
EFFIGY
TREMOR
SHRAPNEL
SICKLE
YOU'RE EXACTLY RIGHT! THIS IS A MURDER WORLD!
THE CHECKMATE THUGS AND THOSE OTHER MAGGOT-SACKS IN THE SO-CALLED SUICIDE SQUAD LIED TO US.
THIS PLANET IS ONE GIANT DEATH TRAP.

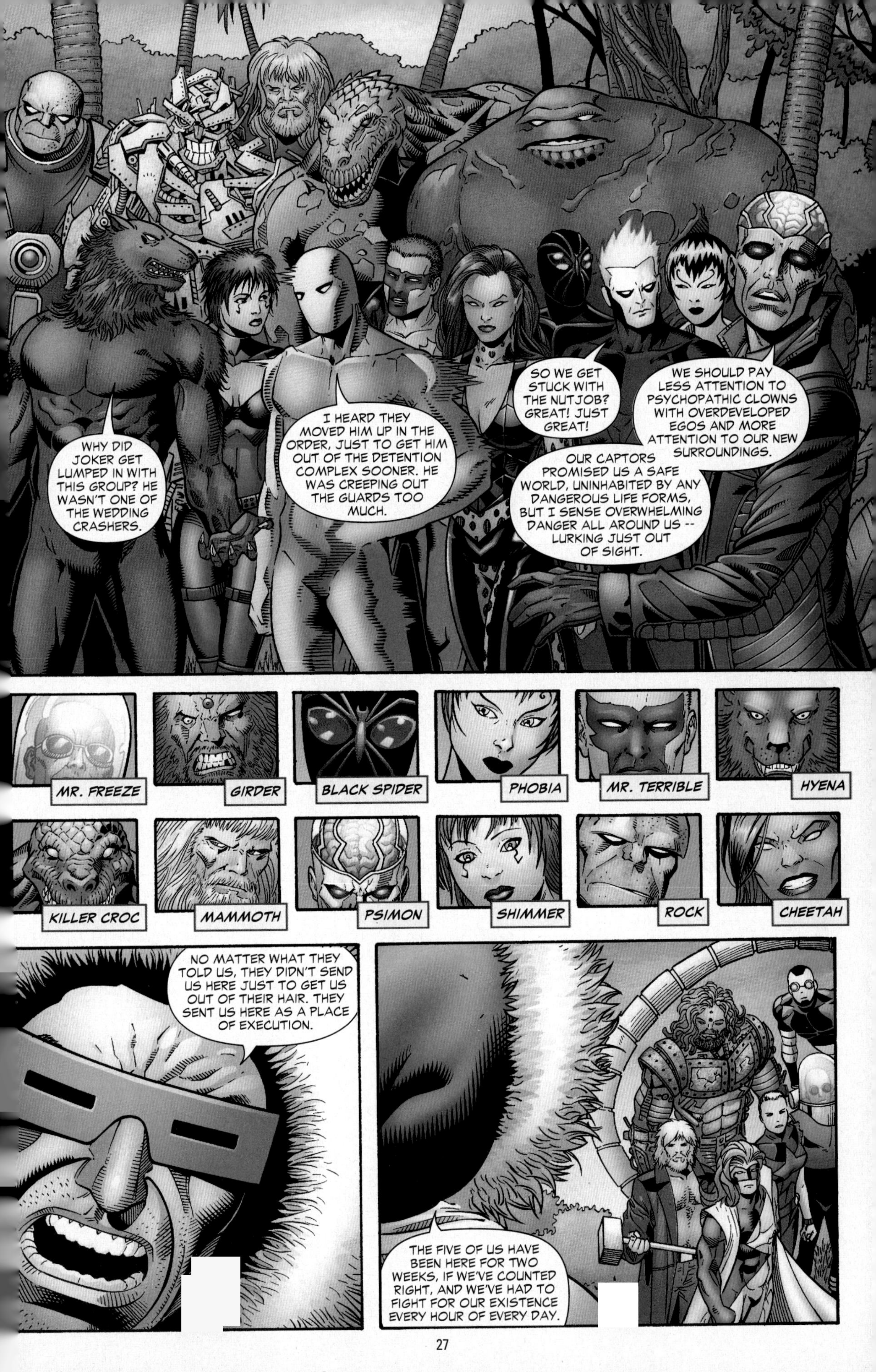
WHY DID JOKER GET LUMPED IN WITH THIS GROUP? HE WASN'T ONE OF THE WEDDING CRASHERS.
I HEARD THEY MOVED HIM UP IN THE ORDER, JUST TO GET HIM OUT OF THE DETENTION COMPLEX SOONER. HE WAS CREEPING OUT THE GUARDS TOO MUCH.
SO WE GET STUCK WITH THE NUTJOB? GREAT! JUST GREAT!
WE SHOULD PAY LESS ATTENTION TO PSYCHOPATHIC CLOWNS WITH OVERDEVELOPED EGOS AND MORE ATTENTION TO OUR NEW SURROUNDINGS.
OUR CAPTORS PROMISED US A SAFE WORLD, UNINHABITED BY ANY DANGEROUS LIFE FORMS, BUT I SENSE OVERWHELMING DANGER ALL AROUND US -- LURKING JUST OUT OF SIGHT.
MR. FREEZE
GIRDER
BLACK SPIDER
PHOBIA
MR. TERRIBLE
HYENA
KILLER CROC
MAMMOTH
PSIMON
SHIMMER
ROCK
CHEETAH
NO MATTER WHAT THEY TOLD US, THEY DIDN'T SEND US HERE JUST TO GET US OUT OF THEIR HAIR. THEY SENT US HERE AS A PLACE OF EXECUTION.
THE FIVE OF US HAVE BEEN HERE FOR TWO WEEKS, IF WE'VE COUNTED RIGHT, AND WE'VE HAD TO FIGHT FOR OUR EXISTENCE EVERY HOUR OF EVERY DAY.

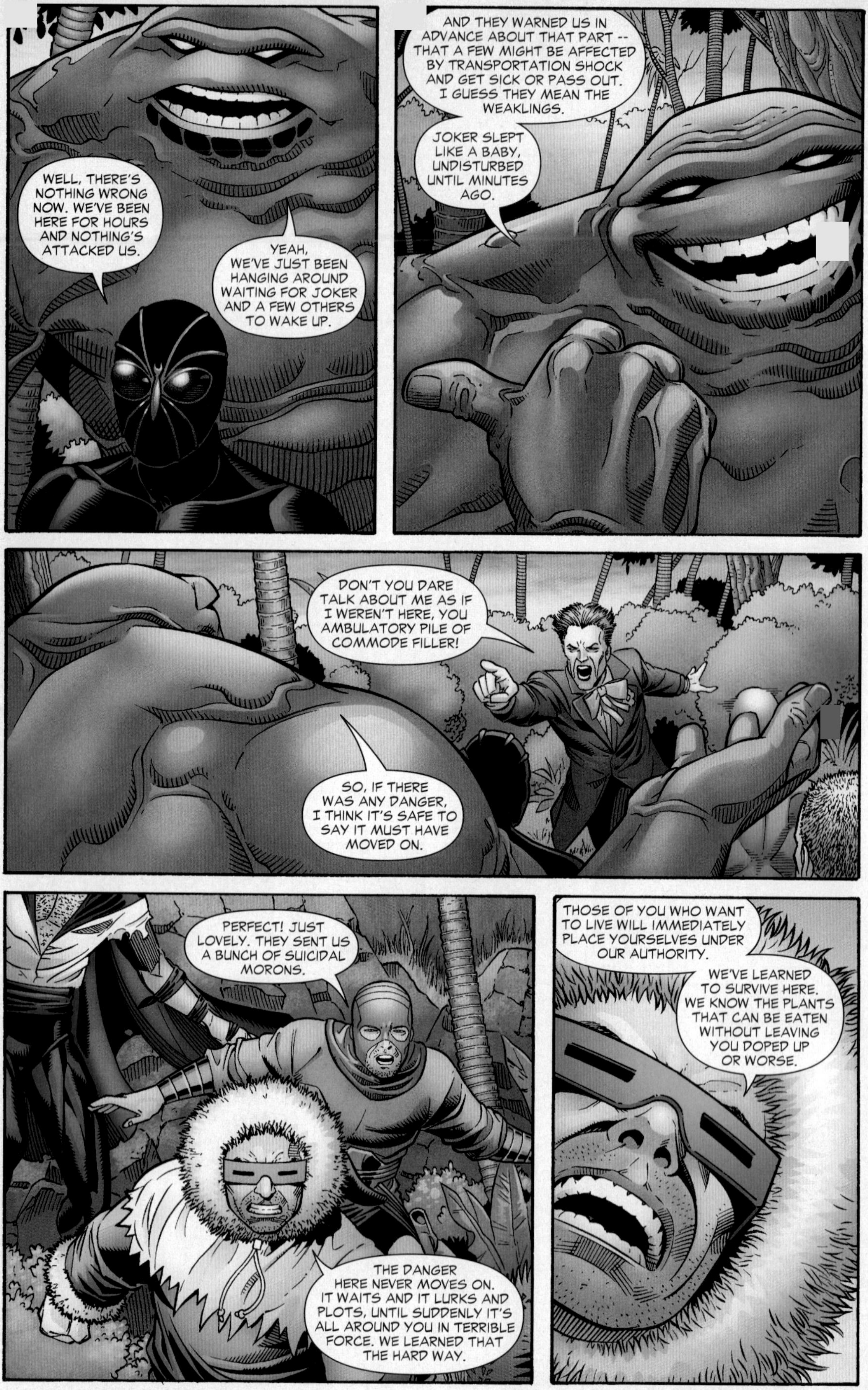
WELL, THERE'S NOTHING WRONG NOW. WE'VE BEEN HERE FOR HOURS AND NOTHING'S ATTACKED US.
YEAH, WE'VE JUST BEEN HANGING AROUND WAITING FOR JOKER AND A FEW OTHERS TO WAKE UP.
AND THEY WARNED US IN ADVANCE ABOUT THAT PART -- THAT A FEW MIGHT BE AFFECTED BY TRANSPORTATION SHOCK AND GET SICK OR PASS OUT. I GUESS THEY MEAN THE WEAKLINGS.
JOKER SLEPT LIKE A BABY, UNDISTURBED UNTIL MINUTES AGO.
DON'T YOU DARE TALK ABOUT ME AS IF I WEREN'T HERE, YOU AMBULATORY PILE OF COMMODE FILLER!
SO, IF THERE WAS ANY DANGER, I THINK IT'S SAFE TO SAY IT MUST HAVE MOVED ON.
PERFECT! JUST LOVELY. THEY SENT US A BUNCH OF SUICIDAL MORONS.
THE DANGER HERE NEVER MOVES ON. IT WAITS AND IT LURKS AND PLOTS, UNTIL SUDDENLY IT'S ALL AROUND YOU IN TERRIBLE FORCE. WE LEARNED THAT THE HARD WAY.
THOSE OF YOU WHO WANT TO LIVE WILL IMMEDIATELY PLACE YOURSELVES UNDER OUR AUTHORITY.
WE'VE LEARNED TO SURVIVE HERE. WE KNOW THE PLANTS THAT CAN BE EATEN WITHOUT LEAVING YOU DOPED UP OR WORSE.

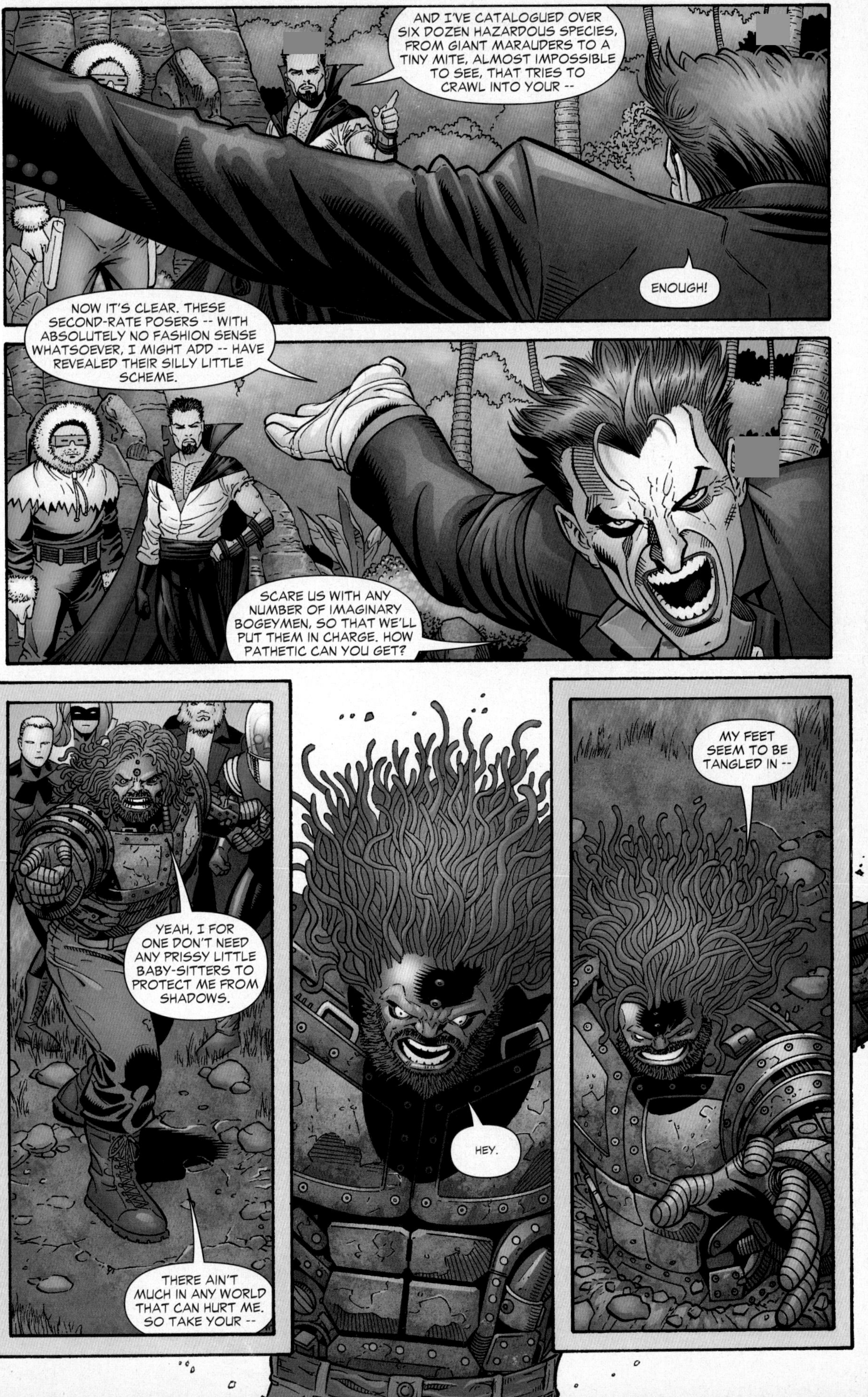
AND I'VE CATALOGUED OVER SIX DOZEN HAZARDOUS SPECIES, FROM GIANT MARAUDERS TO A TINY MITE, ALMOST IMPOSSIBLE TO SEE, THAT TRIES TO CRAWL INTO YOUR --
ENOUGH!
NOW IT'S CLEAR. THESE SECOND-RATE POSERS -- WITH ABSOLUTELY NO FASHION SENSE WHATSOEVER, I MIGHT ADD -- HAVE REVEALED THEIR SILLY LITTLE SCHEME.
SCARE US WITH ANY NUMBER OF IMAGINARY BOGEYMEN, SO THAT WE'LL PUT THEM IN CHARGE. HOW PATHETIC CAN YOU GET?
YEAH, I FOR ONE DON'T NEED ANY PRISSY LITTLE BABY-SITTERS TO PROTECT ME FROM SHADOWS.
THERE AIN'T MUCH IN ANY WORLD THAT CAN HURT ME. SO TAKE YOUR --
HEY.
MY FEET SEEM TO BE TANGLED IN --

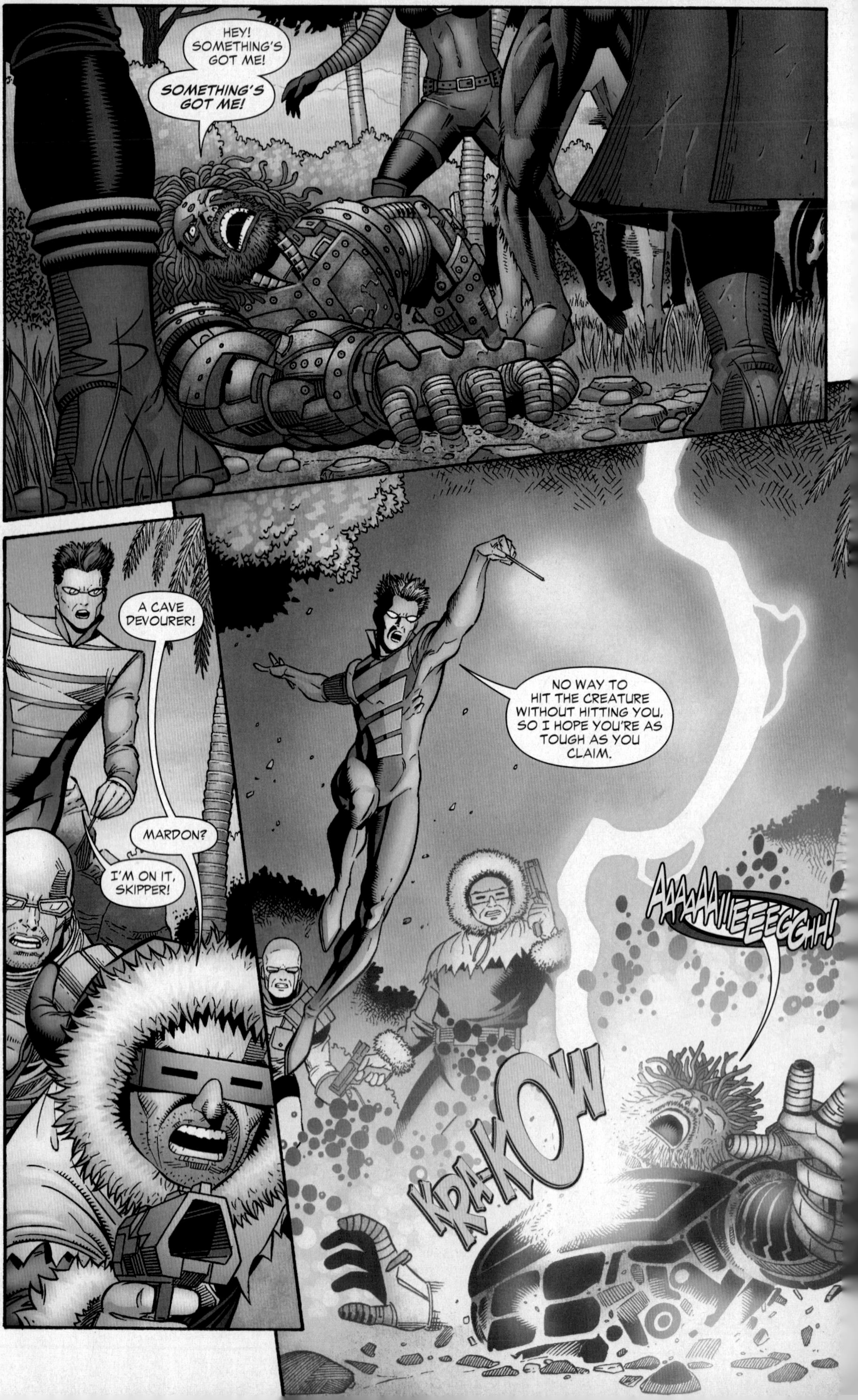
HEY! SOMETHING'S GOT ME!
SOMETHING'S GOT ME!
A CAVE DEVOURER!
MARDON?
I'M ON IT, SKIPPER!
NO WAY TO HIT THE CREATURE WITHOUT HITTING YOU, SO I HOPE YOU'RE AS TOUGH AS YOU CLAIM.
AAAAAIIEEEGGHH!
KRA-KOW

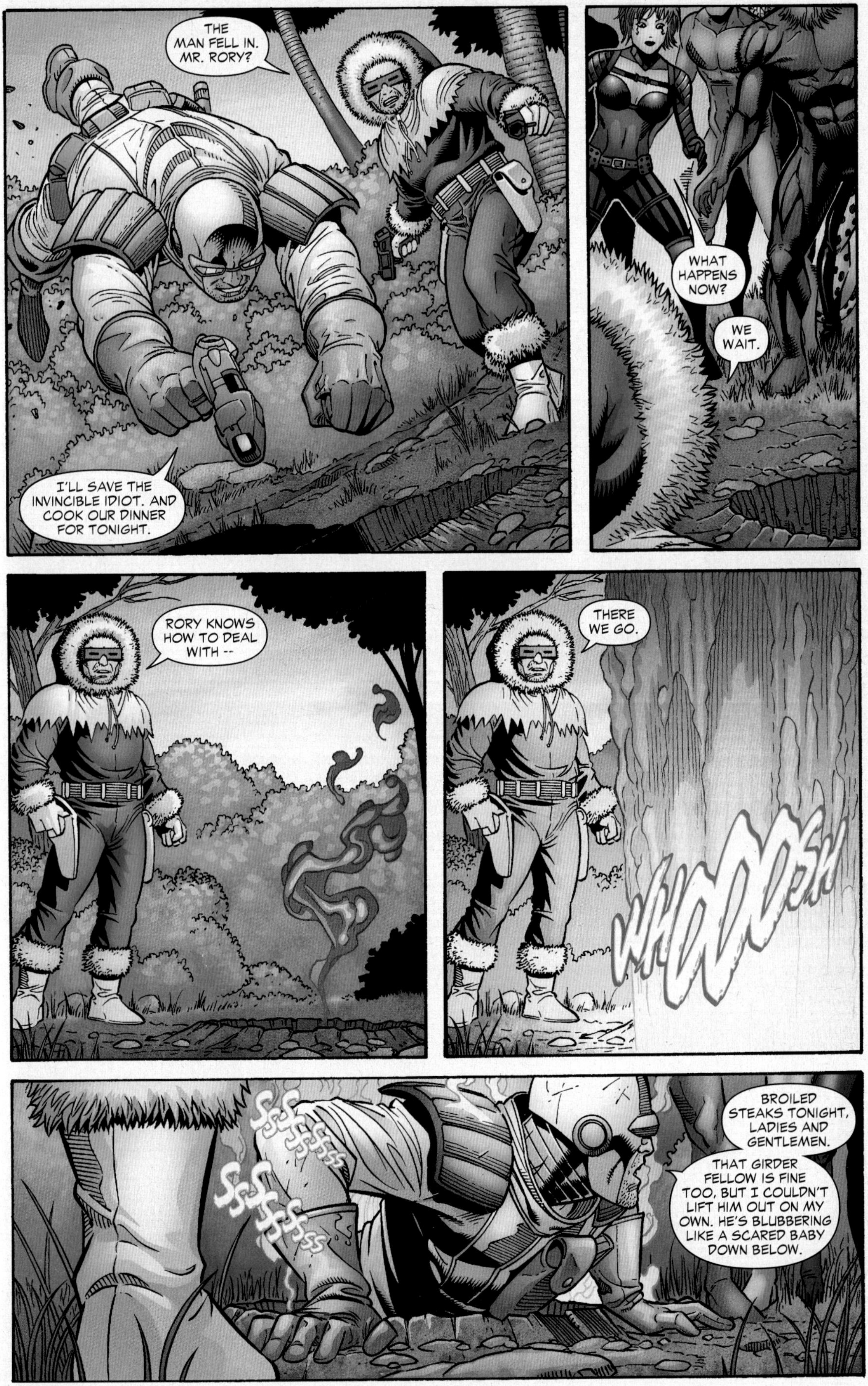
THE MAN FELL IN. MR. RORY?
I'LL SAVE THE INVINCIBLE IDIOT. AND COOK OUR DINNER FOR TONIGHT.
WHAT HAPPENS NOW?
WE WAIT.
RORY KNOWS HOW TO DEAL WITH --
THERE WE GO.
WHOOSH
SSSSSSSS
BROILED STEAKS TONIGHT, LADIES AND GENTLEMEN.
THAT GIRDER FELLOW IS FINE TOO, BUT I COULDN'T LIFT HIM OUT ON MY OWN. HE'S BLUBBERING LIKE A SCARED BABY DOWN BELOW.

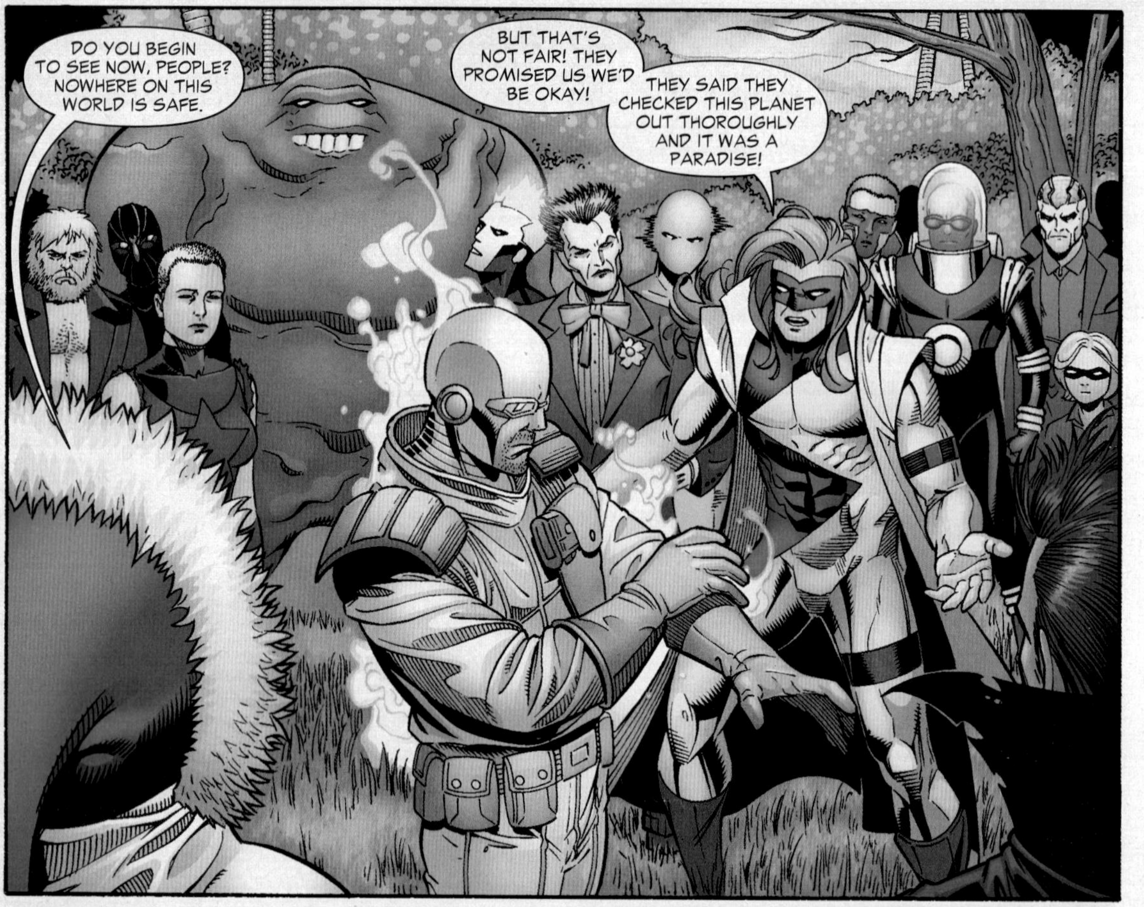
DO YOU BEGIN TO SEE NOW, PEOPLE? NOWHERE ON THIS WORLD IS SAFE.
BUT THAT'S NOT FAIR! THEY PROMISED US WE'D BE OKAY!
THEY SAID THEY CHECKED THIS PLANET OUT THOROUGHLY AND IT WAS A PARADISE!

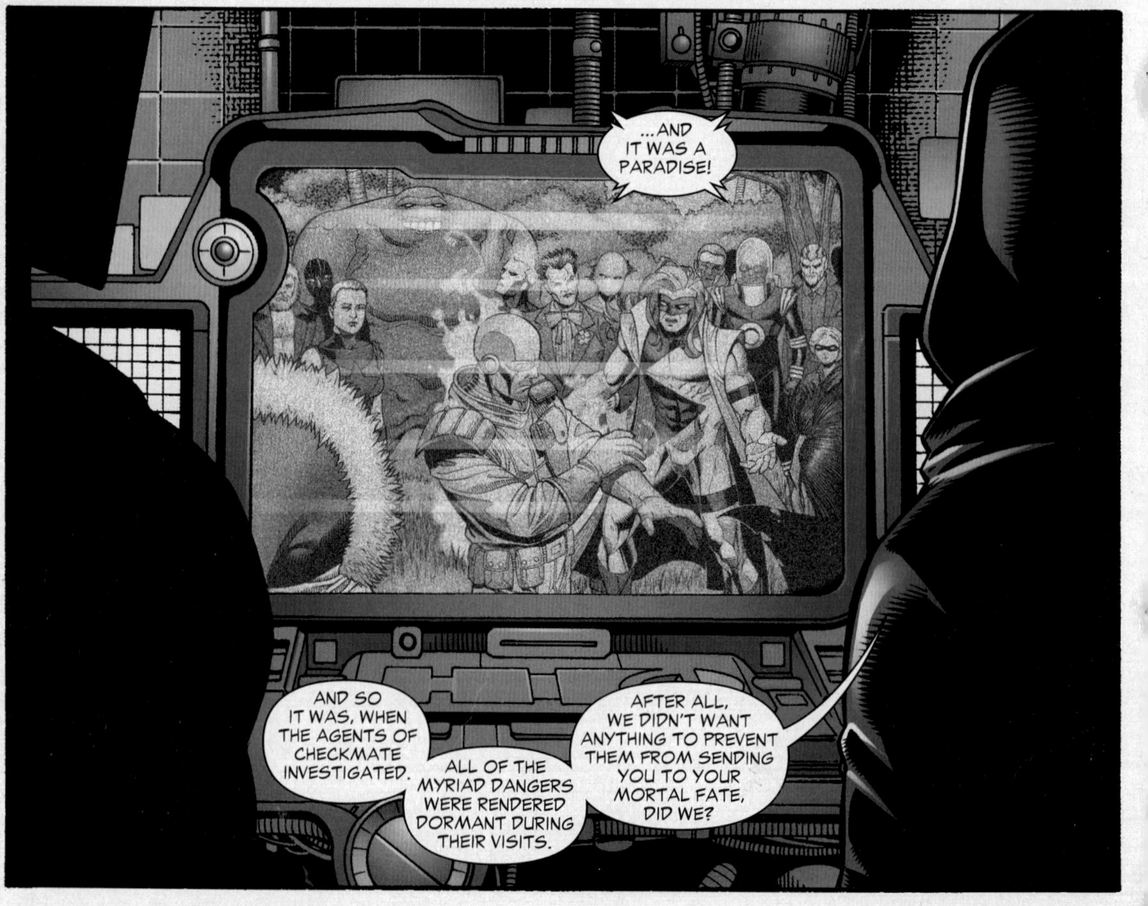
...AND IT WAS A PARADISE!
AND SO IT WAS, WHEN THE AGENTS OF CHECKMATE INVESTIGATED.
ALL OF THE MYRIAD DANGERS WERE RENDERED DORMANT DURING THEIR VISITS.
AFTER ALL, WE DIDN'T WANT ANYTHING TO PREVENT THEM FROM SENDING YOU TO YOUR MORTAL FATE, DID WE?

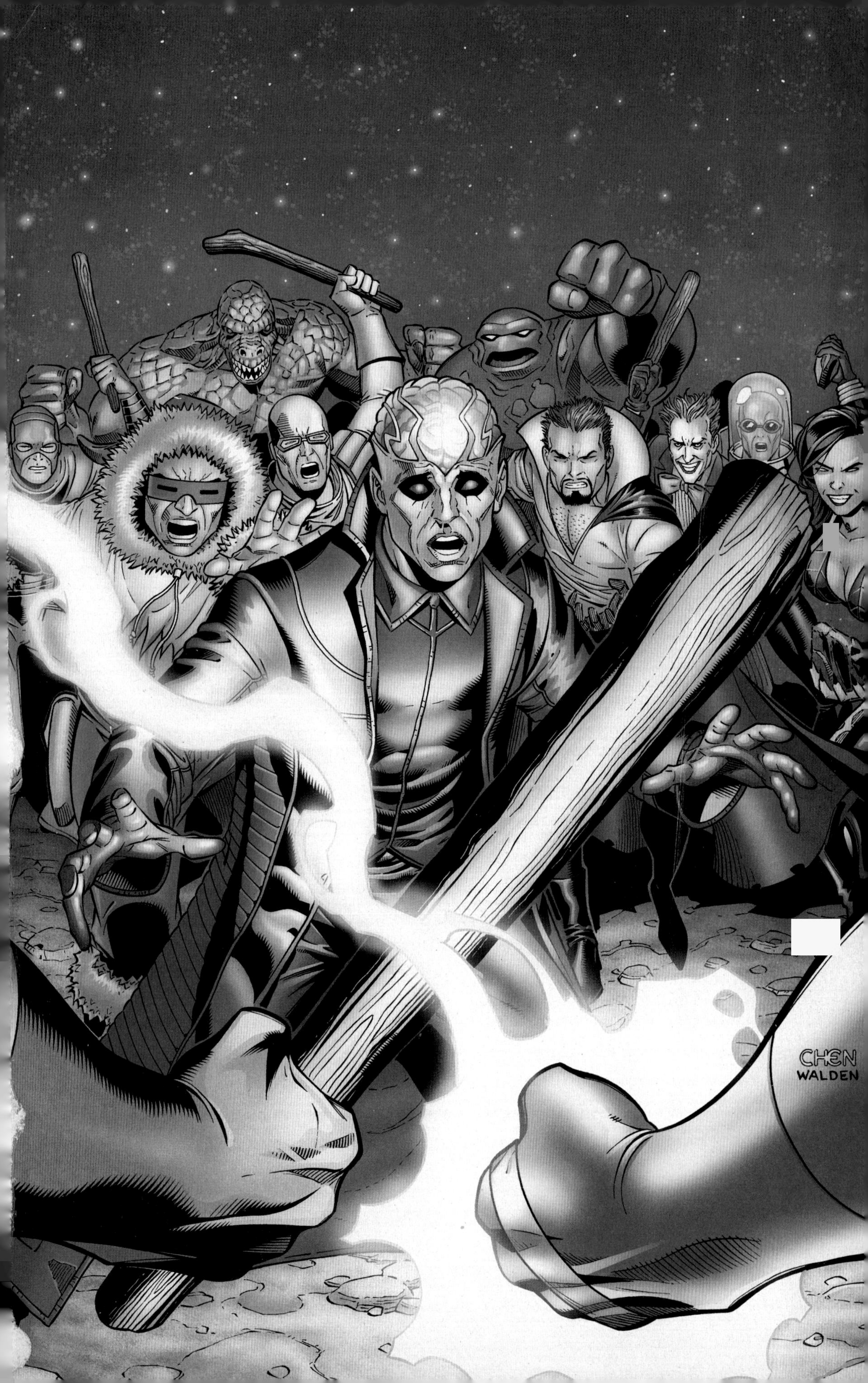
CHEN
WALDEN

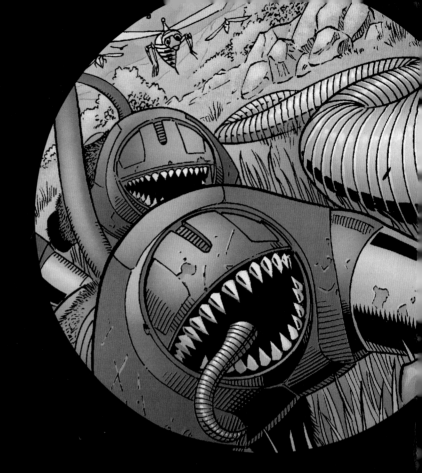

Bill Willingham
Writer

Sean Chen
Penciller

Walden Wong
Inker

John Kalisz
Colorist

Steve Wands
Letterer

CHAPTER TWO

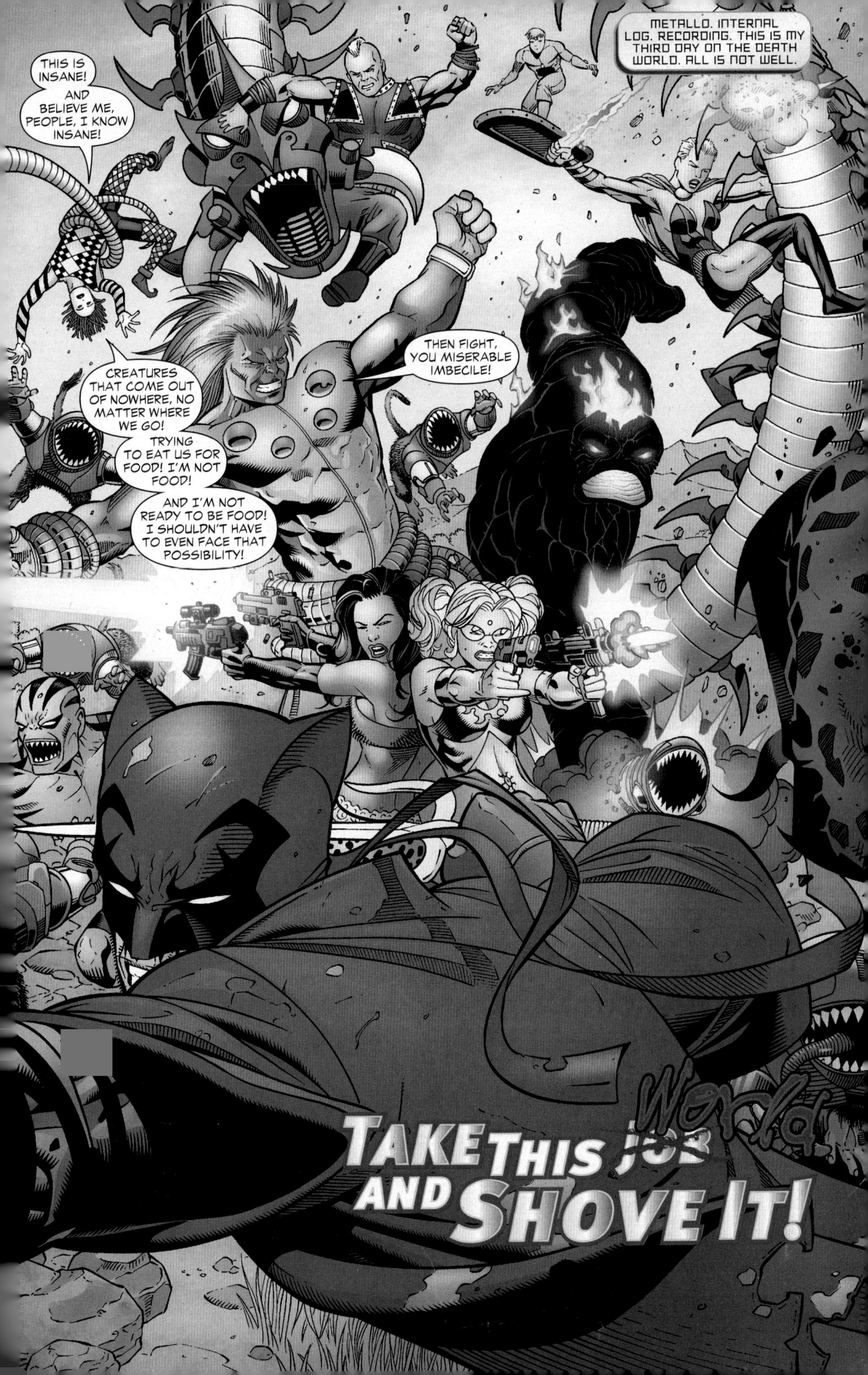
METALLO. INTERNAL LOG. RECORDING. THIS IS MY THIRD DAY ON THE DEATH WORLD. ALL IS NOT WELL.
THIS IS INSANE!
AND BELIEVE ME, PEOPLE, I KNOW INSANE!
CREATURES THAT COME OUT OF NOWHERE, NO MATTER WHERE WE GO!
TRYING TO EAT US FOR FOOD! I'M NOT FOOD!
AND I'M NOT READY TO BE FOOD! I SHOULDN'T HAVE TO EVEN FACE THAT POSSIBILITY!
THEN FIGHT, YOU MISERABLE IMBECILE!
TAKE THIS ~~JOB~~ World AND SHOVE IT!

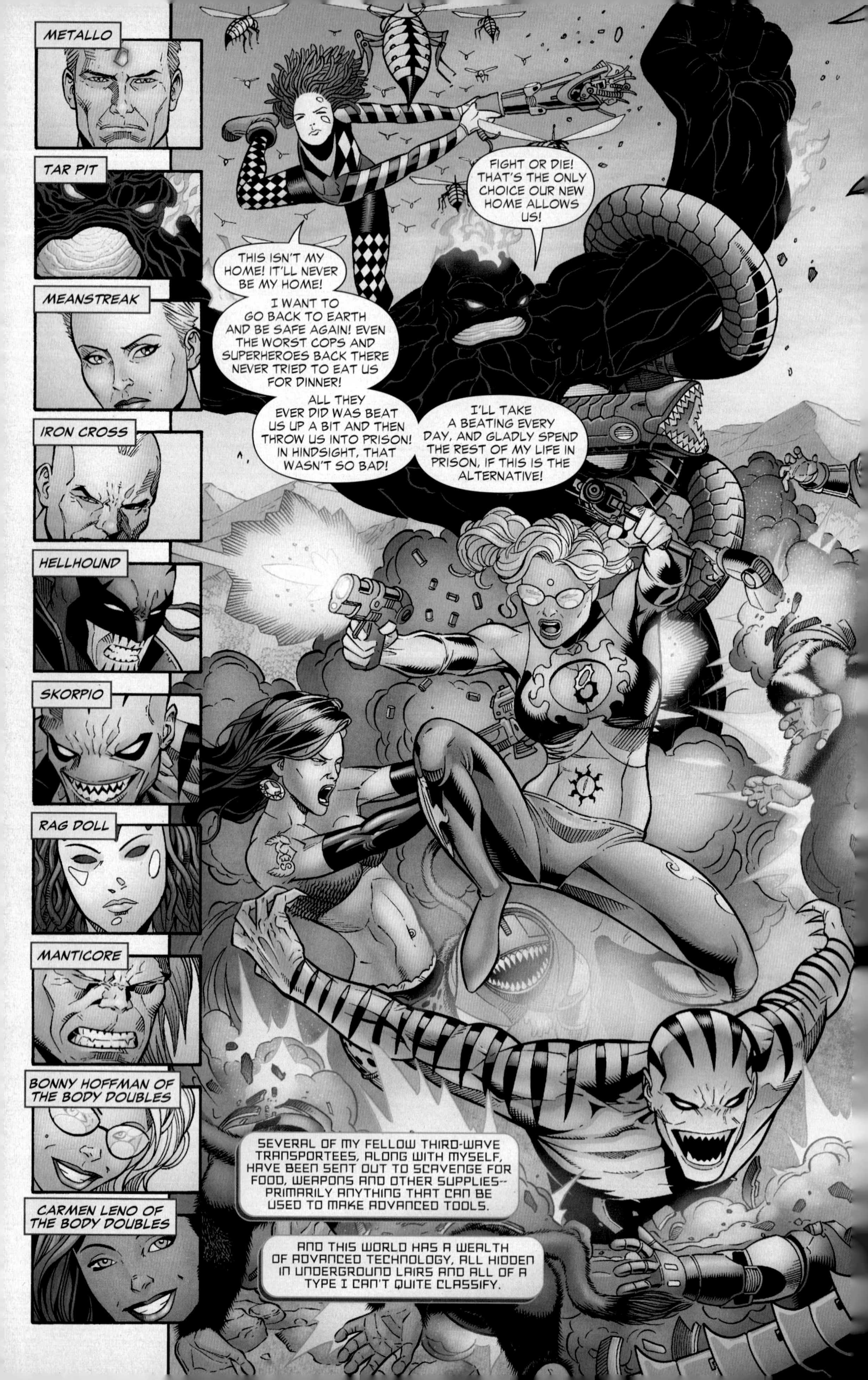
METALLO
TAR PIT
MEANSTREAK
IRON CROSS
HELLHOUND
SKORPIO
RAG DOLL
MANTICORE
BONNY HOFFMAN OF THE BODY DOUBLES
CARMEN LENO OF THE BODY DOUBLES
FIGHT OR DIE! THAT'S THE ONLY CHOICE OUR NEW HOME ALLOWS US!
THIS ISN'T MY HOME! IT'LL NEVER BE MY HOME!
I WANT TO GO BACK TO EARTH AND BE SAFE AGAIN! EVEN THE WORST COPS AND SUPERHEROES BACK THERE NEVER TRIED TO EAT US FOR DINNER!
ALL THEY EVER DID WAS BEAT US UP A BIT AND THEN THROW US INTO PRISON! IN HINDSIGHT, THAT WASN'T SO BAD!
I'LL TAKE A BEATING EVERY DAY, AND GLADLY SPEND THE REST OF MY LIFE IN PRISON, IF THIS IS THE ALTERNATIVE!
SEVERAL OF MY FELLOW THIRD-WAVE TRANSPORTEES, ALONG WITH MYSELF, HAVE BEEN SENT OUT TO SCAVENGE FOR FOOD, WEAPONS AND OTHER SUPPLIES-- PRIMARILY ANYTHING THAT CAN BE USED TO MAKE ADVANCED TOOLS.
AND THIS WORLD HAS A WEALTH OF ADVANCED TECHNOLOGY, ALL HIDDEN IN UNDERGROUND LAIRS AND ALL OF A TYPE I CAN'T QUITE CLASSIFY.

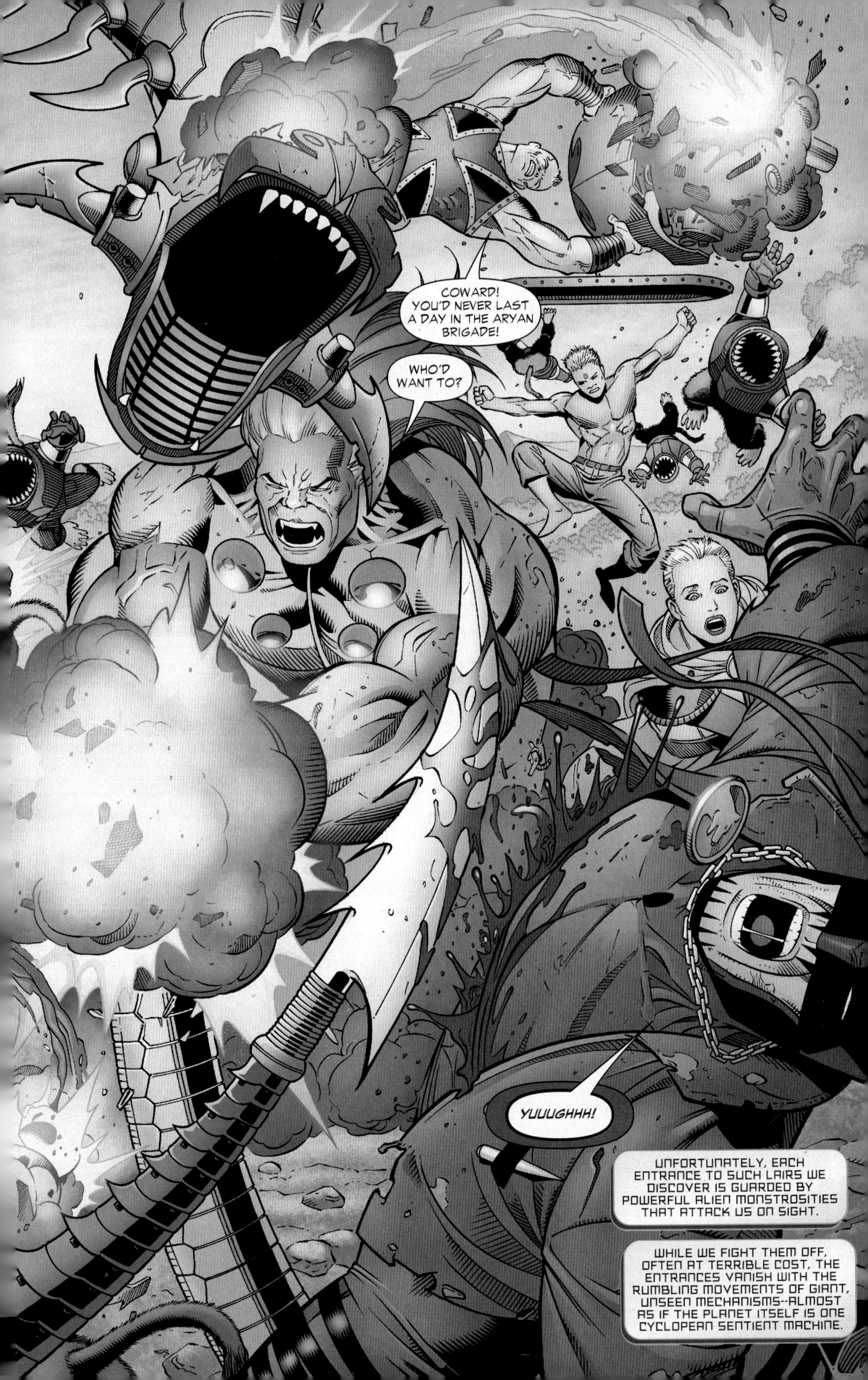
COWARD! YOU'D NEVER LAST A DAY IN THE ARYAN BRIGADE!
WHO'D WANT TO?
YUUUGHHH!
UNFORTUNATELY, EACH ENTRANCE TO SUCH LAIRS WE DISCOVER IS GUARDED BY POWERFUL ALIEN MONSTROSITIES THAT ATTACK US ON SIGHT.
WHILE WE FIGHT THEM OFF, OFTEN AT TERRIBLE COST, THE ENTRANCES VANISH WITH THE RUMBLING MOVEMENTS OF GIANT, UNSEEN MECHANISMS--ALMOST AS IF THE PLANET ITSELF IS ONE CYCLOPEAN SENTIENT MACHINE.

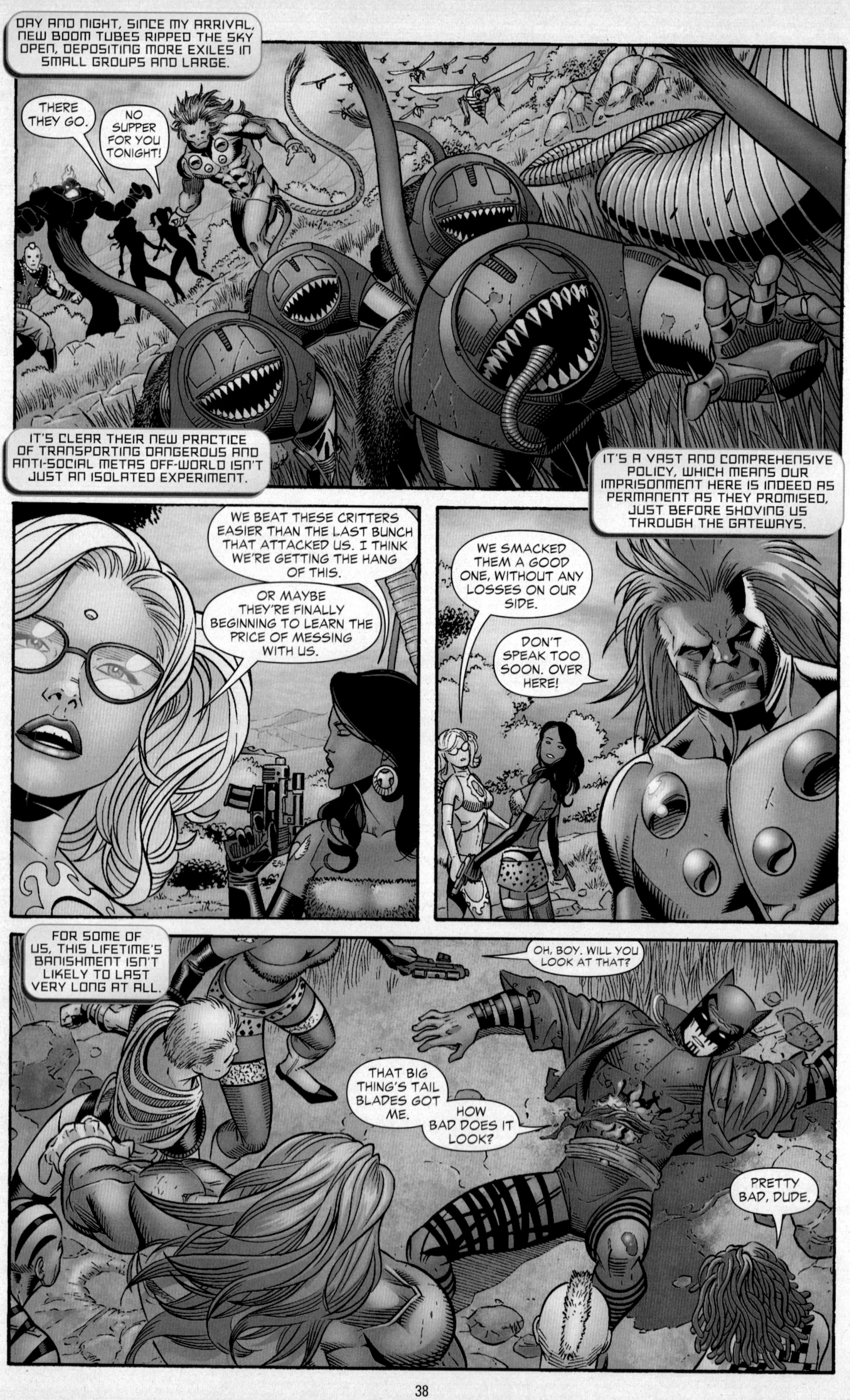
DAY AND NIGHT, SINCE MY ARRIVAL, NEW BOOM TUBES RIPPED THE SKY OPEN, DEPOSITING MORE EXILES IN SMALL GROUPS AND LARGE.
THERE THEY GO.
NO SUPPER FOR YOU TONIGHT!
IT'S CLEAR THEIR NEW PRACTICE OF TRANSPORTING DANGEROUS AND ANTI-SOCIAL METAS OFF-WORLD ISN'T JUST AN ISOLATED EXPERIMENT.
IT'S A VAST AND COMPREHENSIVE POLICY, WHICH MEANS OUR IMPRISONMENT HERE IS INDEED AS PERMANENT AS THEY PROMISED, JUST BEFORE SHOVING US THROUGH THE GATEWAYS.
WE BEAT THESE CRITTERS EASIER THAN THE LAST BUNCH THAT ATTACKED US. I THINK WE'RE GETTING THE HANG OF THIS.
OR MAYBE THEY'RE FINALLY BEGINNING TO LEARN THE PRICE OF MESSING WITH US.
WE SMACKED THEM A GOOD ONE, WITHOUT ANY LOSSES ON OUR SIDE.
DON'T SPEAK TOO SOON. OVER HERE!
FOR SOME OF US, THIS LIFETIME'S BANISHMENT ISN'T LIKELY TO LAST VERY LONG AT ALL.
OH, BOY. WILL YOU LOOK AT THAT?
THAT BIG THING'S TAIL BLADES GOT ME.
HOW BAD DOES IT LOOK?
PRETTY BAD, DUDE.

BEING WELL-ARMORED AND LARGELY COMPOSED OF INORGANIC MATERIAL, I'LL PROBABLY SURVIVE LONGER THAN MOST.

HE'S TOAST. LET'S LEAVE HIM AND GO.

NO! DON'T LEAVE ME! I CAN SURVIVE THIS! IT HARDLY HURTS AT ALL!

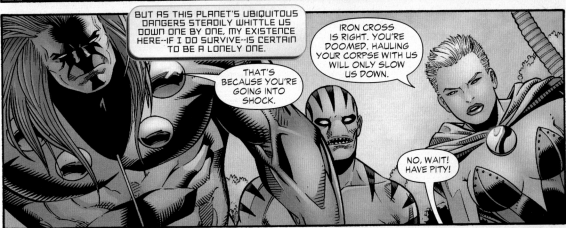

BUT AS THIS PLANET'S UBIQUITOUS DANGERS STEADILY WHITTLE US DOWN ONE BY ONE, MY EXISTENCE HERE--IF I DO SURVIVE--IS CERTAIN TO BE A LONELY ONE.

IRON CROSS IS RIGHT. YOU'RE DOOMED. HAULING YOUR CORPSE WITH US WILL ONLY SLOW US DOWN.

THAT'S BECAUSE YOU'RE GOING INTO SHOCK.

NO, WAIT! HAVE PITY!

YEAH, WE'D BETTER GET GOING.

NO WE DON'T. WE AREN'T LEAVING HELLHOUND BEHIND.

CARMEN'S RIGHT. WE'RE GOING TO BIND HIS WOUNDS AND TAKE HIM WITH US.

ARE YOU TWO INSANE? LOOK AT HIM! HE'S ALREADY AS GOOD AS DEAD!

WE AREN'T GOING TO SURVIVE THIS PLACE UNLESS WE STICK TOGETHER. AND WE CAN'T DO THAT BY ABANDONING OUR WOUNDED.

YEAH. WE CAN CARRY HELLHOUND WITH US ON METALLO'S ROCKET SCOOTER. EASY AS PIE.

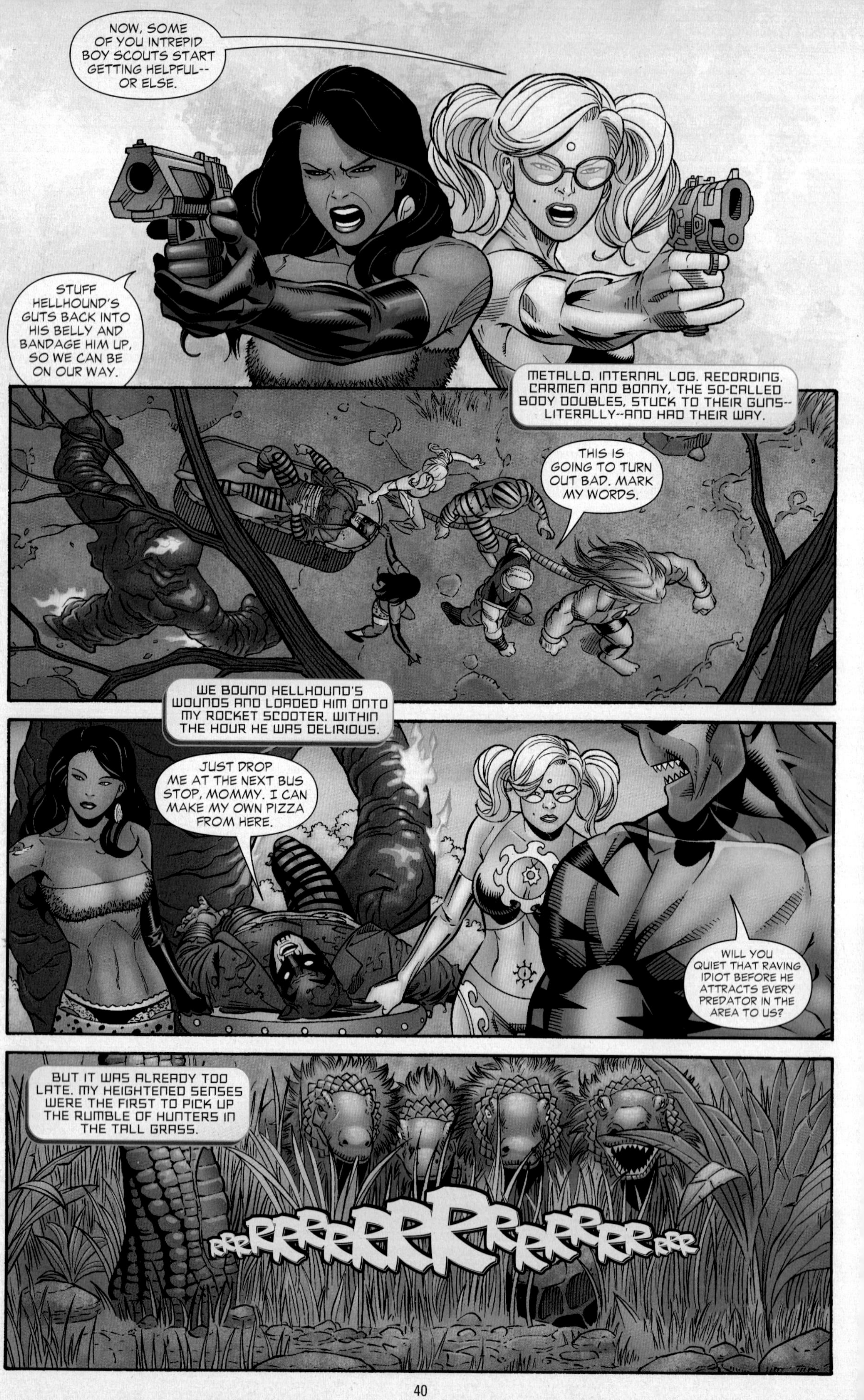
NOW, SOME OF YOU INTREPID BOY SCOUTS START GETTING HELPFUL-- OR ELSE.
STUFF HELLHOUND'S GUTS BACK INTO HIS BELLY AND BANDAGE HIM UP, SO WE CAN BE ON OUR WAY.
METALLO. INTERNAL LOG. RECORDING. CARMEN AND BONNY, THE SO-CALLED BODY DOUBLES, STUCK TO THEIR GUNS-- LITERALLY--AND HAD THEIR WAY.
THIS IS GOING TO TURN OUT BAD. MARK MY WORDS.
WE BOUND HELLHOUND'S WOUNDS AND LOADED HIM ONTO MY ROCKET SCOOTER. WITHIN THE HOUR HE WAS DELIRIOUS.
JUST DROP ME AT THE NEXT BUS STOP, MOMMY. I CAN MAKE MY OWN PIZZA FROM HERE.
WILL YOU QUIET THAT RAVING IDIOT BEFORE HE ATTRACTS EVERY PREDATOR IN THE AREA TO US?
BUT IT WAS ALREADY TOO LATE. MY HEIGHTENED SENSES WERE THE FIRST TO PICK UP THE RUMBLE OF HUNTERS IN THE TALL GRASS.
RRRRRRRRRRRRRRRRRRRRRRRR

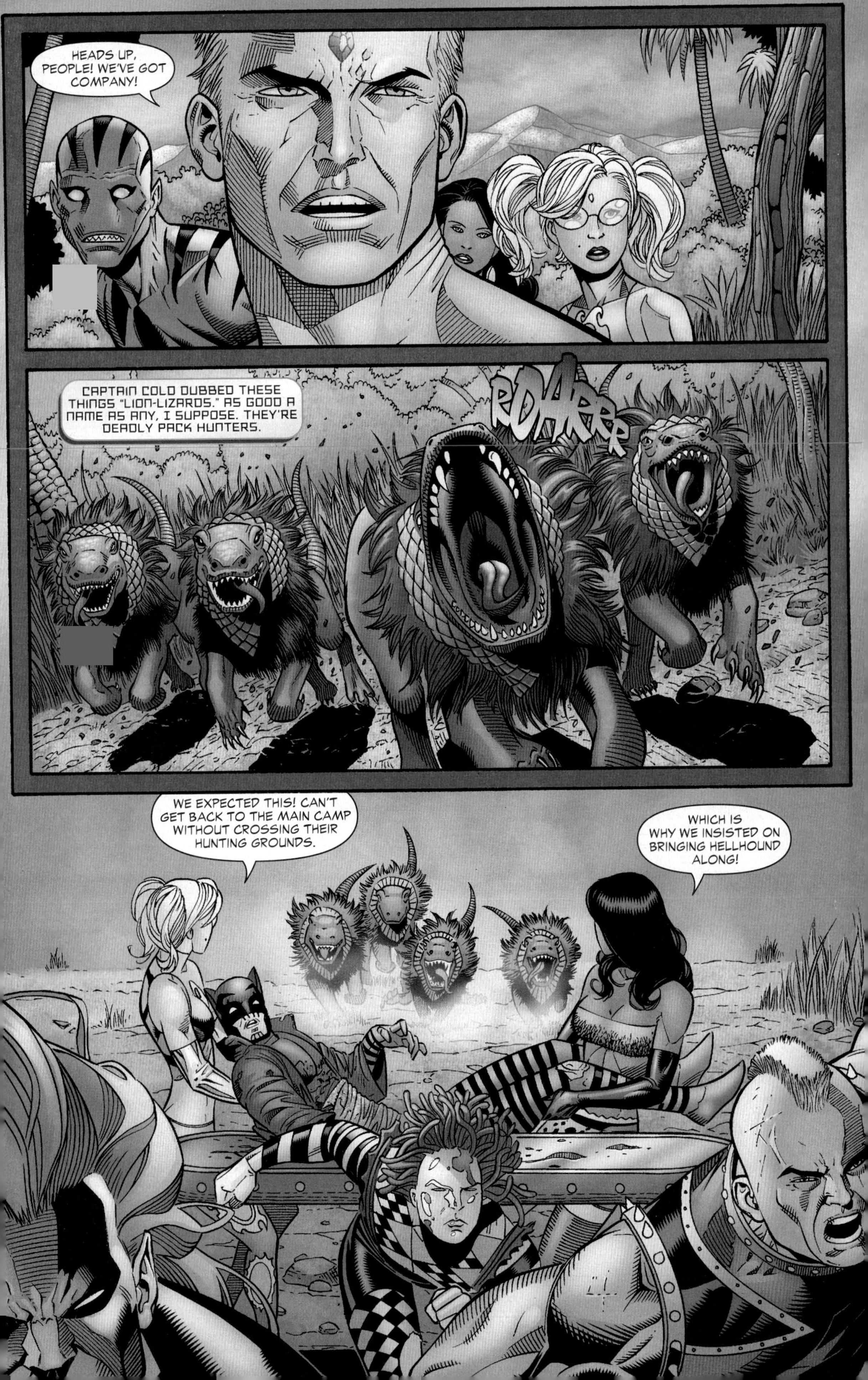
HEADS UP, PEOPLE! WE'VE GOT COMPANY!
CAPTAIN COLD DUBBED THESE THINGS "LION-LIZARDS." AS GOOD A NAME AS ANY, I SUPPOSE. THEY'RE DEADLY PACK HUNTERS.
ROARRR
WE EXPECTED THIS! CAN'T GET BACK TO THE MAIN CAMP WITHOUT CROSSING THEIR HUNTING GROUNDS.
WHICH IS WHY WE INSISTED ON BRINGING HELLHOUND ALONG!

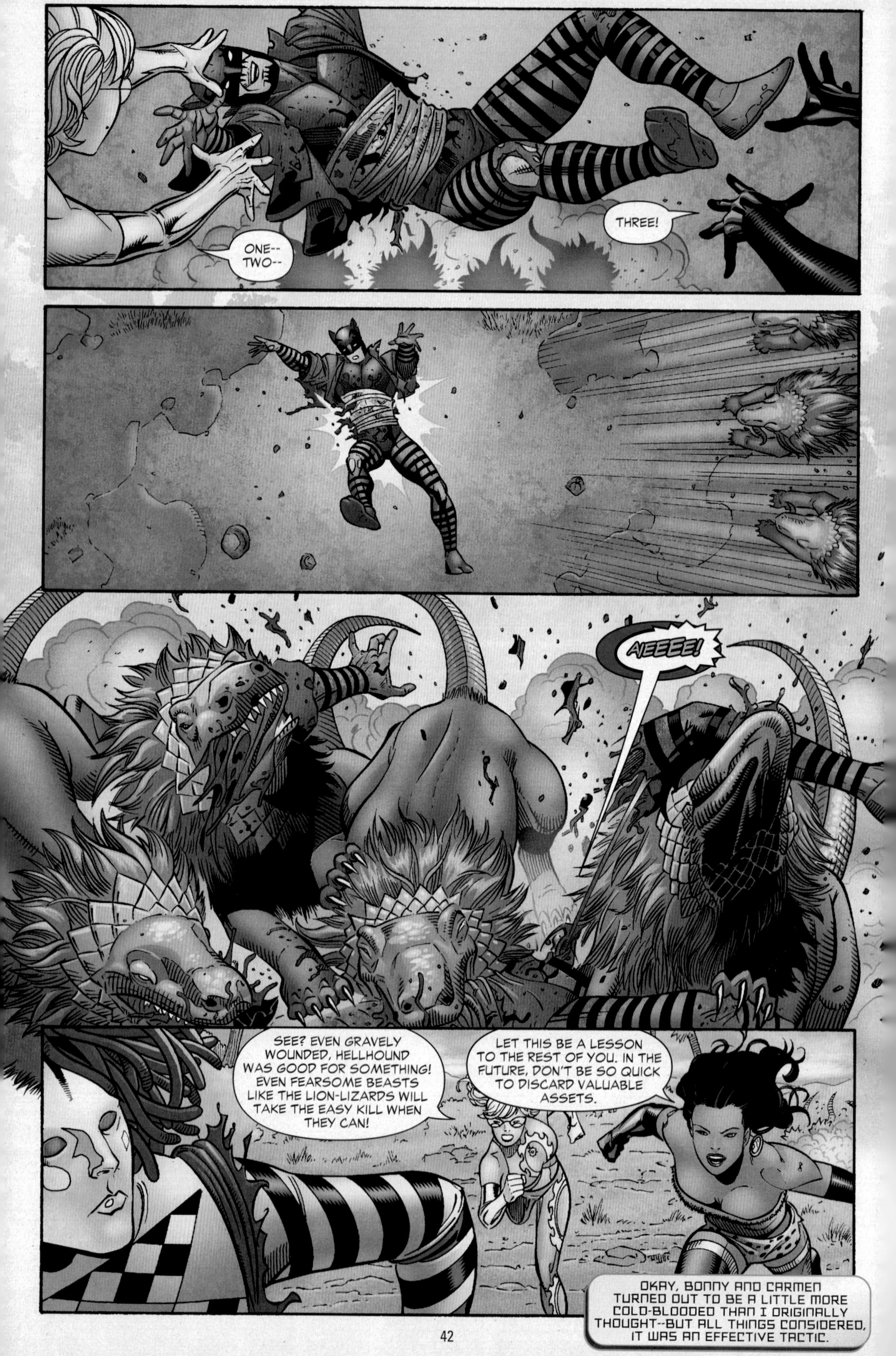
ONE--
TWO--
THREE!
AIEEEE!
SEE? EVEN GRAVELY WOUNDED, HELLHOUND WAS GOOD FOR SOMETHING! EVEN FEARSOME BEASTS LIKE THE LION-LIZARDS WILL TAKE THE EASY KILL WHEN THEY CAN!
LET THIS BE A LESSON TO THE REST OF YOU. IN THE FUTURE, DON'T BE SO QUICK TO DISCARD VALUABLE ASSETS.
OKAY, BONNY AND CARMEN TURNED OUT TO BE A LITTLE MORE COLD-BLOODED THAN I ORIGINALLY THOUGHT--BUT ALL THINGS CONSIDERED, IT WAS AN EFFECTIVE TACTIC.

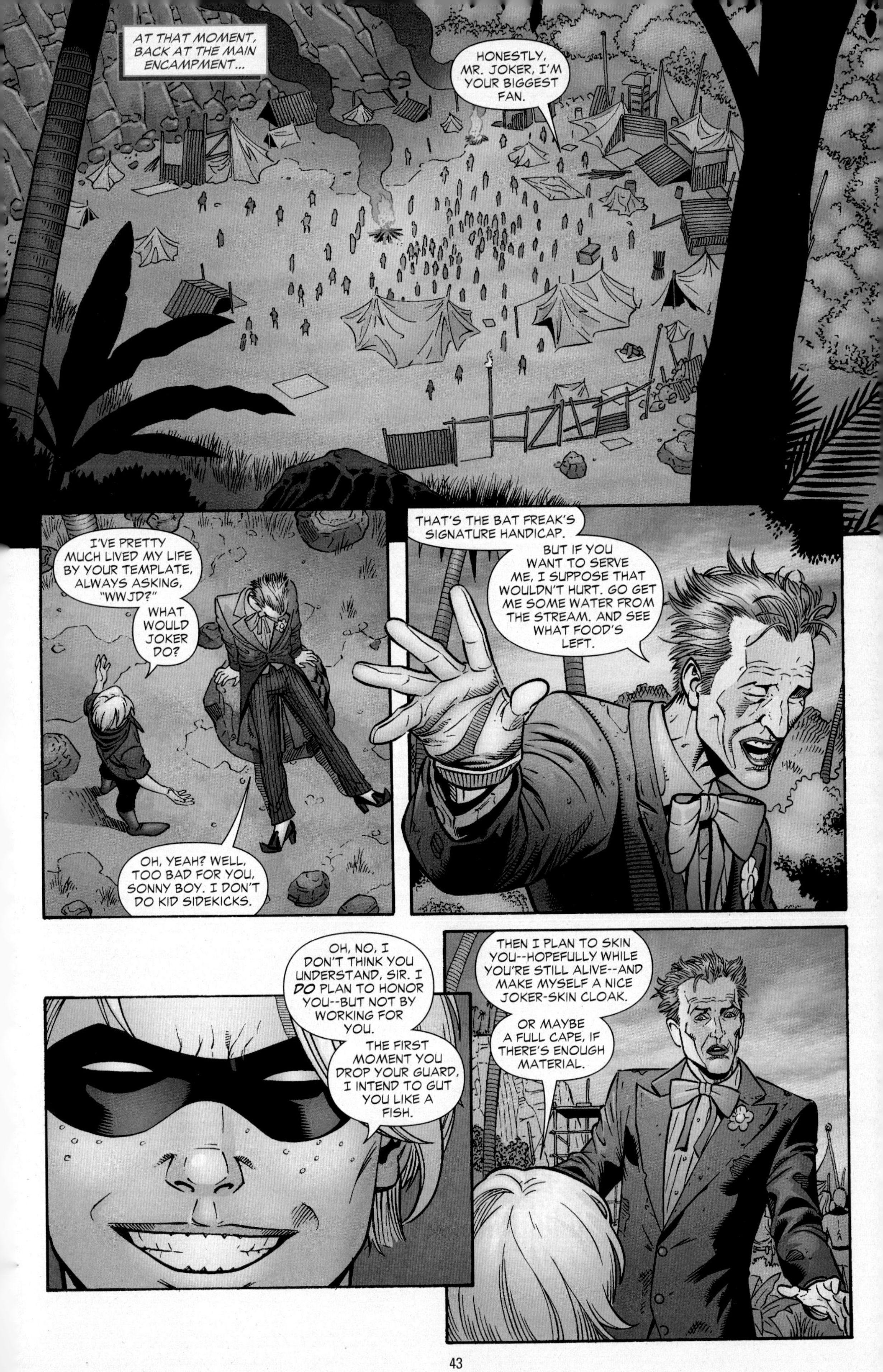
AT THAT MOMENT, BACK AT THE MAIN ENCAMPMENT...
HONESTLY, MR. JOKER, I'M YOUR BIGGEST FAN.
I'VE PRETTY MUCH LIVED MY LIFE BY YOUR TEMPLATE, ALWAYS ASKING, "WWJD?"
WHAT WOULD JOKER DO?
OH, YEAH? WELL, TOO BAD FOR YOU, SONNY BOY. I DON'T DO KID SIDEKICKS.
THAT'S THE BAT FREAK'S SIGNATURE HANDICAP.
BUT IF YOU WANT TO SERVE ME, I SUPPOSE THAT WOULDN'T HURT. GO GET ME SOME WATER FROM THE STREAM. AND SEE WHAT FOOD'S LEFT.
OH, NO, I DON'T THINK YOU UNDERSTAND, SIR. I *DO* PLAN TO HONOR YOU--BUT NOT BY WORKING FOR YOU.
THE FIRST MOMENT YOU DROP YOUR GUARD, I INTEND TO GUT YOU LIKE A FISH.
THEN I PLAN TO SKIN YOU--HOPEFULLY WHILE YOU'RE STILL ALIVE--AND MAKE MYSELF A NICE JOKER-SKIN CLOAK.
OR MAYBE A FULL CAPE, IF THERE'S ENOUGH MATERIAL.

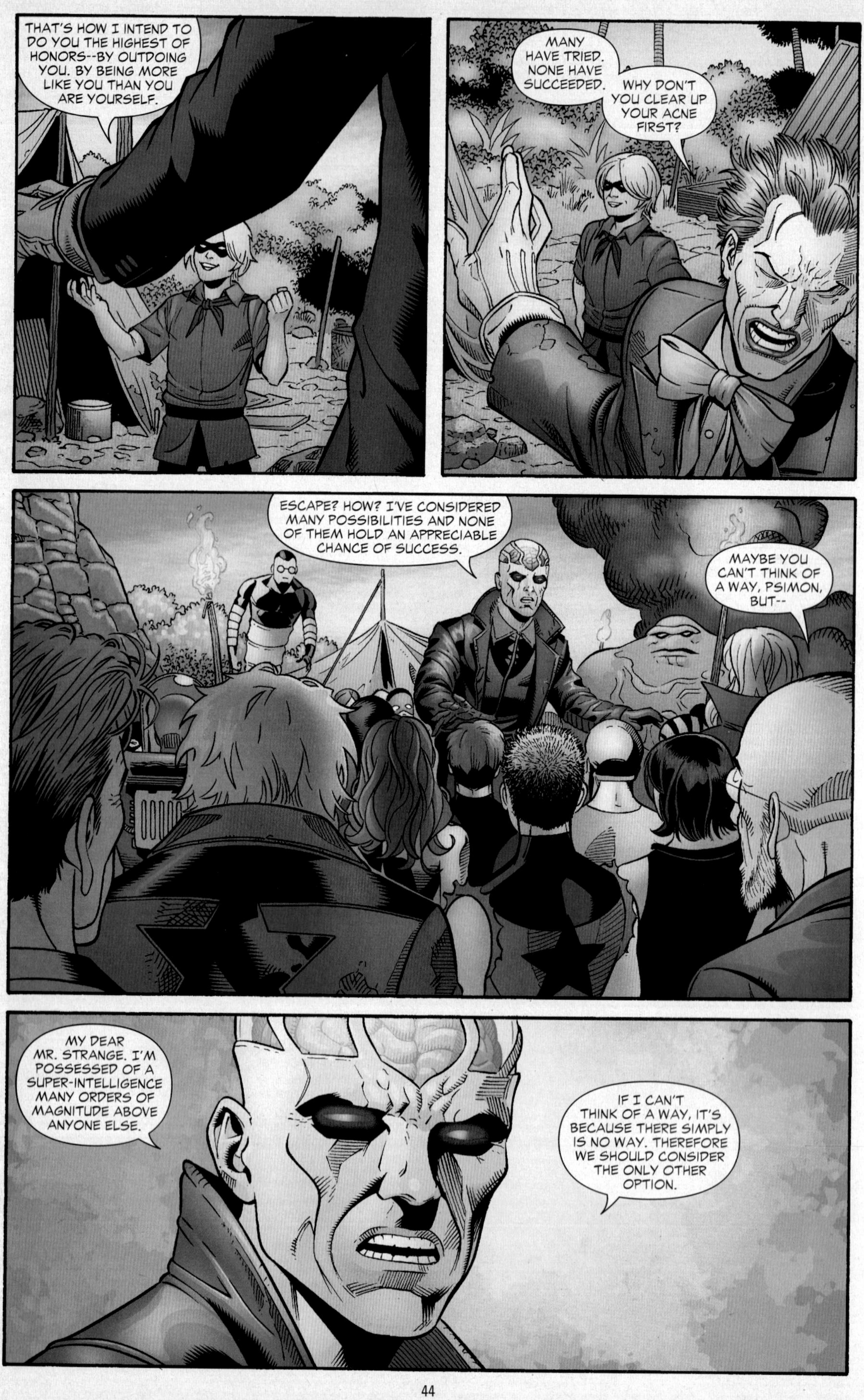
THAT'S HOW I INTEND TO DO YOU THE HIGHEST OF HONORS--BY OUTDOING YOU. BY BEING MORE LIKE YOU THAN YOU ARE YOURSELF.
MANY HAVE TRIED. NONE HAVE SUCCEEDED.
WHY DON'T YOU CLEAR UP YOUR ACNE FIRST?
ESCAPE? HOW? I'VE CONSIDERED MANY POSSIBILITIES AND NONE OF THEM HOLD AN APPRECIABLE CHANCE OF SUCCESS.
MAYBE YOU CAN'T THINK OF A WAY, PSIMON, BUT--
MY DEAR MR. STRANGE. I'M POSSESSED OF A SUPER-INTELLIGENCE MANY ORDERS OF MAGNITUDE ABOVE ANYONE ELSE.
IF I CAN'T THINK OF A WAY, IT'S BECAUSE THERE SIMPLY IS NO WAY. THEREFORE WE SHOULD CONSIDER THE ONLY OTHER OPTION.

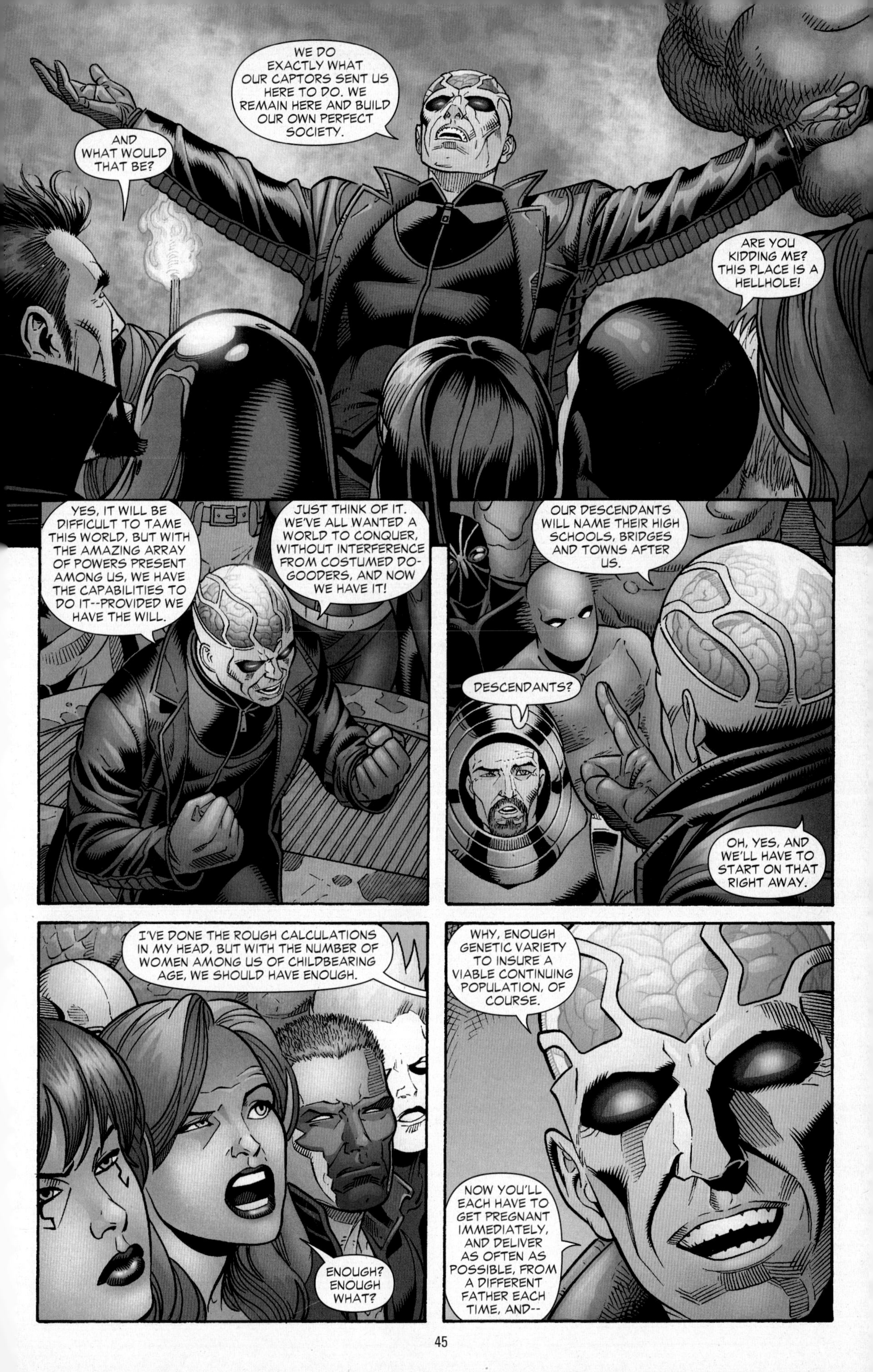
WE DO EXACTLY WHAT OUR CAPTORS SENT US HERE TO DO. WE REMAIN HERE AND BUILD OUR OWN PERFECT SOCIETY.
AND WHAT WOULD THAT BE?
ARE YOU KIDDING ME? THIS PLACE IS A HELLHOLE!
YES, IT WILL BE DIFFICULT TO TAME THIS WORLD, BUT WITH THE AMAZING ARRAY OF POWERS PRESENT AMONG US, WE HAVE THE CAPABILITIES TO DO IT--PROVIDED WE HAVE THE WILL.
JUST THINK OF IT. WE'VE ALL WANTED A WORLD TO CONQUER, WITHOUT INTERFERENCE FROM COSTUMED DO-GOODERS, AND NOW WE HAVE IT!
OUR DESCENDANTS WILL NAME THEIR HIGH SCHOOLS, BRIDGES AND TOWNS AFTER US.
DESCENDANTS?
OH, YES, AND WE'LL HAVE TO START ON THAT RIGHT AWAY.
I'VE DONE THE ROUGH CALCULATIONS IN MY HEAD, BUT WITH THE NUMBER OF WOMEN AMONG US OF CHILDBEARING AGE, WE SHOULD HAVE ENOUGH.
ENOUGH? ENOUGH WHAT?
WHY, ENOUGH GENETIC VARIETY TO INSURE A VIABLE CONTINUING POPULATION, OF COURSE.
NOW YOU'LL EACH HAVE TO GET PREGNANT IMMEDIATELY, AND DELIVER AS OFTEN AS POSSIBLE, FROM A DIFFERENT FATHER EACH TIME, AND--

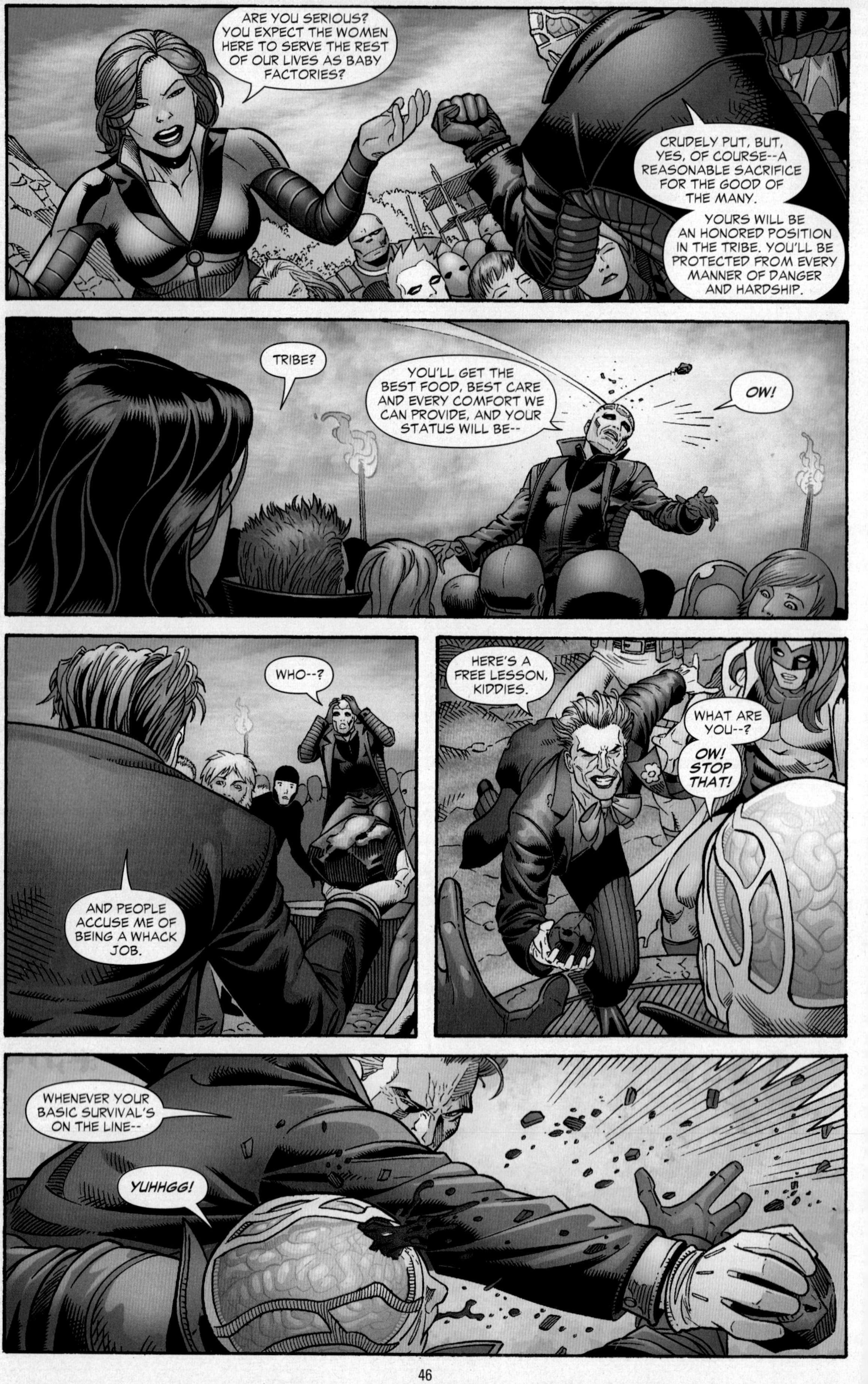
ARE YOU SERIOUS? YOU EXPECT THE WOMEN HERE TO SERVE THE REST OF OUR LIVES AS BABY FACTORIES?
CRUDELY PUT, BUT, YES, OF COURSE--A REASONABLE SACRIFICE FOR THE GOOD OF THE MANY.
YOURS WILL BE AN HONORED POSITION IN THE TRIBE. YOU'LL BE PROTECTED FROM EVERY MANNER OF DANGER AND HARDSHIP.
TRIBE?
YOU'LL GET THE BEST FOOD, BEST CARE AND EVERY COMFORT WE CAN PROVIDE, AND YOUR STATUS WILL BE--
OW!
WHO--?
AND PEOPLE ACCUSE ME OF BEING A WHACK JOB.
HERE'S A FREE LESSON, KIDDIES.
WHAT ARE YOU--?
OW! STOP THAT!
WHENEVER YOUR BASIC SURVIVAL'S ON THE LINE--
YUHHGG!

--LOSE THE IDIOTS AS SOON AS POSSIBLE!

IMMEDIATELY DIVEST YOURSELVES OF ALL LOSERS, DREAMERS, WISHFUL THINKERS, AND HAPPY HUGGERS!

THEY'LL ONLY DRAG YOU DOWN!

THEY SIMPLY AREN'T PRACTICAL.

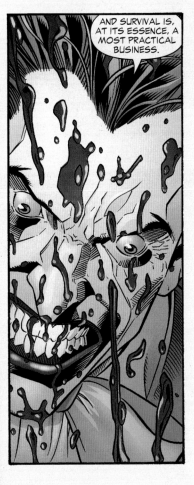

AND SURVIVAL IS, AT ITS ESSENCE, A MOST PRACTICAL BUSINESS.

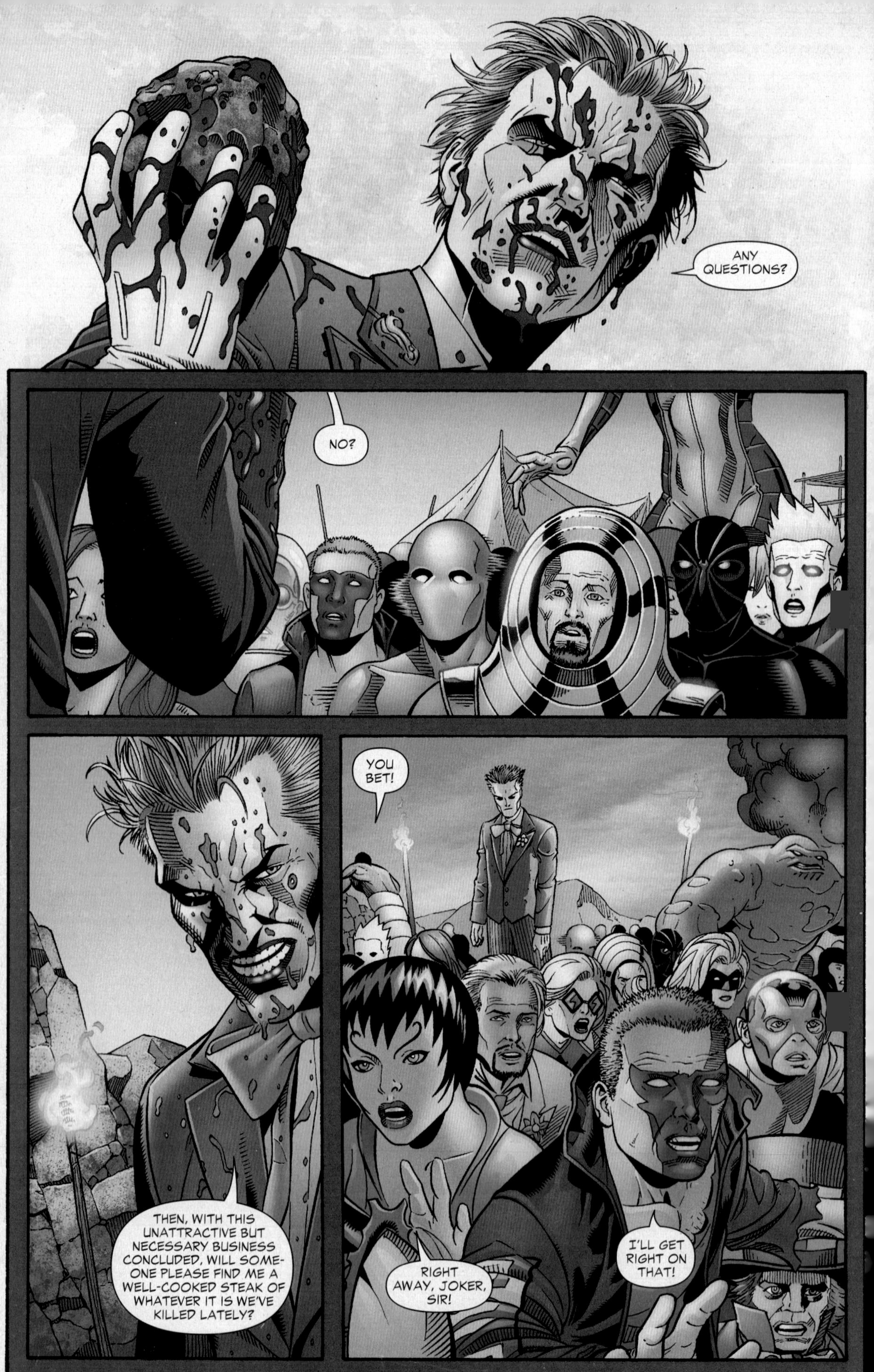
ANY QUESTIONS?
NO?
THEN, WITH THIS UNATTRACTIVE BUT NECESSARY BUSINESS CONCLUDED, WILL SOMEONE PLEASE FIND ME A WELL-COOKED STEAK OF WHATEVER IT IS WE'VE KILLED LATELY?
YOU BET!
RIGHT AWAY, JOKER, SIR!
I'LL GET RIGHT ON THAT!

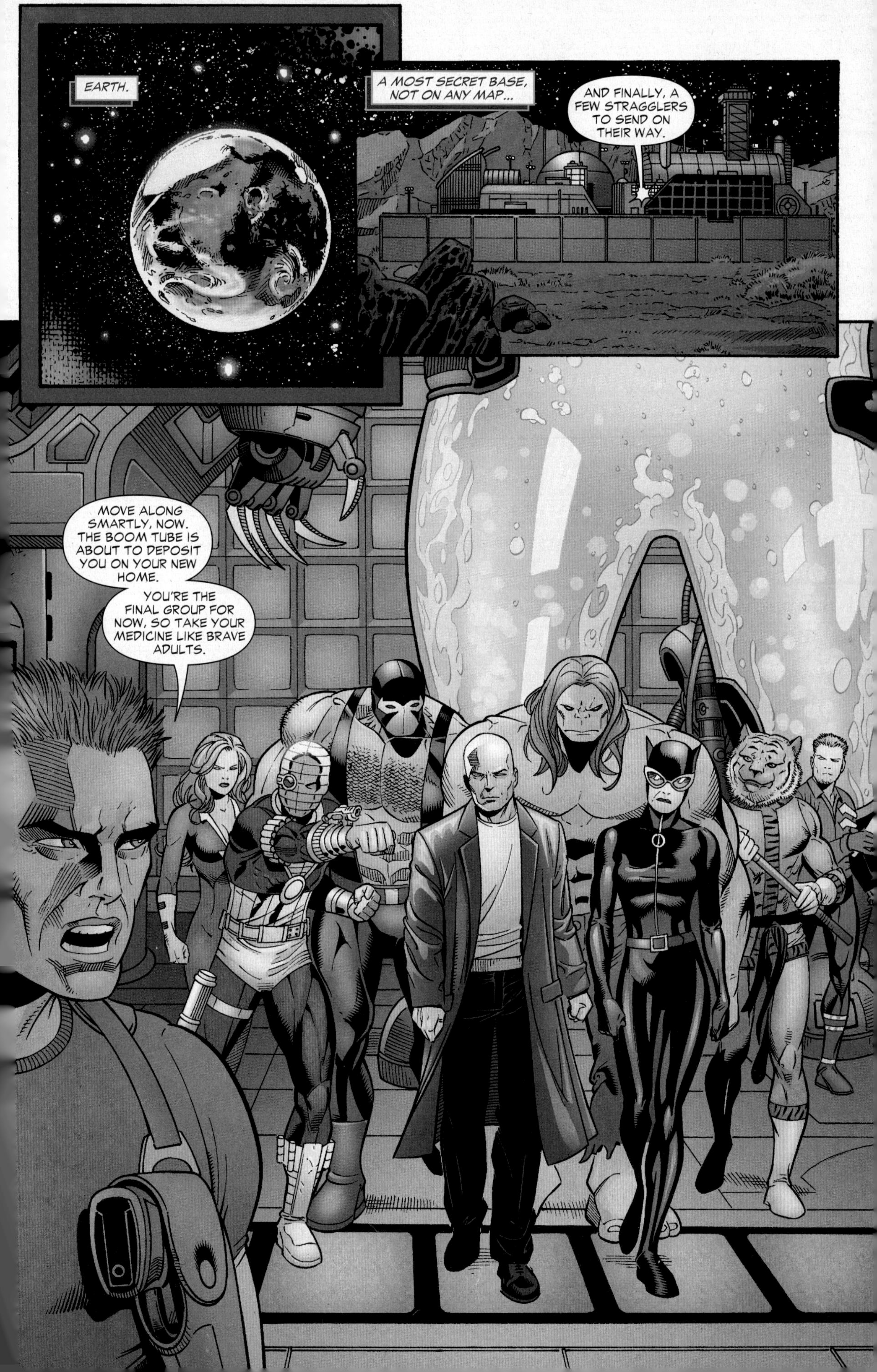
EARTH.
A MOST SECRET BASE, NOT ON ANY MAP...
AND FINALLY, A FEW STRAGGLERS TO SEND ON THEIR WAY.
MOVE ALONG SMARTLY, NOW. THE BOOM TUBE IS ABOUT TO DEPOSIT YOU ON YOUR NEW HOME.
YOU'RE THE FINAL GROUP FOR NOW, SO TAKE YOUR MEDICINE LIKE BRAVE ADULTS.

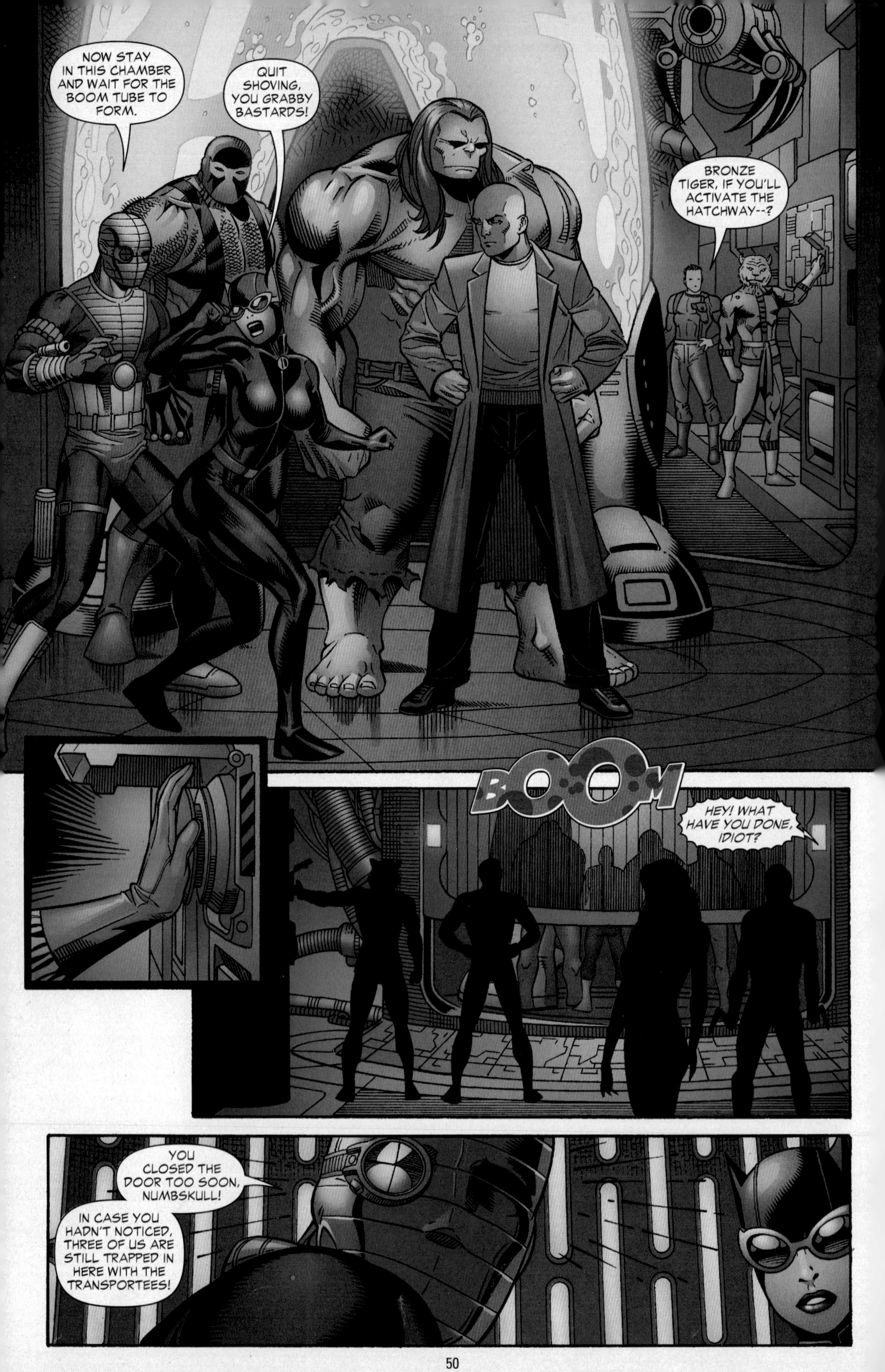
NOW STAY IN THIS CHAMBER AND WAIT FOR THE BOOM TUBE TO FORM.
QUIT SHOVING, YOU GRABBY BASTARDS!
BRONZE TIGER, IF YOU'LL ACTIVATE THE HATCHWAY--?
BOOOM
HEY! WHAT HAVE YOU DONE, IDIOT?
YOU CLOSED THE DOOR TOO SOON, NUMBSKULL!
IN CASE YOU HADN'T NOTICED, THREE OF US ARE STILL TRAPPED IN HERE WITH THE TRANSPORTEES!

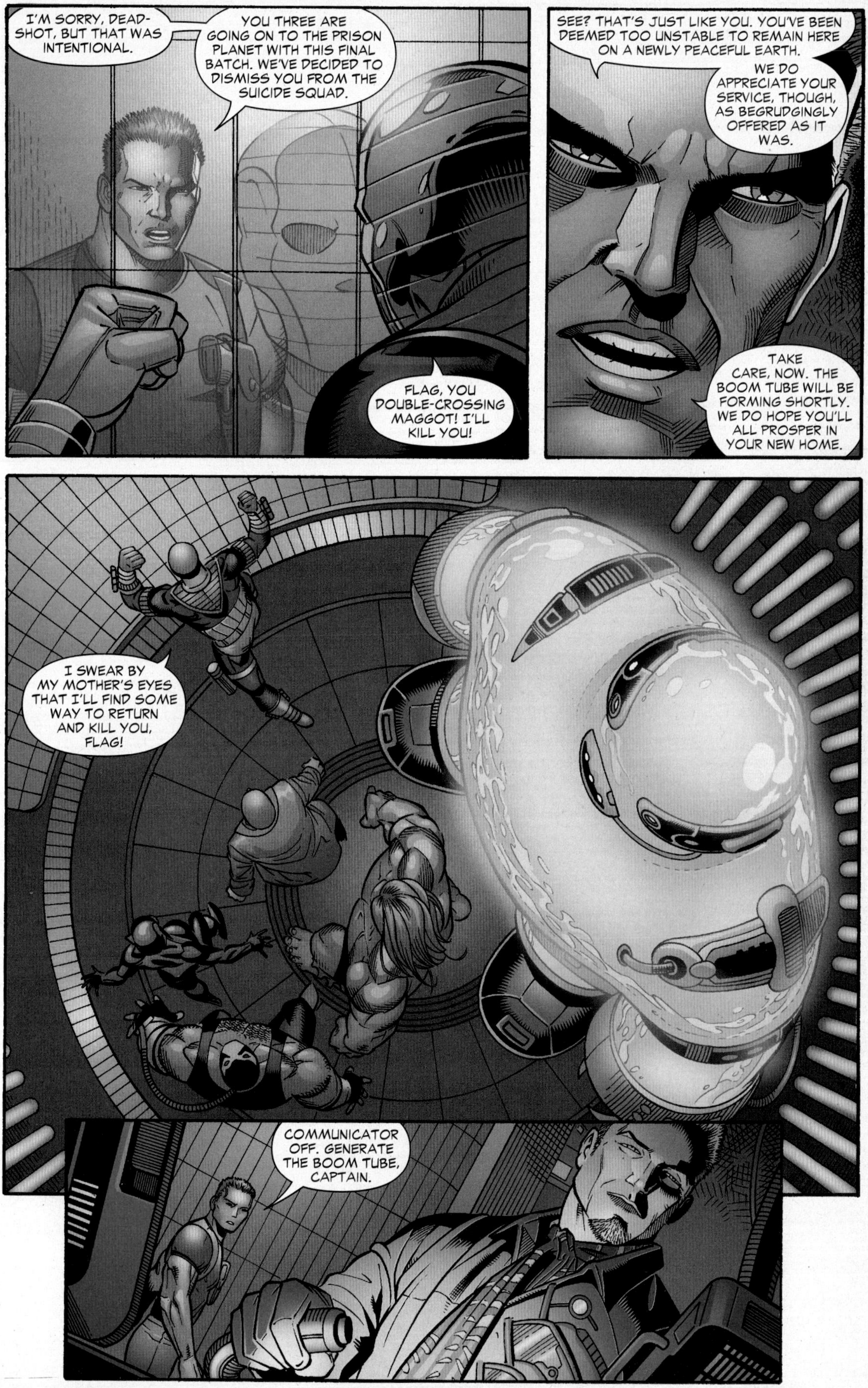
I'M SORRY, DEAD-SHOT, BUT THAT WAS INTENTIONAL.
YOU THREE ARE GOING ON TO THE PRISON PLANET WITH THIS FINAL BATCH. WE'VE DECIDED TO DISMISS YOU FROM THE SUICIDE SQUAD.
FLAG, YOU DOUBLE-CROSSING MAGGOT! I'LL KILL YOU!
SEE? THAT'S JUST LIKE YOU. YOU'VE BEEN DEEMED TOO UNSTABLE TO REMAIN HERE ON A NEWLY PEACEFUL EARTH.
WE DO APPRECIATE YOUR SERVICE, THOUGH, AS BEGRUDGINGLY OFFERED AS IT WAS.
TAKE CARE, NOW. THE BOOM TUBE WILL BE FORMING SHORTLY. WE DO HOPE YOU'LL ALL PROSPER IN YOUR NEW HOME.
I SWEAR BY MY MOTHER'S EYES THAT I'LL FIND SOME WAY TO RETURN AND KILL YOU, FLAG!
COMMUNICATOR OFF. GENERATE THE BOOM TUBE, CAPTAIN.

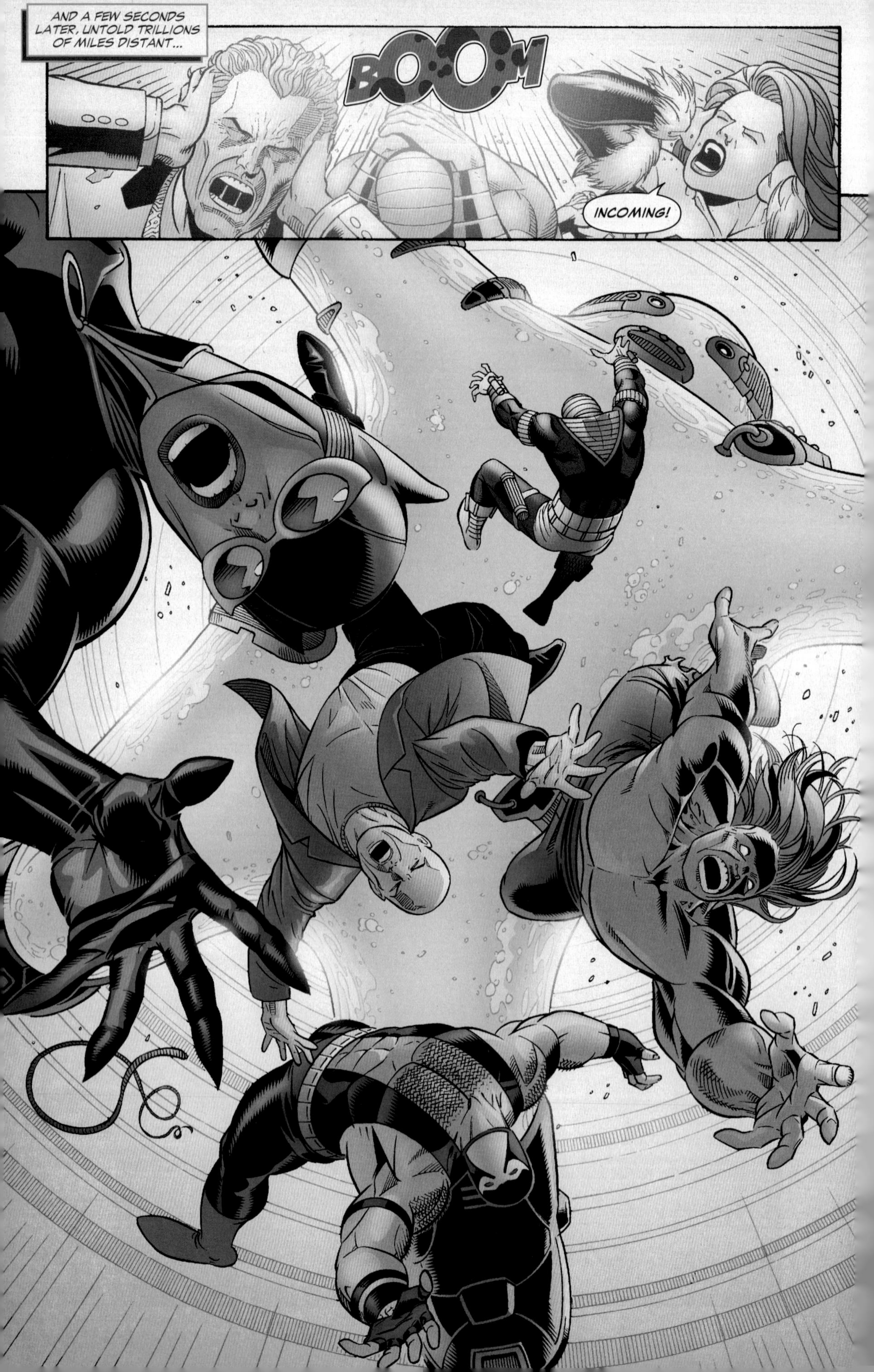
AND A FEW SECONDS LATER, UNTOLD TRILLIONS OF MILES DISTANT...
BOOOM
INCOMING!

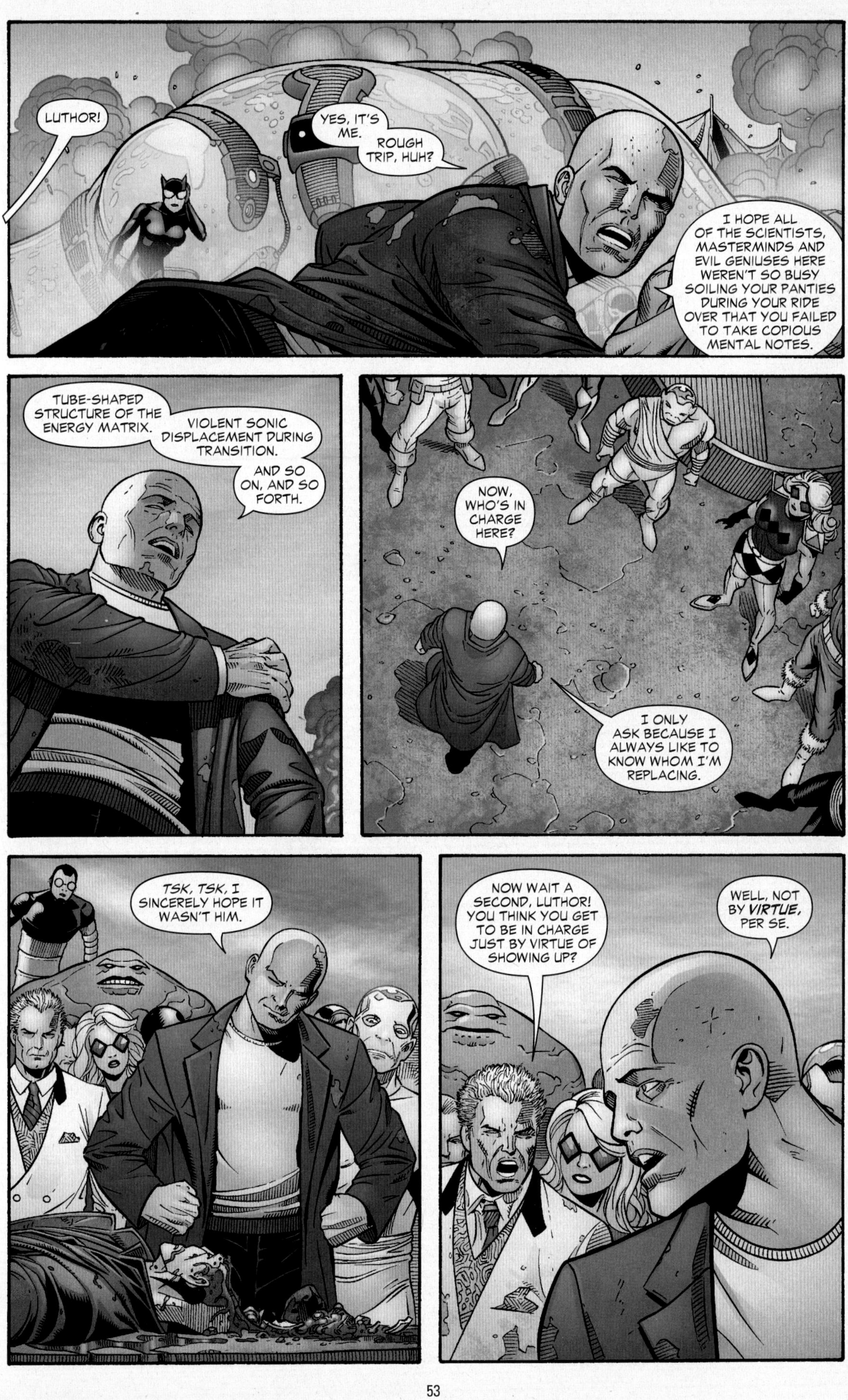
LUTHOR!
YES, IT'S ME.
ROUGH TRIP, HUH?
I HOPE ALL OF THE SCIENTISTS, MASTERMINDS AND EVIL GENIUSES HERE WEREN'T SO BUSY SOILING YOUR PANTIES DURING YOUR RIDE OVER THAT YOU FAILED TO TAKE COPIOUS MENTAL NOTES.
TUBE-SHAPED STRUCTURE OF THE ENERGY MATRIX.
VIOLENT SONIC DISPLACEMENT DURING TRANSITION.
AND SO ON, AND SO FORTH.
NOW, WHO'S IN CHARGE HERE?
I ONLY ASK BECAUSE I ALWAYS LIKE TO KNOW WHOM I'M REPLACING.
TSK, TSK, I SINCERELY HOPE IT WASN'T HIM.
NOW WAIT A SECOND, LUTHOR! YOU THINK YOU GET TO BE IN CHARGE JUST BY VIRTUE OF SHOWING UP?
WELL, NOT BY VIRTUE, PER SE.

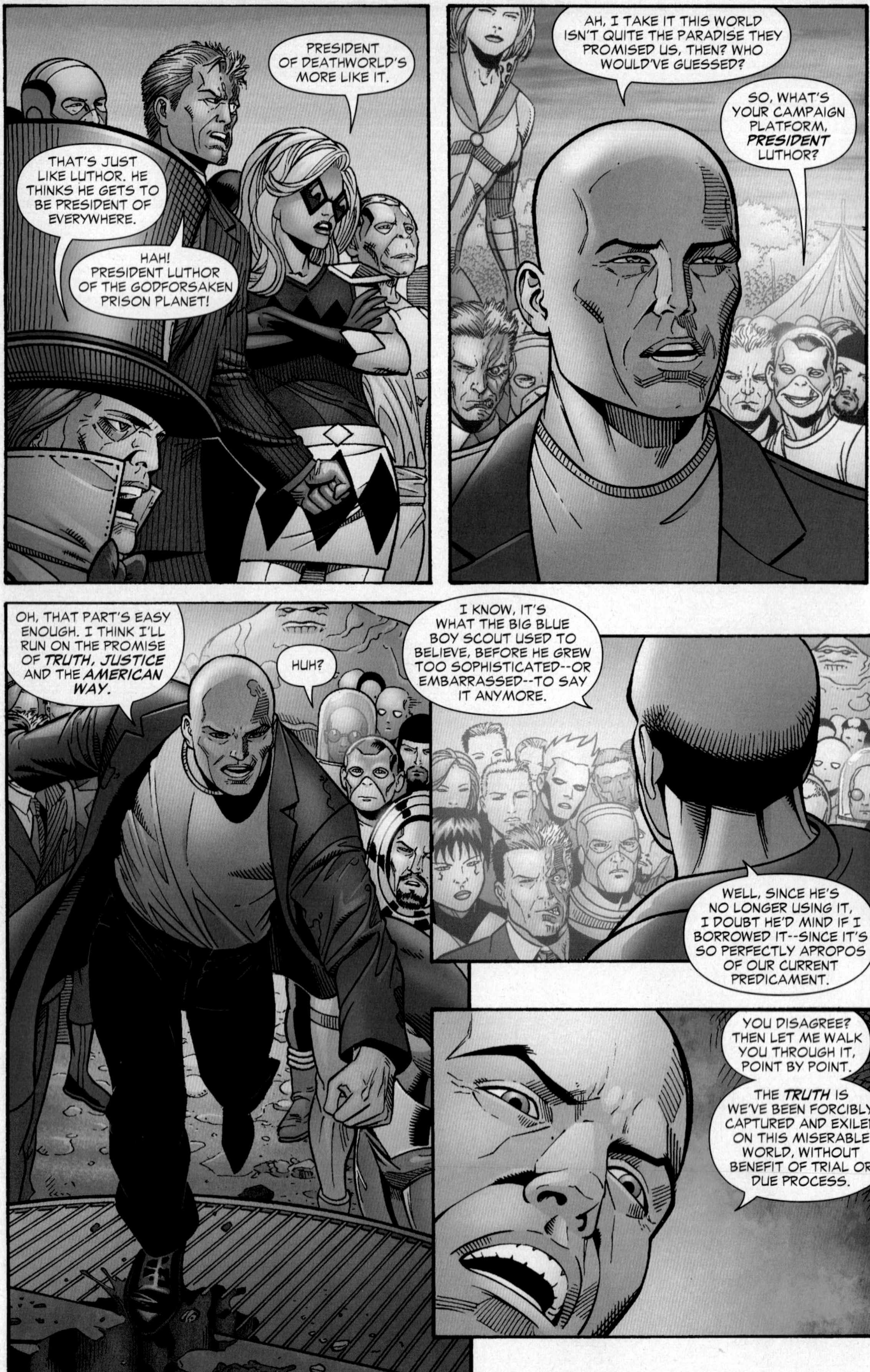
PRESIDENT OF DEATHWORLD'S MORE LIKE IT.
THAT'S JUST LIKE LUTHOR. HE THINKS HE GETS TO BE PRESIDENT OF EVERYWHERE.
HAH! PRESIDENT LUTHOR OF THE GODFORSAKEN PRISON PLANET!
AH, I TAKE IT THIS WORLD ISN'T QUITE THE PARADISE THEY PROMISED US, THEN? WHO WOULD'VE GUESSED?
SO, WHAT'S YOUR CAMPAIGN PLATFORM, PRESIDENT LUTHOR?
OH, THAT PART'S EASY ENOUGH. I THINK I'LL RUN ON THE PROMISE OF TRUTH, JUSTICE AND THE AMERICAN WAY.
HUH?
I KNOW, IT'S WHAT THE BIG BLUE BOY SCOUT USED TO BELIEVE, BEFORE HE GREW TOO SOPHISTICATED--OR EMBARRASSED--TO SAY IT ANYMORE.
WELL, SINCE HE'S NO LONGER USING IT, I DOUBT HE'D MIND IF I BORROWED IT--SINCE IT'S SO PERFECTLY APROPOS OF OUR CURRENT PREDICAMENT.
YOU DISAGREE? THEN LET ME WALK YOU THROUGH IT, POINT BY POINT.
THE TRUTH IS WE'VE BEEN FORCIBLY CAPTURED AND EXILED ON THIS MISERABLE WORLD, WITHOUT BENEFIT OF TRIAL OR DUE PROCESS.

THE ONES WHO DUMPED US HERE EXPECT US TO LIVE OUT THE REST OF OUR SORRY LIVES, SURVIVING PERHAPS, BUT MOST LIKELY DYING HORRIBLE, ALIEN DEATHS.

IT DOESN'T MATTER TO THEM, AS LONG AS WE NEVER DARKEN THEIR DOOR-STEP AGAIN.

BUT THE *JUSTICE* WOULD OCCUR IN FINDING A WAY TO CONFOUND THEIR SCHEMES, TO GET BACK TO OUR OWN WORLD AND EXACT OUR VERY *JUST* REVENGE ON THEM.

PERSONALLY, I'D BE PARTIAL TO FEEDING EACH AND EVERY ONE OF THE SCUM INTO THEIR OWN BOOM TUBE GENERATOR--BUT SELECTING EMPTY SPACE AS THE EXIT POINT.

NOW, I'VE BEEN A LOYAL AMERICAN ALL OF MY LIFE, LONG ENOUGH TO REALIZE WHAT THE TRUE *AMERICAN WAY* IS.

THE TRUE *AMERICAN WAY* IS A SIMPLE FUNCTION OF APPETITE. WHEN I SEE SOMETHING I WANT, I TAKE IT--AS MUCH OF IT AS I WANT.

AND I DON'T CARE A BIT IF THAT DOESN'T LEAVE ENOUGH FOR ANYONE ELSE.

AND IF WHAT I WANT DOESN'T EXIST YET, THEN I FIND A WAY TO BUILD IT.

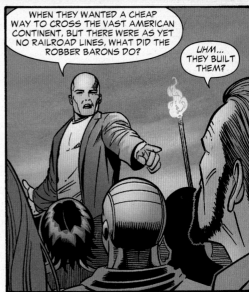

WHEN THEY WANTED A CHEAP WAY TO CROSS THE VAST AMERICAN CONTINENT, BUT THERE WERE AS YET NO RAILROAD LINES, WHAT DID THE ROBBER BARONS DO?

UHM... THEY BUILT THEM?

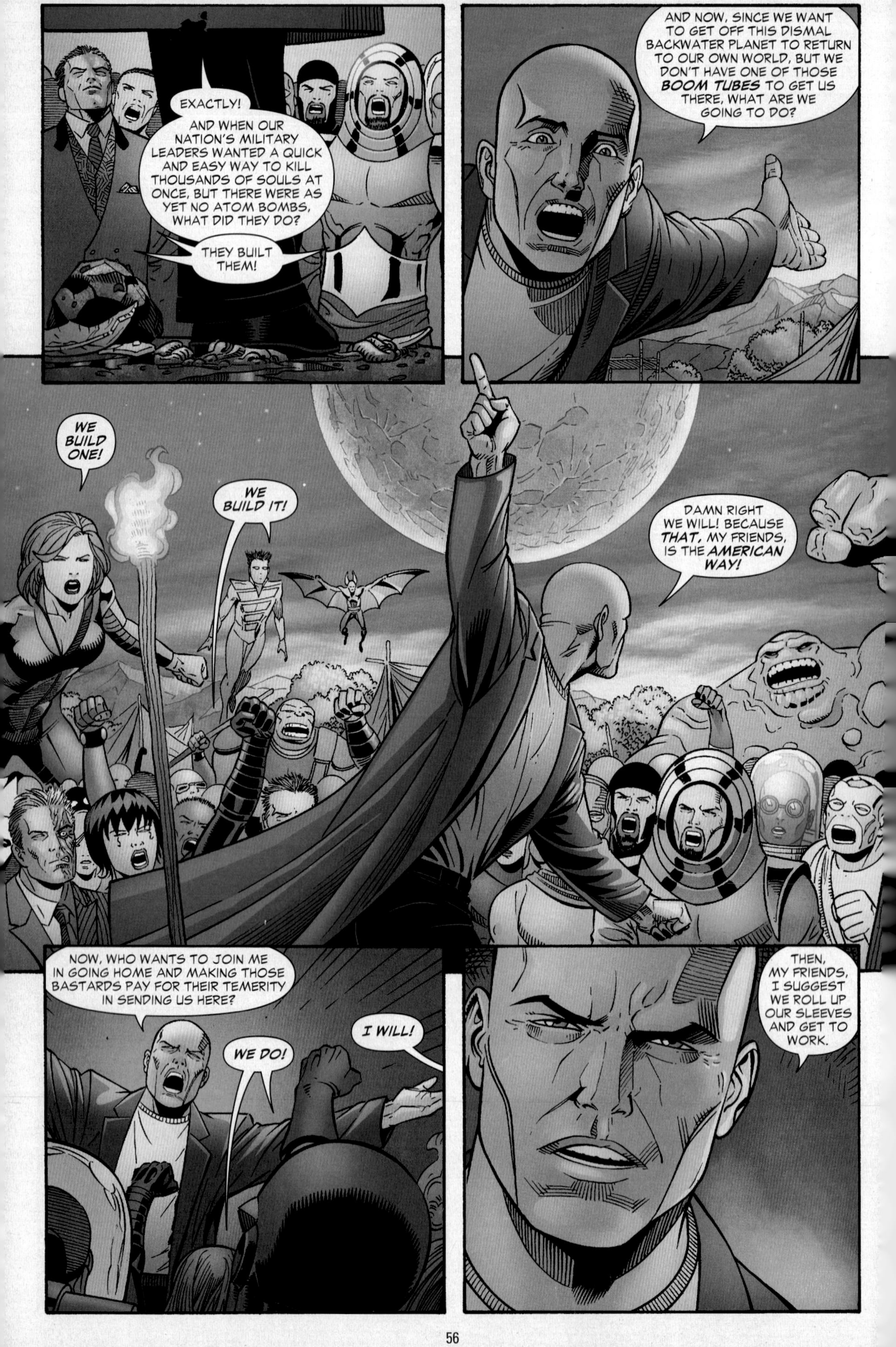

EXACTLY!
AND WHEN OUR NATION'S MILITARY LEADERS WANTED A QUICK AND EASY WAY TO KILL THOUSANDS OF SOULS AT ONCE, BUT THERE WERE AS YET NO ATOM BOMBS, WHAT DID THEY DO?
THEY BUILT THEM!
AND NOW, SINCE WE WANT TO GET OFF THIS DISMAL BACKWATER PLANET TO RETURN TO OUR OWN WORLD, BUT WE DON'T HAVE ONE OF THOSE BOOM TUBES TO GET US THERE, WHAT ARE WE GOING TO DO?
WE BUILD ONE!
WE BUILD IT!
DAMN RIGHT WE WILL! BECAUSE THAT, MY FRIENDS, IS THE AMERICAN WAY!
NOW, WHO WANTS TO JOIN ME IN GOING HOME AND MAKING THOSE BASTARDS PAY FOR THEIR TEMERITY IN SENDING US HERE?
WE DO!
I WILL!
THEN, MY FRIENDS, I SUGGEST WE ROLL UP OUR SLEEVES AND GET TO WORK.

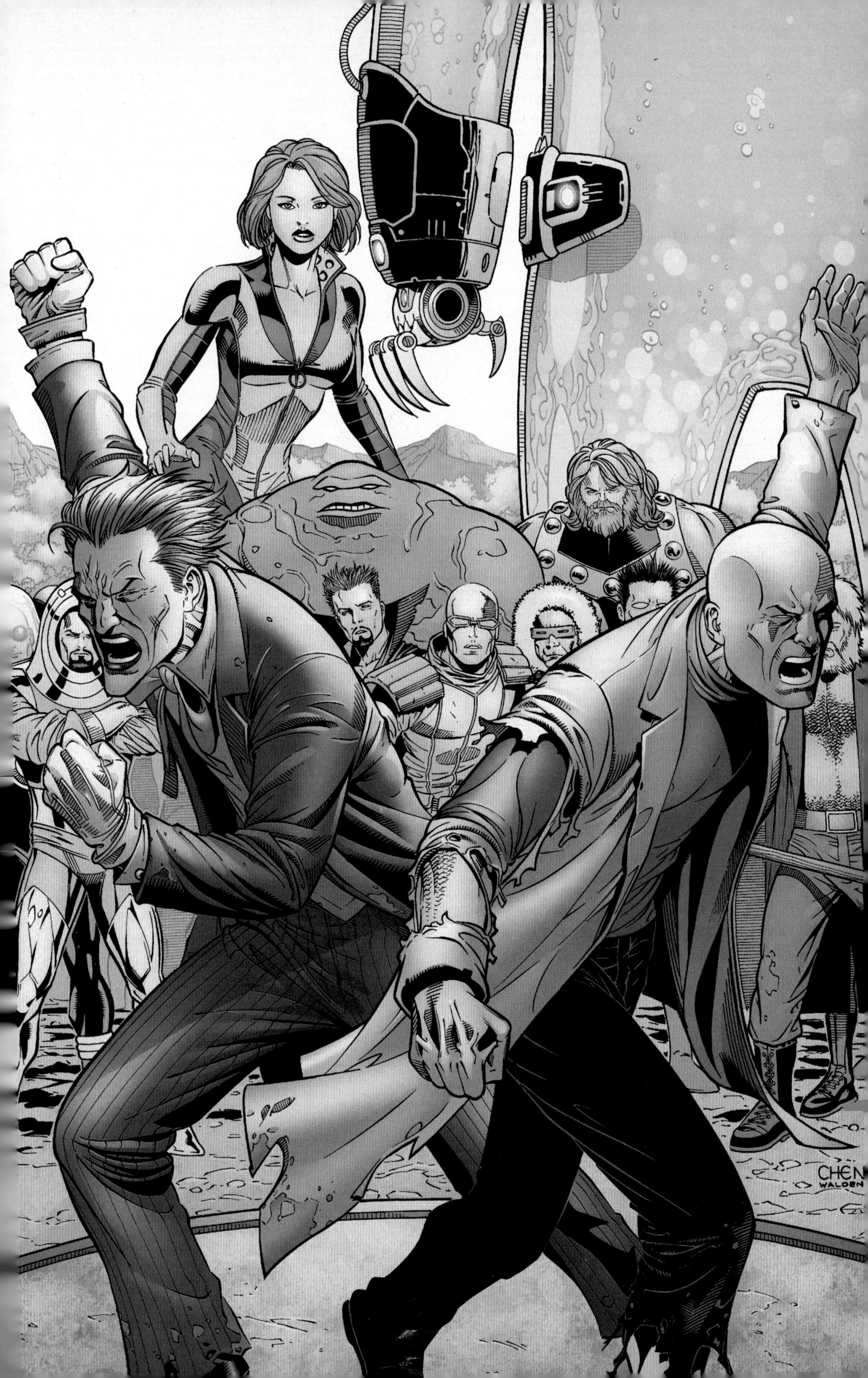
CHEN
WALDEN

Matthew Sturges
Writer

Sean Chen
Penciller

Walden Wong
Inker

John Kalisz
Colorist

Steve Wands
Letterer

CHAPTER THREE

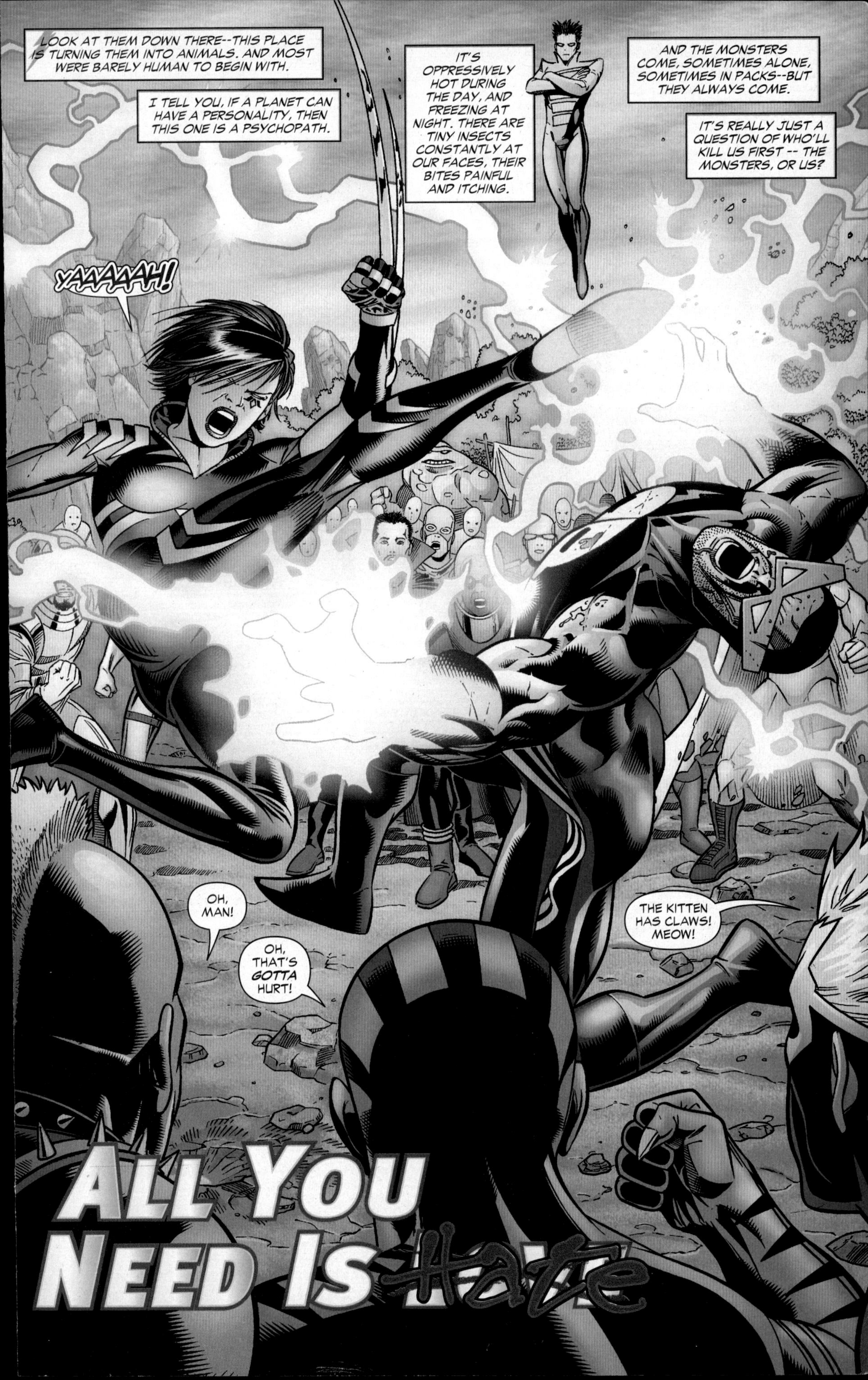

LOOK AT THEM DOWN THERE--THIS PLACE IS TURNING THEM INTO ANIMALS. AND MOST WERE BARELY HUMAN TO BEGIN WITH.
I TELL YOU, IF A PLANET CAN HAVE A PERSONALITY, THEN THIS ONE IS A PSYCHOPATH.
IT'S OPPRESSIVELY HOT DURING THE DAY, AND FREEZING AT NIGHT. THERE ARE TINY INSECTS CONSTANTLY AT OUR FACES, THEIR BITES PAINFUL AND ITCHING.
AND THE MONSTERS COME, SOMETIMES ALONE, SOMETIMES IN PACKS--BUT THEY ALWAYS COME.
IT'S REALLY JUST A QUESTION OF WHO'LL KILL US FIRST -- THE MONSTERS, OR US?
YAAAAAH!
OH, MAN!
OH, THAT'S GOTTA HURT!
THE KITTEN HAS CLAWS! MEOW!
ALL YOU NEED IS Hate

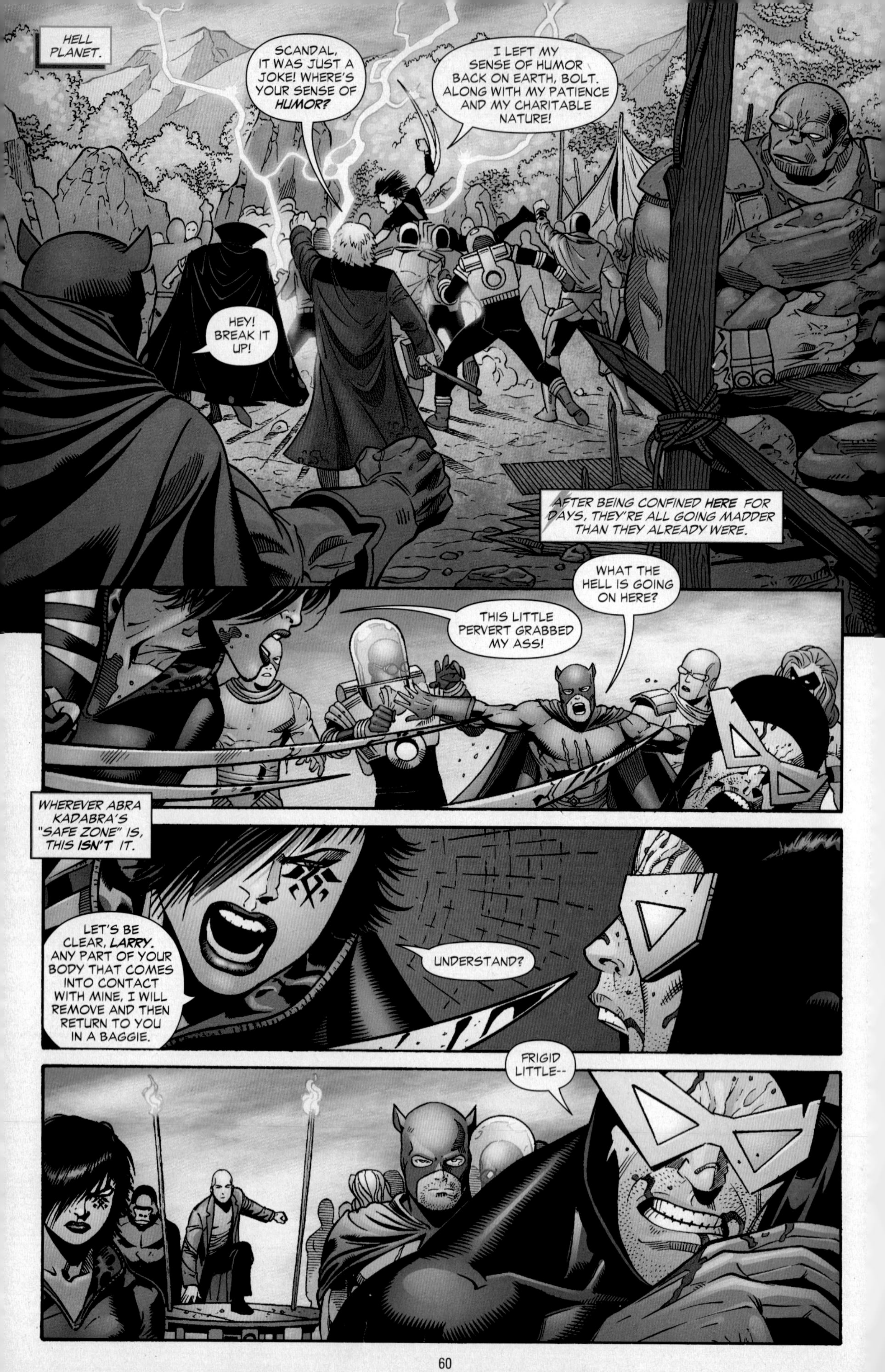
HELL PLANET.
SCANDAL, IT WAS JUST A JOKE! WHERE'S YOUR SENSE OF HUMOR?
I LEFT MY SENSE OF HUMOR BACK ON EARTH, BOLT. ALONG WITH MY PATIENCE AND MY CHARITABLE NATURE!
HEY! BREAK IT UP!
AFTER BEING CONFINED HERE FOR DAYS, THEY'RE ALL GOING MADDER THAN THEY ALREADY WERE.
WHAT THE HELL IS GOING ON HERE?
THIS LITTLE PERVERT GRABBED MY ASS!
WHEREVER ABRA KADABRA'S "SAFE ZONE" IS, THIS ISN'T IT.
LET'S BE CLEAR, LARRY. ANY PART OF YOUR BODY THAT COMES INTO CONTACT WITH MINE, I WILL REMOVE AND THEN RETURN TO YOU IN A BAGGIE.
UNDERSTAND?
FRIGID LITTLE--

LEX LUTHOR IS THE UNDISPUTED LEADER OF THIS GROUP IN ALL BUT NAME.

LADIES AND GENTLEMEN! YOUR ATTENTION, PLEASE!

NOBODY'S CHALLENGED HIM OPENLY--YET. BUT OPINIONS ARE LIKE--WELL, LIKE *WEATHER*-- AND THEY CAN CHANGE IN THE BLINK OF AN EYE...

I REALIZE THAT WE'RE ALL UNDER A GREAT DEAL OF STRESS, AND THAT TEMPERS ARE GETTING SHORTER BY THE MINUTE.

AND SOME OF YOU ARE PROBABLY WONDERING IF YOU'RE GOING TO BE SPENDING THE REST OF YOUR LIVES HERE.

WELL, I'M HERE TO TELL YOU THAT I HAVE FINALLY DEVISED A WAY TO GET US OFF THIS ROCK.

WITH THE VERY ABLE ASSISTANCE OF DR. SIVANA, GENERAL IMMORTUS, AND PROFESSOR IVO, OF COURSE.

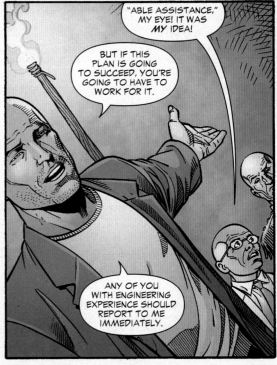

"ABLE ASSISTANCE," MY EYE! IT WAS *MY* IDEA!

BUT IF THIS PLAN IS GOING TO SUCCEED, YOU'RE GOING TO HAVE TO WORK FOR IT.

ANY OF YOU WITH ENGINEERING EXPERIENCE SHOULD REPORT TO ME IMMEDIATELY.

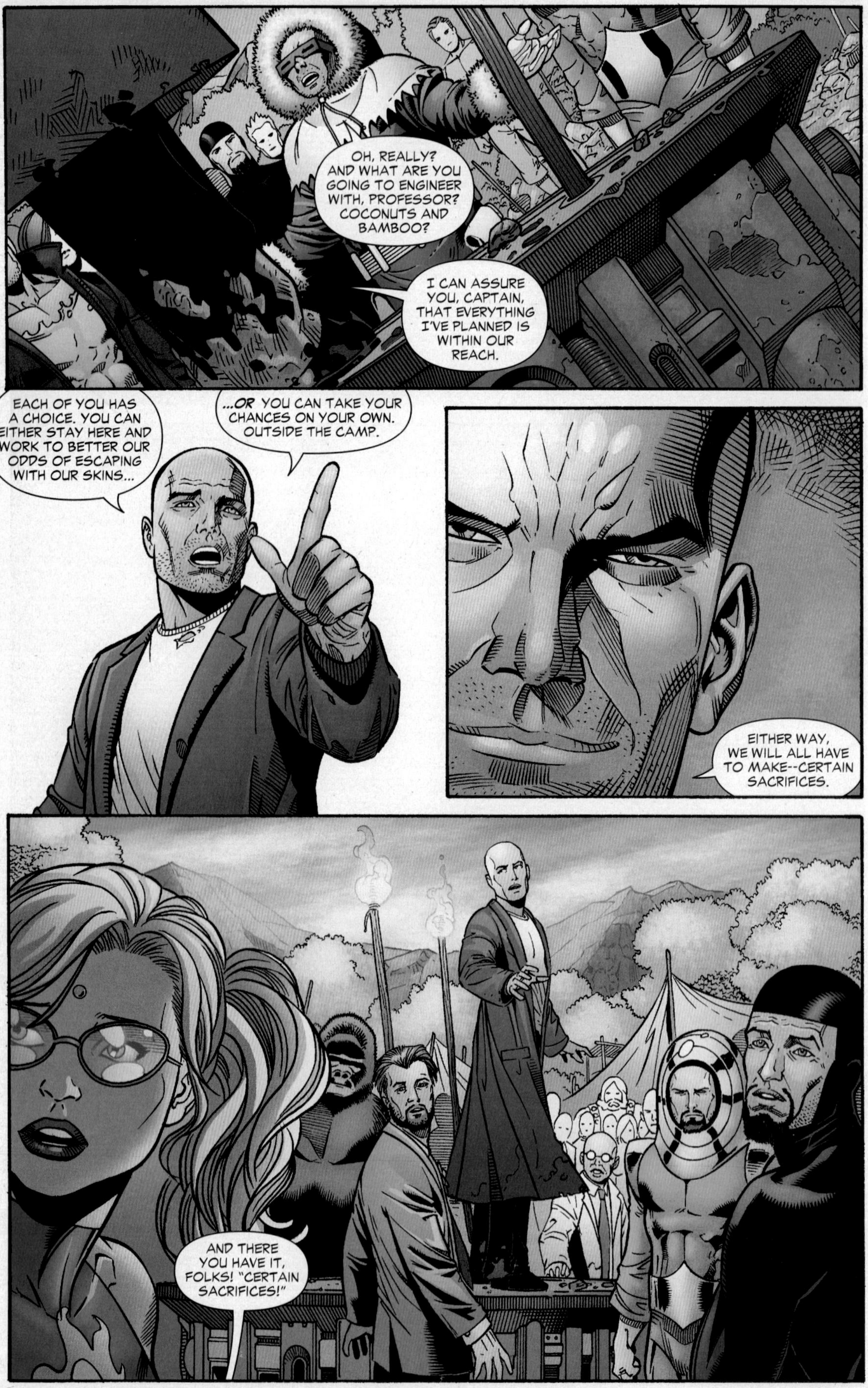
OH, REALLY? AND WHAT ARE YOU GOING TO ENGINEER WITH, PROFESSOR? COCONUTS AND BAMBOO?
I CAN ASSURE YOU, CAPTAIN, THAT EVERYTHING I'VE PLANNED IS WITHIN OUR REACH.
EACH OF YOU HAS A CHOICE. YOU CAN EITHER STAY HERE AND WORK TO BETTER OUR ODDS OF ESCAPING WITH OUR SKINS...
...OR YOU CAN TAKE YOUR CHANCES ON YOUR OWN. OUTSIDE THE CAMP.
EITHER WAY, WE WILL ALL HAVE TO MAKE--CERTAIN SACRIFICES.
AND THERE YOU HAVE IT, FOLKS! "CERTAIN SACRIFICES!"

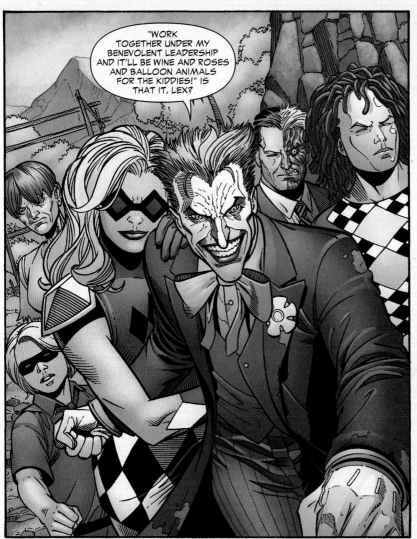

"WORK TOGETHER UNDER MY BENEVOLENT LEADERSHIP AND IT'LL BE WINE AND ROSES AND BALLOON ANIMALS FOR THE KIDDIES!" IS THAT IT, LEX?

IF YOU DON'T MIND, THE *GROWN-UPS* ARE TRYING TO HAVE A CONVERSATION.

NO, NO, SIVANA. WE'LL SORT THIS OUT RIGHT NOW.

I'VE NEVER LIKED YOU, JOKER. YOU'RE DANGEROUS AND UNSTABLE.

PSIMON COULD HAVE HELPED US GET OFF THIS PLANET AND YOU BLUDGEONED HIM TO DEATH FOR NOTHING! THAT KIND OF IDIOCY WILL GET US *ALL* KILLED.

PSIMON? BUT HE WAS SO *OBNOXIOUS!* AND THAT VISIBLE BRAIN OF HIS MADE ME ANXIOUS--I ALWAYS FELT LIKE IT WAS... THROBBING AT ME.

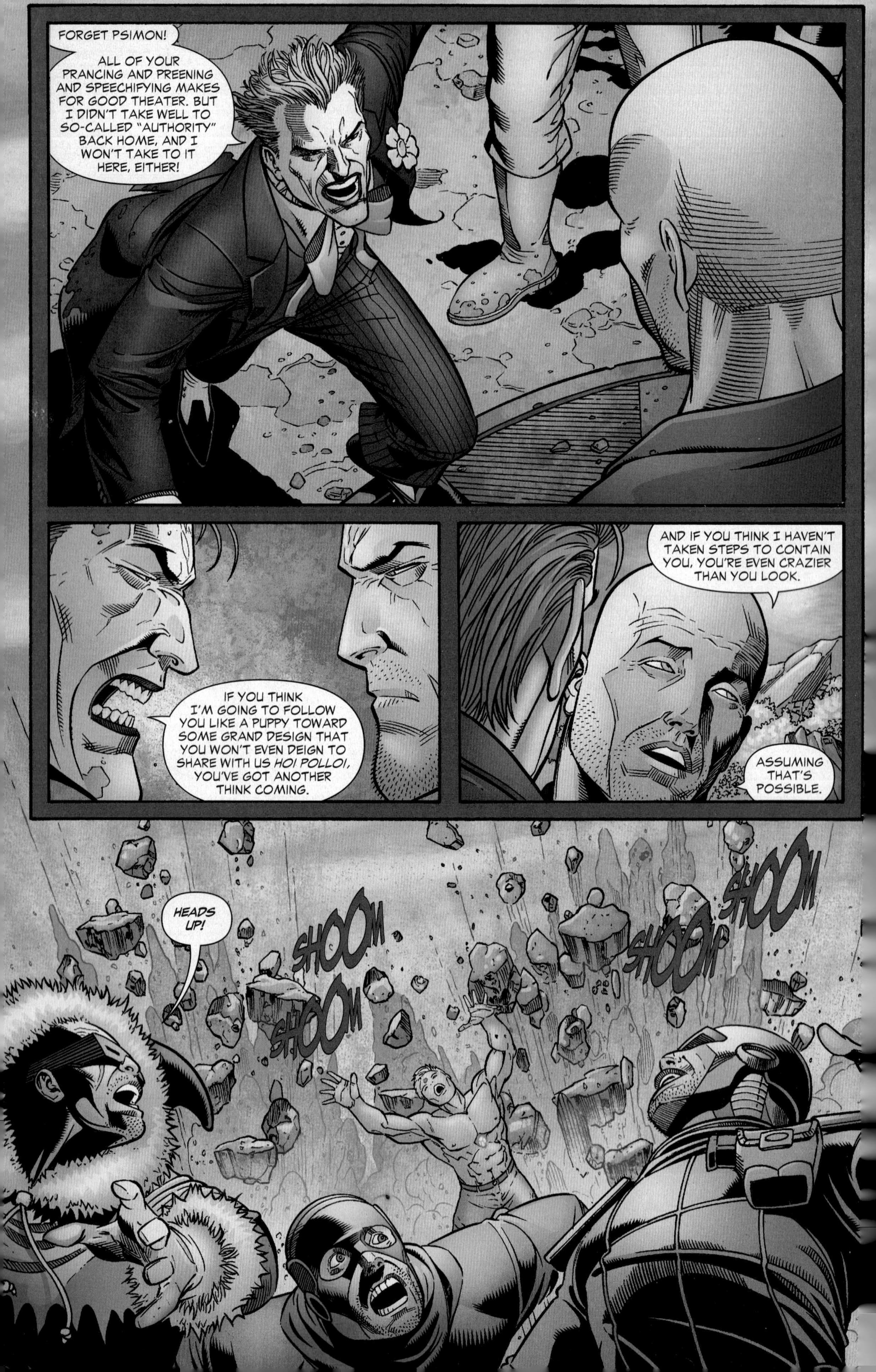
FORGET PSIMON!
ALL OF YOUR PRANCING AND PREENING AND SPEECHIFYING MAKES FOR GOOD THEATER. BUT I DIDN'T TAKE WELL TO SO-CALLED "AUTHORITY" BACK HOME, AND I WON'T TAKE TO IT HERE, EITHER!
IF YOU THINK I'M GOING TO FOLLOW YOU LIKE A PUPPY TOWARD SOME GRAND DESIGN THAT YOU WON'T EVEN DEIGN TO SHARE WITH US *HOI POLLOI*, YOU'VE GOT ANOTHER THINK COMING.
AND IF YOU THINK I HAVEN'T TAKEN STEPS TO CONTAIN YOU, YOU'RE EVEN CRAZIER THAN YOU LOOK.
ASSUMING THAT'S POSSIBLE.
HEADS UP!
SHOOM
SHOOM
SHOOM
SHOOM

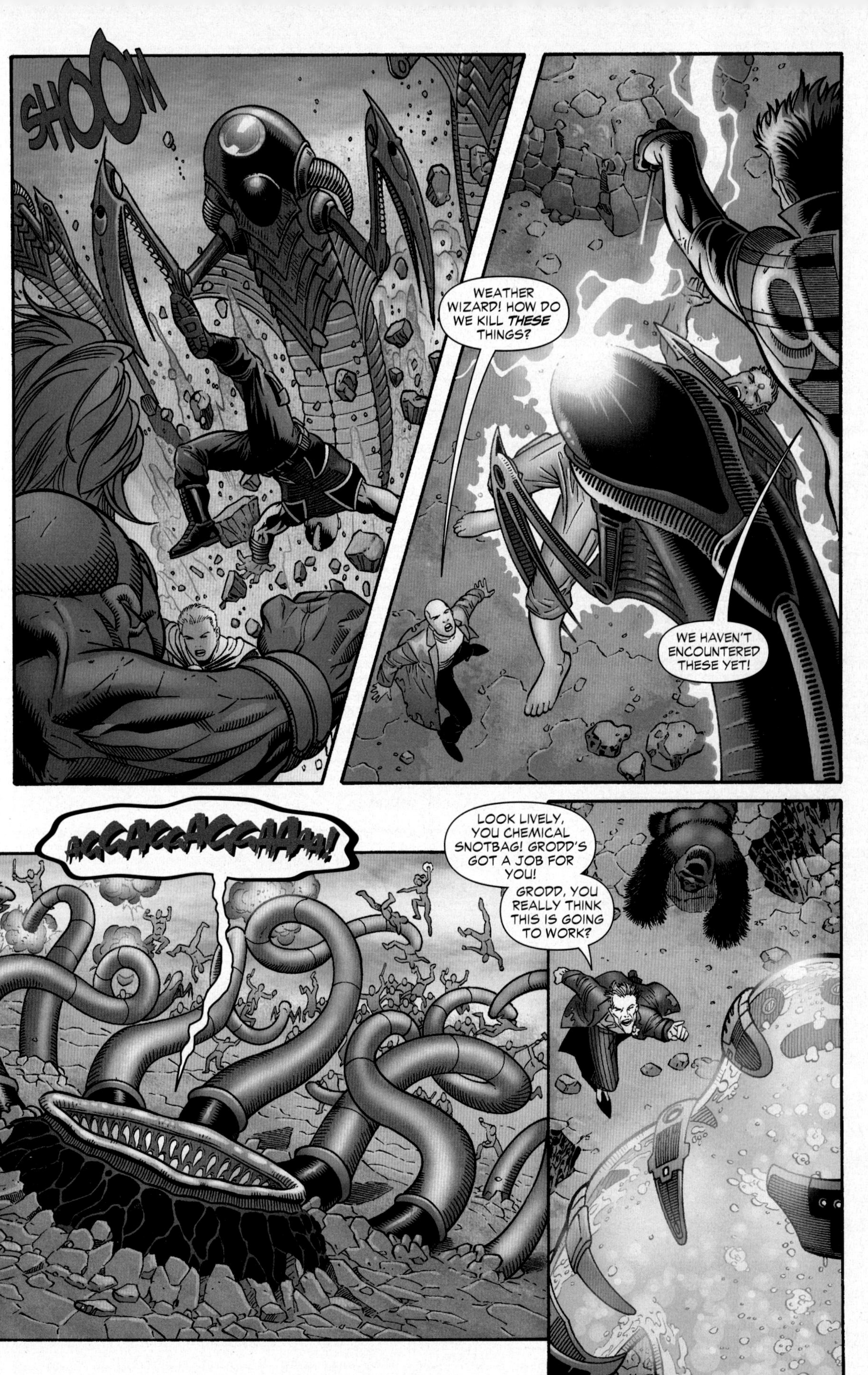
SHOOM
WEATHER WIZARD! HOW DO WE KILL THESE THINGS?
WE HAVEN'T ENCOUNTERED THESE YET!
AGGAGGAGGAAAA!
LOOK LIVELY, YOU CHEMICAL SNOTBAG! GRODD'S GOT A JOB FOR YOU!
GRODD, YOU REALLY THINK THIS IS GOING TO WORK?

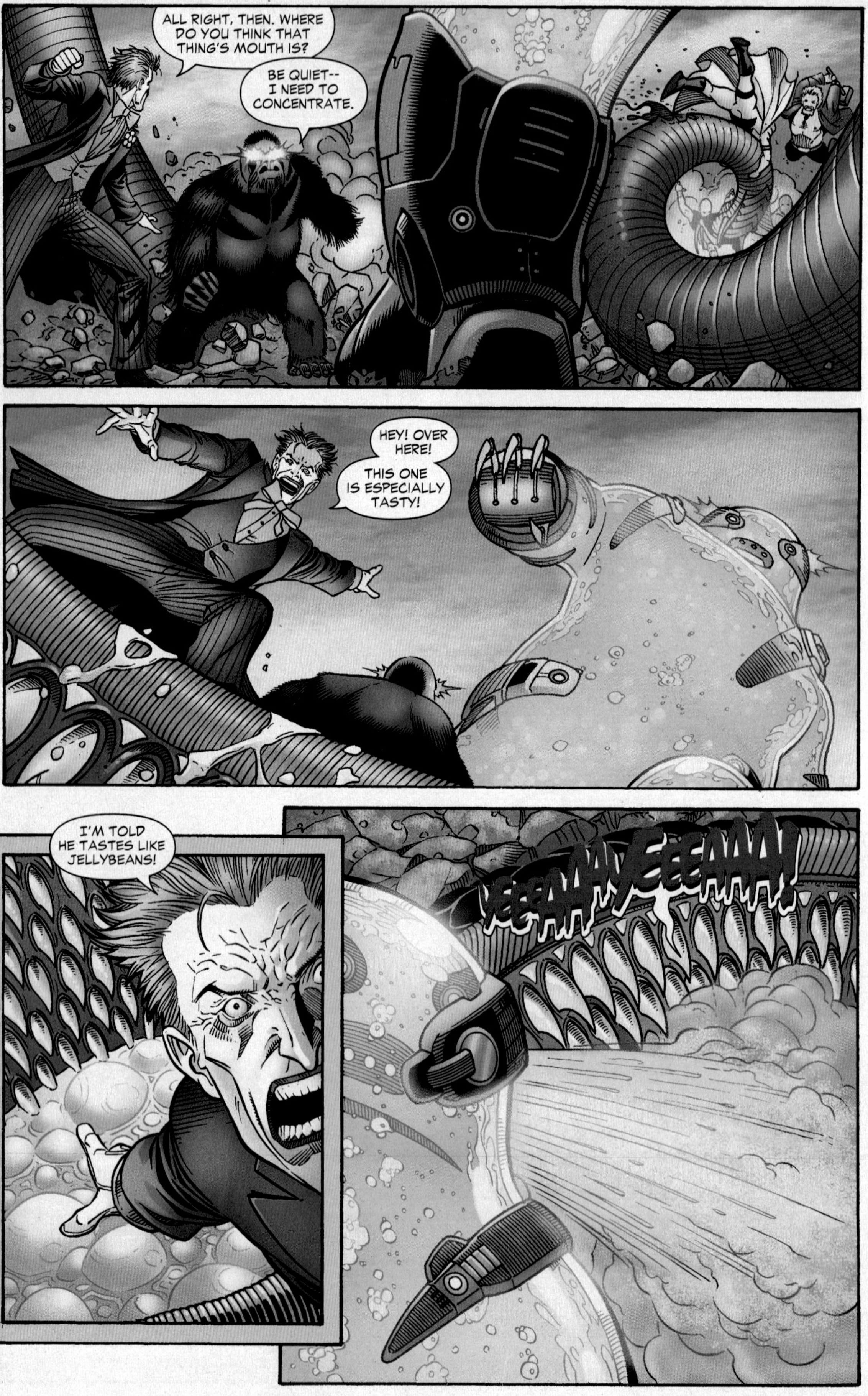
ALL RIGHT, THEN. WHERE DO YOU THINK THAT THING'S MOUTH IS?
BE QUIET-- I NEED TO CONCENTRATE.
HEY! OVER HERE!
THIS ONE IS ESPECIALLY TASTY!
I'M TOLD HE TASTES LIKE JELLYBEANS!
YEEEAAAHYEEEAAAA!

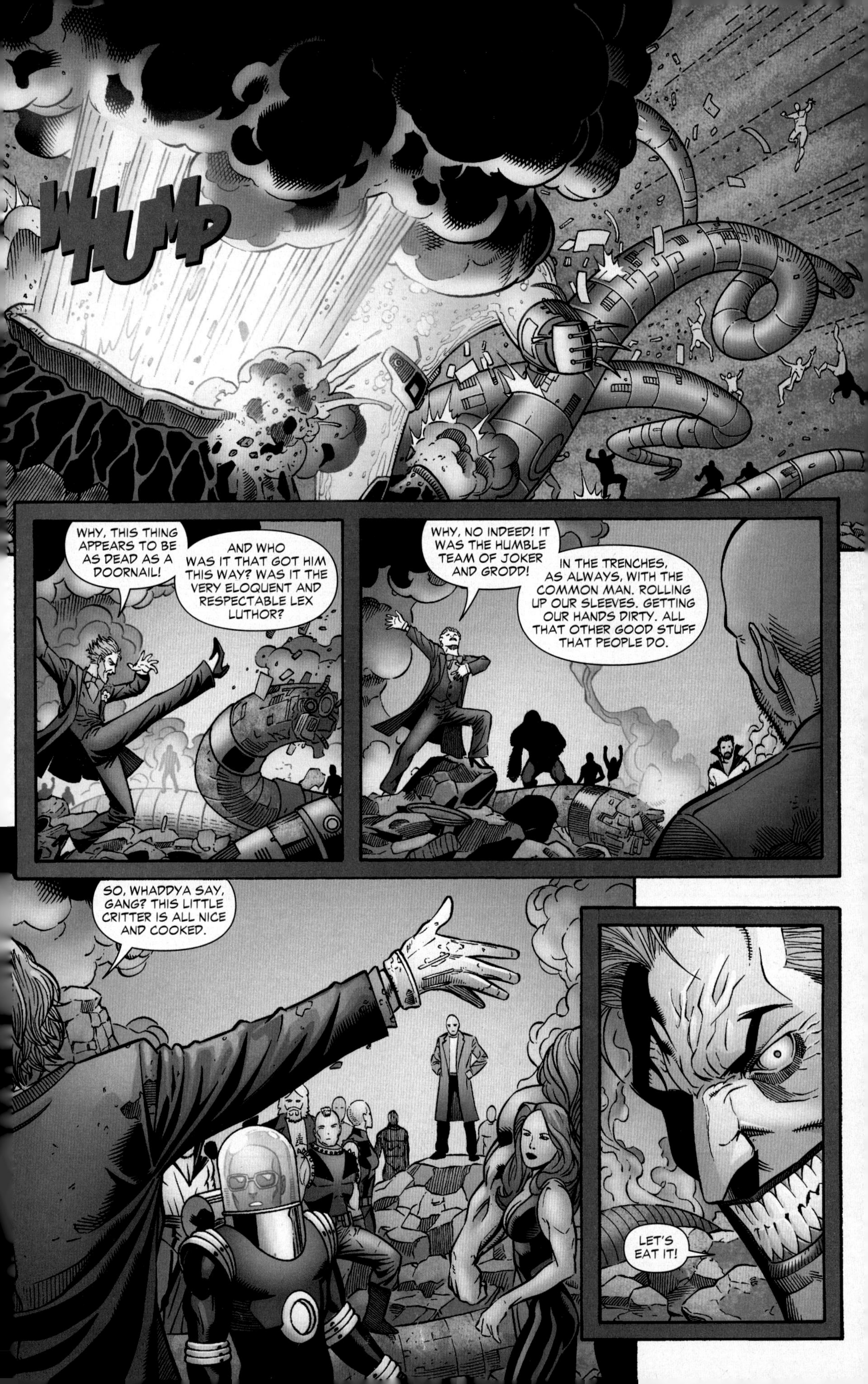
WHUMP
WHY, THIS THING APPEARS TO BE AS DEAD AS A DOORNAIL!
AND WHO WAS IT THAT GOT HIM THIS WAY? WAS IT THE VERY ELOQUENT AND RESPECTABLE LEX LUTHOR?
WHY, NO INDEED! IT WAS THE HUMBLE TEAM OF JOKER AND GRODD!
IN THE TRENCHES, AS ALWAYS, WITH THE COMMON MAN. ROLLING UP OUR SLEEVES. GETTING OUR HANDS DIRTY. ALL THAT OTHER GOOD STUFF THAT PEOPLE DO.
SO, WHADDYA SAY, GANG? THIS LITTLE CRITTER IS ALL NICE AND COOKED.
LET'S EAT IT!

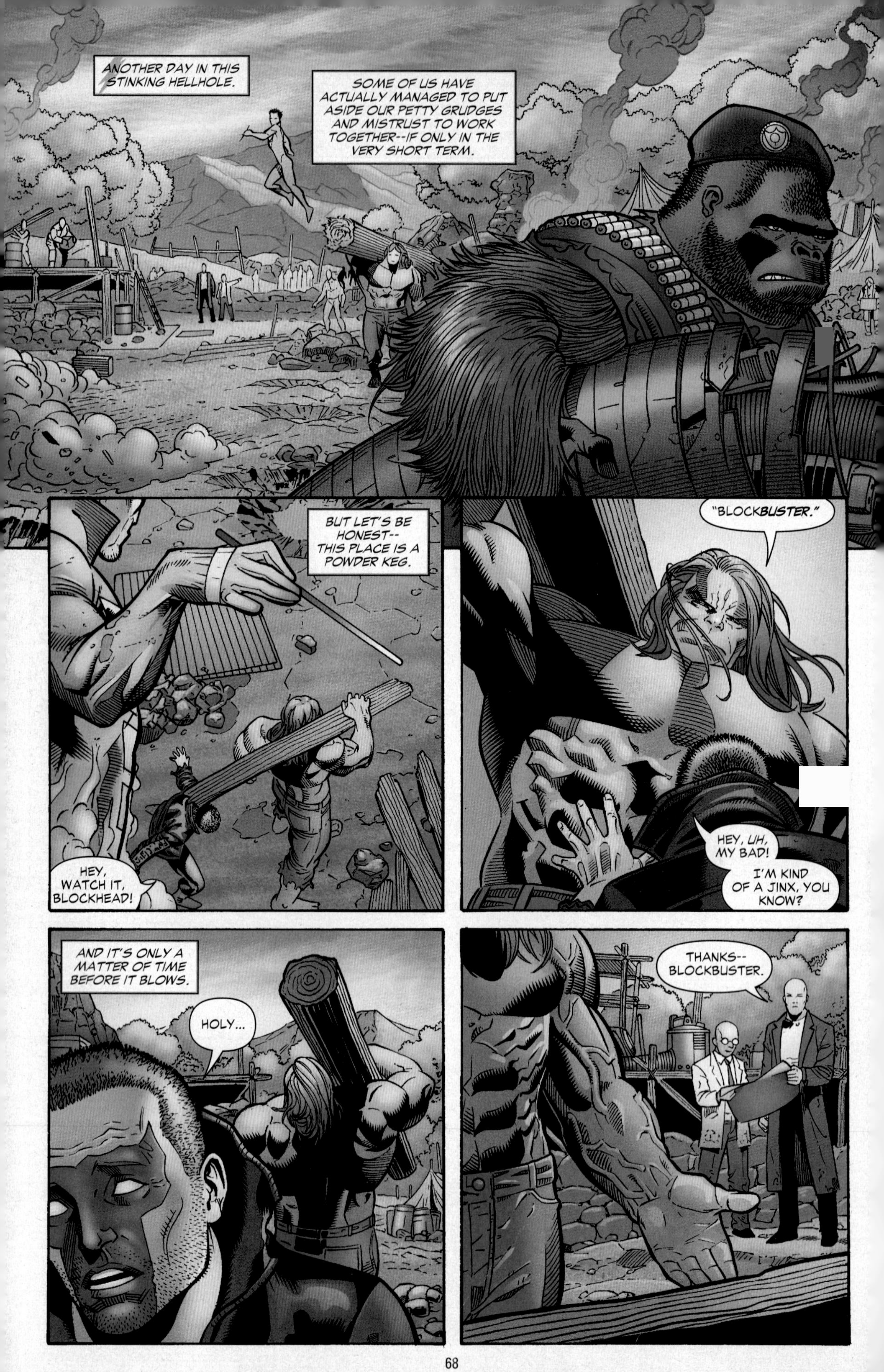

ANOTHER DAY IN THIS STINKING HELLHOLE.
SOME OF US HAVE ACTUALLY MANAGED TO PUT ASIDE OUR PETTY GRUDGES AND MISTRUST TO WORK TOGETHER--IF ONLY IN THE VERY SHORT TERM.
BUT LET'S BE HONEST-- THIS PLACE IS A POWDER KEG.
HEY, WATCH IT, BLOCKHEAD!
"BLOCKBUSTER."
HEY, UH, MY BAD!
I'M KIND OF A JINX, YOU KNOW?
AND IT'S ONLY A MATTER OF TIME BEFORE IT BLOWS.
HOLY...
THANKS-- BLOCKBUSTER.

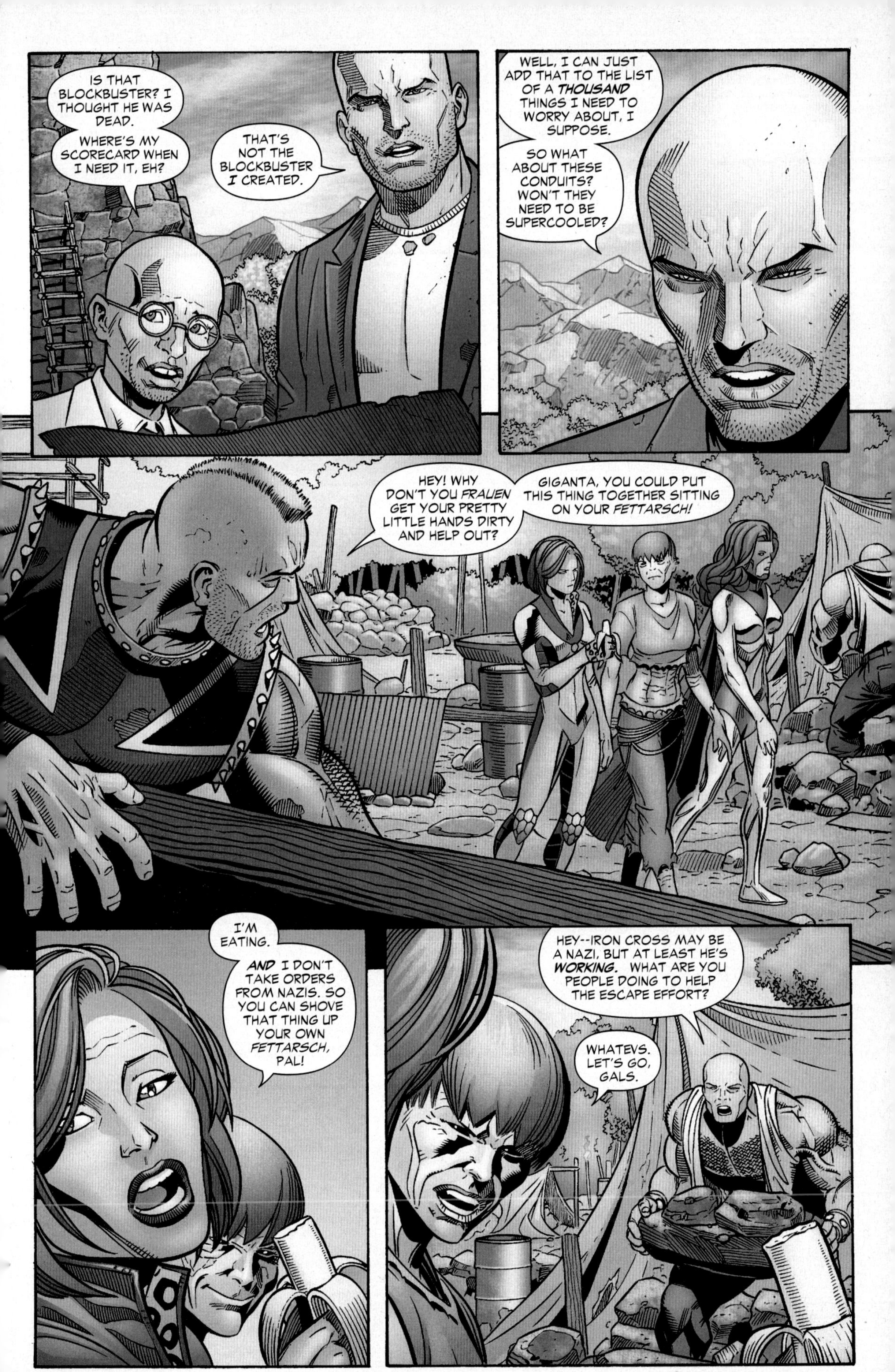

IS THAT BLOCKBUSTER? I THOUGHT HE WAS DEAD.
WHERE'S MY SCORECARD WHEN I NEED IT, EH?
THAT'S NOT THE BLOCKBUSTER *I* CREATED.
WELL, I CAN JUST ADD THAT TO THE LIST OF A ***THOUSAND*** THINGS I NEED TO WORRY ABOUT, I SUPPOSE.
SO WHAT ABOUT THESE CONDUITS? WON'T THEY NEED TO BE SUPERCOOLED?
HEY! WHY DON'T YOU *FRAUEN* GET YOUR PRETTY LITTLE HANDS DIRTY AND HELP OUT?
GIGANTA, YOU COULD PUT THIS THING TOGETHER SITTING ON YOUR *FETTARSCH!*
I'M EATING.
AND I DON'T TAKE ORDERS FROM NAZIS. SO YOU CAN SHOVE THAT THING UP YOUR OWN *FETTARSCH,* PAL!
HEY--IRON CROSS MAY BE A NAZI, BUT AT LEAST HE'S ***WORKING.*** WHAT ARE YOU PEOPLE DOING TO HELP THE ESCAPE EFFORT?
WHATEVS. LET'S GO, GALS.

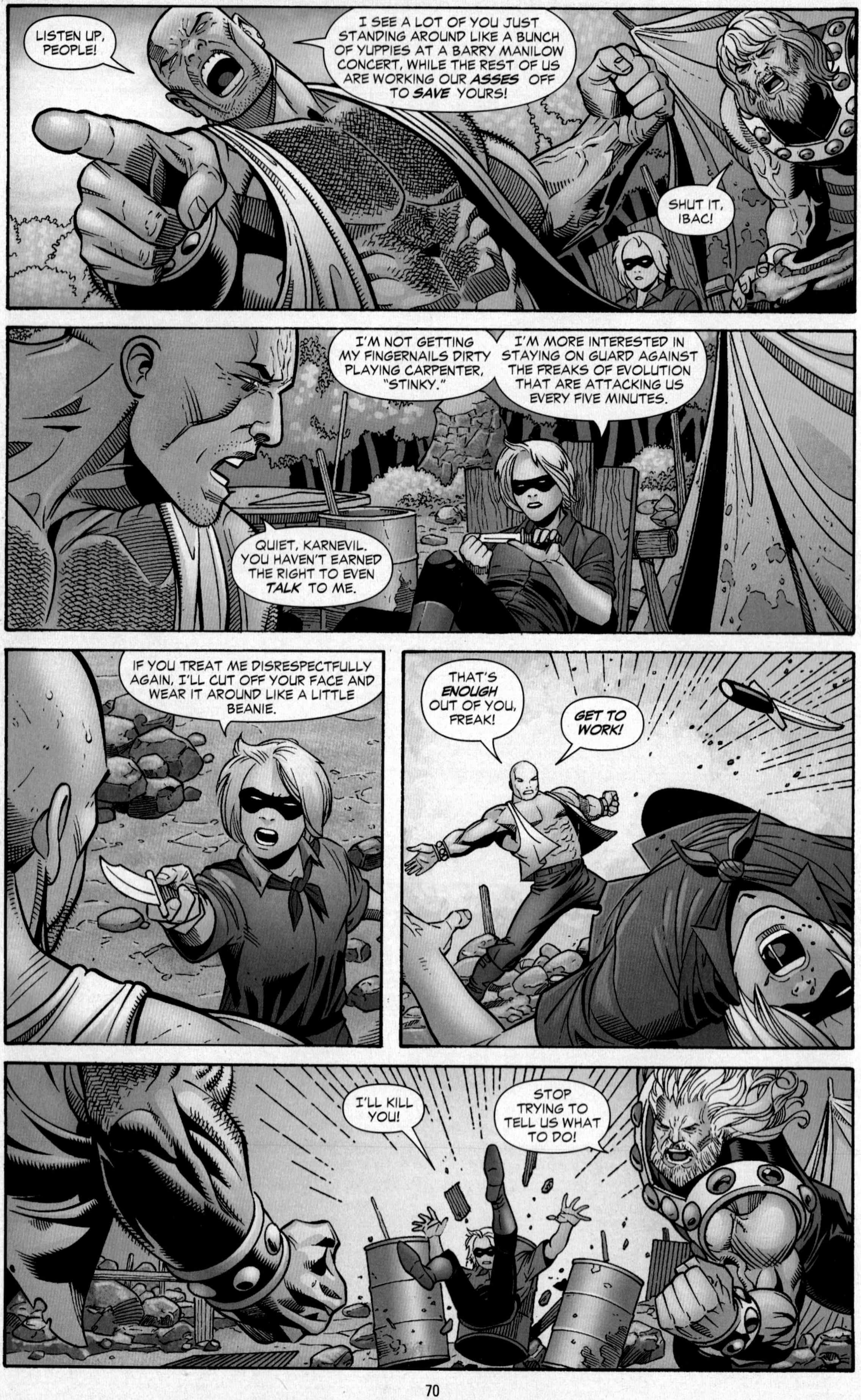
LISTEN UP, PEOPLE!
I SEE A LOT OF YOU JUST STANDING AROUND LIKE A BUNCH OF YUPPIES AT A BARRY MANILOW CONCERT, WHILE THE REST OF US ARE WORKING OUR ASSES OFF TO SAVE YOURS!
SHUT IT, IBAC!
I'M NOT GETTING MY FINGERNAILS DIRTY PLAYING CARPENTER, "STINKY."
I'M MORE INTERESTED IN STAYING ON GUARD AGAINST THE FREAKS OF EVOLUTION THAT ARE ATTACKING US EVERY FIVE MINUTES.
QUIET, KARNEVIL. YOU HAVEN'T EARNED THE RIGHT TO EVEN TALK TO ME.
IF YOU TREAT ME DISRESPECTFULLY AGAIN, I'LL CUT OFF YOUR FACE AND WEAR IT AROUND LIKE A LITTLE BEANIE.
THAT'S ENOUGH OUT OF YOU, FREAK!
GET TO WORK!
I'LL KILL YOU!
STOP TRYING TO TELL US WHAT TO DO!

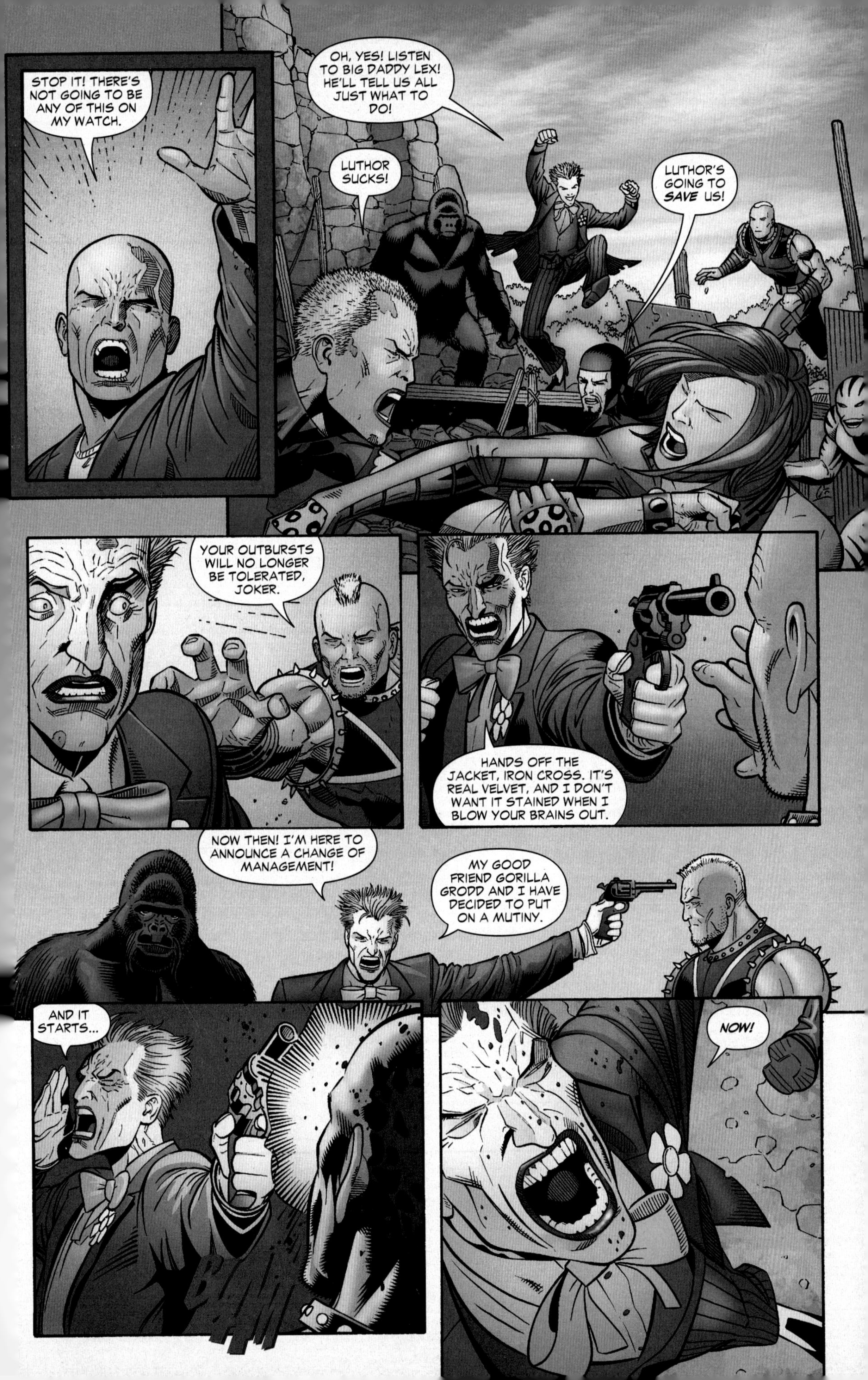
STOP IT! THERE'S NOT GOING TO BE ANY OF THIS ON MY WATCH.
OH, YES! LISTEN TO BIG DADDY LEX! HE'LL TELL US ALL JUST WHAT TO DO!
LUTHOR SUCKS!
LUTHOR'S GOING TO SAVE US!
YOUR OUTBURSTS WILL NO LONGER BE TOLERATED, JOKER.
HANDS OFF THE JACKET, IRON CROSS. IT'S REAL VELVET, AND I DON'T WANT IT STAINED WHEN I BLOW YOUR BRAINS OUT.
NOW THEN! I'M HERE TO ANNOUNCE A CHANGE OF MANAGEMENT!
MY GOOD FRIEND GORILLA GRODD AND I HAVE DECIDED TO PUT ON A MUTINY.
AND IT STARTS...
NOW!

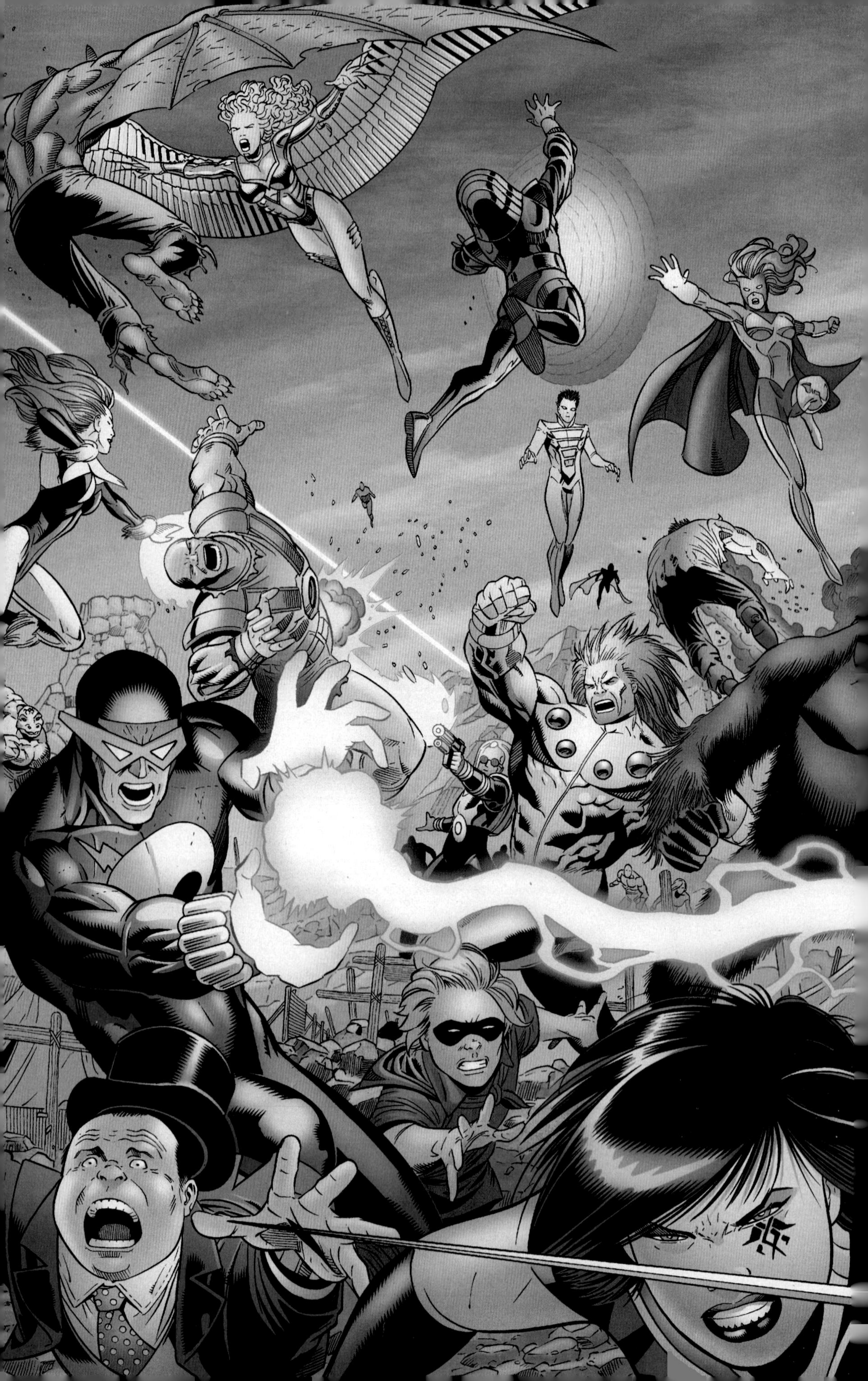

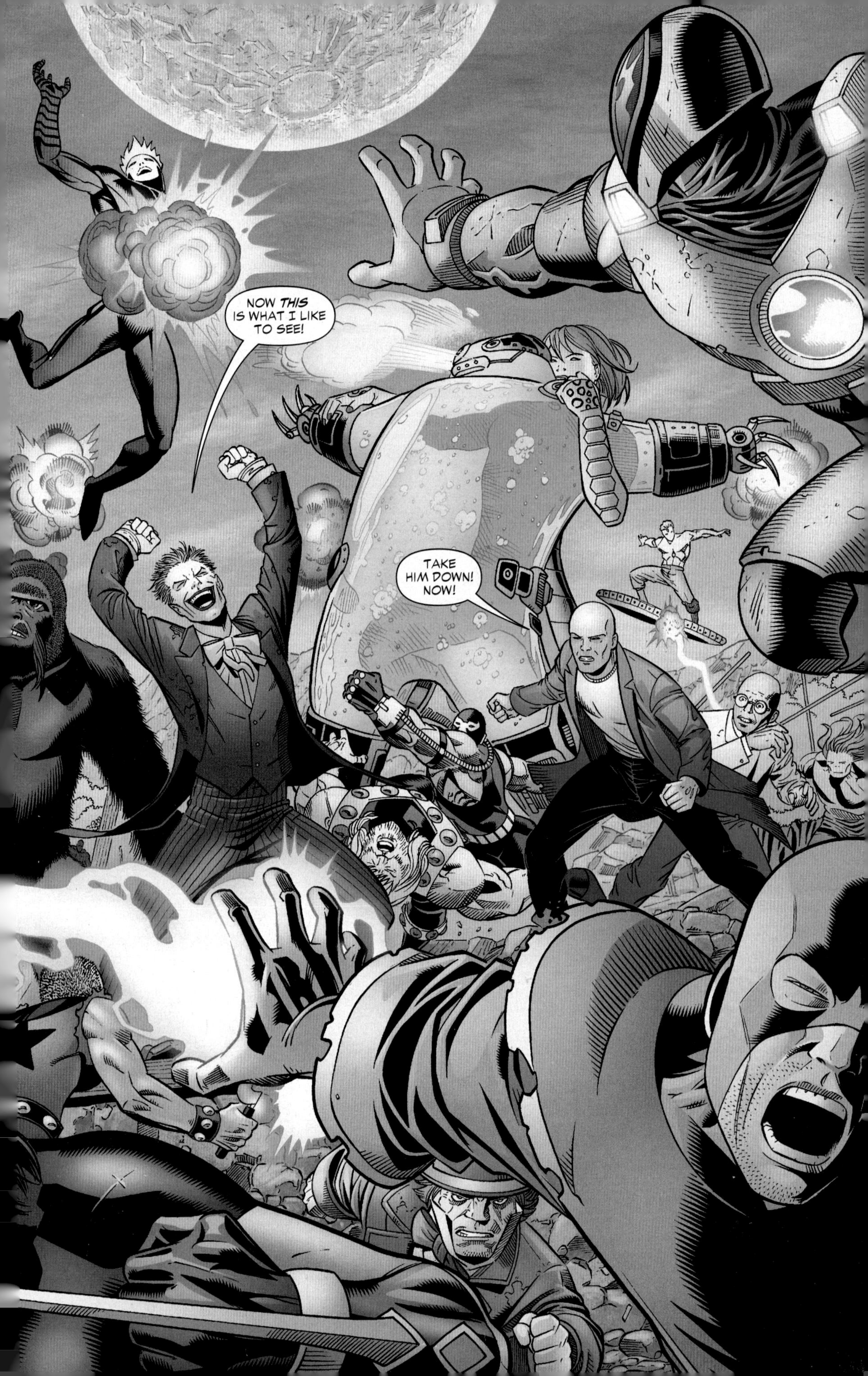
NOW THIS IS WHAT I LIKE TO SEE!
TAKE HIM DOWN! NOW!

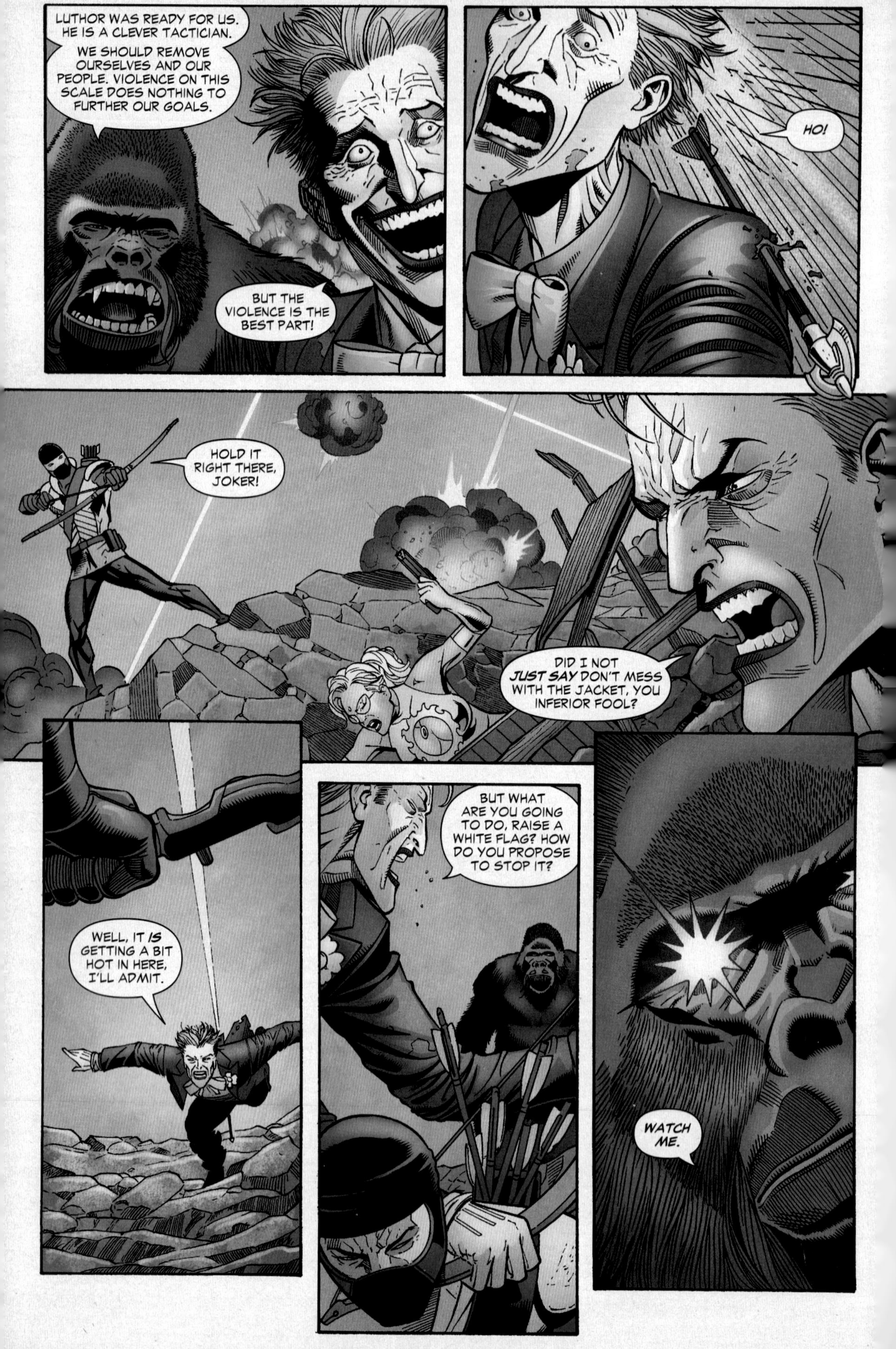
LUTHOR WAS READY FOR US. HE IS A CLEVER TACTICIAN.
WE SHOULD REMOVE OURSELVES AND OUR PEOPLE. VIOLENCE ON THIS SCALE DOES NOTHING TO FURTHER OUR GOALS.
BUT THE VIOLENCE IS THE BEST PART!
HO!
HOLD IT RIGHT THERE, JOKER!
DID I NOT *JUST SAY* DON'T MESS WITH THE JACKET, YOU INFERIOR FOOL?
WELL, IT *IS* GETTING A BIT HOT IN HERE, I'LL ADMIT.
BUT WHAT ARE YOU GOING TO DO, RAISE A WHITE FLAG? HOW DO YOU PROPOSE TO STOP IT?
WATCH ME.

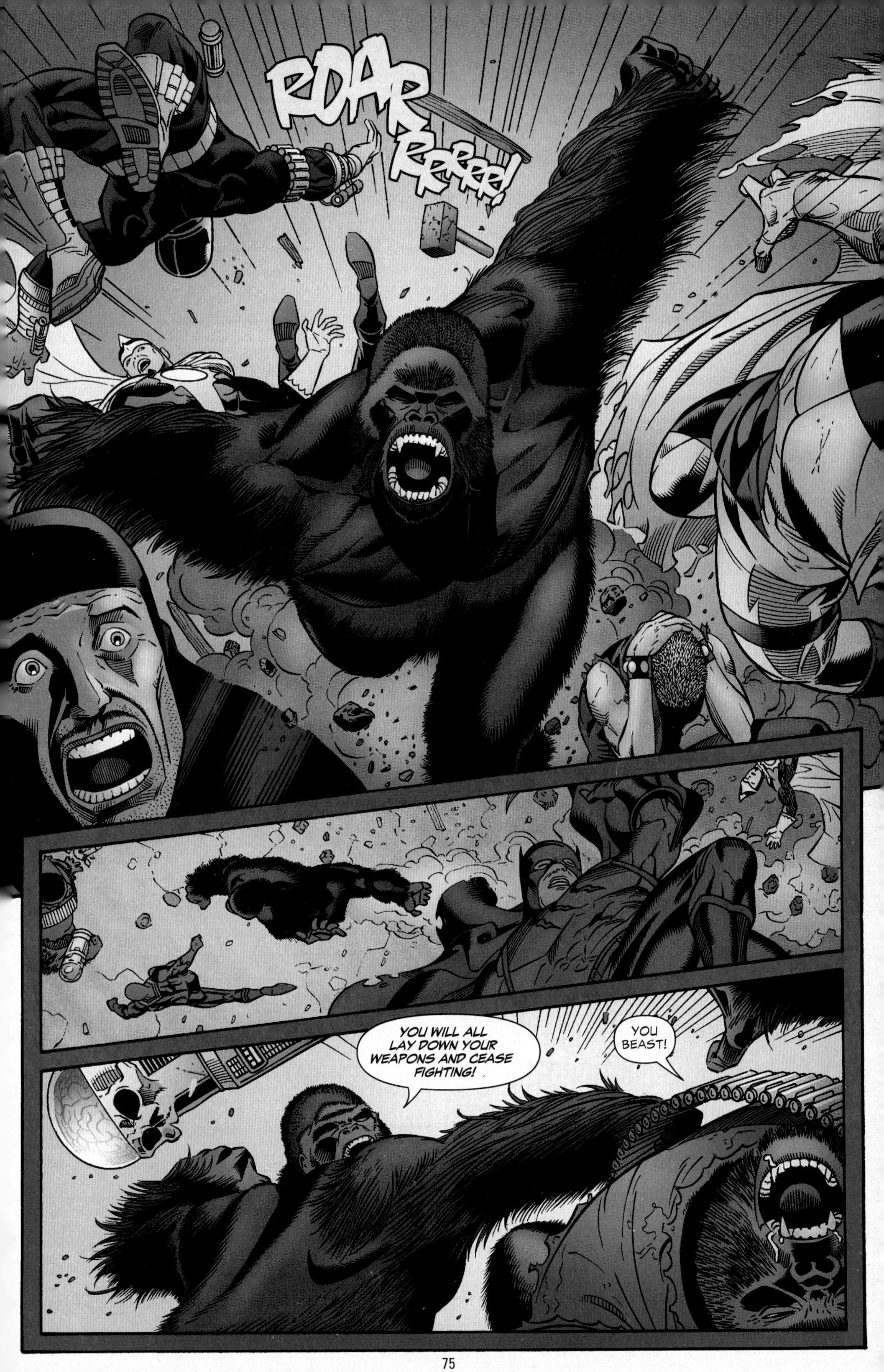
ROAR RRRRR!
YOU WILL ALL LAY DOWN YOUR WEAPONS AND CEASE FIGHTING!
YOU BEAST!

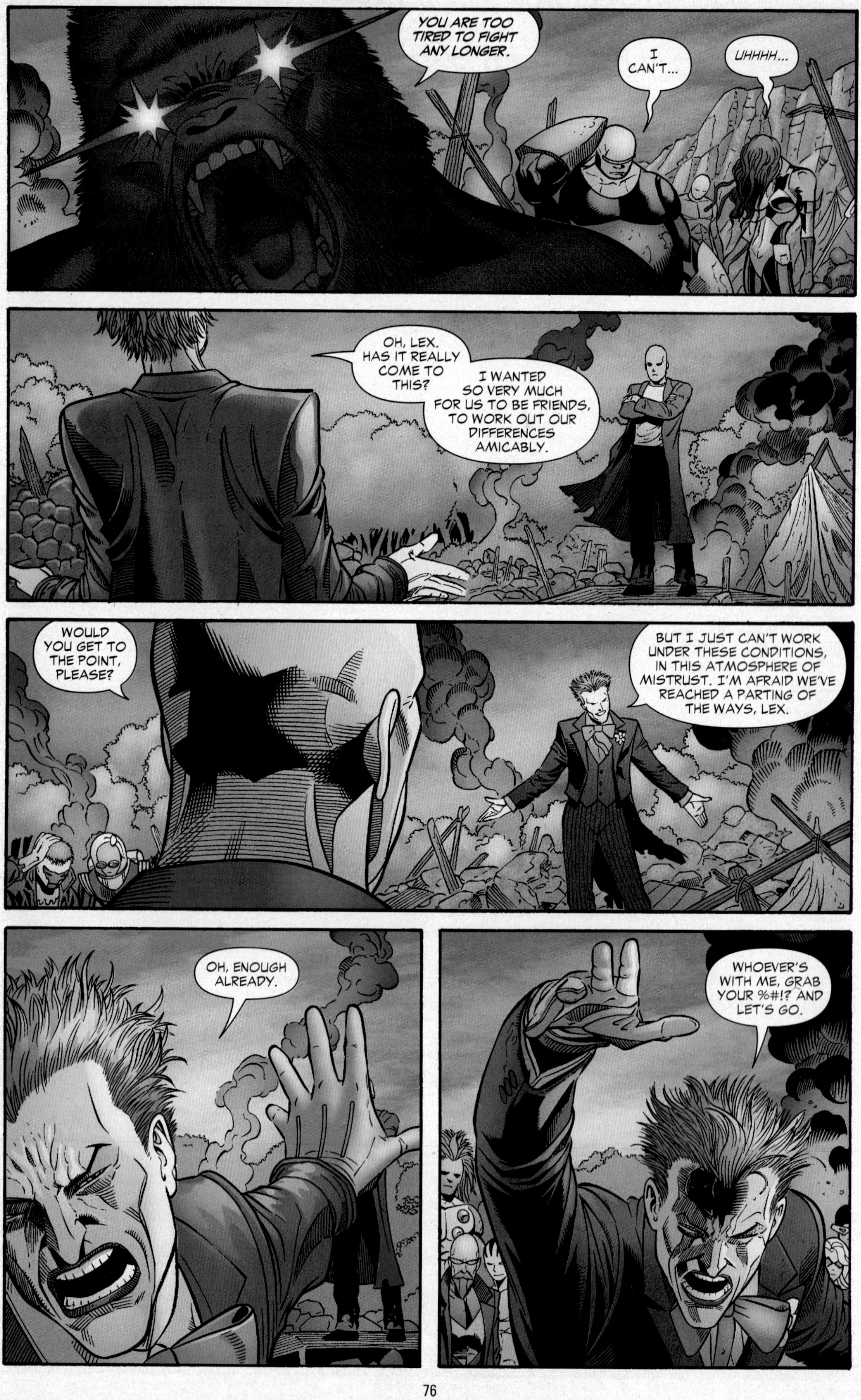
YOU ARE TOO TIRED TO FIGHT ANY LONGER.
I CAN'T...
UHHHH...
OH, LEX. HAS IT REALLY COME TO THIS?
I WANTED SO VERY MUCH FOR US TO BE FRIENDS, TO WORK OUT OUR DIFFERENCES AMICABLY.
WOULD YOU GET TO THE POINT, PLEASE?
BUT I JUST CAN'T WORK UNDER THESE CONDITIONS, IN THIS ATMOSPHERE OF MISTRUST. I'M AFRAID WE'VE REACHED A PARTING OF THE WAYS, LEX.
OH, ENOUGH ALREADY.
WHOEVER'S WITH ME, GRAB YOUR %#!? AND LET'S GO.

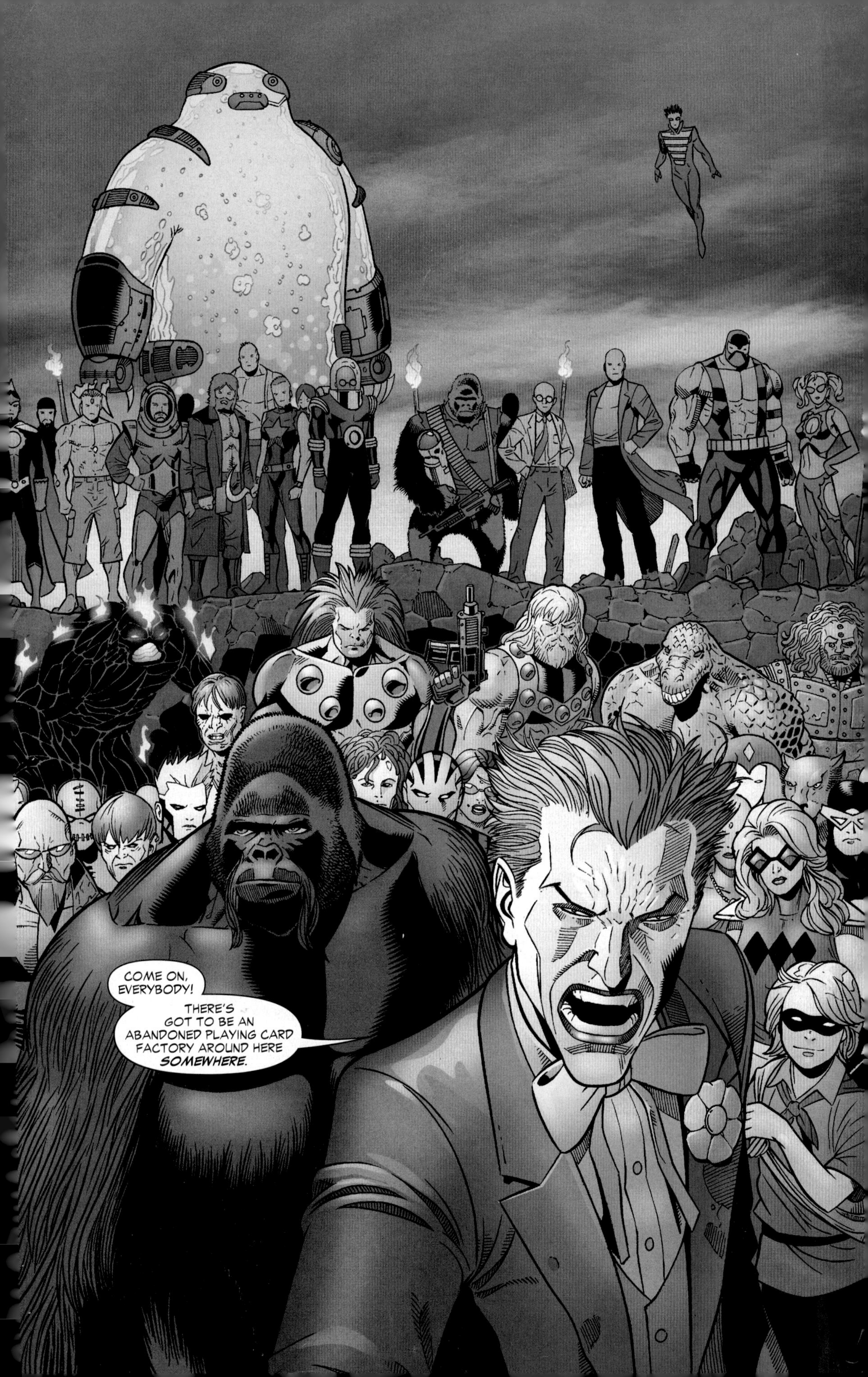
COME ON, EVERYBODY!
THERE'S GOT TO BE AN ABANDONED PLAYING CARD FACTORY AROUND HERE *SOMEWHERE*.

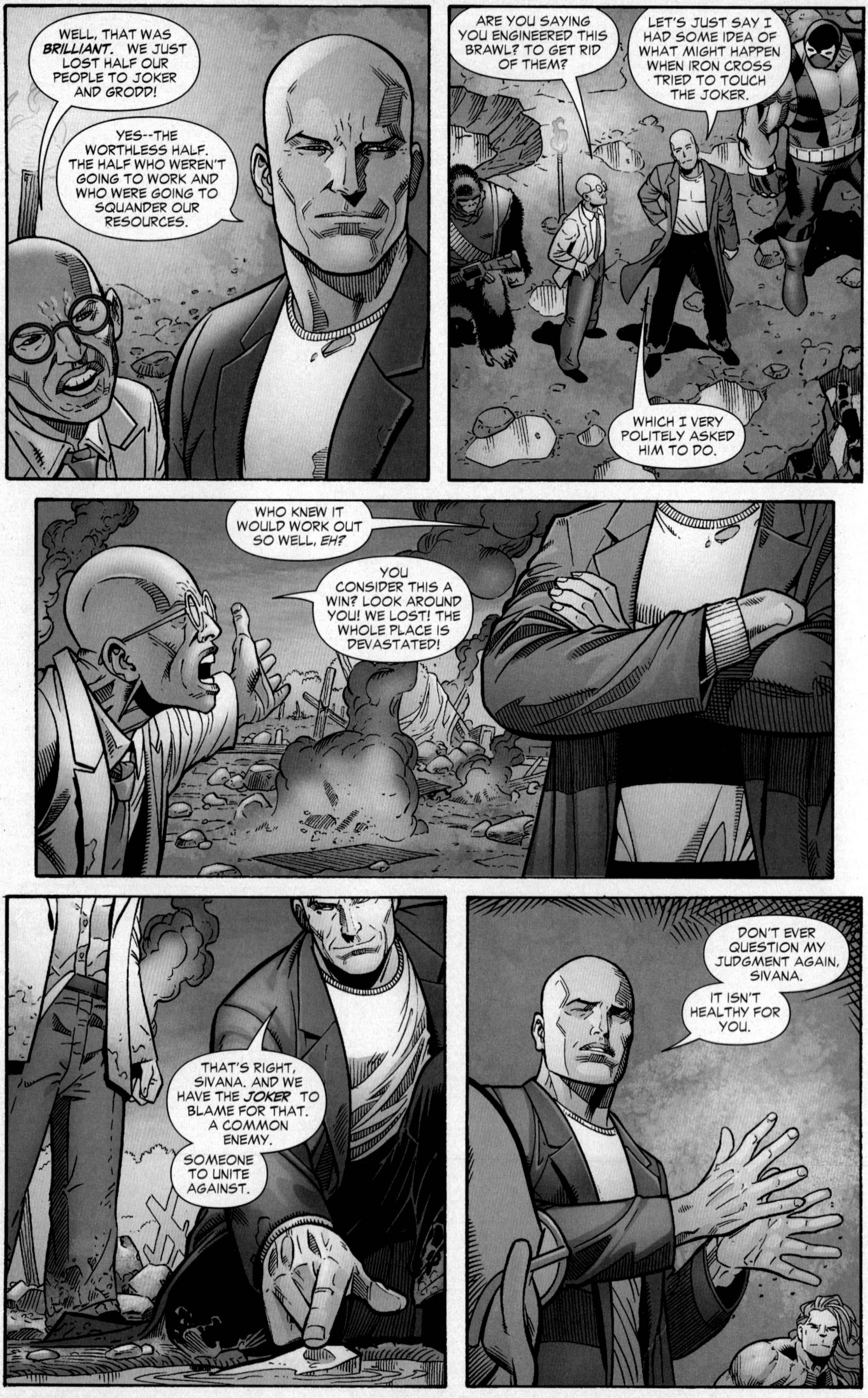
WELL, THAT WAS *BRILLIANT.* WE JUST LOST HALF OUR PEOPLE TO JOKER AND GRODD!
YES--THE WORTHLESS HALF. THE HALF WHO WEREN'T GOING TO WORK AND WHO WERE GOING TO SQUANDER OUR RESOURCES.
ARE YOU SAYING YOU ENGINEERED THIS BRAWL? TO GET RID OF THEM?
LET'S JUST SAY I HAD SOME IDEA OF WHAT MIGHT HAPPEN WHEN IRON CROSS TRIED TO TOUCH THE JOKER.
WHICH I VERY POLITELY ASKED HIM TO DO.
WHO KNEW IT WOULD WORK OUT SO WELL, *EH?*
YOU CONSIDER THIS A WIN? LOOK AROUND YOU! WE LOST! THE WHOLE PLACE IS DEVASTATED!
THAT'S RIGHT, SIVANA. AND WE HAVE THE *JOKER* TO BLAME FOR THAT. A COMMON ENEMY.
SOMEONE TO UNITE AGAINST.
DON'T EVER QUESTION MY JUDGMENT AGAIN, SIVANA.
IT ISN'T HEALTHY FOR YOU.

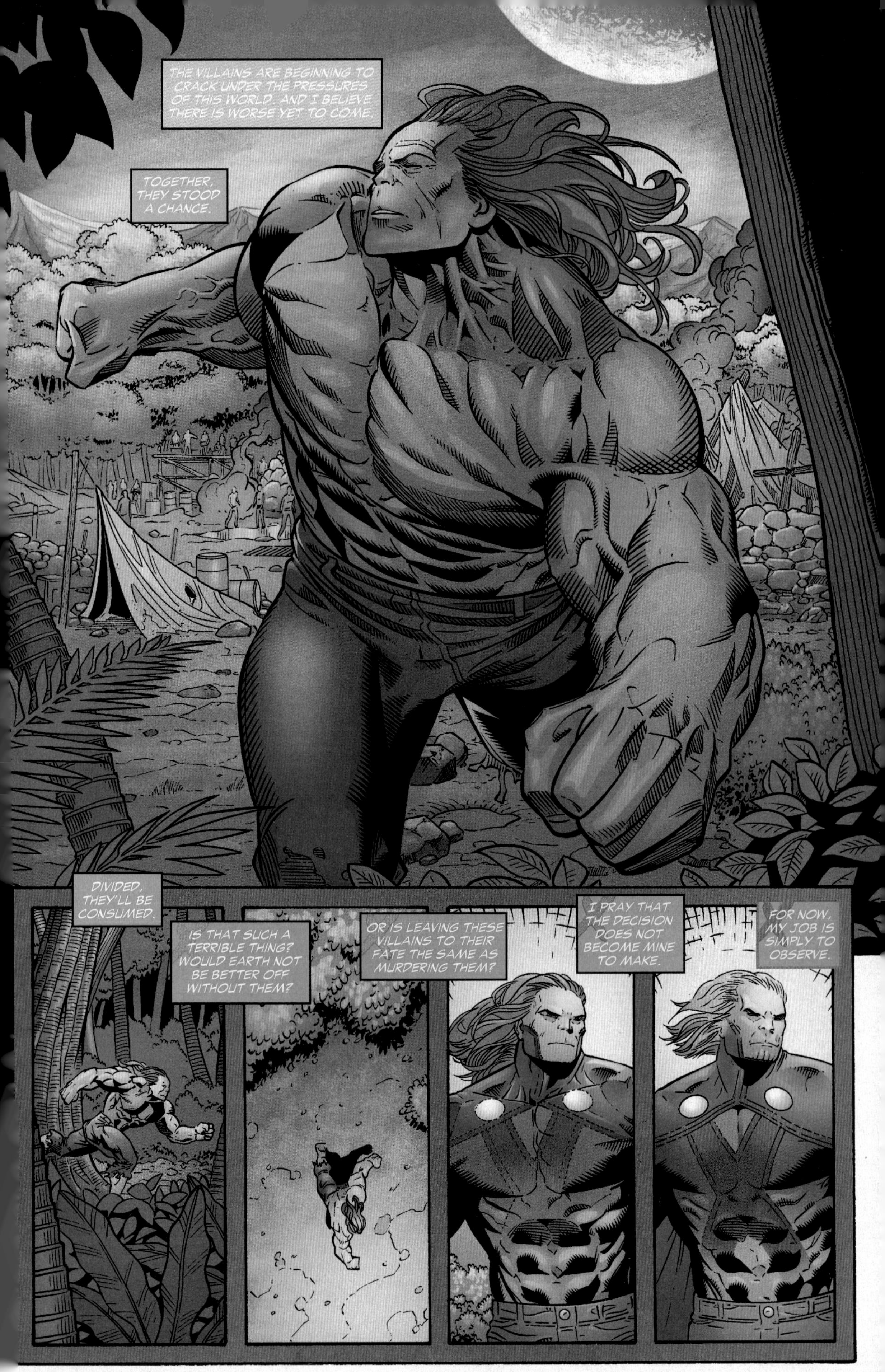
THE VILLAINS ARE BEGINNING TO CRACK UNDER THE PRESSURES OF THIS WORLD. AND I BELIEVE THERE IS WORSE YET TO COME.
TOGETHER, THEY STOOD A CHANCE.
DIVIDED, THEY'LL BE CONSUMED.
IS THAT SUCH A TERRIBLE THING? WOULD EARTH NOT BE BETTER OFF WITHOUT THEM?
OR IS LEAVING THESE VILLAINS TO THEIR FATE THE SAME AS MURDERING THEM?
I PRAY THAT THE DECISION DOES NOT BECOME MINE TO MAKE.
FOR NOW, MY JOB IS SIMPLY TO OBSERVE.

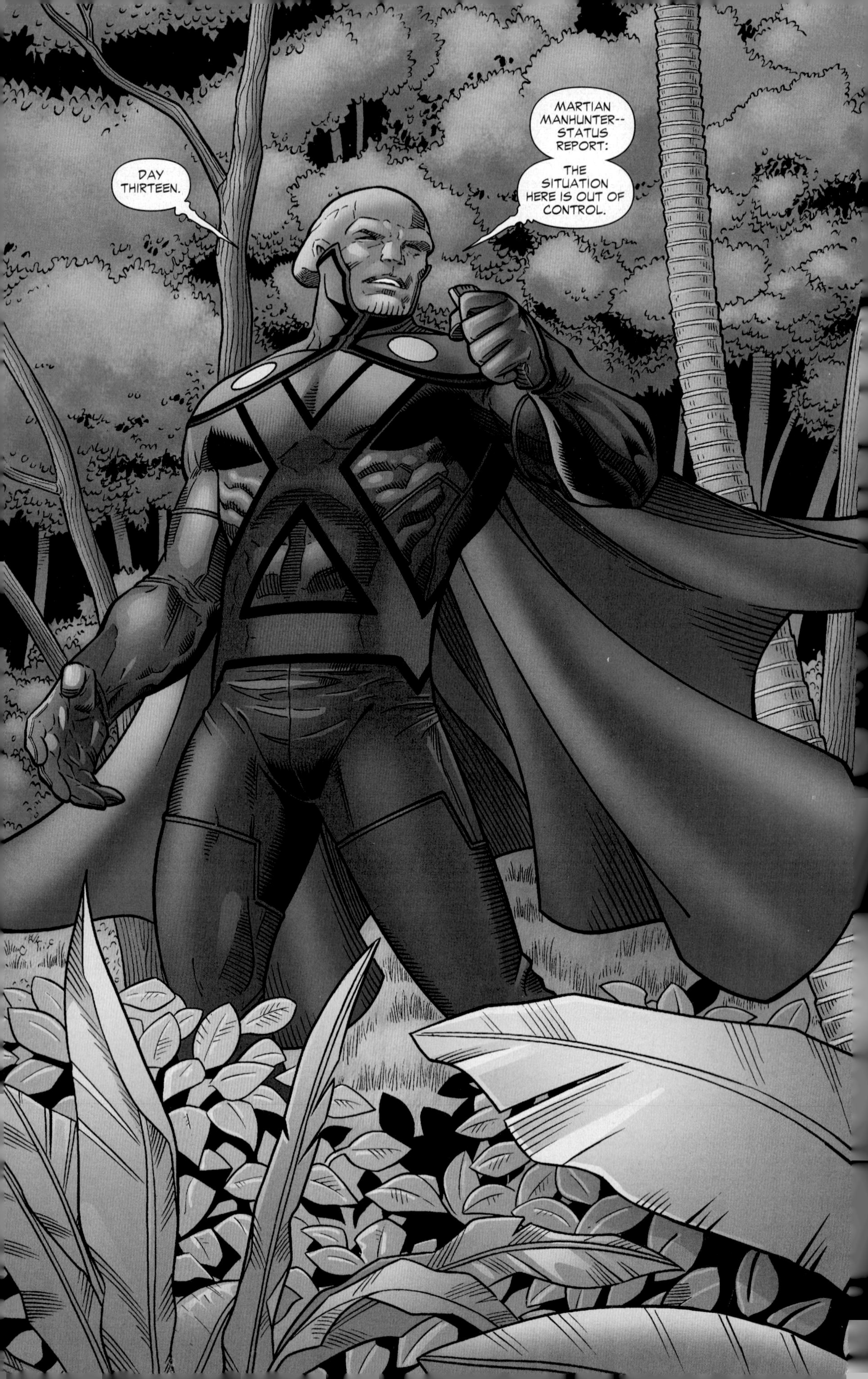
DAY THIRTEEN.
MARTIAN MANHUNTER-- STATUS REPORT:
THE SITUATION HERE IS OUT OF CONTROL.

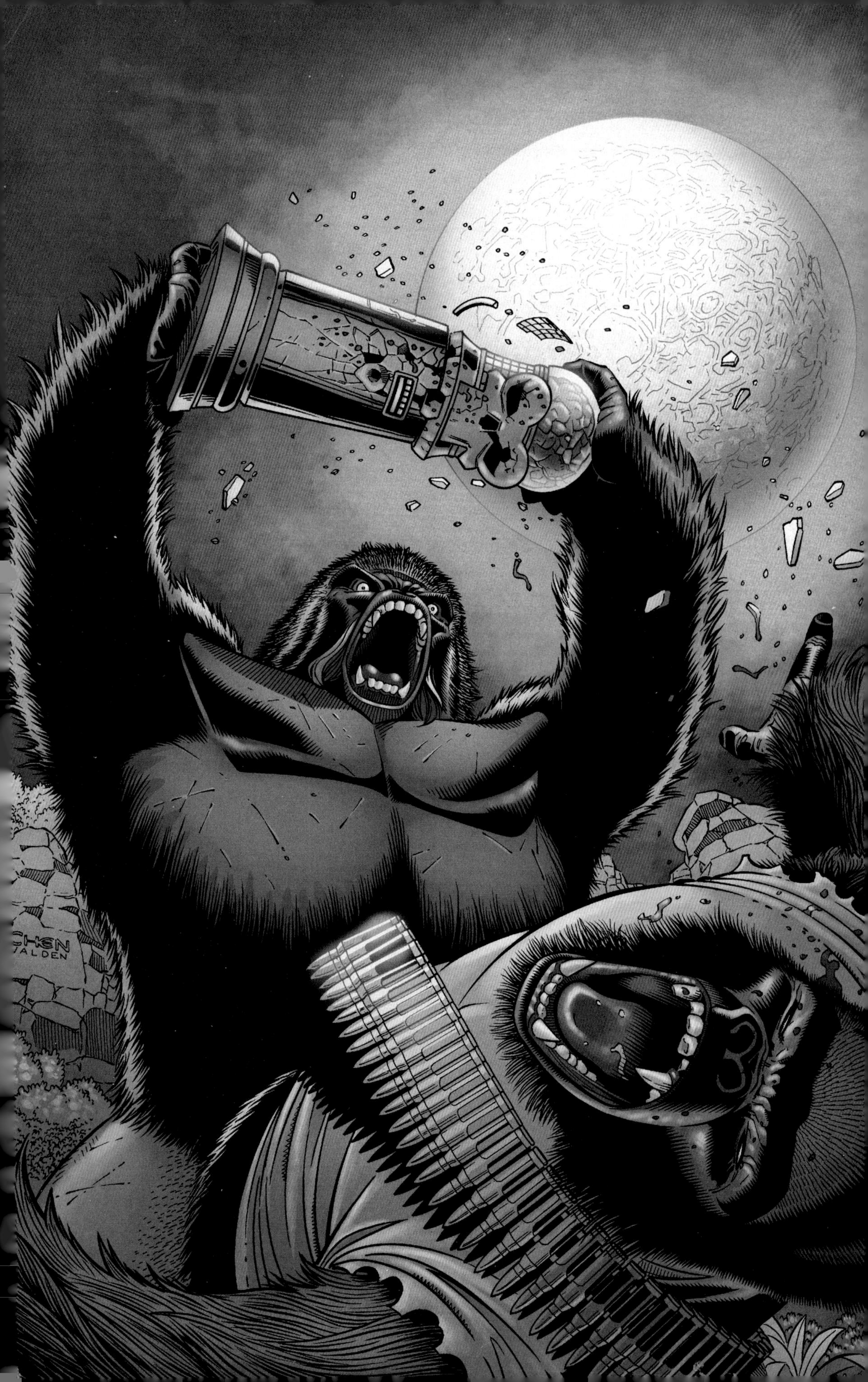
CHEN
WALDEN

Matthew Sturges
Writer

Sean Chen
Penciller

Walden Wong
Inker

John Kalisz
Colorist

Steve Wands
Letterer

CHAPTER FOUR

HELL PLANET.

THIS PLANET IS UNLIKE ANYTHING I'VE EVER SEEN.

THE ORGANISMS HERE APPEAR TO BE ENGINEERED. IT SEEMS *HIGHLY* IMPROBABLE THAT SUCH THINGS COULD HAVE EVOLVED ON THEIR OWN.

AND MAKE NO MISTAKE: IF THE CREATURES ON THIS PLANET *WERE* ENGINEERED, THEY WERE DESIGNED TO BE DEADLY.

PERHAPS MOST DISTRESSING IS THAT NO ONE--NOT EVEN LUTHOR--APPEARS TO HAVE ANY IDEA *WHERE* THIS PLANET IS.

NONE OF THE VISIBLE STARS ARE FAMILIAR TO ANYONE HERE.

BATMAN, AT THIS DISTANCE I DON'T KNOW IF YOU'RE EVEN RECEIVING THIS--BUT IF YOU ARE, I STRONGLY URGE YOU TO TAKE ACTION.

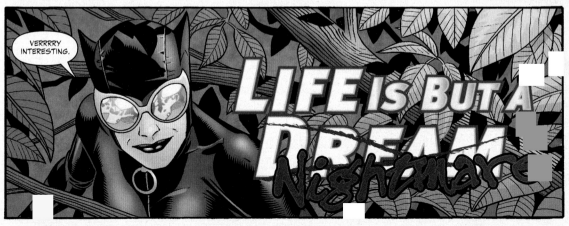

VERRRRY INTERESTING.

LIFE IS BUT A DREAM Nightmare

83

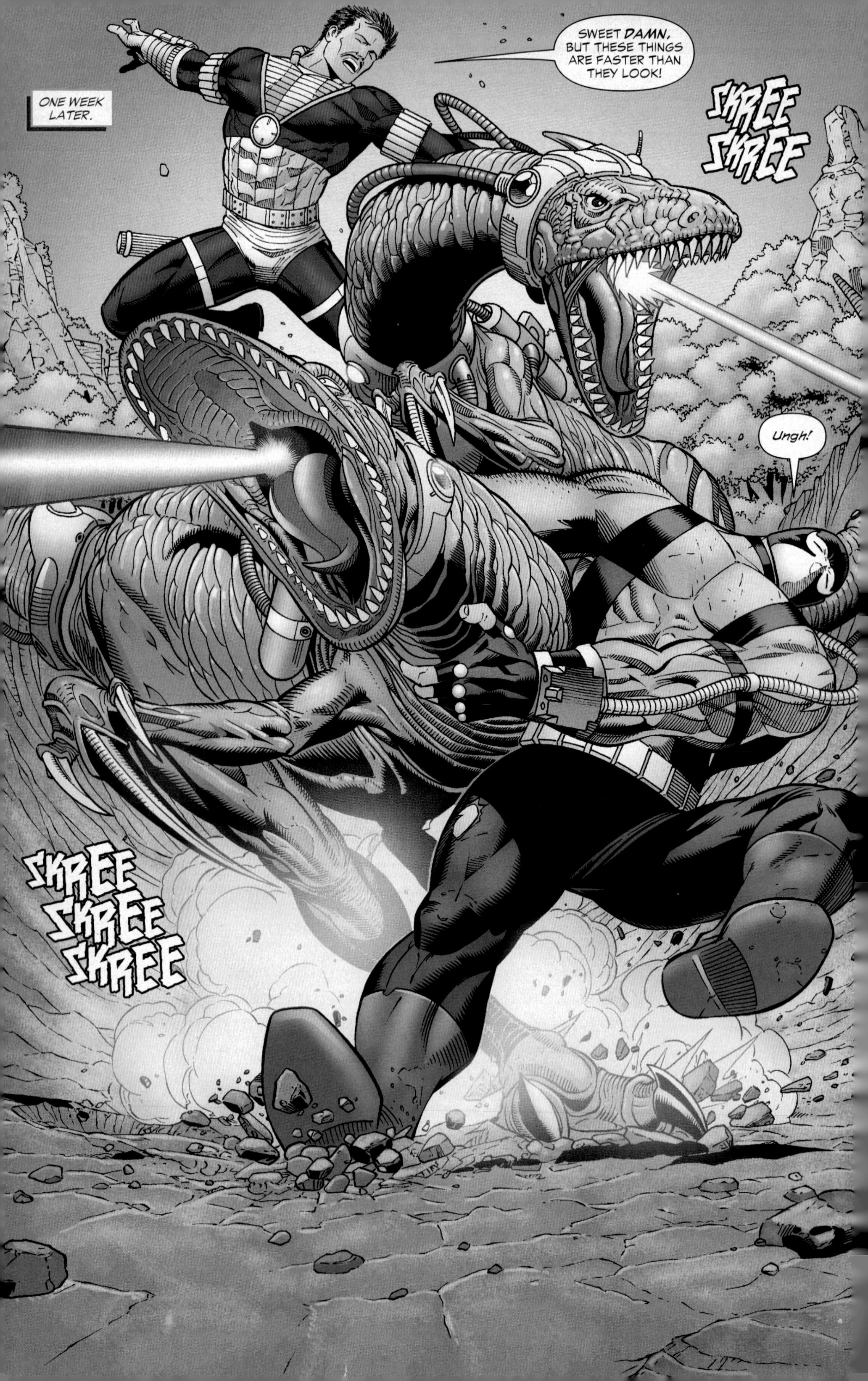
ONE WEEK LATER.
SWEET DAMN, BUT THESE THINGS ARE FASTER THAN THEY LOOK!
SKREE SKREE
Ungh!
SKREE SKREE SKREE

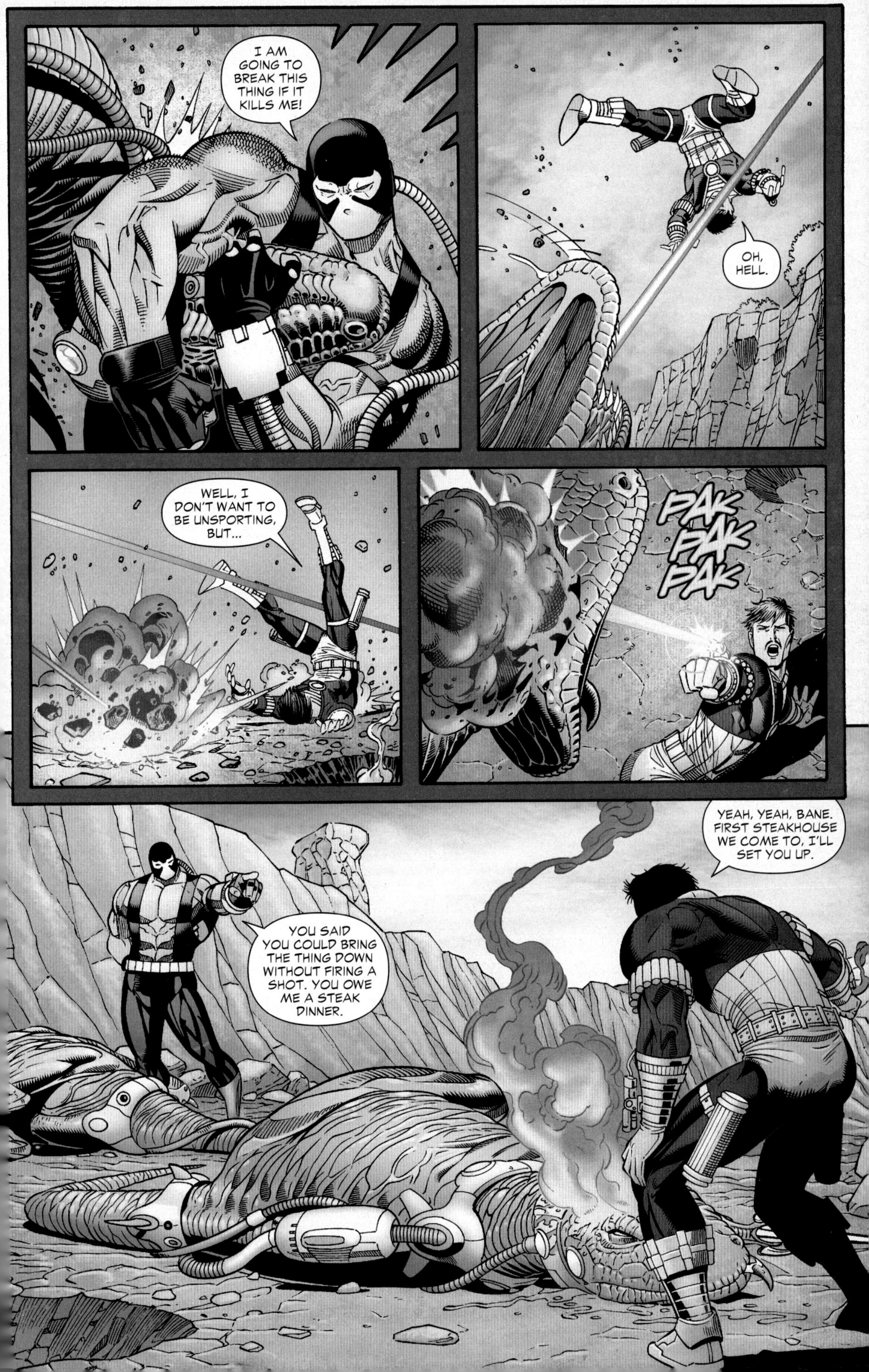
I AM GOING TO BREAK THIS THING IF IT KILLS ME!
OH, HELL.
WELL, I DON'T WANT TO BE UNSPORTING, BUT...
PAK PAK PAK
YEAH, YEAH, BANE. FIRST STEAKHOUSE WE COME TO, I'LL SET YOU UP.
YOU SAID YOU COULD BRING THE THING DOWN WITHOUT FIRING A SHOT. YOU OWE ME A STEAK DINNER.

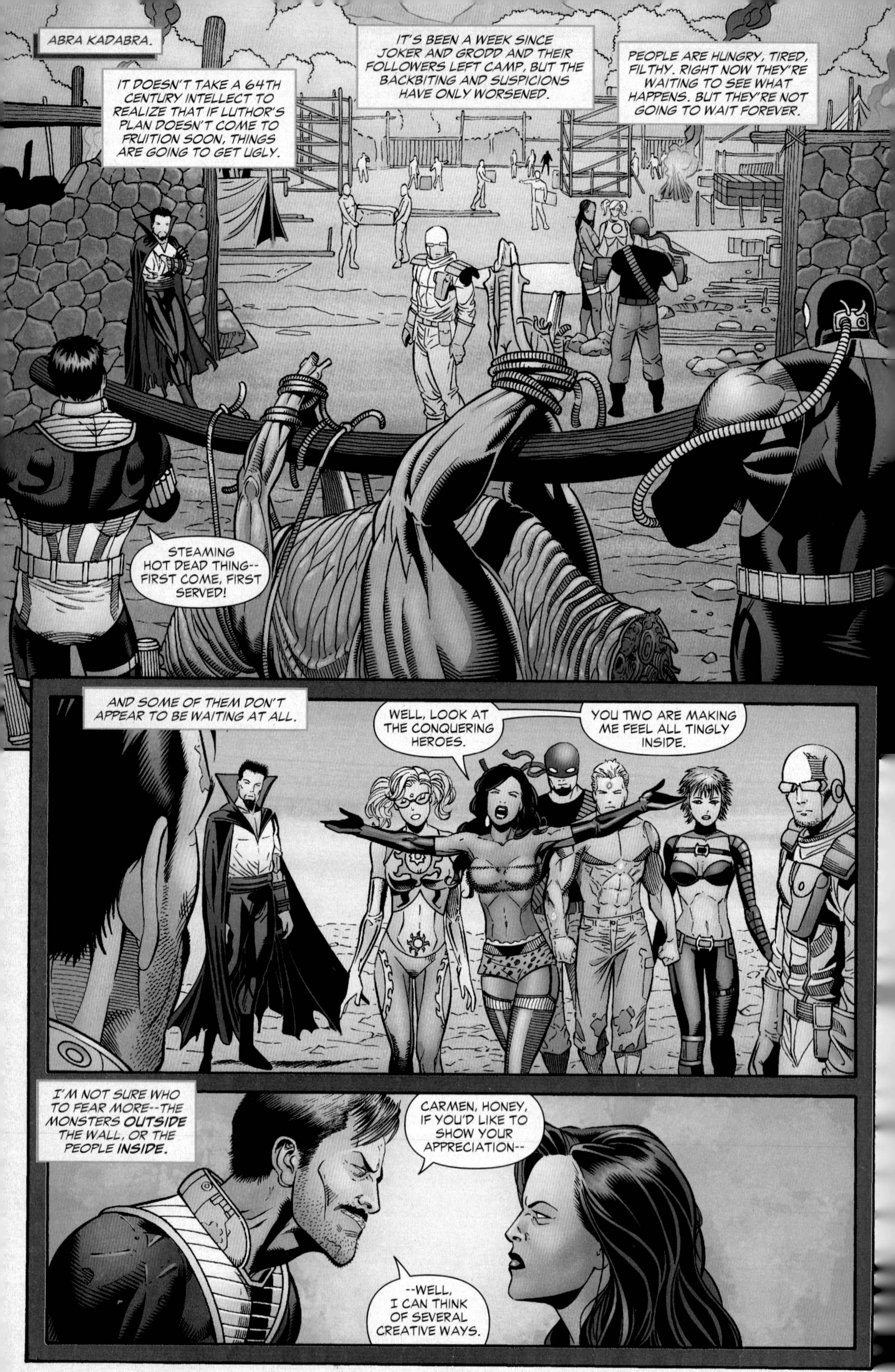
ABRA KADABRA.
IT DOESN'T TAKE A 64TH CENTURY INTELLECT TO REALIZE THAT IF LUTHOR'S PLAN DOESN'T COME TO FRUITION SOON, THINGS ARE GOING TO GET UGLY.
IT'S BEEN A WEEK SINCE JOKER AND GRODD AND THEIR FOLLOWERS LEFT CAMP, BUT THE BACKBITING AND SUSPICIONS HAVE ONLY WORSENED.
PEOPLE ARE HUNGRY, TIRED, FILTHY. RIGHT NOW THEY'RE WAITING TO SEE WHAT HAPPENS. BUT THEY'RE NOT GOING TO WAIT FOREVER.
STEAMING HOT DEAD THING--FIRST COME, FIRST SERVED!
AND SOME OF THEM DON'T APPEAR TO BE WAITING AT ALL.
WELL, LOOK AT THE CONQUERING HEROES.
YOU TWO ARE MAKING ME FEEL ALL TINGLY INSIDE.
I'M NOT SURE WHO TO FEAR MORE--THE MONSTERS OUTSIDE THE WALL, OR THE PEOPLE INSIDE.
CARMEN, HONEY, IF YOU'D LIKE TO SHOW YOUR APPRECIATION--
--WELL, I CAN THINK OF SEVERAL CREATIVE WAYS.

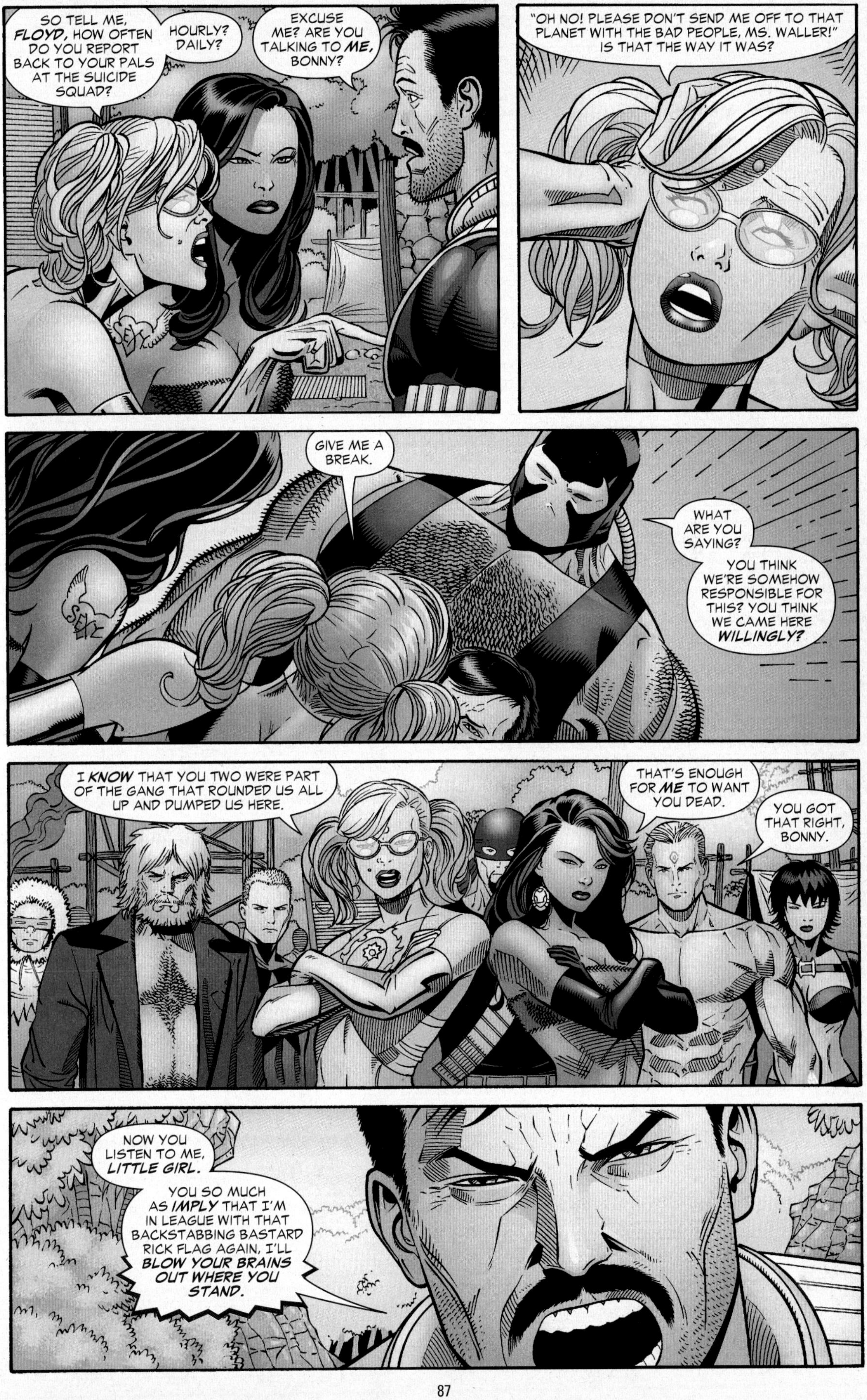
SO TELL ME, FLOYD, HOW OFTEN DO YOU REPORT BACK TO YOUR PALS AT THE SUICIDE SQUAD?
HOURLY? DAILY?
EXCUSE ME? ARE YOU TALKING TO ME, BONNY?
"OH NO! PLEASE DON'T SEND ME OFF TO THAT PLANET WITH THE BAD PEOPLE, MS. WALLER!" IS THAT THE WAY IT WAS?
GIVE ME A BREAK.
WHAT ARE YOU SAYING?
YOU THINK WE'RE SOMEHOW RESPONSIBLE FOR THIS? YOU THINK WE CAME HERE WILLINGLY?
I KNOW THAT YOU TWO WERE PART OF THE GANG THAT ROUNDED US ALL UP AND DUMPED US HERE.
THAT'S ENOUGH FOR ME TO WANT YOU DEAD.
YOU GOT THAT RIGHT, BONNY.
NOW YOU LISTEN TO ME, LITTLE GIRL.
YOU SO MUCH AS IMPLY THAT I'M IN LEAGUE WITH THAT BACKSTABBING BASTARD RICK FLAG AGAIN, I'LL BLOW YOUR BRAINS OUT WHERE YOU STAND.

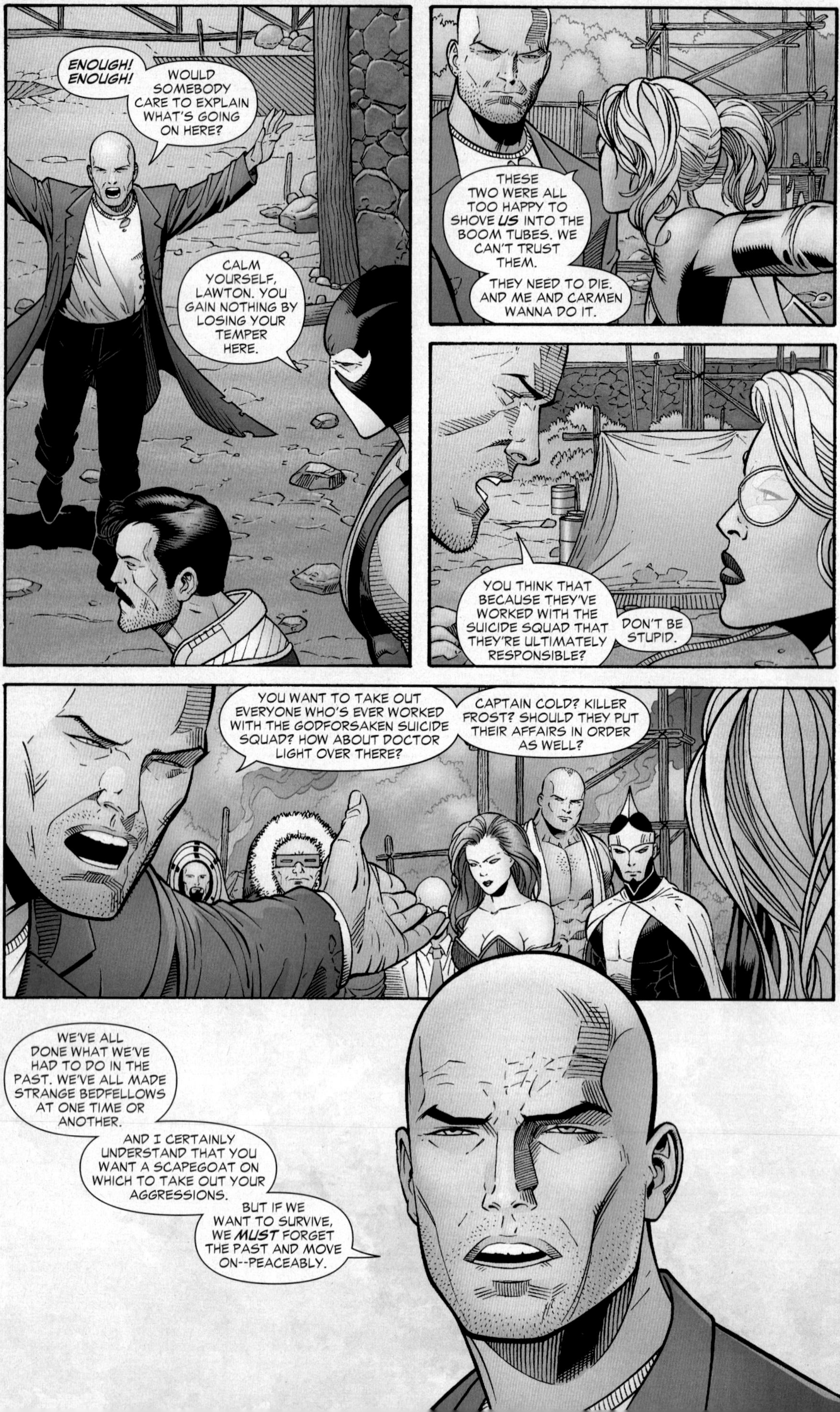
ENOUGH! ENOUGH!
WOULD SOMEBODY CARE TO EXPLAIN WHAT'S GOING ON HERE?
CALM YOURSELF, LAWTON. YOU GAIN NOTHING BY LOSING YOUR TEMPER HERE.
THESE TWO WERE ALL TOO HAPPY TO SHOVE *US* INTO THE BOOM TUBES. WE CAN'T TRUST THEM.
THEY NEED TO DIE. AND ME AND CARMEN WANNA DO IT.
YOU THINK THAT BECAUSE THEY'VE WORKED WITH THE SUICIDE SQUAD THAT THEY'RE ULTIMATELY RESPONSIBLE?
DON'T BE STUPID.
YOU WANT TO TAKE OUT EVERYONE WHO'S EVER WORKED WITH THE GODFORSAKEN SUICIDE SQUAD? HOW ABOUT DOCTOR LIGHT OVER THERE?
CAPTAIN COLD? KILLER FROST? SHOULD THEY PUT THEIR AFFAIRS IN ORDER AS WELL?
WE'VE ALL DONE WHAT WE'VE HAD TO DO IN THE PAST. WE'VE ALL MADE STRANGE BEDFELLOWS AT ONE TIME OR ANOTHER.
AND I CERTAINLY UNDERSTAND THAT YOU WANT A SCAPEGOAT ON WHICH TO TAKE OUT YOUR AGGRESSIONS.
BUT IF WE WANT TO SURVIVE, WE *MUST* FORGET THE PAST AND MOVE ON--PEACEABLY.

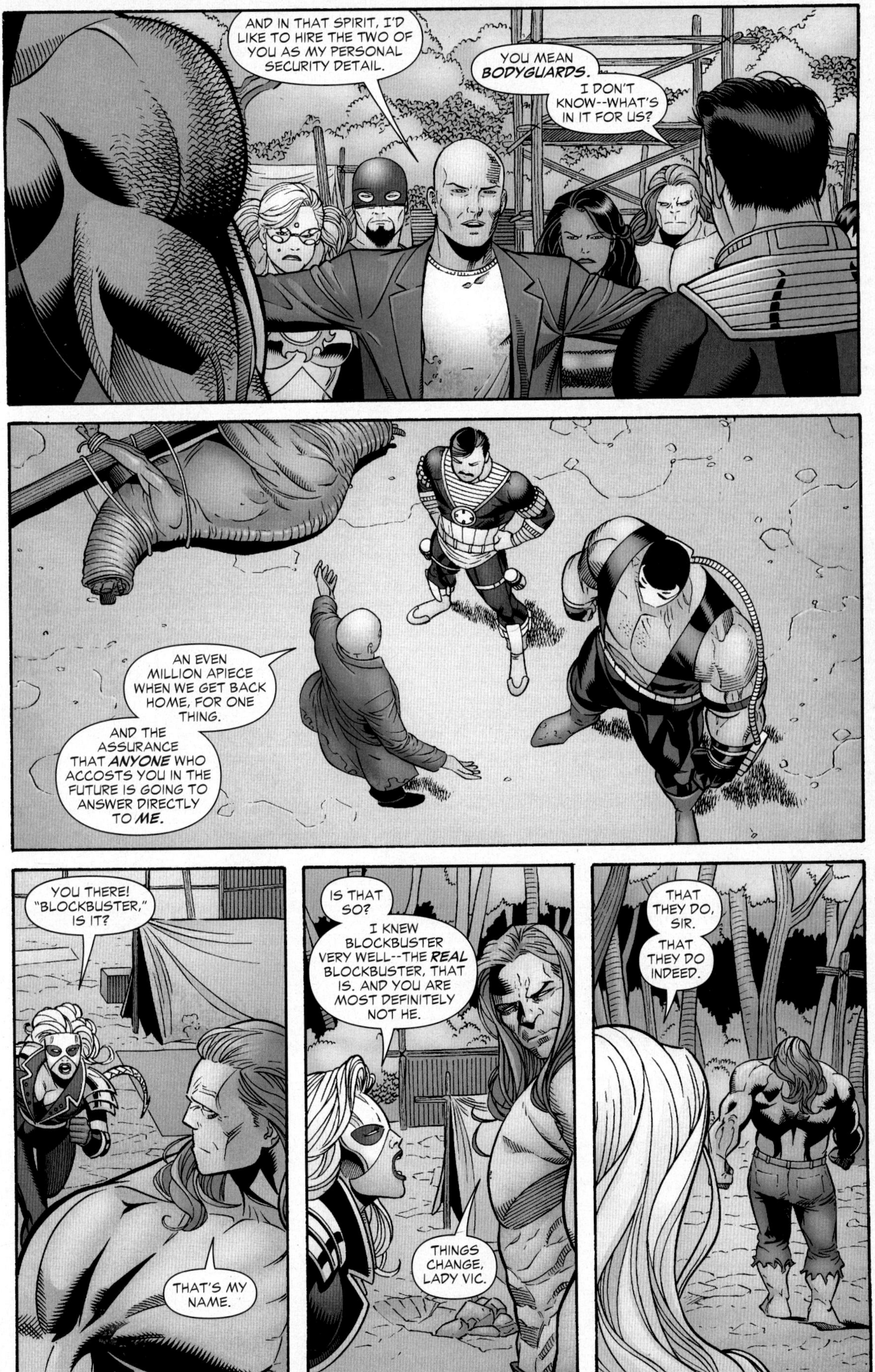
AND IN THAT SPIRIT, I'D LIKE TO HIRE THE TWO OF YOU AS MY PERSONAL SECURITY DETAIL.
YOU MEAN BODYGUARDS.
I DON'T KNOW--WHAT'S IN IT FOR US?
AN EVEN MILLION APIECE WHEN WE GET BACK HOME, FOR ONE THING.
AND THE ASSURANCE THAT ANYONE WHO ACCOSTS YOU IN THE FUTURE IS GOING TO ANSWER DIRECTLY TO ME.
YOU THERE! "BLOCKBUSTER," IS IT?
THAT'S MY NAME.
IS THAT SO?
I KNEW BLOCKBUSTER VERY WELL--THE REAL BLOCKBUSTER, THAT IS. AND YOU ARE MOST DEFINITELY NOT HE.
THINGS CHANGE, LADY VIC.
THAT THEY DO, SIR.
THAT THEY DO INDEED.

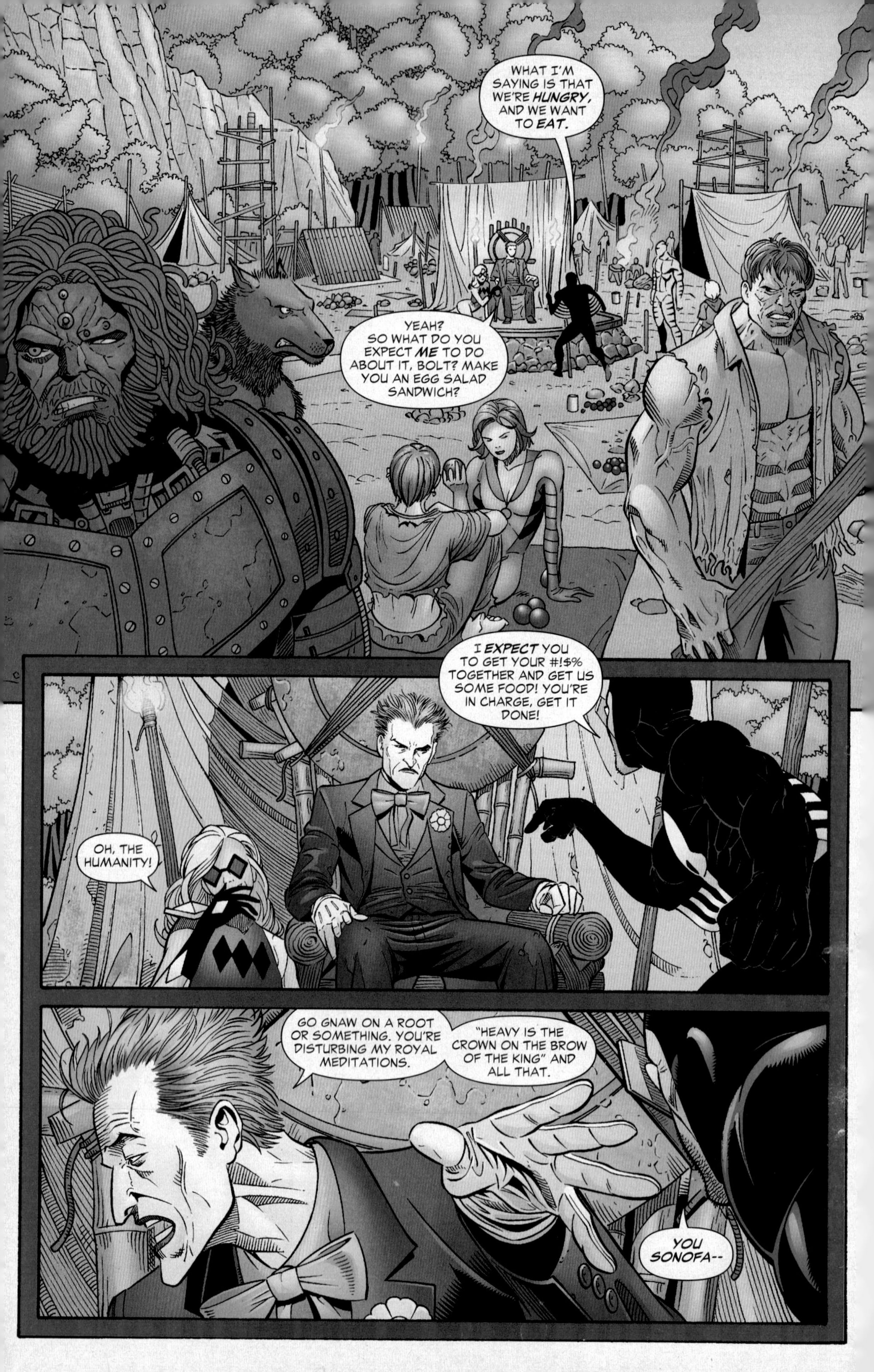
WHAT I'M SAYING IS THAT WE'RE HUNGRY, AND WE WANT TO EAT.
YEAH? SO WHAT DO YOU EXPECT ME TO DO ABOUT IT, BOLT? MAKE YOU AN EGG SALAD SANDWICH?
I EXPECT YOU TO GET YOUR #!$% TOGETHER AND GET US SOME FOOD! YOU'RE IN CHARGE, GET IT DONE!
OH, THE HUMANITY!
GO GNAW ON A ROOT OR SOMETHING. YOU'RE DISTURBING MY ROYAL MEDITATIONS.
"HEAVY IS THE CROWN ON THE BROW OF THE KING" AND ALL THAT.
YOU SONOFA--

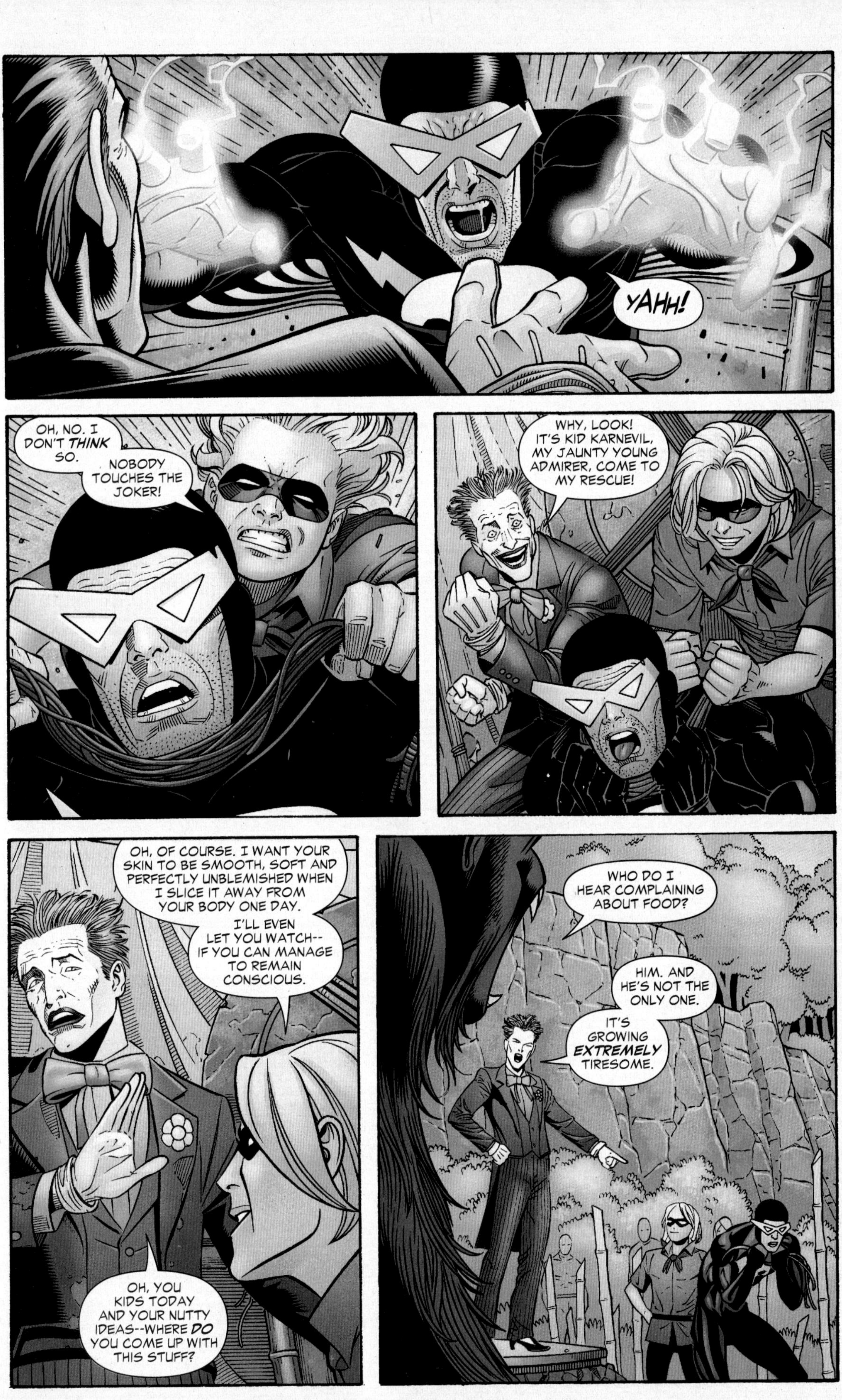
yAHH!
OH, NO. I DON'T *THINK* SO.
NOBODY TOUCHES THE JOKER!
WHY, LOOK! IT'S KID KARNEVIL, MY JAUNTY YOUNG ADMIRER, COME TO MY RESCUE!
OH, OF COURSE. I WANT YOUR SKIN TO BE SMOOTH, SOFT AND PERFECTLY UNBLEMISHED WHEN I SLICE IT AWAY FROM YOUR BODY ONE DAY.
I'LL EVEN LET YOU WATCH-- IF YOU CAN MANAGE TO REMAIN CONSCIOUS.
OH, YOU KIDS TODAY AND YOUR NUTTY IDEAS--WHERE *DO* YOU COME UP WITH THIS STUFF?
WHO DO I HEAR COMPLAINING ABOUT FOOD?
HIM. AND HE'S NOT THE ONLY ONE.
IT'S GROWING *EXTREMELY* TIRESOME.

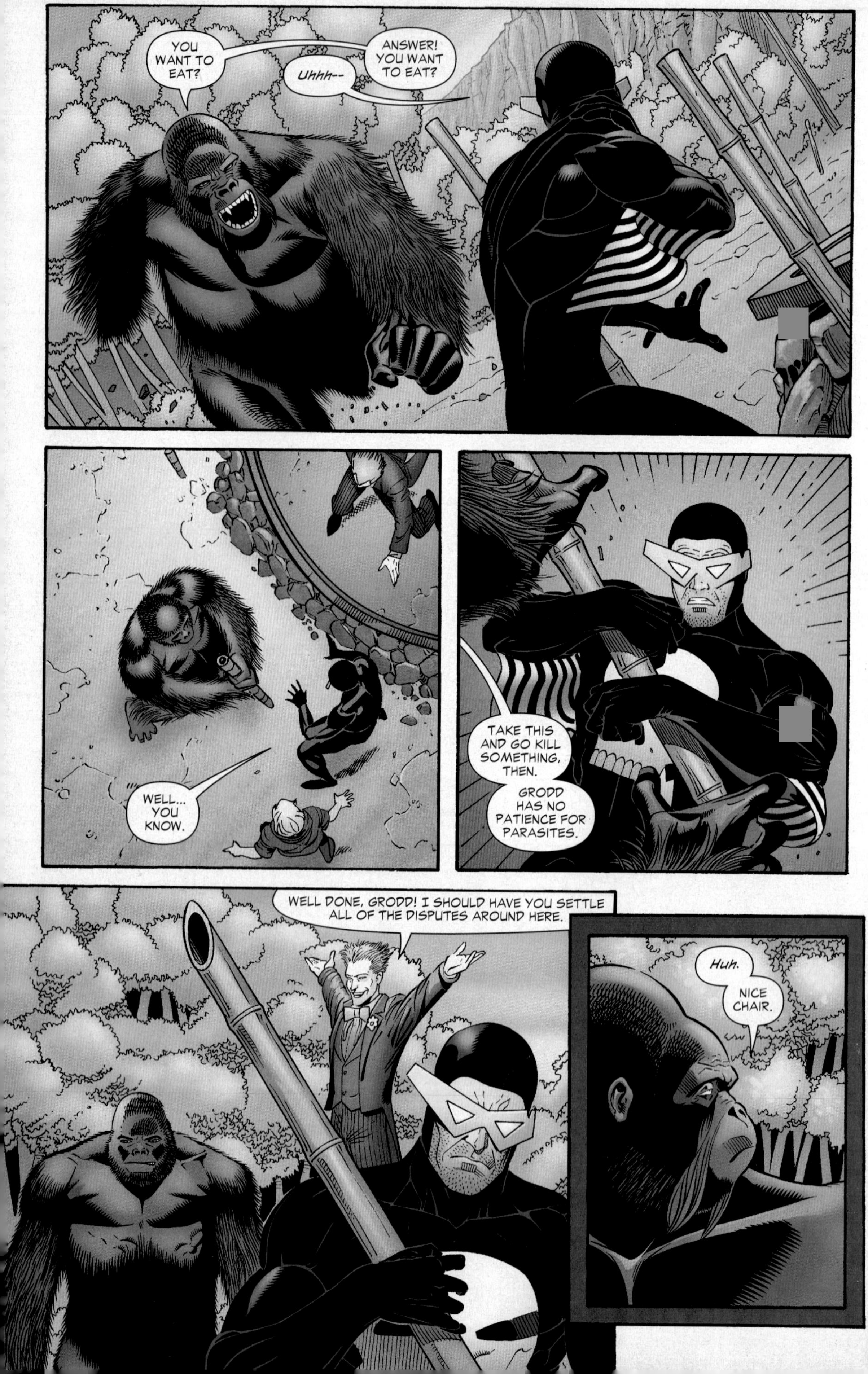
YOU WANT TO EAT?
ANSWER! YOU WANT TO EAT?
Uhhh--
WELL... YOU KNOW.
TAKE THIS AND GO KILL SOMETHING, THEN.
GRODD HAS NO PATIENCE FOR PARASITES.
WELL DONE, GRODD! I SHOULD HAVE YOU SETTLE ALL OF THE DISPUTES AROUND HERE.
Huh.
NICE CHAIR.

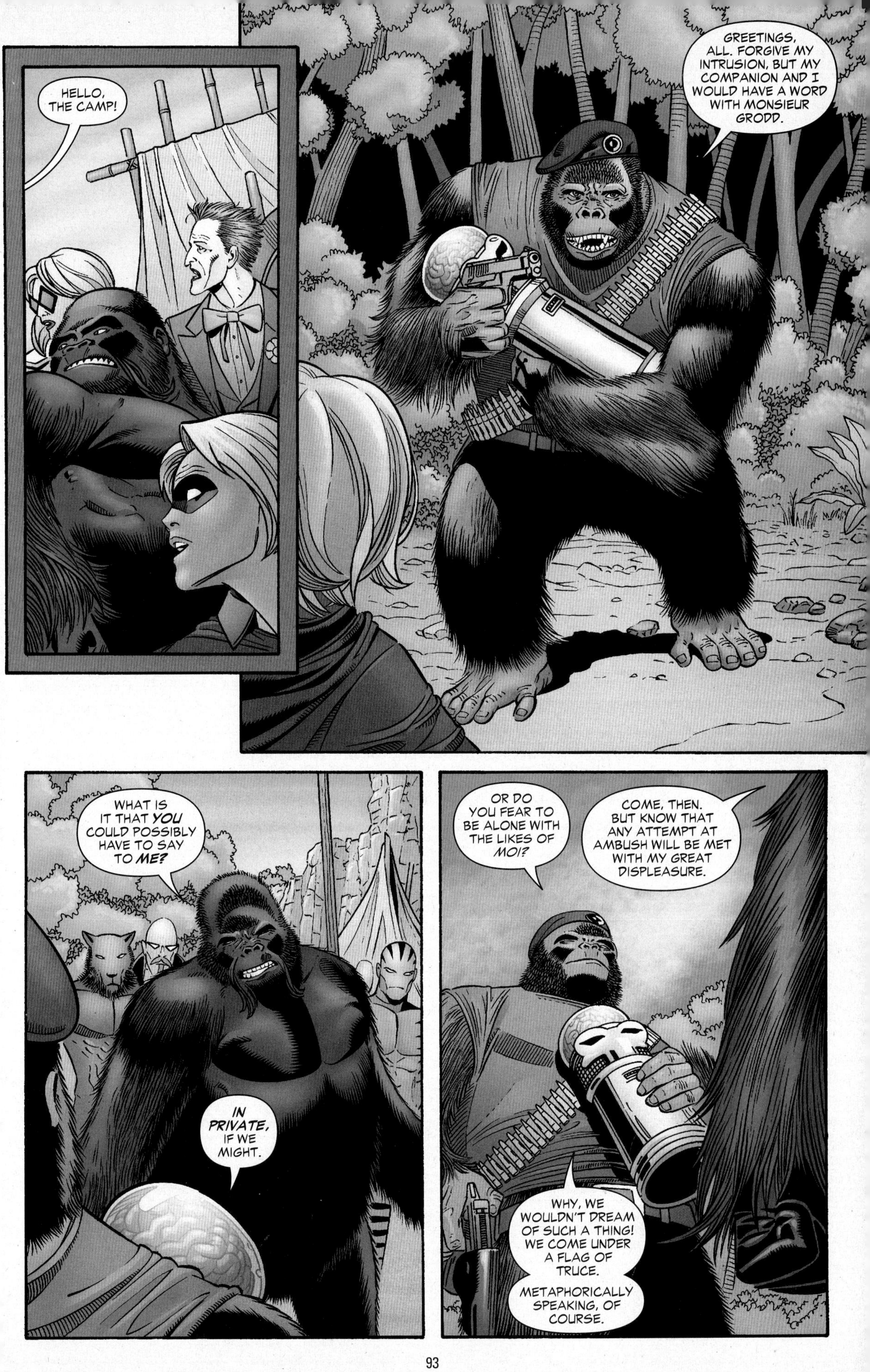
HELLO, THE CAMP!
GREETINGS, ALL. FORGIVE MY INTRUSION, BUT MY COMPANION AND I WOULD HAVE A WORD WITH MONSIEUR GRODD.
WHAT IS IT THAT *YOU* COULD POSSIBLY HAVE TO SAY TO *ME?*
IN PRIVATE, IF WE MIGHT.
OR DO YOU FEAR TO BE ALONE WITH THE LIKES OF *MOI!?*
COME, THEN. BUT KNOW THAT ANY ATTEMPT AT AMBUSH WILL BE MET WITH MY GREAT DISPLEASURE.
WHY, WE WOULDN'T DREAM OF SUCH A THING! WE COME UNDER A FLAG OF TRUCE.
METAPHORICALLY SPEAKING, OF COURSE.

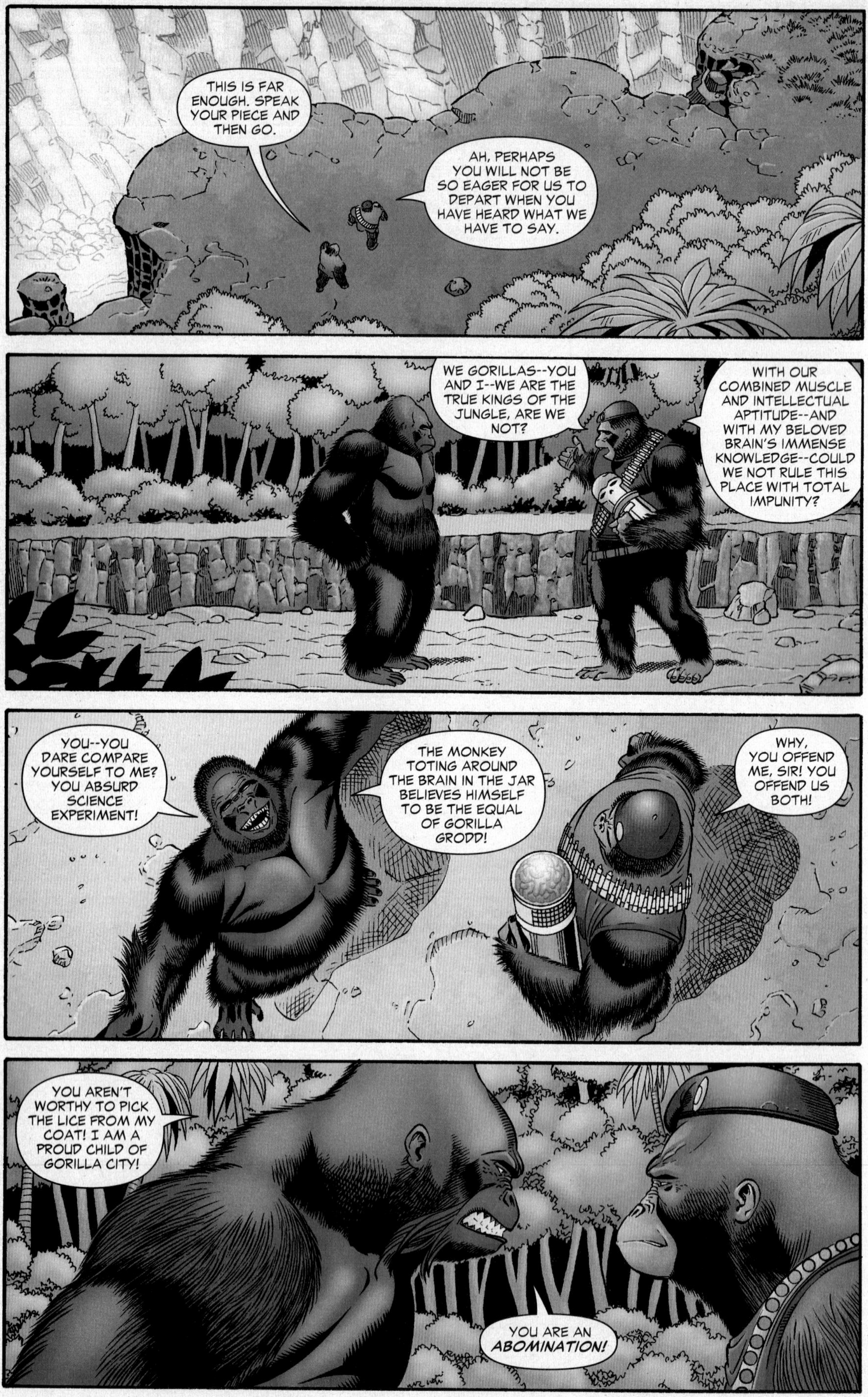
THIS IS FAR ENOUGH. SPEAK YOUR PIECE AND THEN GO.
AH, PERHAPS YOU WILL NOT BE SO EAGER FOR US TO DEPART WHEN YOU HAVE HEARD WHAT WE HAVE TO SAY.
WE GORILLAS--YOU AND I--WE ARE THE TRUE KINGS OF THE JUNGLE, ARE WE NOT?
WITH OUR COMBINED MUSCLE AND INTELLECTUAL APTITUDE--AND WITH MY BELOVED BRAIN'S IMMENSE KNOWLEDGE--COULD WE NOT RULE THIS PLACE WITH TOTAL IMPUNITY?
YOU--YOU DARE COMPARE YOURSELF TO ME? YOU ABSURD SCIENCE EXPERIMENT!
THE MONKEY TOTING AROUND THE BRAIN IN THE JAR BELIEVES HIMSELF TO BE THE EQUAL OF GORILLA GRODD!
WHY, YOU OFFEND ME, SIR! YOU OFFEND US BOTH!
YOU AREN'T WORTHY TO PICK THE LICE FROM MY COAT! I AM A PROUD CHILD OF GORILLA CITY!
YOU ARE AN *ABOMINATION!*

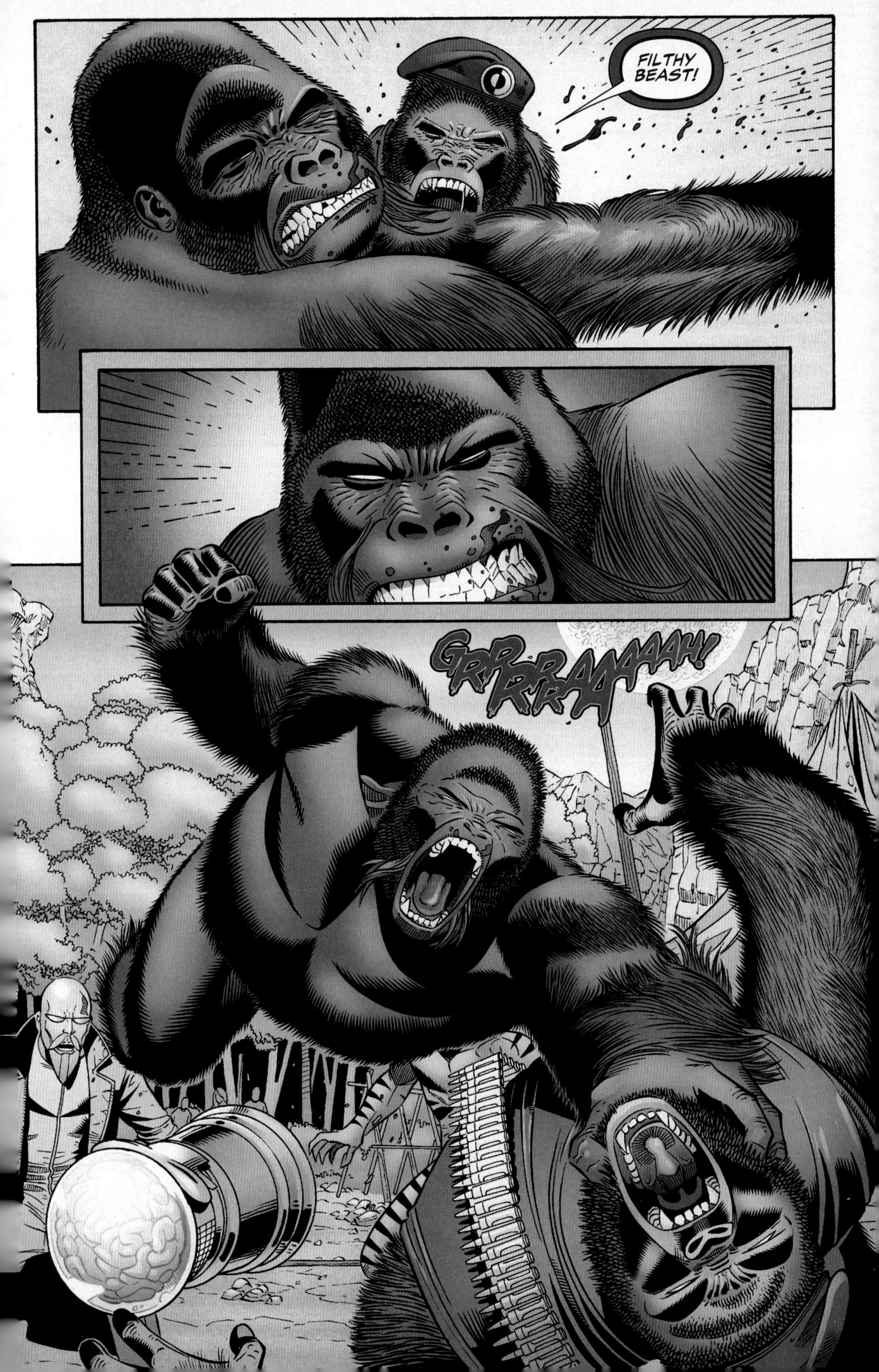
FILTHY BEAST!
GRRRRRAAAAAAH!

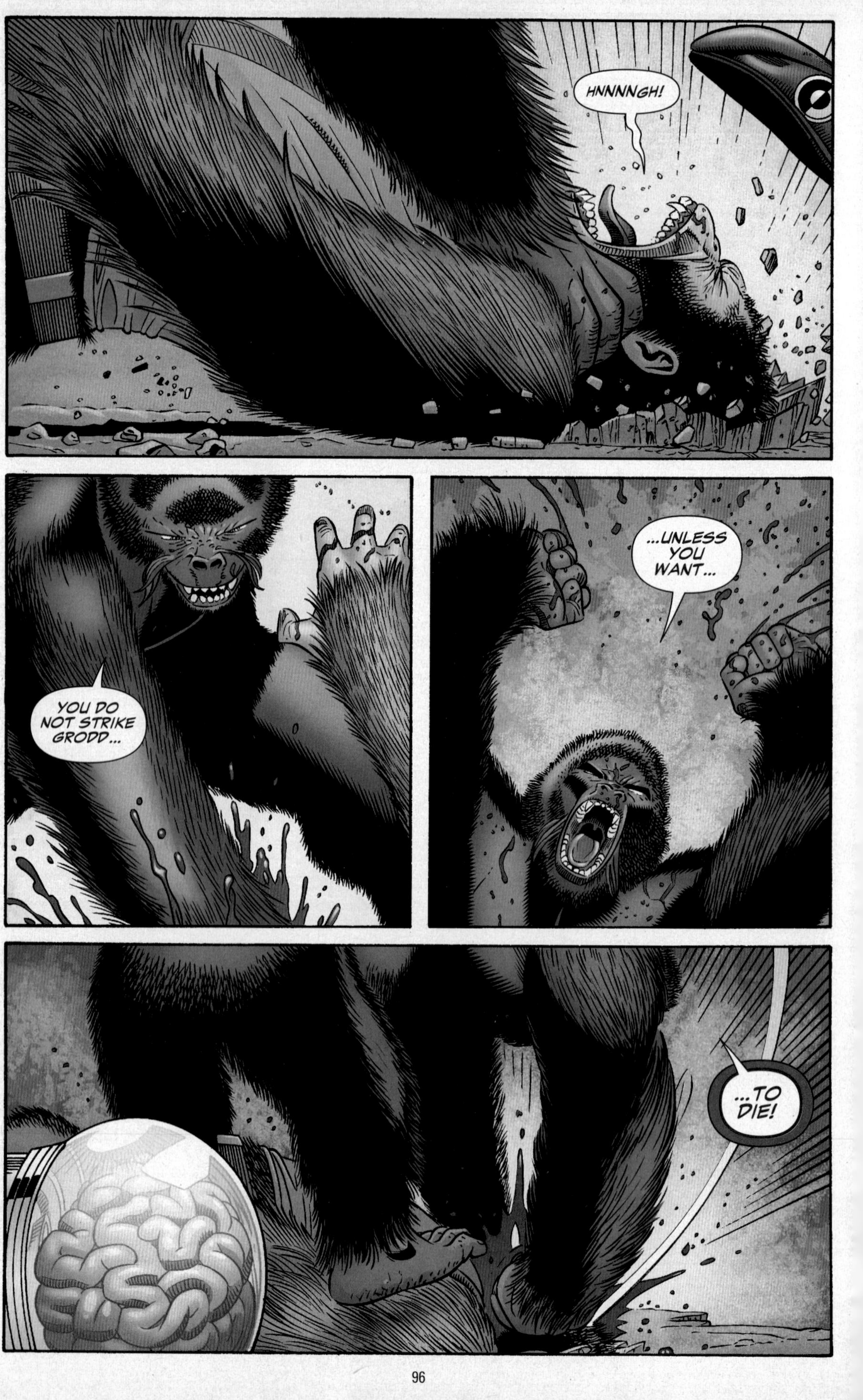
HNNNNGH!
YOU DO NOT STRIKE GRODD...
...UNLESS YOU WANT...
...TO DIE!

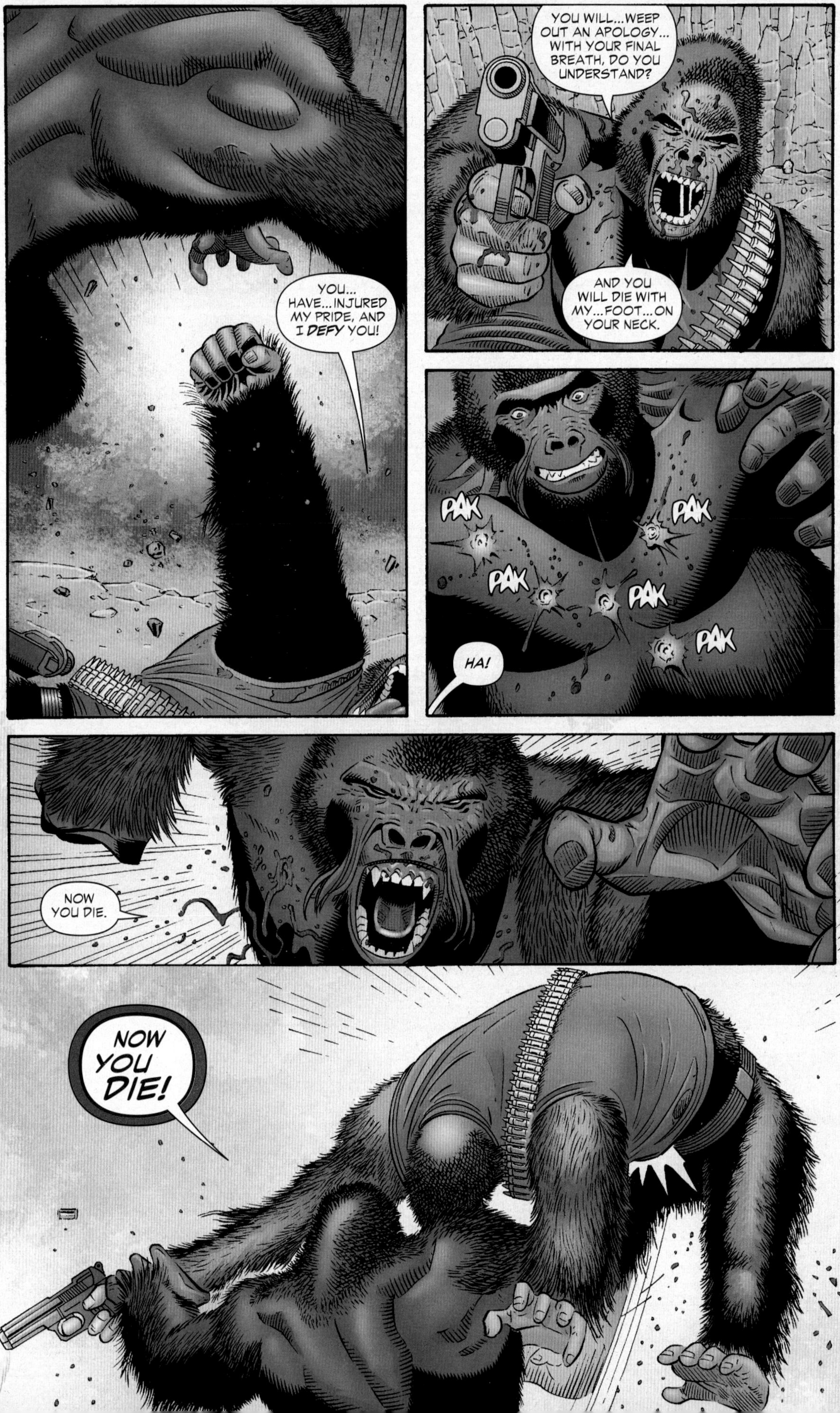
YOU... HAVE...INJURED MY PRIDE, AND I DEFY YOU!
YOU WILL...WEEP OUT AN APOLOGY... WITH YOUR FINAL BREATH, DO YOU UNDERSTAND?
AND YOU WILL DIE WITH MY...FOOT...ON YOUR NECK.
PAK
PAK
PAK
PAK
PAK
HA!
NOW YOU DIE.
NOW YOU DIE!

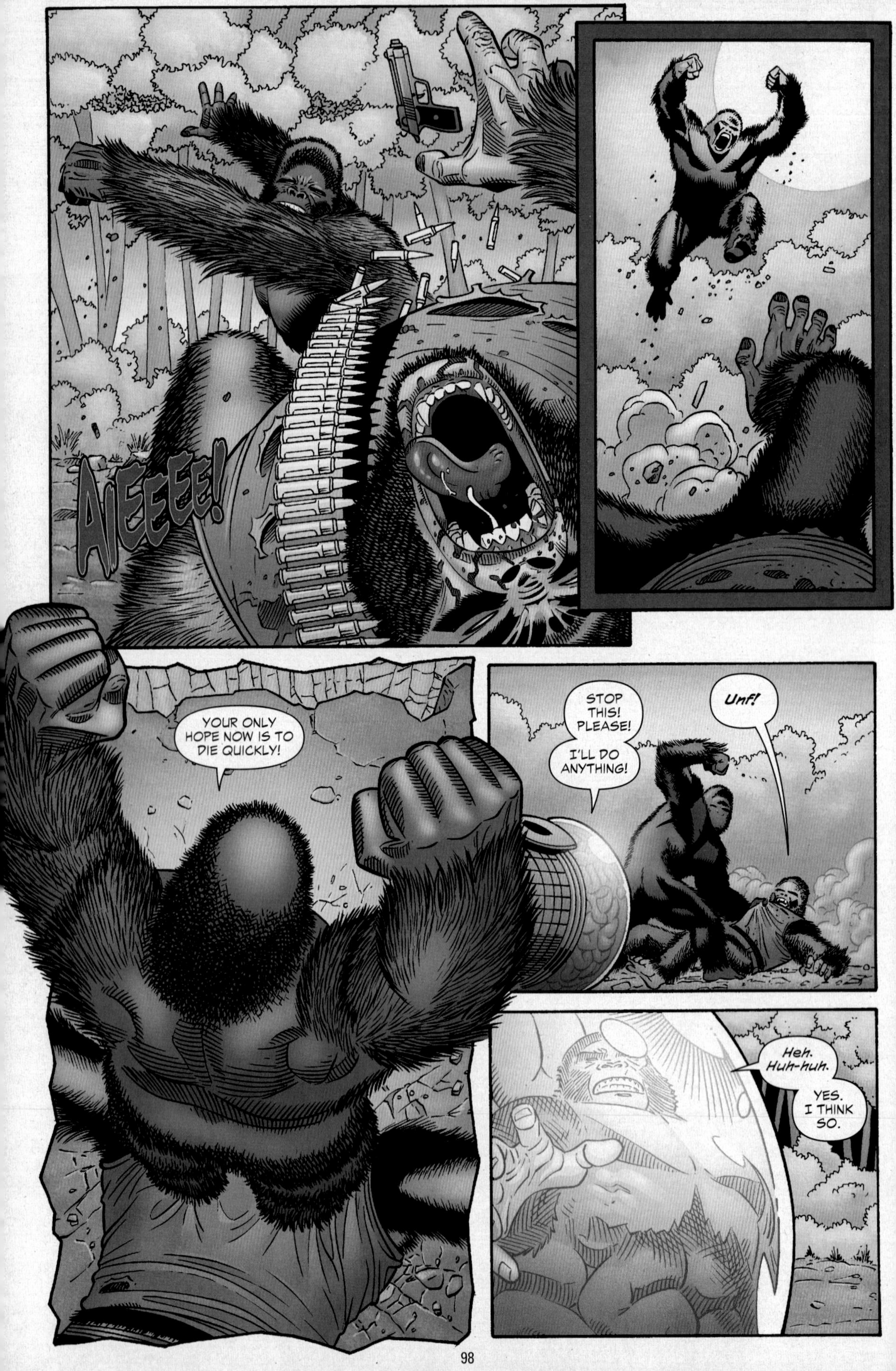
AIEEEEE!
YOUR ONLY HOPE NOW IS TO DIE QUICKLY!
STOP THIS! PLEASE!
I'LL DO ANYTHING!
Unf!
Heh. Huh-huh.
YES. I THINK SO.

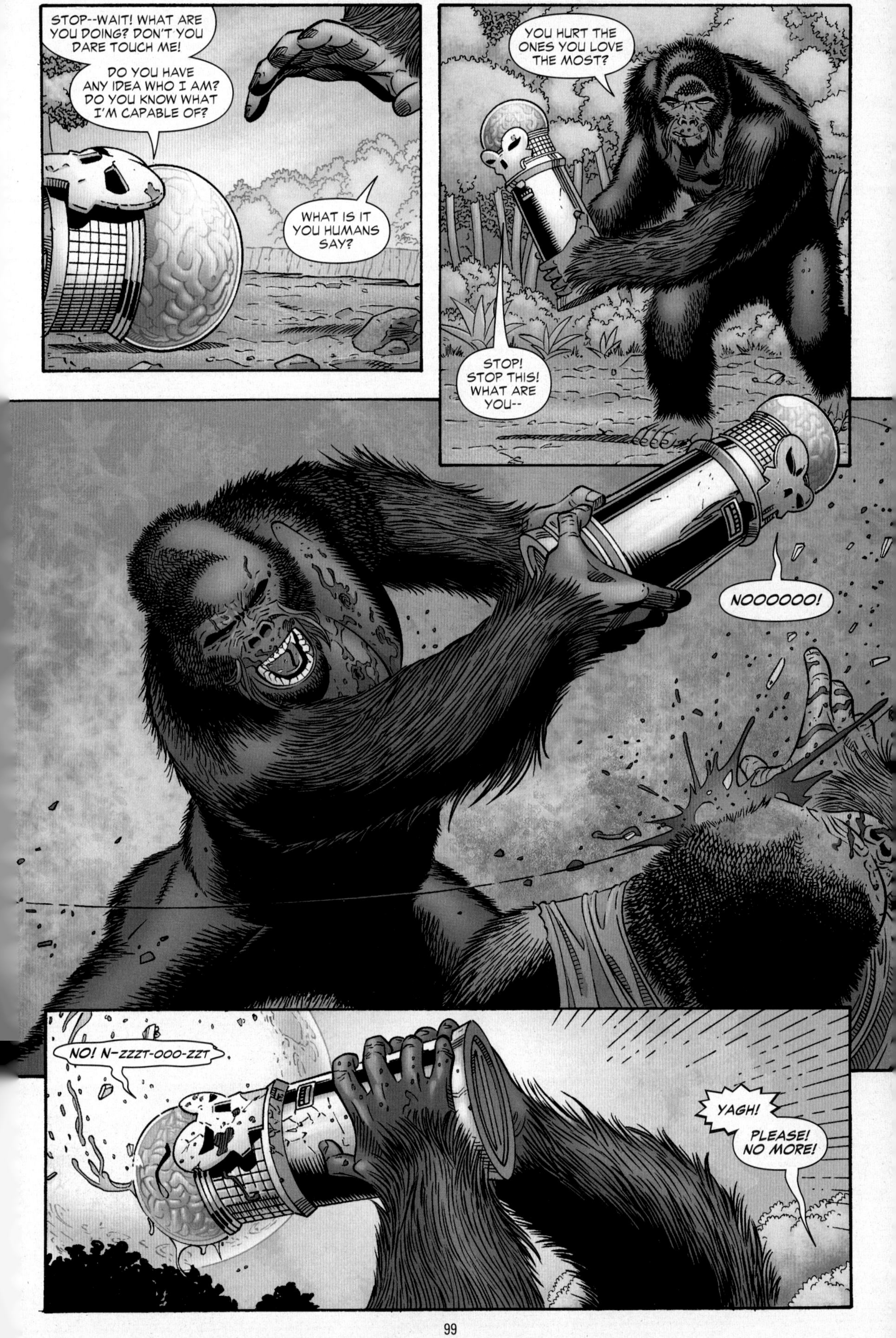
STOP--WAIT! WHAT ARE YOU DOING? DON'T YOU DARE TOUCH ME!
DO YOU HAVE ANY IDEA WHO I AM? DO YOU KNOW WHAT I'M CAPABLE OF?
WHAT IS IT YOU HUMANS SAY?
YOU HURT THE ONES YOU LOVE THE MOST?
STOP! STOP THIS! WHAT ARE YOU--
NOOOOOO!
NO! N-ZZZT-OOO-ZZT
YAGH!
PLEASE! NO MORE!

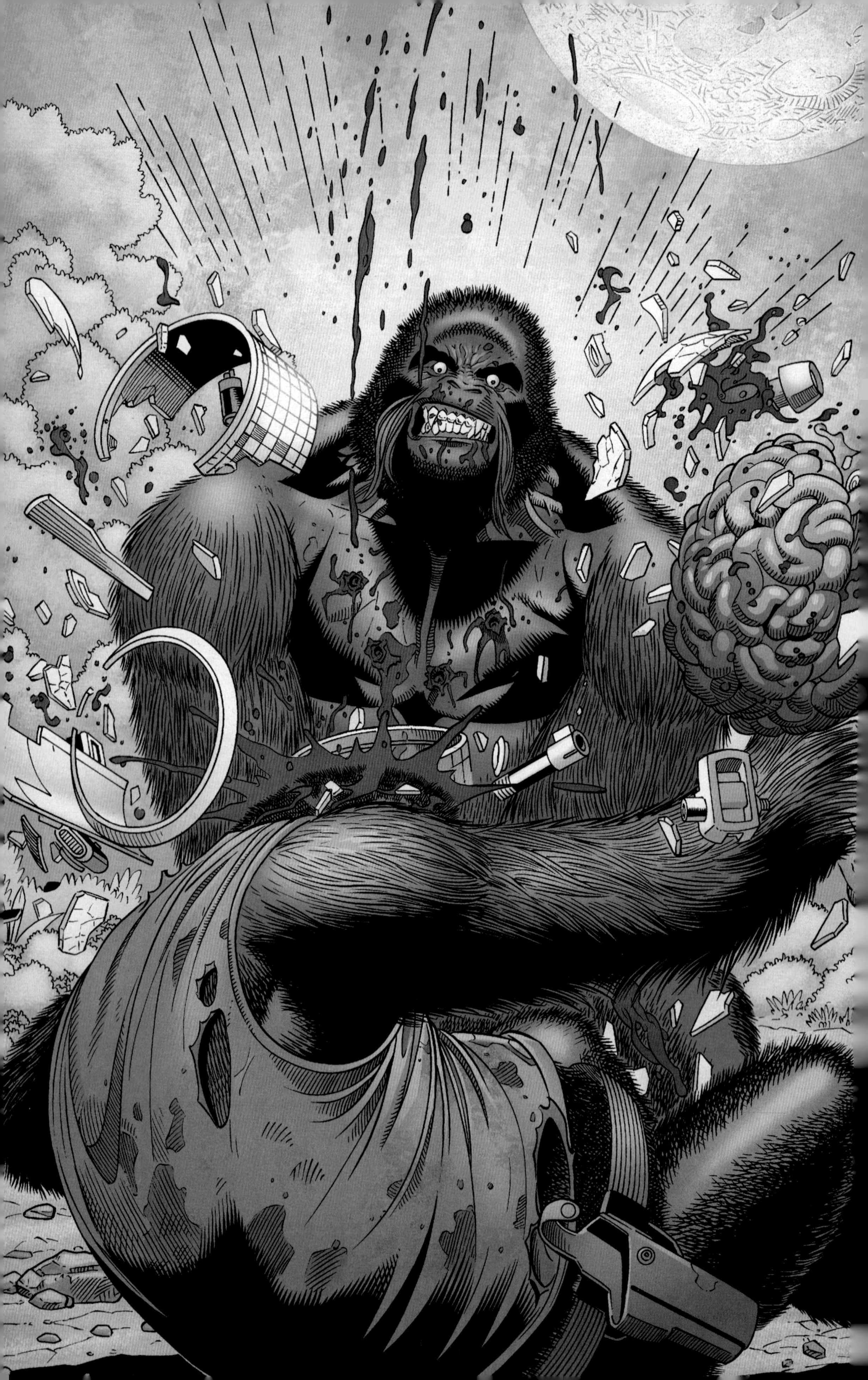

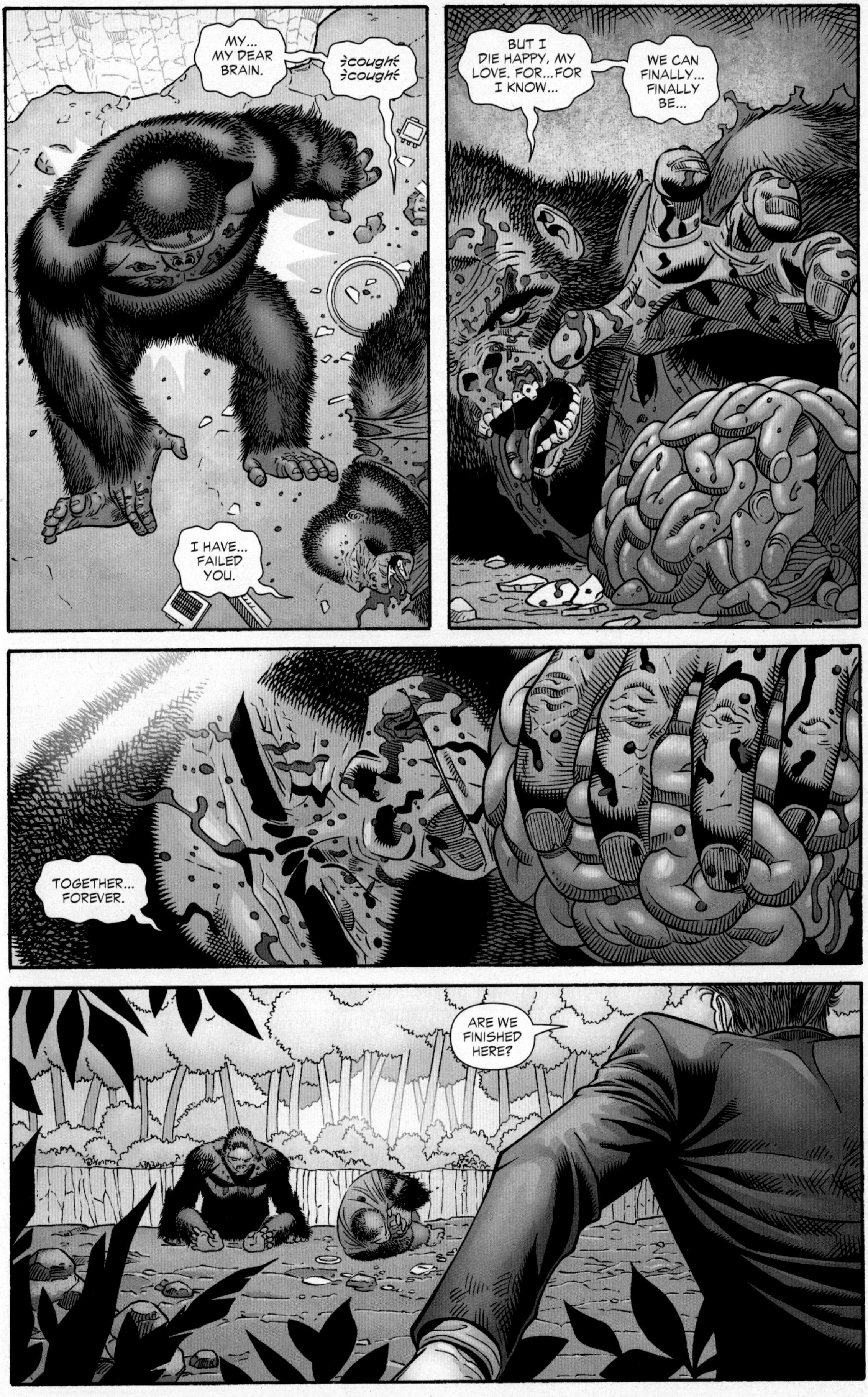
MY... MY DEAR BRAIN.
cough *cough*
I HAVE... FAILED YOU.
BUT I DIE HAPPY, MY LOVE. FOR...FOR I KNOW...
WE CAN FINALLY... FINALLY BE...
TOGETHER... FOREVER.
ARE WE FINISHED HERE?

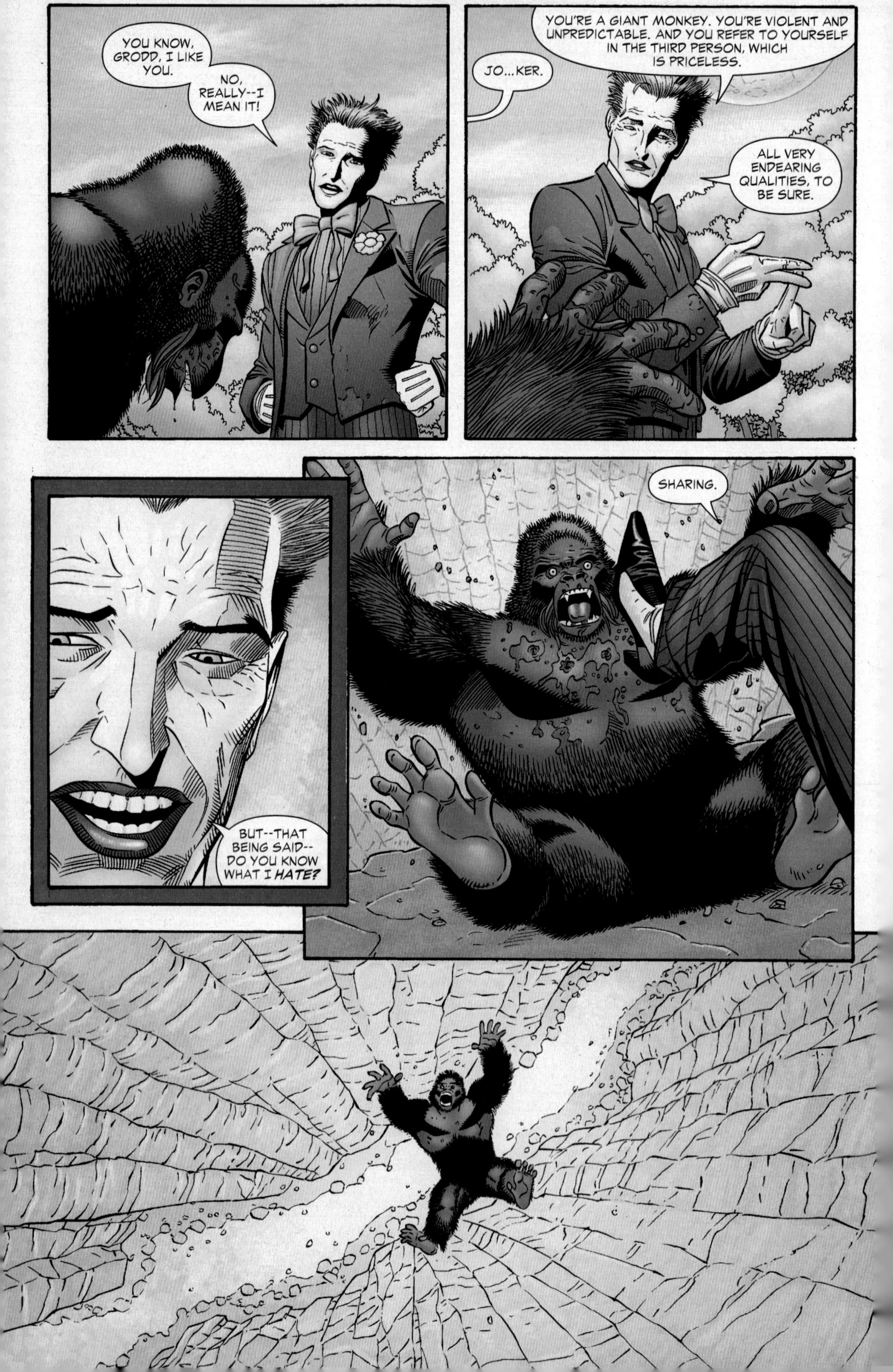
YOU KNOW, GRODD, I LIKE YOU.
NO, REALLY--I MEAN IT!
JO...KER.
YOU'RE A GIANT MONKEY. YOU'RE VIOLENT AND UNPREDICTABLE. AND YOU REFER TO YOURSELF IN THE THIRD PERSON, WHICH IS PRICELESS.
ALL VERY ENDEARING QUALITIES, TO BE SURE.
BUT--THAT BEING SAID--DO YOU KNOW WHAT I HATE?
SHARING.

IS IT MUCH FARTHER? I'M AFRAID I LEFT MY HIKING BOOTS AT HOME, AND THESE HEELS AREN'T MUCH FOR MOUNTAIN CLIMBING.

JUST THROUGH THIS PASS, UNLESS I MISS MY GUESS. WHICH IS TO SAY, JUST THROUGH THIS PASS.

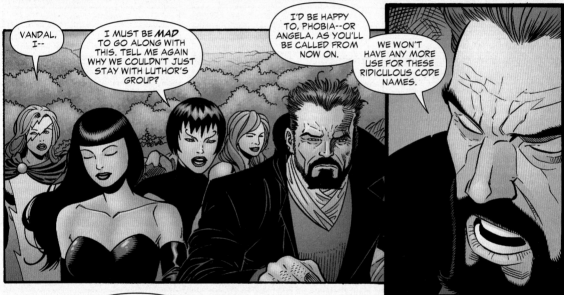

VANDAL, I--

I MUST BE *MAD* TO GO ALONG WITH THIS. TELL ME AGAIN WHY WE COULDN'T JUST STAY WITH LUTHOR'S GROUP?

I'D BE HAPPY TO, PHOBIA--OR ANGELA, AS YOU'LL BE CALLED FROM NOW ON.

WE WON'T HAVE ANY MORE USE FOR THESE RIDICULOUS CODE NAMES.

EMPIRES FAIL FOR ONE OF THREE REASONS, MY FRIENDS. THE FIRST IS CONQUEST BY A STRONGER EMPIRE, WHICH IS CLEARLY NOT AN ISSUE ON THIS GODFORSAKEN ROCK.

THE SECOND IS A LACK OF ORGANIZATION.

TAKE GRODD AND THE JOKER, FOR INSTANCE. ONE OF THEM IS CERTAIN TO BETRAY THE OTHER--IN FACT, I WOULDN'T BE SURPRISED IF ONE OR BOTH OF THEM WERE ALREADY DEAD.

OH, GREAT. JUST WHAT I NEED-- A HISTORY LESSON.

THOSE LUNATICS WILL BE ROASTING EACH OTHER AND WORSHIPPING PIG SKULLS WITHIN THE YEAR.

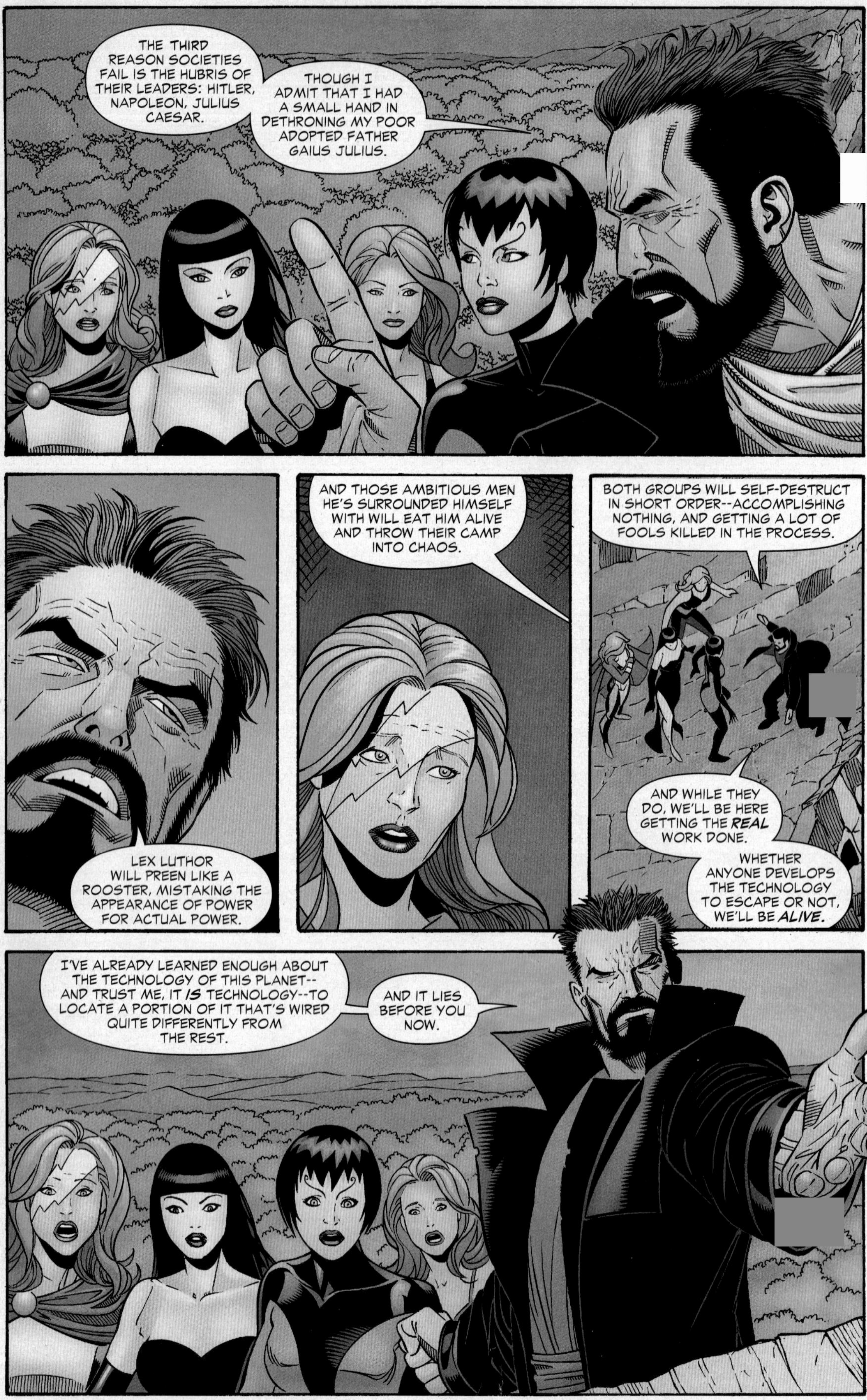
THE THIRD REASON SOCIETIES FAIL IS THE HUBRIS OF THEIR LEADERS: HITLER, NAPOLEON, JULIUS CAESAR.
THOUGH I ADMIT THAT I HAD A SMALL HAND IN DETHRONING MY POOR ADOPTED FATHER GAIUS JULIUS.
LEX LUTHOR WILL PREEN LIKE A ROOSTER, MISTAKING THE APPEARANCE OF POWER FOR ACTUAL POWER.
AND THOSE AMBITIOUS MEN HE'S SURROUNDED HIMSELF WITH WILL EAT HIM ALIVE AND THROW THEIR CAMP INTO CHAOS.
BOTH GROUPS WILL SELF-DESTRUCT IN SHORT ORDER--ACCOMPLISHING NOTHING, AND GETTING A LOT OF FOOLS KILLED IN THE PROCESS.
AND WHILE THEY DO, WE'LL BE HERE GETTING THE *REAL* WORK DONE.
WHETHER ANYONE DEVELOPS THE TECHNOLOGY TO ESCAPE OR NOT, WE'LL BE *ALIVE.*
I'VE ALREADY LEARNED ENOUGH ABOUT THE TECHNOLOGY OF THIS PLANET-- AND TRUST ME, IT *IS* TECHNOLOGY--TO LOCATE A PORTION OF IT THAT'S WIRED QUITE DIFFERENTLY FROM THE REST.
AND IT LIES BEFORE YOU NOW.

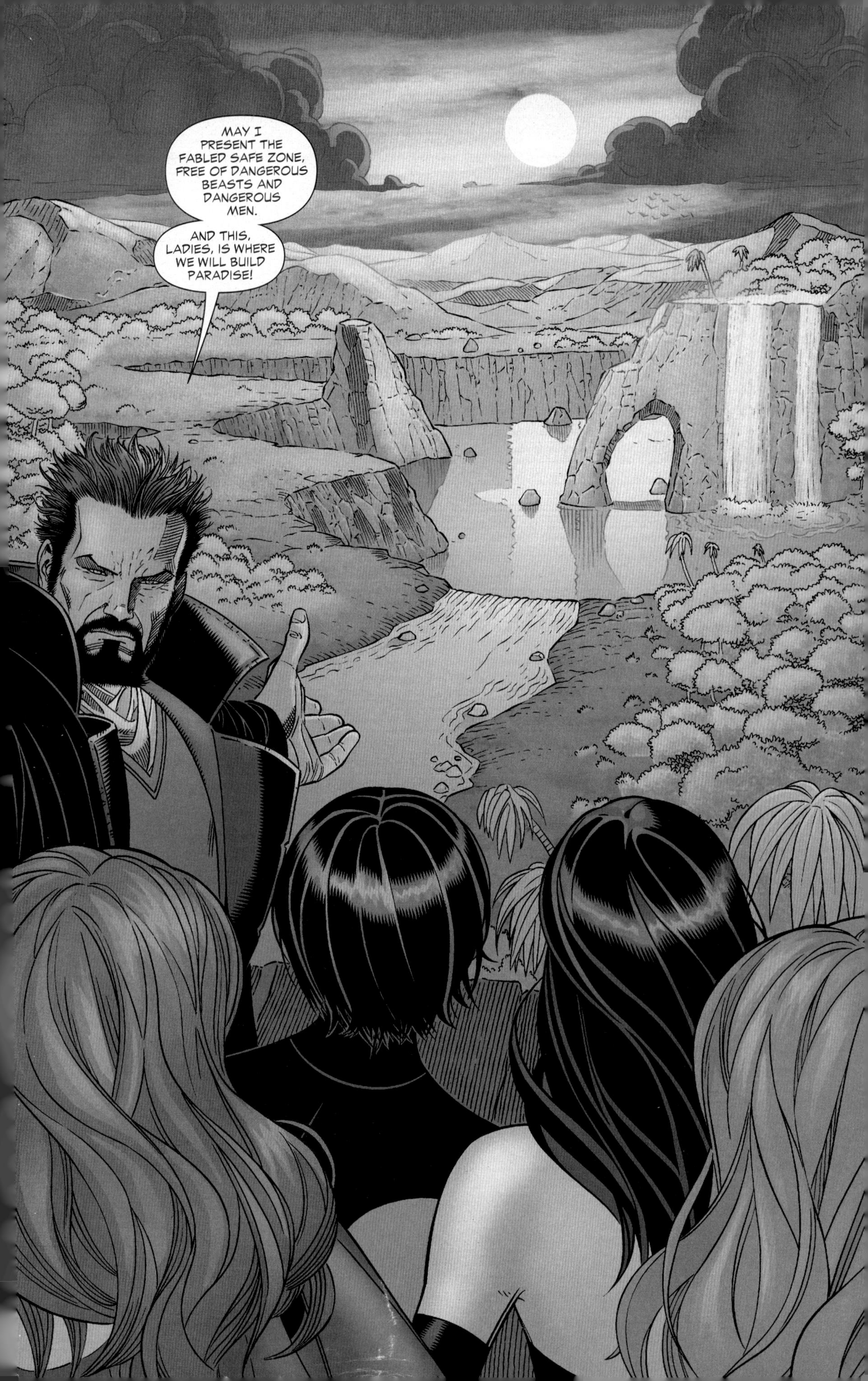
MAY I PRESENT THE FABLED SAFE ZONE, FREE OF DANGEROUS BEASTS AND DANGEROUS MEN.
AND THIS, LADIES, IS WHERE WE WILL BUILD PARADISE!

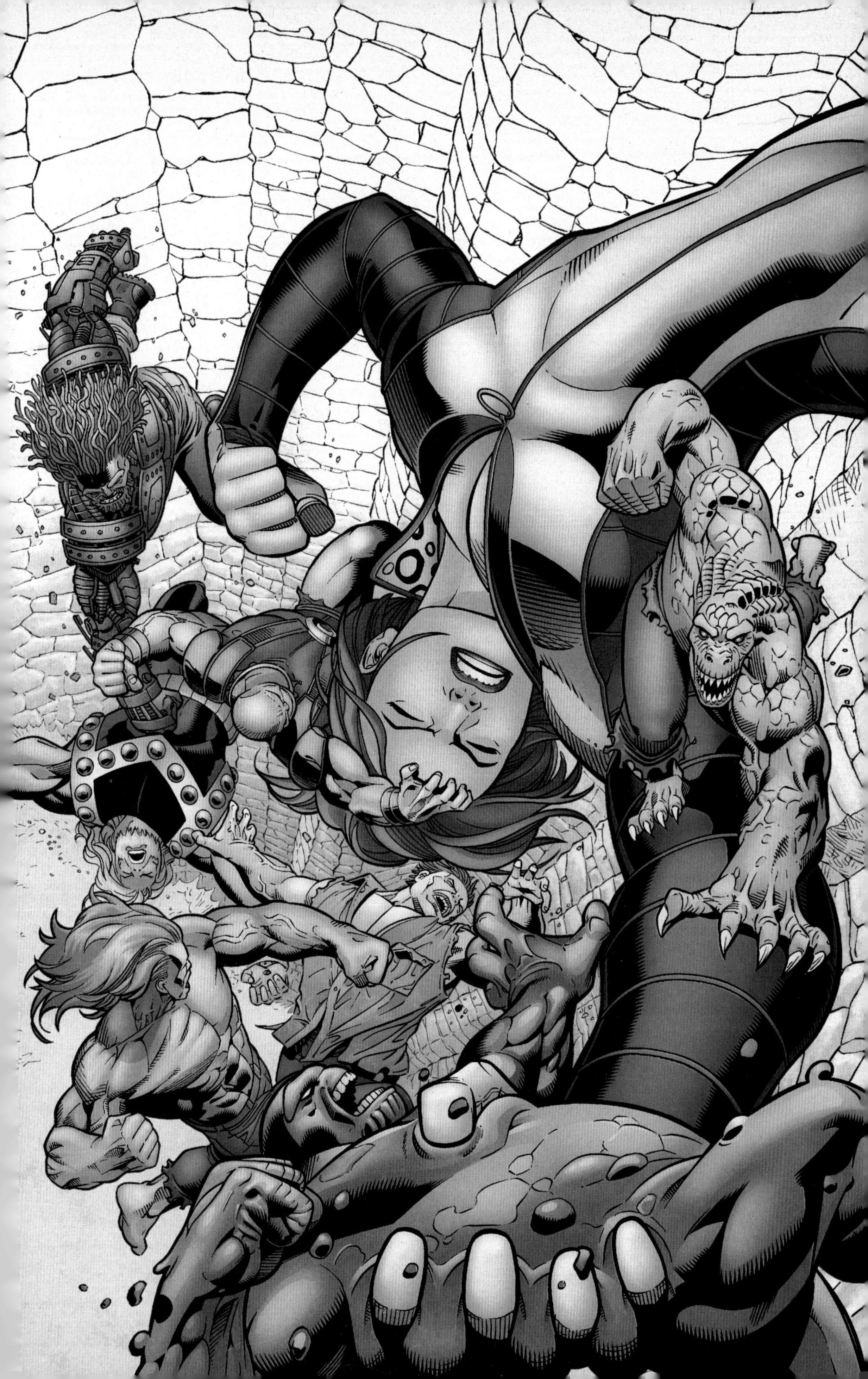

Matthew Sturges
Writer

Joe Bennett
Penciller

Belardino Brabo
Inker

John Kalisz
Colorist

Steve Wands
Letterer

CHAPTER FIVE

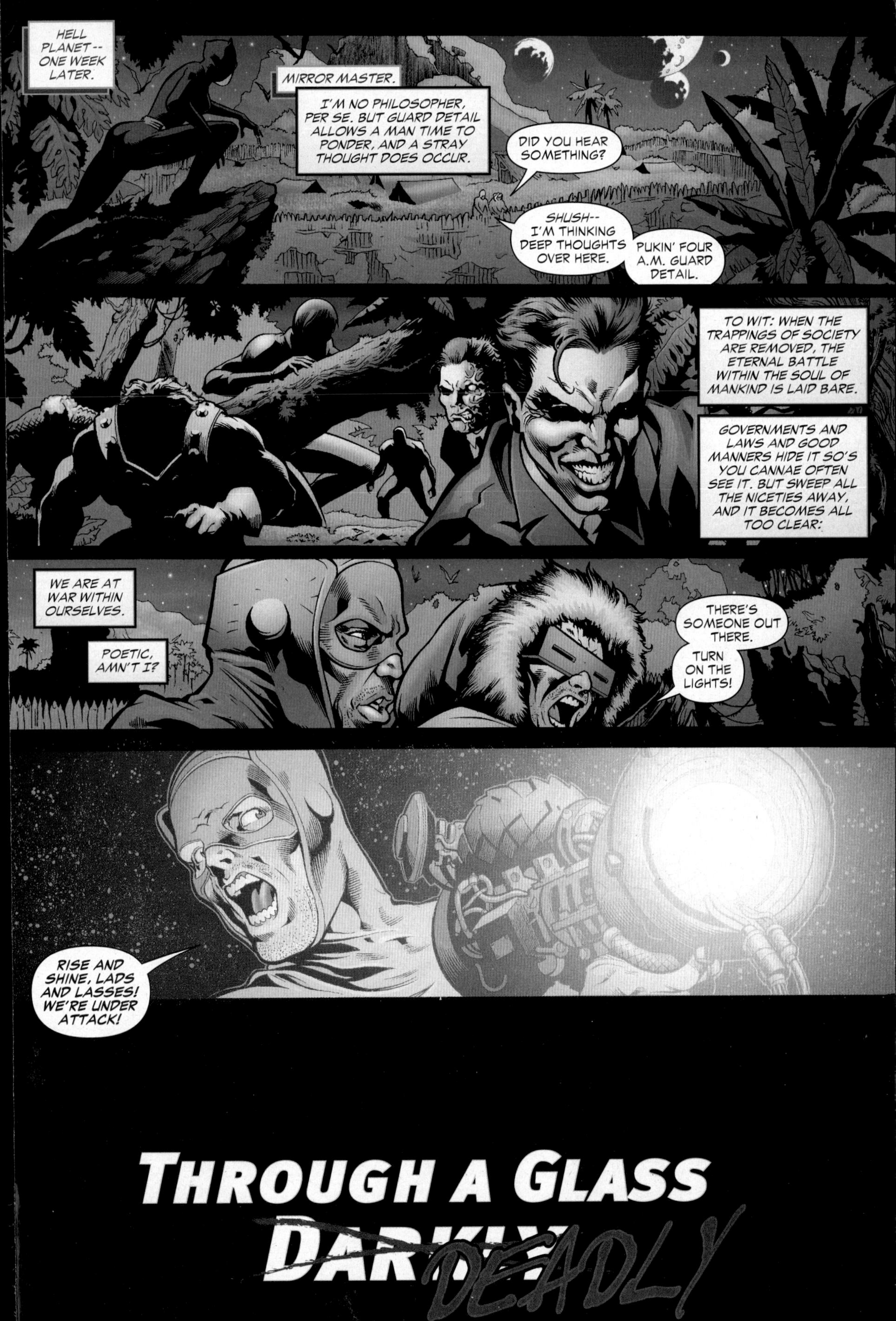
HELL PLANET-- ONE WEEK LATER.
MIRROR MASTER.
I'M NO PHILOSOPHER, PER SE. BUT GUARD DETAIL ALLOWS A MAN TIME TO PONDER, AND A STRAY THOUGHT DOES OCCUR.
DID YOU HEAR SOMETHING?
SHUSH-- I'M THINKING DEEP THOUGHTS OVER HERE.
PUKIN' FOUR A.M. GUARD DETAIL.
TO WIT: WHEN THE TRAPPINGS OF SOCIETY ARE REMOVED, THE ETERNAL BATTLE WITHIN THE SOUL OF MANKIND IS LAID BARE.
GOVERNMENTS AND LAWS AND GOOD MANNERS HIDE IT SO'S YOU CANNAE OFTEN SEE IT. BUT SWEEP ALL THE NICETIES AWAY, AND IT BECOMES ALL TOO CLEAR:
WE ARE AT WAR WITHIN OURSELVES.
POETIC, AMN'T I?
THERE'S SOMEONE OUT THERE.
TURN ON THE LIGHTS!
RISE AND SHINE, LADS AND LASSES! WE'RE UNDER ATTACK!
THROUGH A GLASS DARKLY DEADLY

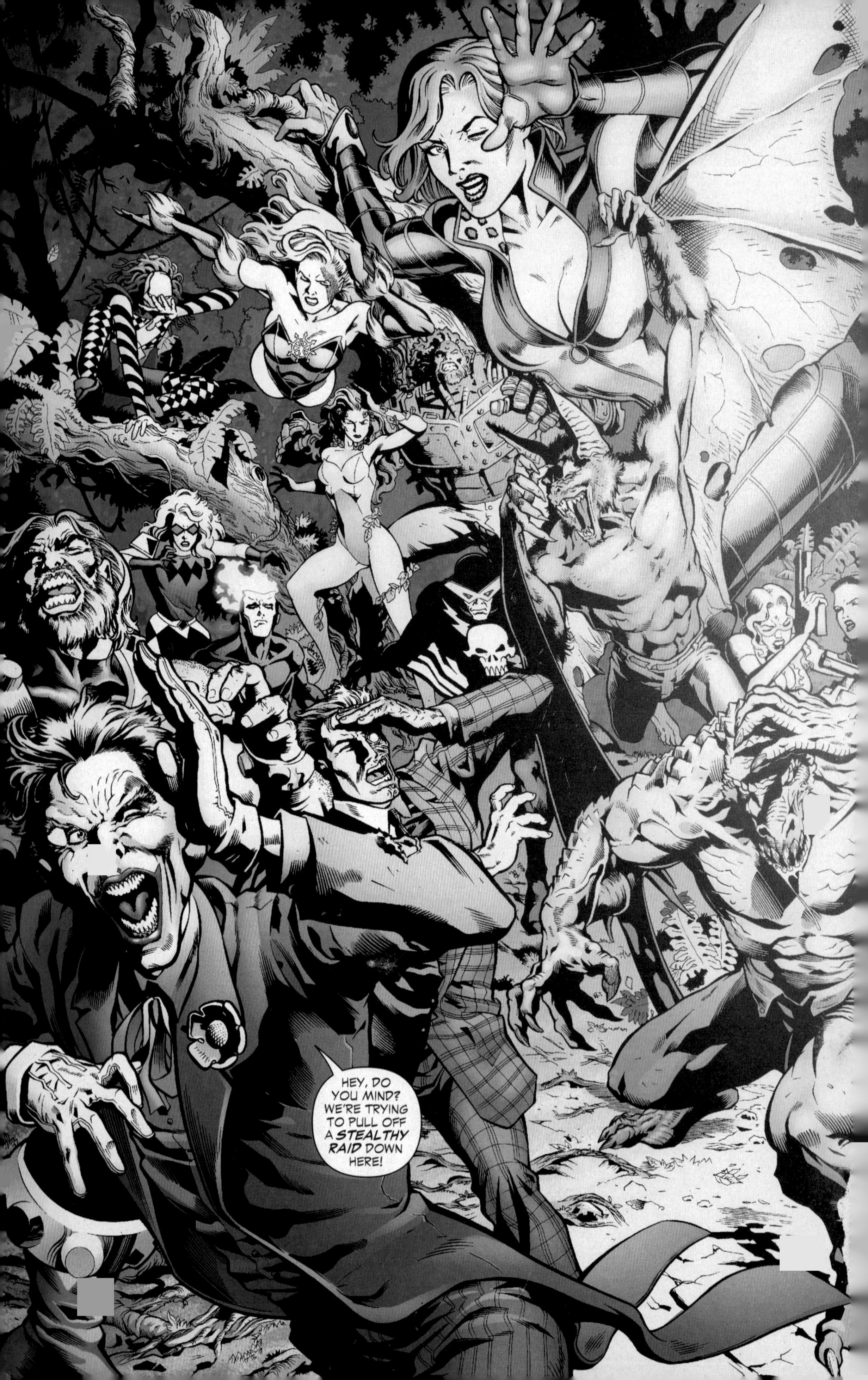
HEY, DO YOU MIND? WE'RE TRYING TO PULL OFF A STEALTHY RAID DOWN HERE!

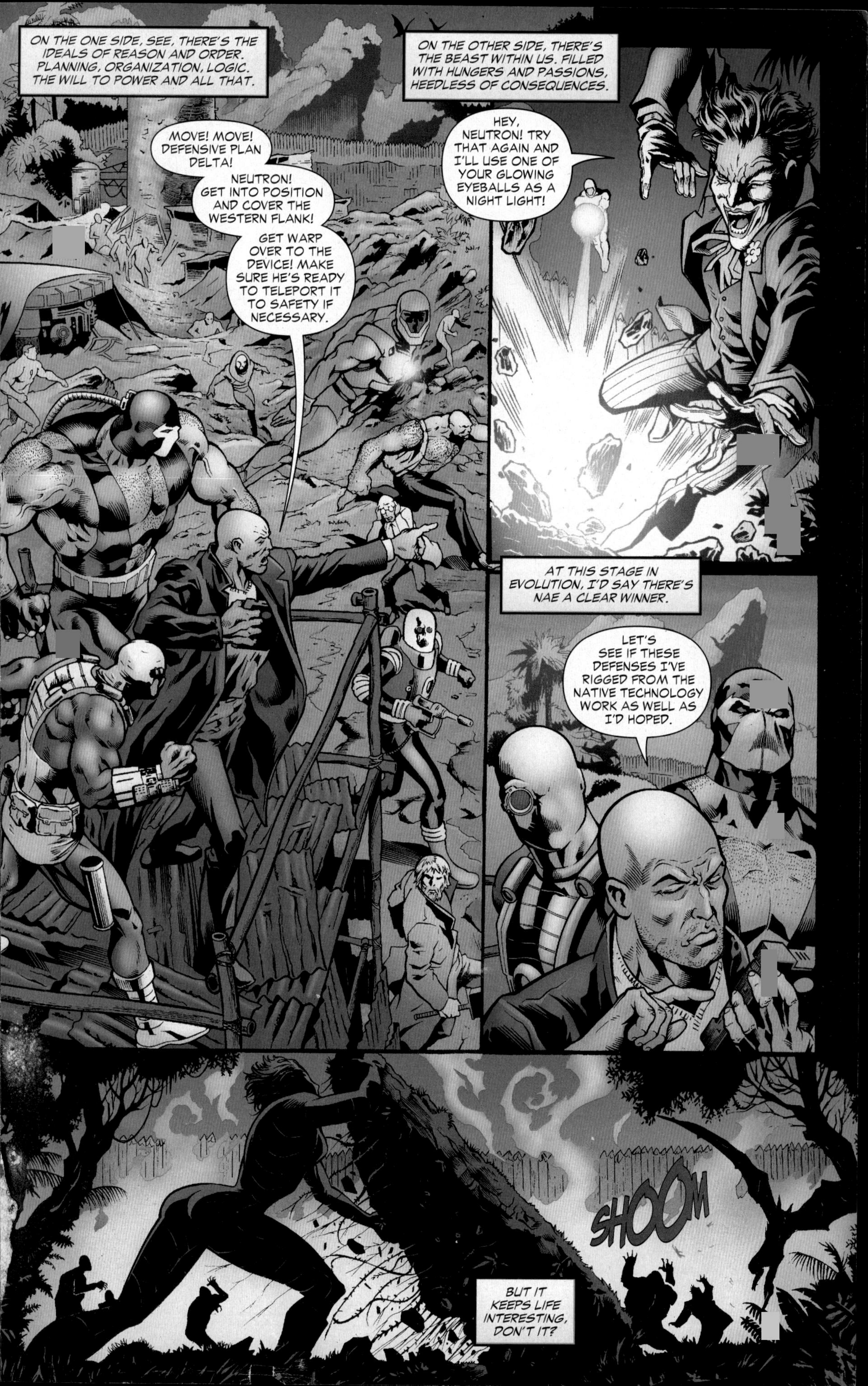
ON THE ONE SIDE, SEE, THERE'S THE IDEALS OF REASON AND ORDER. PLANNING, ORGANIZATION, LOGIC. THE WILL TO POWER AND ALL THAT.
MOVE! MOVE! DEFENSIVE PLAN DELTA!
NEUTRON! GET INTO POSITION AND COVER THE WESTERN FLANK!
GET WARP OVER TO THE DEVICE! MAKE SURE HE'S READY TO TELEPORT IT TO SAFETY IF NECESSARY.
ON THE OTHER SIDE, THERE'S THE BEAST WITHIN US. FILLED WITH HUNGERS AND PASSIONS, HEEDLESS OF CONSEQUENCES.
HEY, NEUTRON! TRY THAT AGAIN AND I'LL USE ONE OF YOUR GLOWING EYEBALLS AS A NIGHT LIGHT!
AT THIS STAGE IN EVOLUTION, I'D SAY THERE'S NAE A CLEAR WINNER.
LET'S SEE IF THESE DEFENSES I'VE RIGGED FROM THE NATIVE TECHNOLOGY WORK AS WELL AS I'D HOPED.
SHOOOM
BUT IT KEEPS LIFE INTERESTING, DON'T IT?

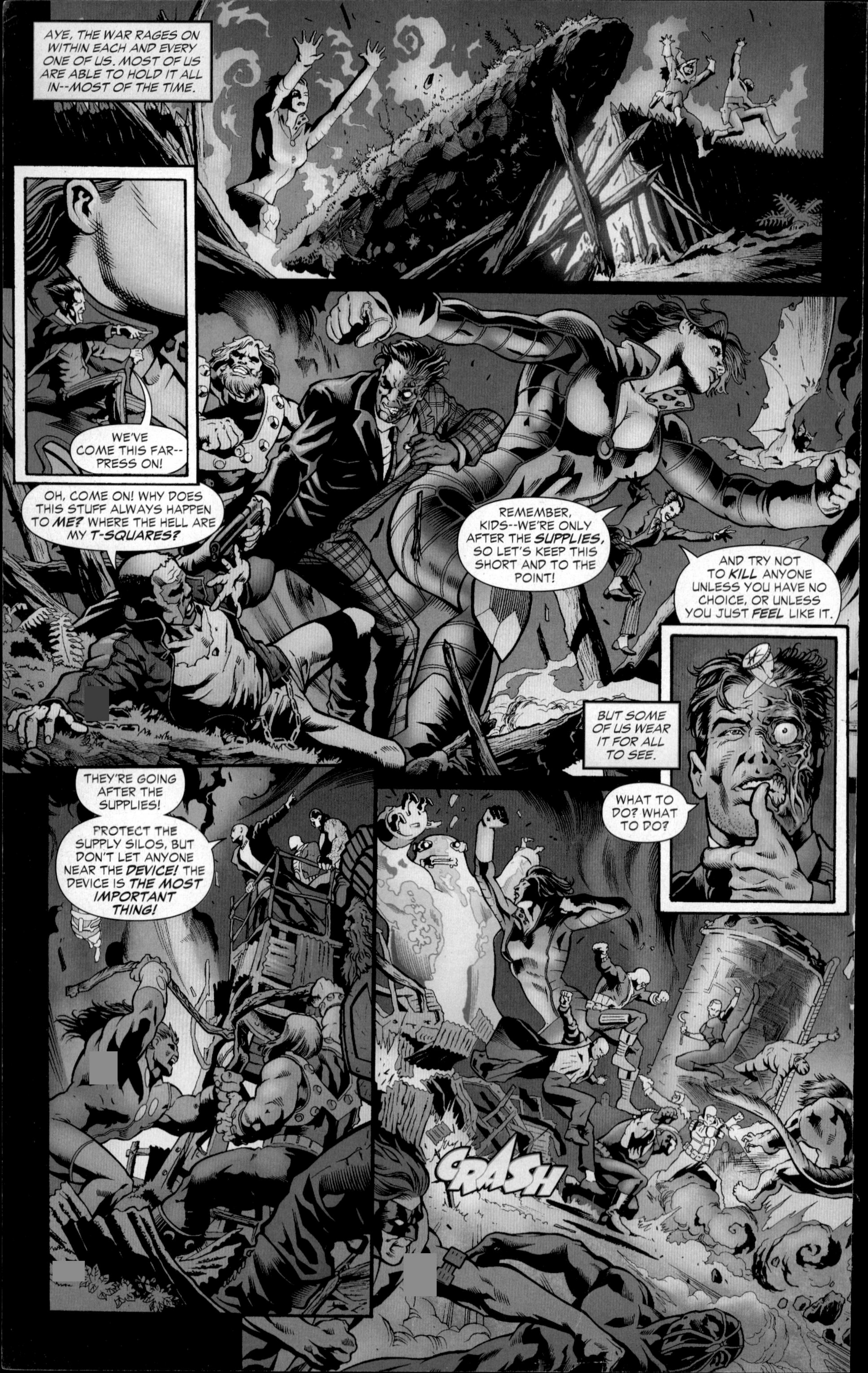
AYE, THE WAR RAGES ON WITHIN EACH AND EVERY ONE OF US. MOST OF US ARE ABLE TO HOLD IT ALL IN--MOST OF THE TIME.
WE'VE COME THIS FAR--PRESS ON!
OH, COME ON! WHY DOES THIS STUFF ALWAYS HAPPEN TO ME? WHERE THE HELL ARE MY T-SQUARES?
REMEMBER, KIDS--WE'RE ONLY AFTER THE SUPPLIES, SO LET'S KEEP THIS SHORT AND TO THE POINT!
AND TRY NOT TO KILL ANYONE UNLESS YOU HAVE NO CHOICE, OR UNLESS YOU JUST FEEL LIKE IT.
BUT SOME OF US WEAR IT FOR ALL TO SEE.
WHAT TO DO? WHAT TO DO?
THEY'RE GOING AFTER THE SUPPLIES!
PROTECT THE SUPPLY SILOS, BUT DON'T LET ANYONE NEAR THE DEVICE! THE DEVICE IS THE MOST IMPORTANT THING!
CRASH

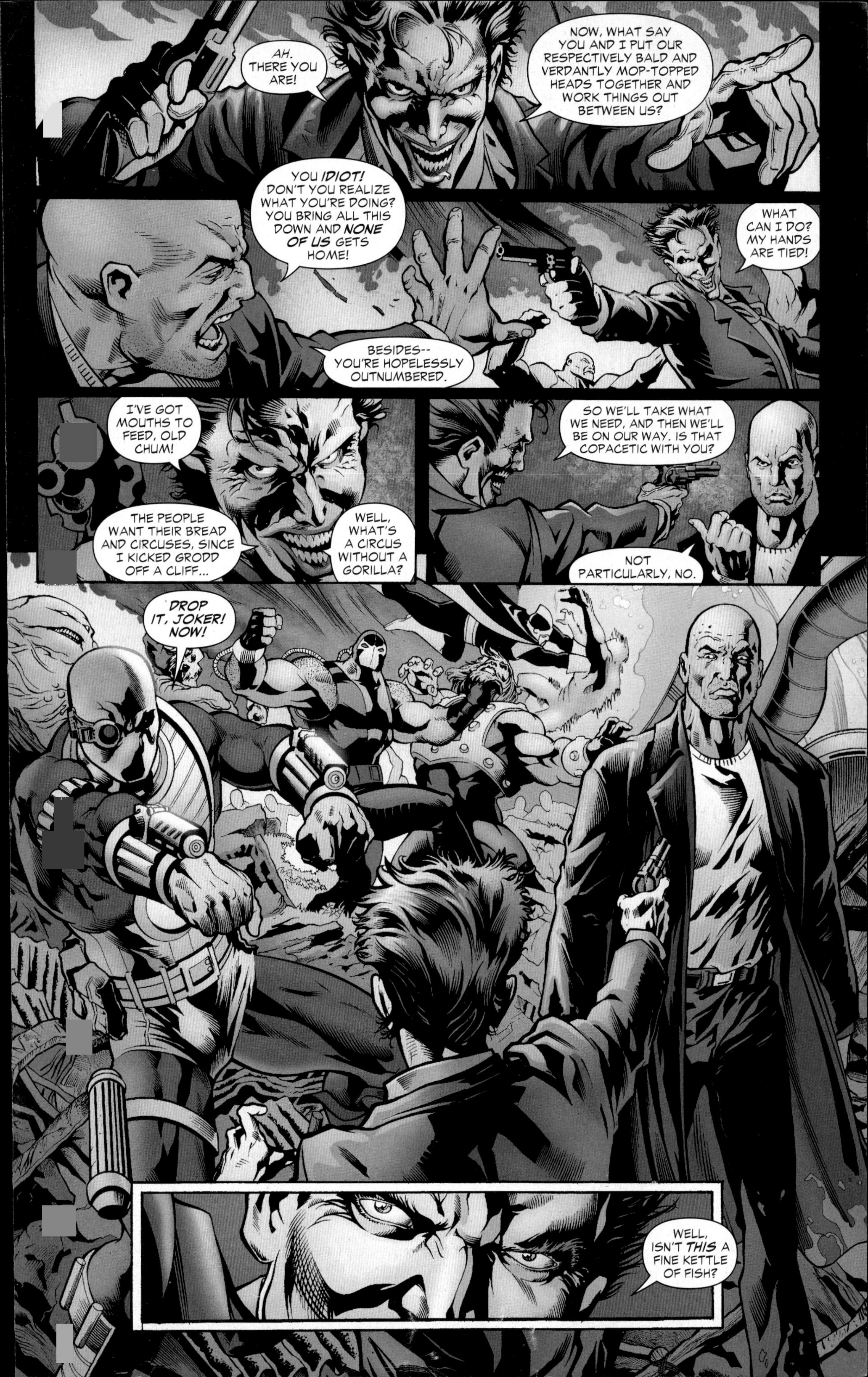
AH. THERE YOU ARE!
NOW, WHAT SAY YOU AND I PUT OUR RESPECTIVELY BALD AND VERDANTLY MOP-TOPPED HEADS TOGETHER AND WORK THINGS OUT BETWEEN US?
YOU *IDIOT!* DON'T YOU REALIZE WHAT YOU'RE DOING? YOU BRING ALL THIS DOWN AND ***NONE OF US*** GETS HOME!
WHAT CAN I DO? MY HANDS ARE TIED!
BESIDES-- YOU'RE HOPELESSLY OUTNUMBERED.
I'VE GOT MOUTHS TO FEED, OLD CHUM!
THE PEOPLE WANT THEIR BREAD AND CIRCUSES, SINCE I KICKED GRODD OFF A CLIFF...
WELL, WHAT'S A CIRCUS WITHOUT A GORILLA?
SO WE'LL TAKE WHAT WE NEED, AND THEN WE'LL BE ON OUR WAY. IS THAT COPACETIC WITH YOU?
NOT PARTICULARLY, NO.
DROP IT, JOKER! NOW!
WELL, ISN'T *THIS* A FINE KETTLE OF FISH?

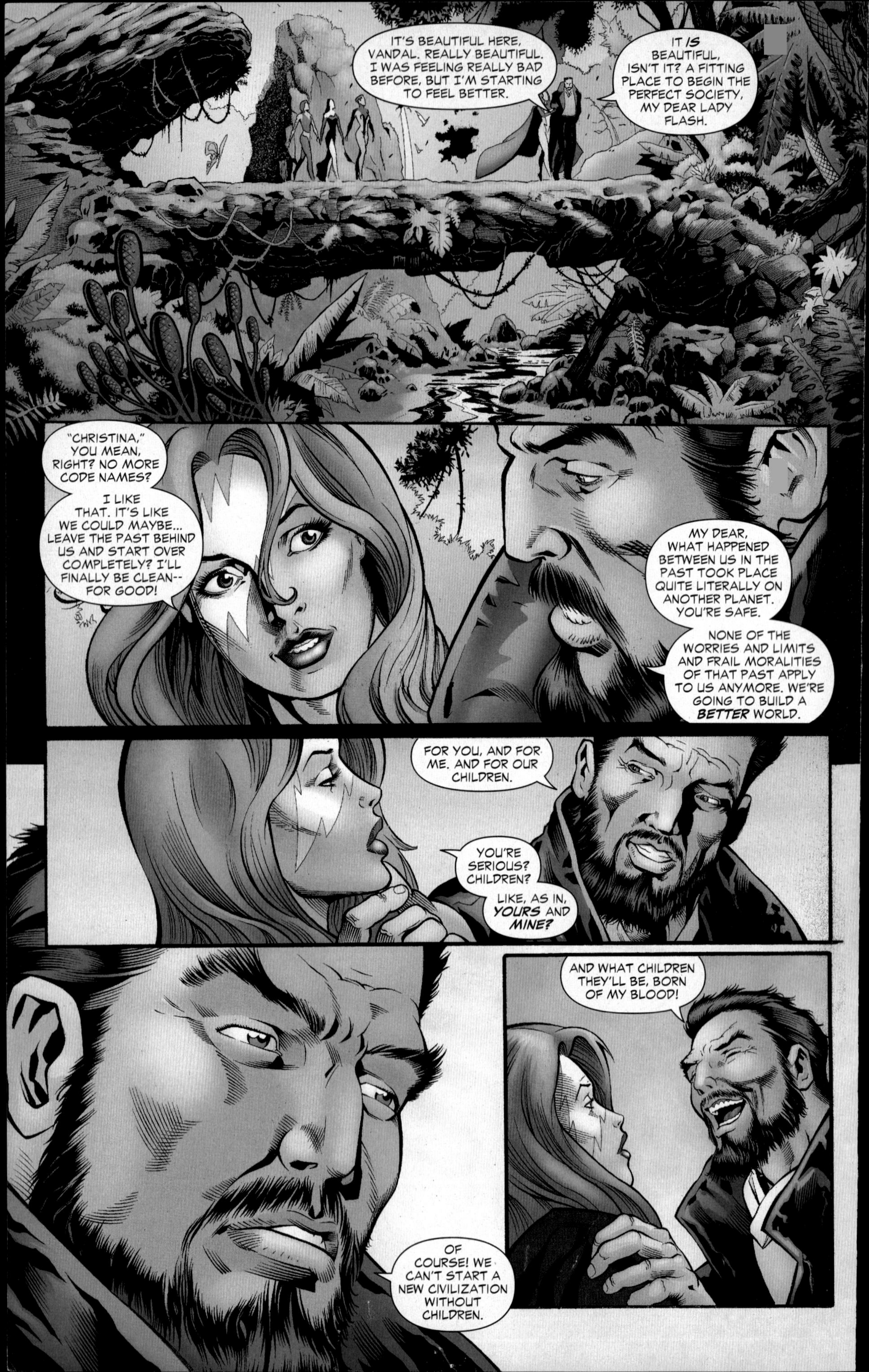
IT'S BEAUTIFUL HERE, VANDAL. REALLY BEAUTIFUL. I WAS FEELING REALLY BAD BEFORE, BUT I'M STARTING TO FEEL BETTER.
IT IS BEAUTIFUL, ISN'T IT? A FITTING PLACE TO BEGIN THE PERFECT SOCIETY, MY DEAR LADY FLASH.
"CHRISTINA," YOU MEAN, RIGHT? NO MORE CODE NAMES?
I LIKE THAT. IT'S LIKE WE COULD MAYBE... LEAVE THE PAST BEHIND US AND START OVER COMPLETELY? I'LL FINALLY BE CLEAN-- FOR GOOD!
MY DEAR, WHAT HAPPENED BETWEEN US IN THE PAST TOOK PLACE QUITE LITERALLY ON ANOTHER PLANET. YOU'RE SAFE.
NONE OF THE WORRIES AND LIMITS AND FRAIL MORALITIES OF THAT PAST APPLY TO US ANYMORE. WE'RE GOING TO BUILD A BETTER WORLD.
FOR YOU, AND FOR ME. AND FOR OUR CHILDREN.
YOU'RE SERIOUS? CHILDREN?
LIKE, AS IN, YOURS AND MINE?
OF COURSE! WE CAN'T START A NEW CIVILIZATION WITHOUT CHILDREN.
AND WHAT CHILDREN THEY'LL BE, BORN OF MY BLOOD!

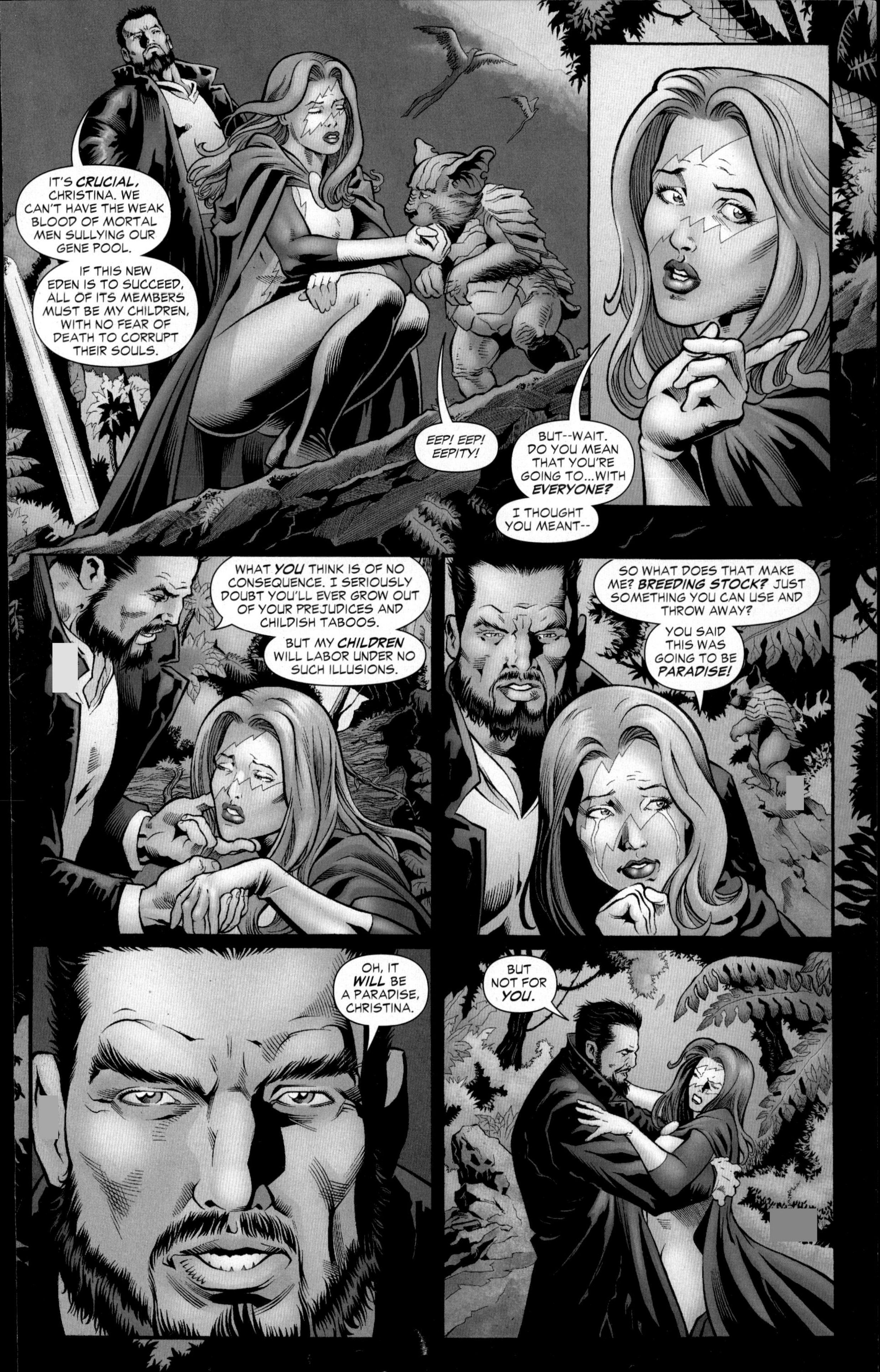
IT'S CRUCIAL, CHRISTINA. WE CAN'T HAVE THE WEAK BLOOD OF MORTAL MEN SULLYING OUR GENE POOL.
IF THIS NEW EDEN IS TO SUCCEED, ALL OF ITS MEMBERS MUST BE MY CHILDREN, WITH NO FEAR OF DEATH TO CORRUPT THEIR SOULS.
EEP! EEP! EEPITY!
BUT--WAIT. DO YOU MEAN THAT YOU'RE GOING TO...WITH EVERYONE?
I THOUGHT YOU MEANT--
WHAT YOU THINK IS OF NO CONSEQUENCE. I SERIOUSLY DOUBT YOU'LL EVER GROW OUT OF YOUR PREJUDICES AND CHILDISH TABOOS.
BUT MY CHILDREN WILL LABOR UNDER NO SUCH ILLUSIONS.
SO WHAT DOES THAT MAKE ME? BREEDING STOCK? JUST SOMETHING YOU CAN USE AND THROW AWAY?
YOU SAID THIS WAS GOING TO BE PARADISE!
OH, IT WILL BE A PARADISE, CHRISTINA.
BUT NOT FOR YOU.

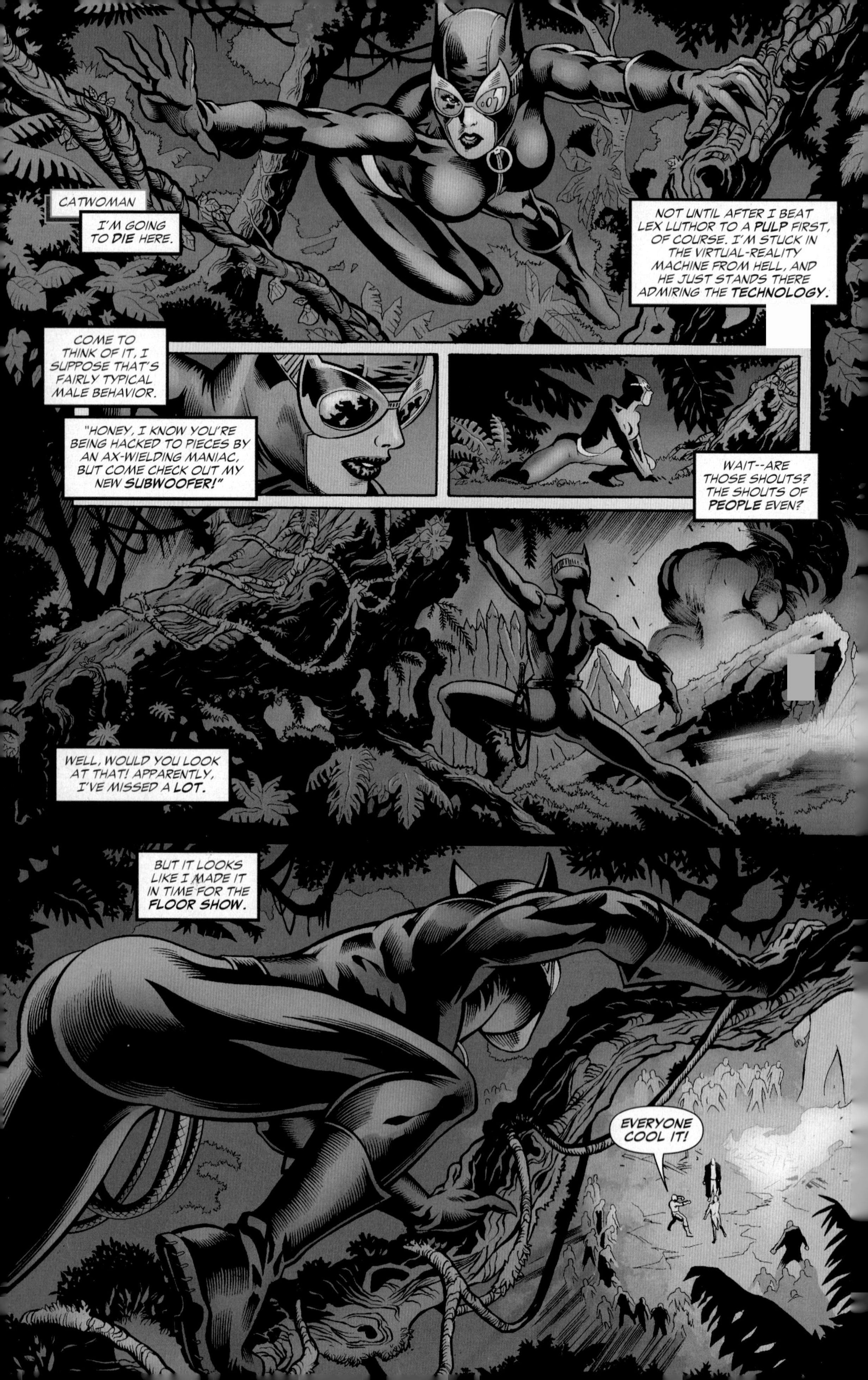
CATWOMAN
I'M GOING TO DIE HERE.
NOT UNTIL AFTER I BEAT LEX LUTHOR TO A PULP FIRST, OF COURSE. I'M STUCK IN THE VIRTUAL-REALITY MACHINE FROM HELL, AND HE JUST STANDS THERE ADMIRING THE TECHNOLOGY.
COME TO THINK OF IT, I SUPPOSE THAT'S FAIRLY TYPICAL MALE BEHAVIOR.
"HONEY, I KNOW YOU'RE BEING HACKED TO PIECES BY AN AX-WIELDING MANIAC, BUT COME CHECK OUT MY NEW SUBWOOFER!"
WAIT--ARE THOSE SHOUTS? THE SHOUTS OF PEOPLE EVEN?
WELL, WOULD YOU LOOK AT THAT! APPARENTLY, I'VE MISSED A LOT.
BUT IT LOOKS LIKE I MADE IT IN TIME FOR THE FLOOR SHOW.
EVERYONE COOL IT!

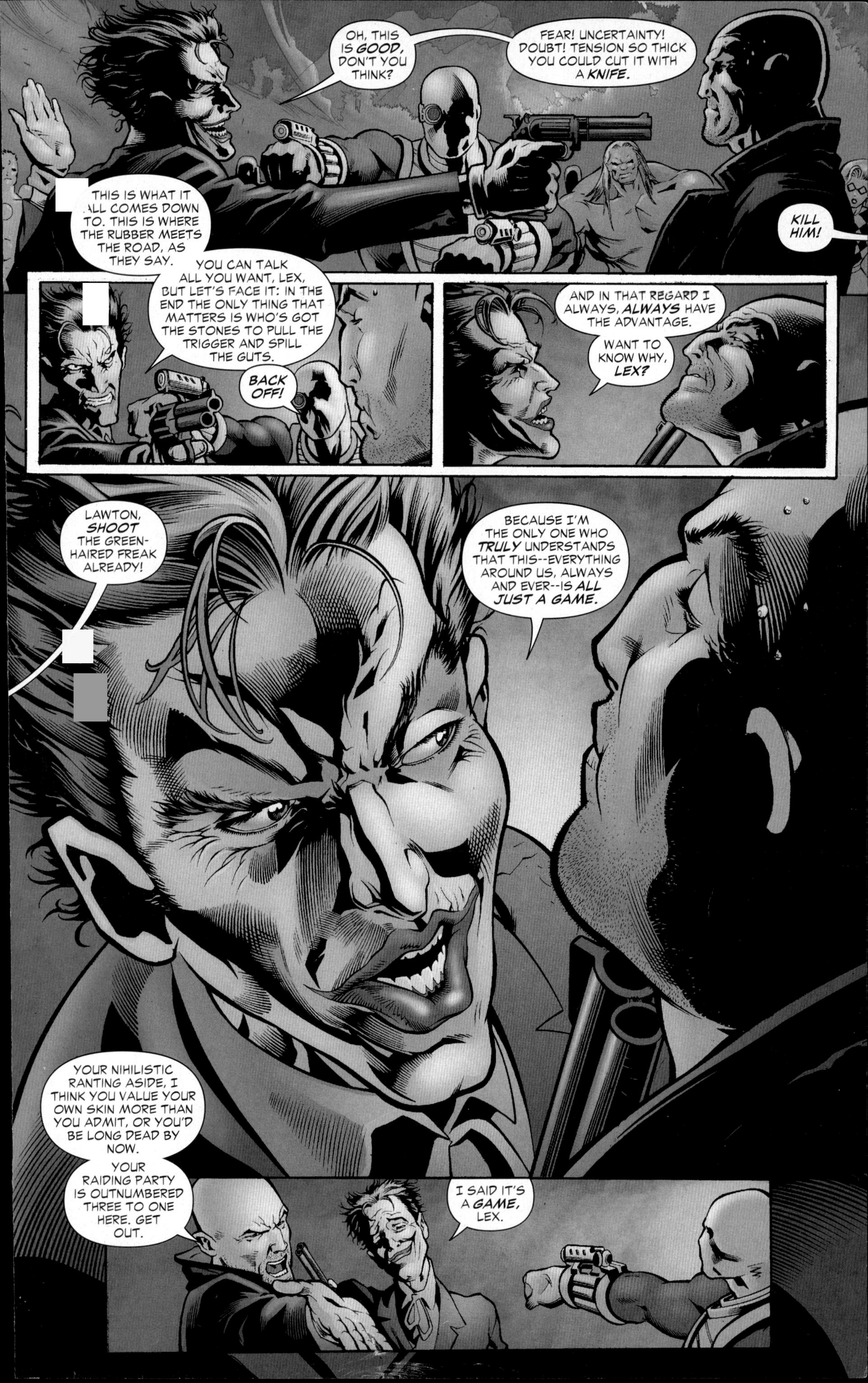
OH, THIS IS GOOD, DON'T YOU THINK?
FEAR! UNCERTAINTY! DOUBT! TENSION SO THICK YOU COULD CUT IT WITH A KNIFE.
THIS IS WHAT IT ALL COMES DOWN TO. THIS IS WHERE THE RUBBER MEETS THE ROAD, AS THEY SAY.
KILL HIM!
YOU CAN TALK ALL YOU WANT, LEX, BUT LET'S FACE IT: IN THE END THE ONLY THING THAT MATTERS IS WHO'S GOT THE STONES TO PULL THE TRIGGER AND SPILL THE GUTS.
BACK OFF!
AND IN THAT REGARD I ALWAYS, ALWAYS HAVE THE ADVANTAGE.
WANT TO KNOW WHY, LEX?
LAWTON, SHOOT THE GREEN-HAIRED FREAK ALREADY!
BECAUSE I'M THE ONLY ONE WHO TRULY UNDERSTANDS THAT THIS--EVERYTHING AROUND US, ALWAYS AND EVER--IS ALL JUST A GAME.
YOUR NIHILISTIC RANTING ASIDE, I THINK YOU VALUE YOUR OWN SKIN MORE THAN YOU ADMIT, OR YOU'D BE LONG DEAD BY NOW.
YOUR RAIDING PARTY IS OUTNUMBERED THREE TO ONE HERE. GET OUT.
I SAID IT'S A GAME, LEX.

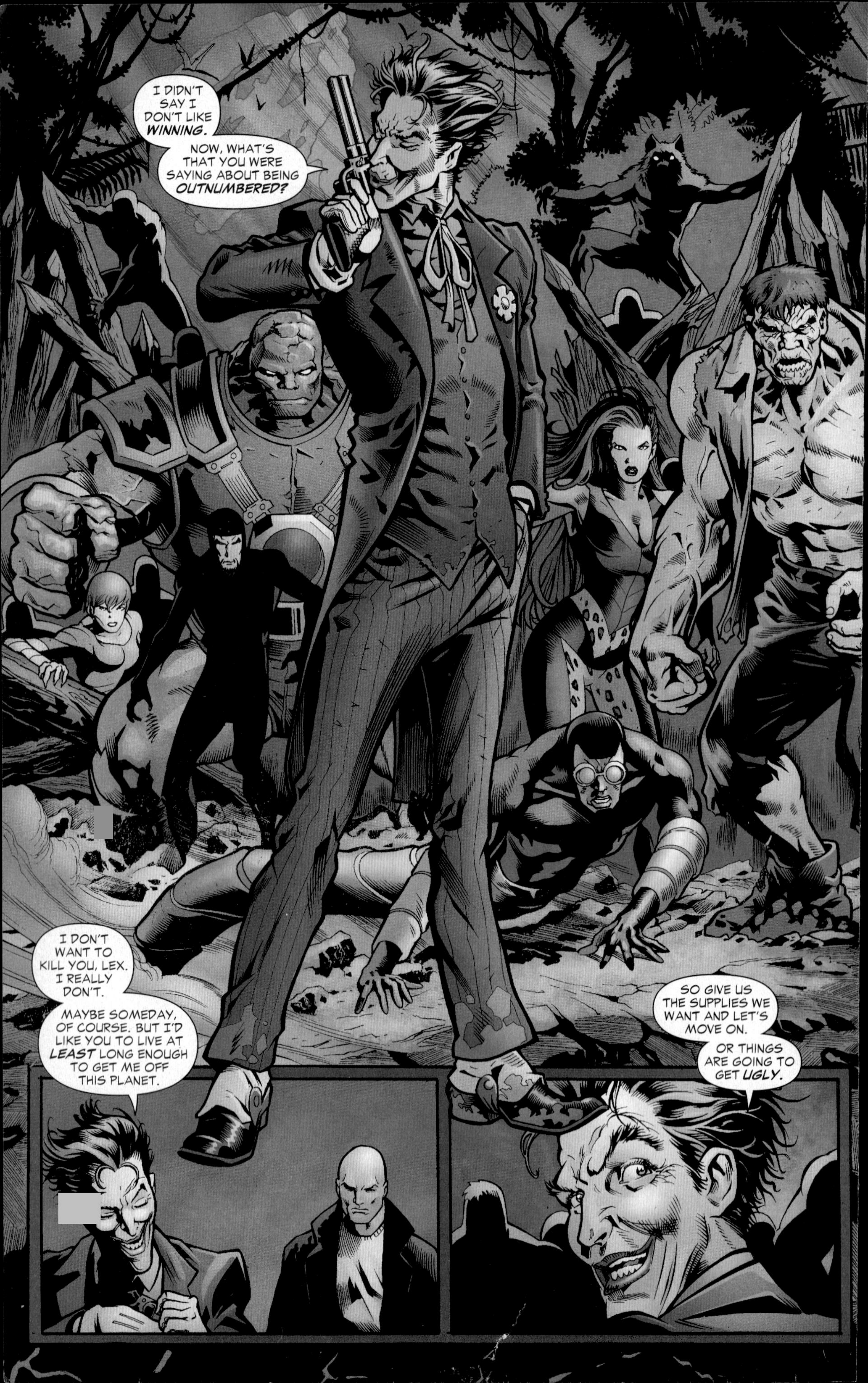
I DIDN'T SAY I DON'T LIKE *WINNING*.
NOW, WHAT'S THAT YOU WERE SAYING ABOUT BEING *OUTNUMBERED?*
I DON'T WANT TO KILL YOU, LEX. I REALLY DON'T.
MAYBE SOMEDAY, OF COURSE. BUT I'D LIKE YOU TO LIVE AT *LEAST* LONG ENOUGH TO GET ME OFF THIS PLANET.
SO GIVE US THE SUPPLIES WE WANT AND LET'S MOVE ON.
OR THINGS ARE GOING TO GET *UGLY*.

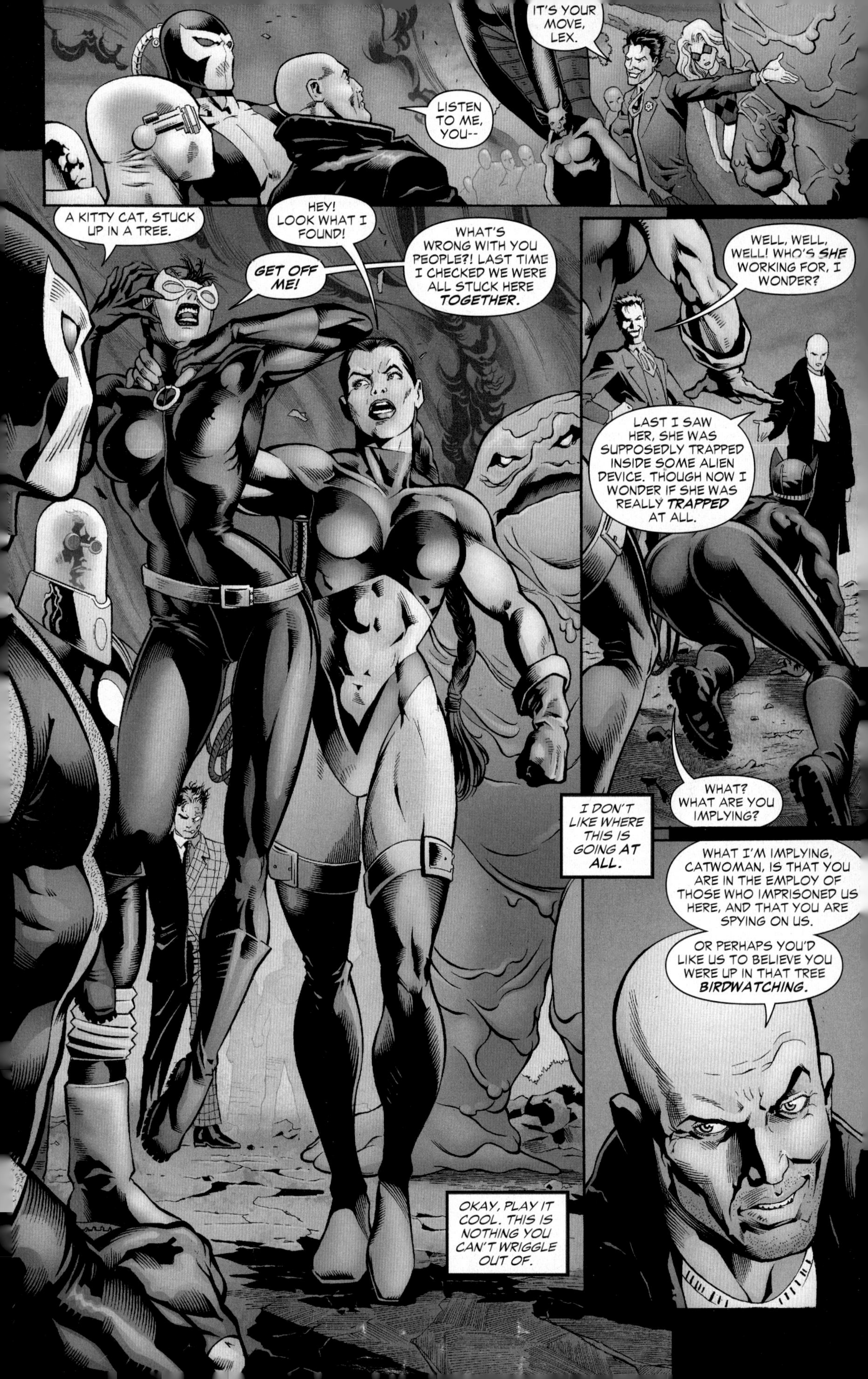
IT'S YOUR MOVE, LEX.
LISTEN TO ME, YOU--
A KITTY CAT, STUCK UP IN A TREE.
HEY! LOOK WHAT I FOUND!
GET OFF ME!
WHAT'S WRONG WITH YOU PEOPLE?! LAST TIME I CHECKED WE WERE ALL STUCK HERE TOGETHER.
WELL, WELL, WELL! WHO'S SHE WORKING FOR, I WONDER?
LAST I SAW HER, SHE WAS SUPPOSEDLY TRAPPED INSIDE SOME ALIEN DEVICE. THOUGH NOW I WONDER IF SHE WAS REALLY TRAPPED AT ALL.
WHAT? WHAT ARE YOU IMPLYING?
I DON'T LIKE WHERE THIS IS GOING AT ALL.
WHAT I'M IMPLYING, CATWOMAN, IS THAT YOU ARE IN THE EMPLOY OF THOSE WHO IMPRISONED US HERE, AND THAT YOU ARE SPYING ON US.
OR PERHAPS YOU'D LIKE US TO BELIEVE YOU WERE UP IN THAT TREE BIRDWATCHING.
OKAY, PLAY IT COOL. THIS IS NOTHING YOU CAN'T WRIGGLE OUT OF.

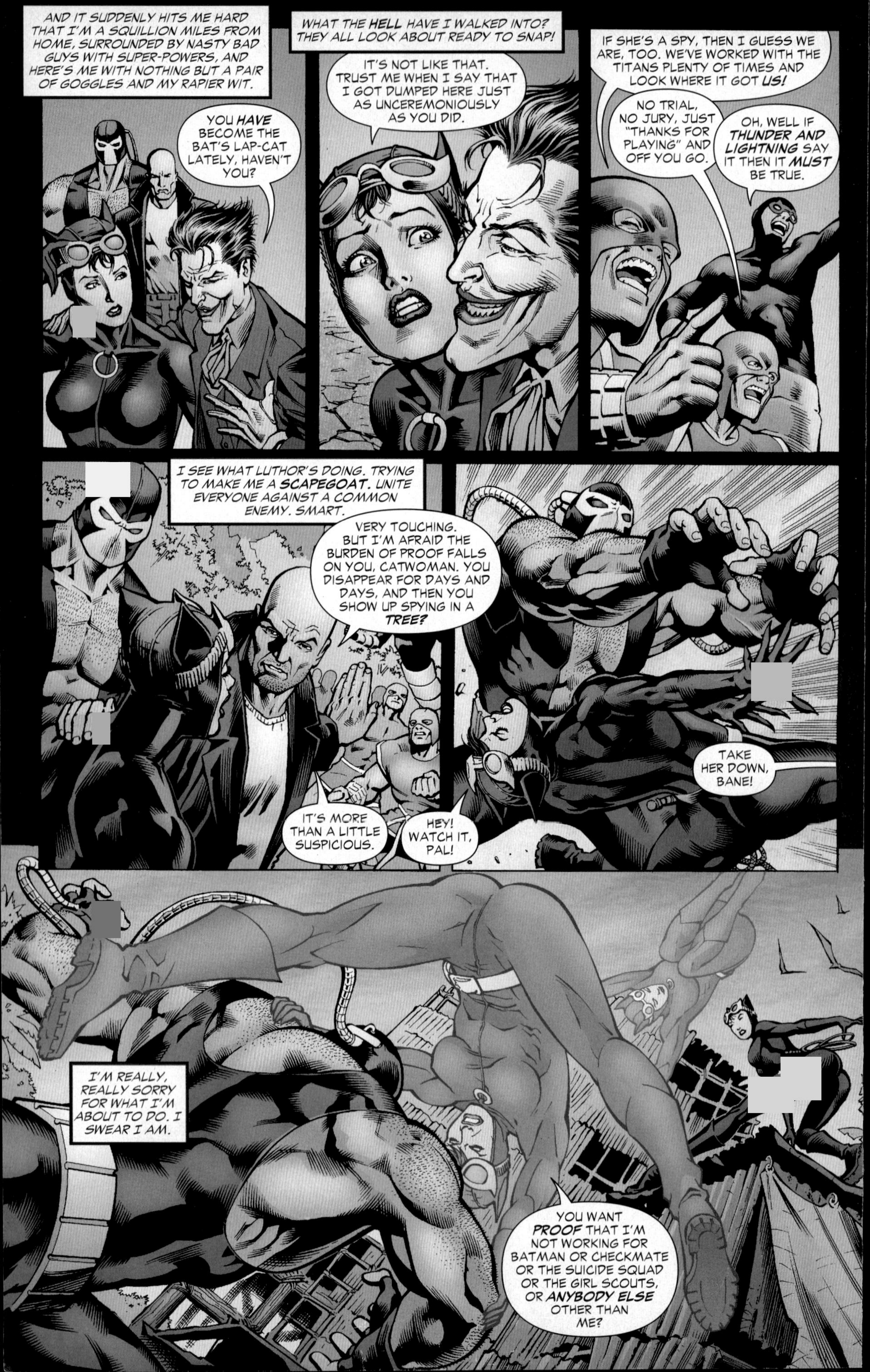
AND IT SUDDENLY HITS ME HARD THAT I'M A SQUILLION MILES FROM HOME, SURROUNDED BY NASTY BAD GUYS WITH SUPER-POWERS, AND HERE'S ME WITH NOTHING BUT A PAIR OF GOGGLES AND MY RAPIER WIT.
YOU HAVE BECOME THE BAT'S LAP-CAT LATELY, HAVEN'T YOU?
WHAT THE HELL HAVE I WALKED INTO? THEY ALL LOOK ABOUT READY TO SNAP!
IT'S NOT LIKE THAT. TRUST ME WHEN I SAY THAT I GOT DUMPED HERE JUST AS UNCEREMONIOUSLY AS YOU DID.
IF SHE'S A SPY, THEN I GUESS WE ARE, TOO. WE'VE WORKED WITH THE TITANS PLENTY OF TIMES AND LOOK WHERE IT GOT US!
NO TRIAL, NO JURY, JUST "THANKS FOR PLAYING" AND OFF YOU GO.
OH, WELL IF THUNDER AND LIGHTNING SAY IT THEN IT MUST BE TRUE.
I SEE WHAT LUTHOR'S DOING. TRYING TO MAKE ME A SCAPEGOAT. UNITE EVERYONE AGAINST A COMMON ENEMY. SMART.
VERY TOUCHING. BUT I'M AFRAID THE BURDEN OF PROOF FALLS ON YOU, CATWOMAN. YOU DISAPPEAR FOR DAYS AND DAYS, AND THEN YOU SHOW UP SPYING IN A TREE?
IT'S MORE THAN A LITTLE SUSPICIOUS.
HEY! WATCH IT, PAL!
TAKE HER DOWN, BANE!
I'M REALLY, REALLY SORRY FOR WHAT I'M ABOUT TO DO. I SWEAR I AM.
YOU WANT PROOF THAT I'M NOT WORKING FOR BATMAN OR CHECKMATE OR THE SUICIDE SQUAD OR THE GIRL SCOUTS, OR ANYBODY ELSE OTHER THAN ME?

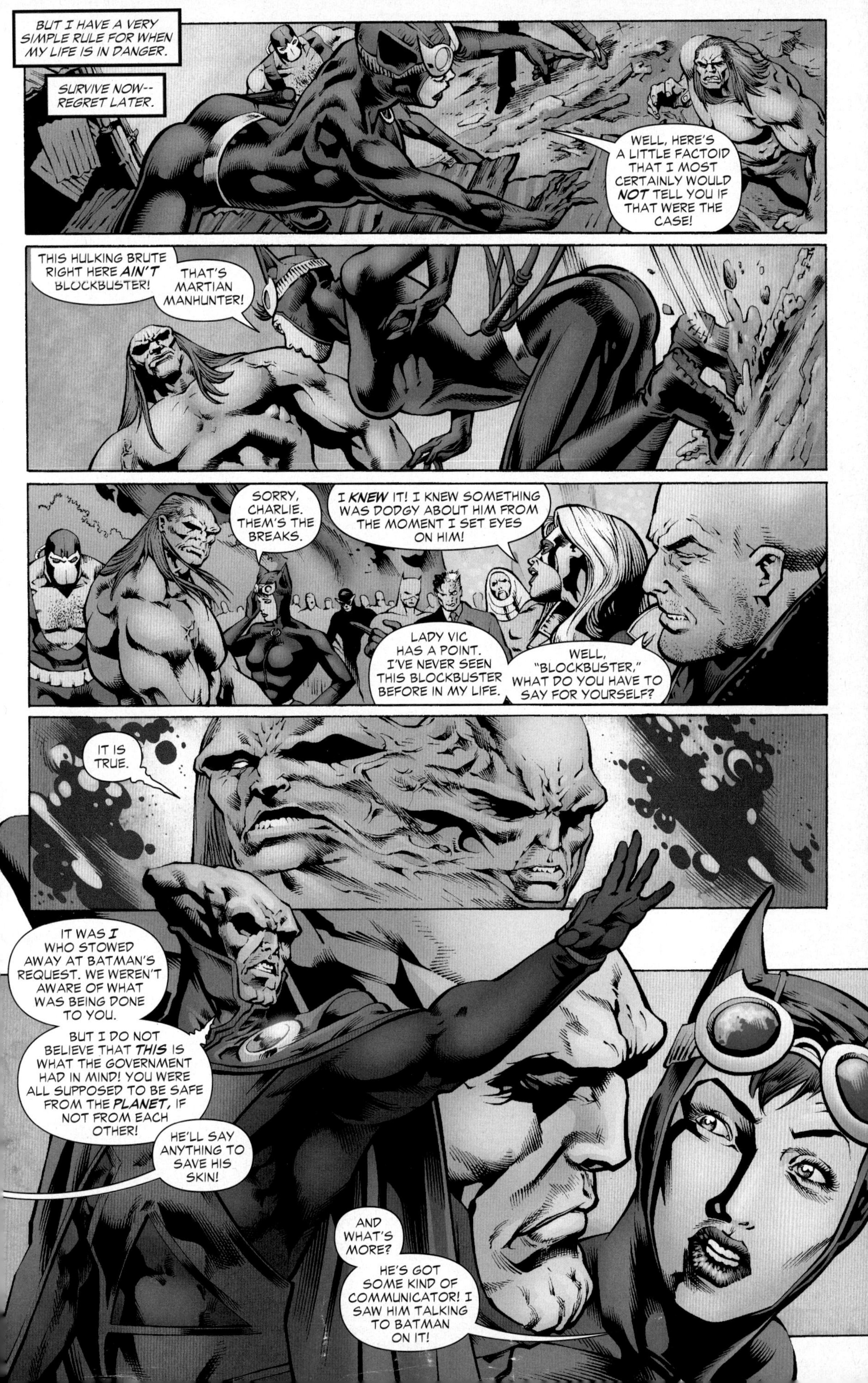

BUT I HAVE A VERY SIMPLE RULE FOR WHEN MY LIFE IS IN DANGER.
SURVIVE NOW-- REGRET LATER.
WELL, HERE'S A LITTLE FACTOID THAT I MOST CERTAINLY WOULD NOT TELL YOU IF THAT WERE THE CASE!
THIS HULKING BRUTE RIGHT HERE AIN'T BLOCKBUSTER!
THAT'S MARTIAN MANHUNTER!
SORRY, CHARLIE. THEM'S THE BREAKS.
I KNEW IT! I KNEW SOMETHING WAS DODGY ABOUT HIM FROM THE MOMENT I SET EYES ON HIM!
LADY VIC HAS A POINT. I'VE NEVER SEEN THIS BLOCKBUSTER BEFORE IN MY LIFE.
WELL, "BLOCKBUSTER," WHAT DO YOU HAVE TO SAY FOR YOURSELF?
IT IS TRUE.
IT WAS I WHO STOWED AWAY AT BATMAN'S REQUEST. WE WEREN'T AWARE OF WHAT WAS BEING DONE TO YOU.
BUT I DO NOT BELIEVE THAT THIS IS WHAT THE GOVERNMENT HAD IN MIND! YOU WERE ALL SUPPOSED TO BE SAFE FROM THE PLANET, IF NOT FROM EACH OTHER!
HE'LL SAY ANYTHING TO SAVE HIS SKIN!
AND WHAT'S MORE?
HE'S GOT SOME KIND OF COMMUNICATOR! I SAW HIM TALKING TO BATMAN ON IT!

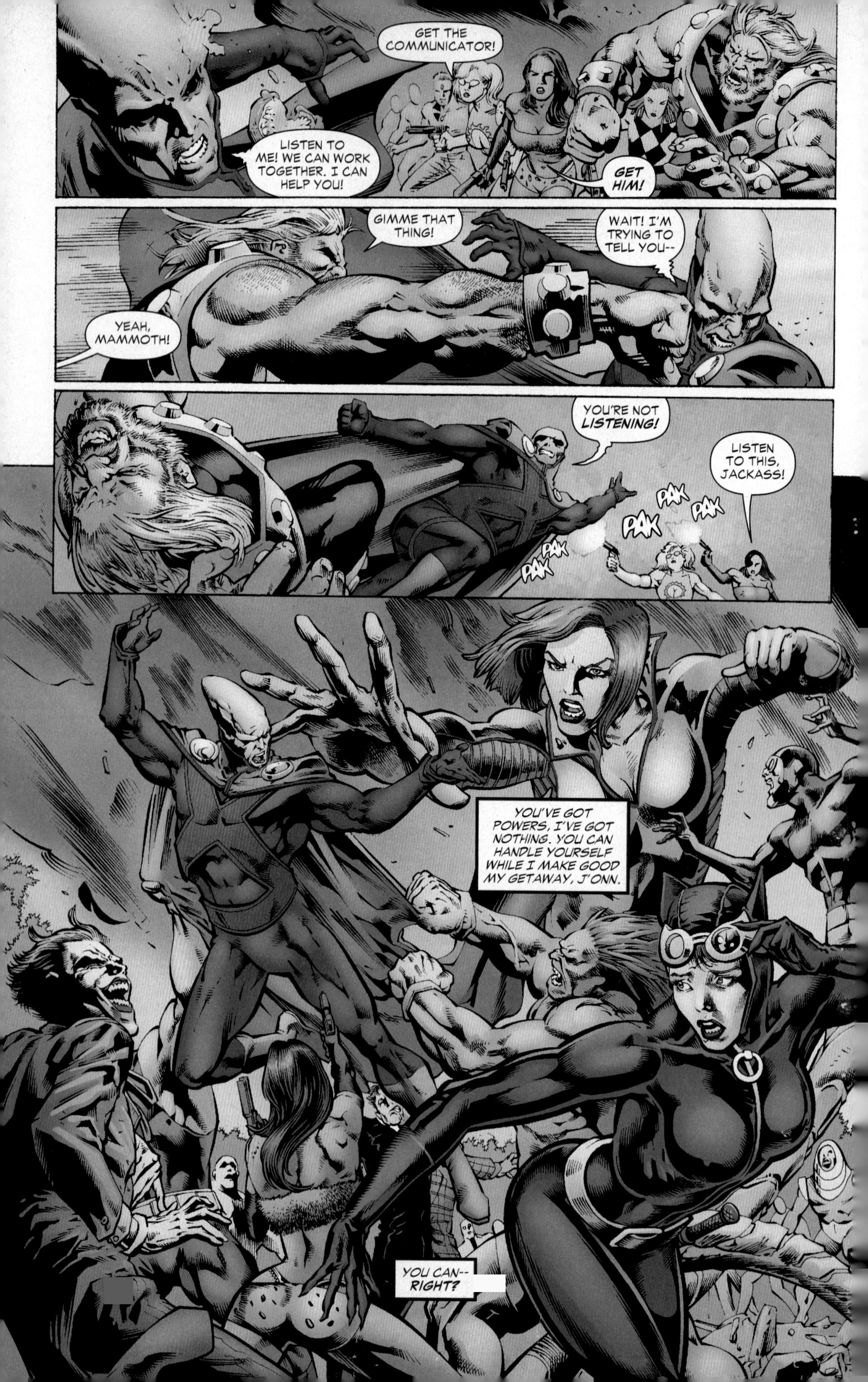
GET THE COMMUNICATOR!
LISTEN TO ME! WE CAN WORK TOGETHER. I CAN HELP YOU!
GET HIM!
GIMME THAT THING!
WAIT! I'M TRYING TO TELL YOU--
YEAH, MAMMOTH!
YOU'RE NOT LISTENING!
LISTEN TO THIS, JACKASS!
PAK PAK PAK PAK PAK PAK
YOU'VE GOT POWERS, I'VE GOT NOTHING. YOU CAN HANDLE YOURSELF WHILE I MAKE GOOD MY GETAWAY, J'ONN.
YOU CAN-- RIGHT?

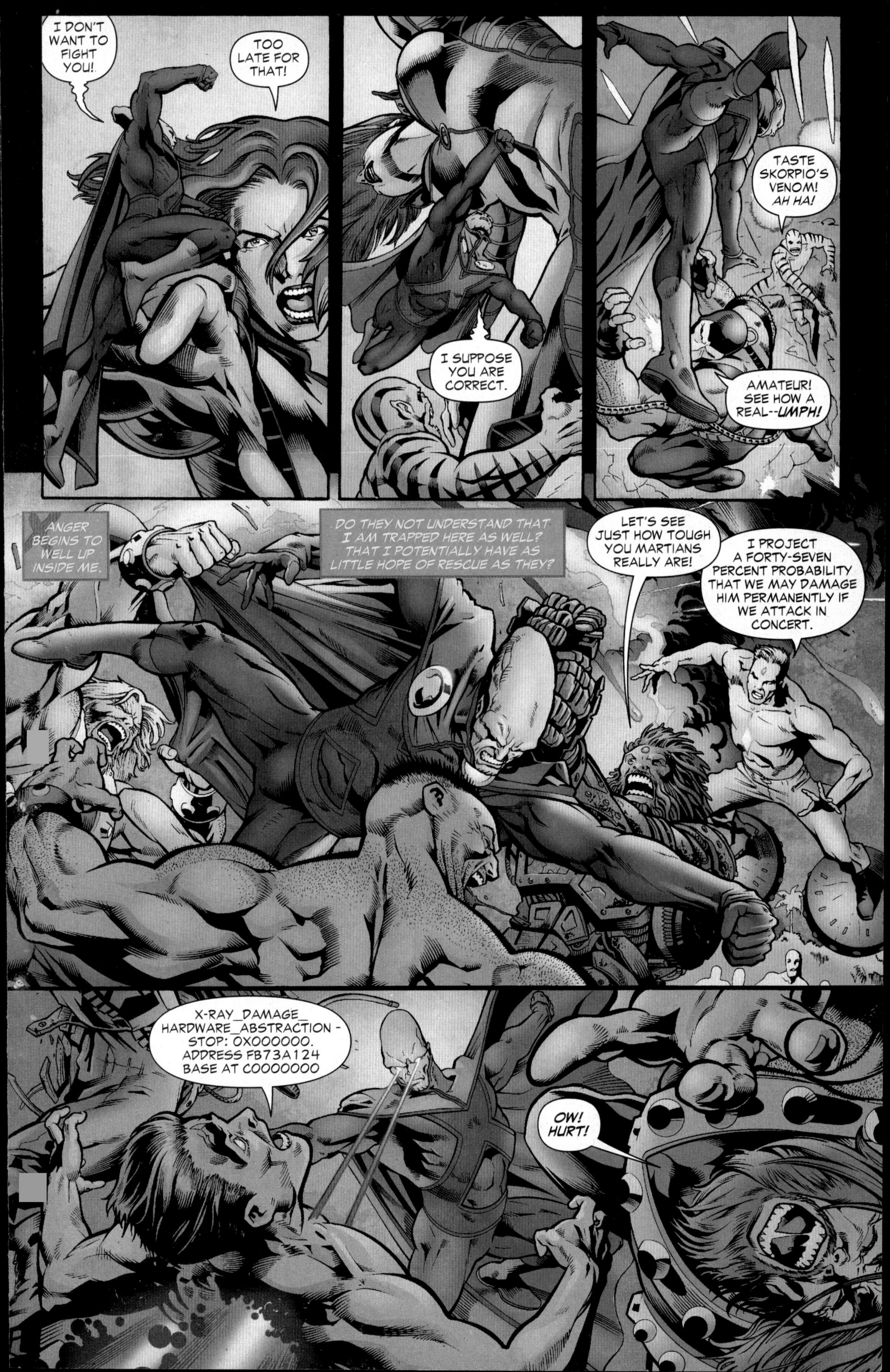
I DON'T WANT TO FIGHT YOU!.
TOO LATE FOR THAT!
I SUPPOSE YOU ARE CORRECT.
TASTE SKORPIO'S VENOM! AH HA!
AMATEUR! SEE HOW A REAL--UMPH!
ANGER BEGINS TO WELL UP INSIDE ME.
..DO THEY NOT UNDERSTAND THAT I AM TRAPPED HERE AS WELL? THAT I POTENTIALLY HAVE AS LITTLE HOPE OF RESCUE AS THEY?
LET'S SEE JUST HOW TOUGH YOU MARTIANS REALLY ARE!
I PROJECT A FORTY-SEVEN PERCENT PROBABILITY THAT WE MAY DAMAGE HIM PERMANENTLY IF WE ATTACK IN CONCERT.
X-RAY_DAMAGE_ HARDWARE_ABSTRACTION - STOP: 0X000000. ADDRESS FB73A124 BASE AT C000000
OW! HURT!

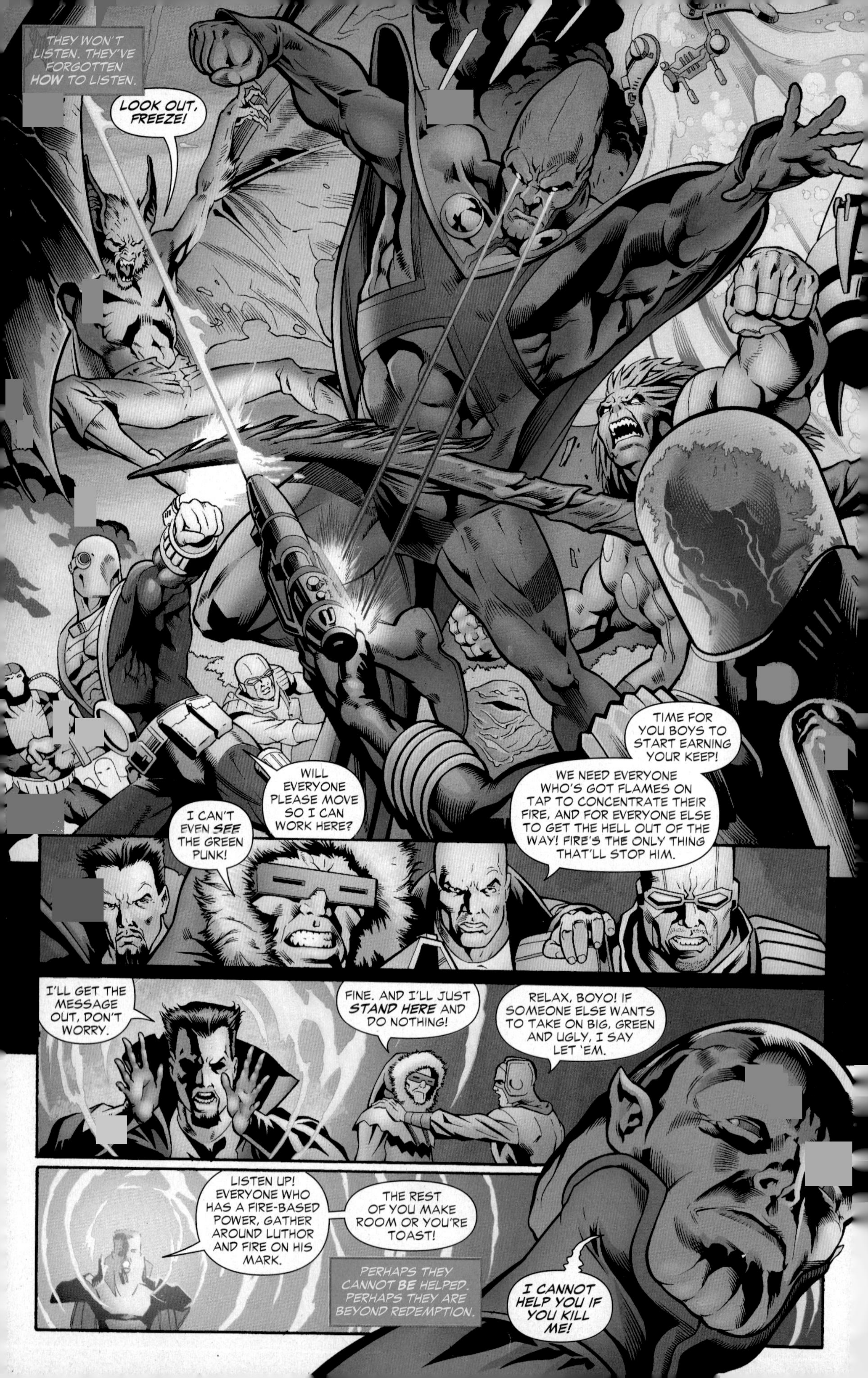
THEY WON'T LISTEN. THEY'VE FORGOTTEN HOW TO LISTEN.
LOOK OUT, FREEZE!
TIME FOR YOU BOYS TO START EARNING YOUR KEEP!
WILL EVERYONE PLEASE MOVE SO I CAN WORK HERE?
I CAN'T EVEN SEE THE GREEN PUNK!
WE NEED EVERYONE WHO'S GOT FLAMES ON TAP TO CONCENTRATE THEIR FIRE, AND FOR EVERYONE ELSE TO GET THE HELL OUT OF THE WAY! FIRE'S THE ONLY THING THAT'LL STOP HIM.
I'LL GET THE MESSAGE OUT, DON'T WORRY.
FINE. AND I'LL JUST STAND HERE AND DO NOTHING!
RELAX, BOYO! IF SOMEONE ELSE WANTS TO TAKE ON BIG, GREEN AND UGLY, I SAY LET 'EM.
LISTEN UP! EVERYONE WHO HAS A FIRE-BASED POWER, GATHER AROUND LUTHOR AND FIRE ON HIS MARK.
THE REST OF YOU MAKE ROOM OR YOU'RE TOAST!
PERHAPS THEY CANNOT BE HELPED. PERHAPS THEY ARE BEYOND REDEMPTION.
I CANNOT HELP YOU IF YOU KILL ME!

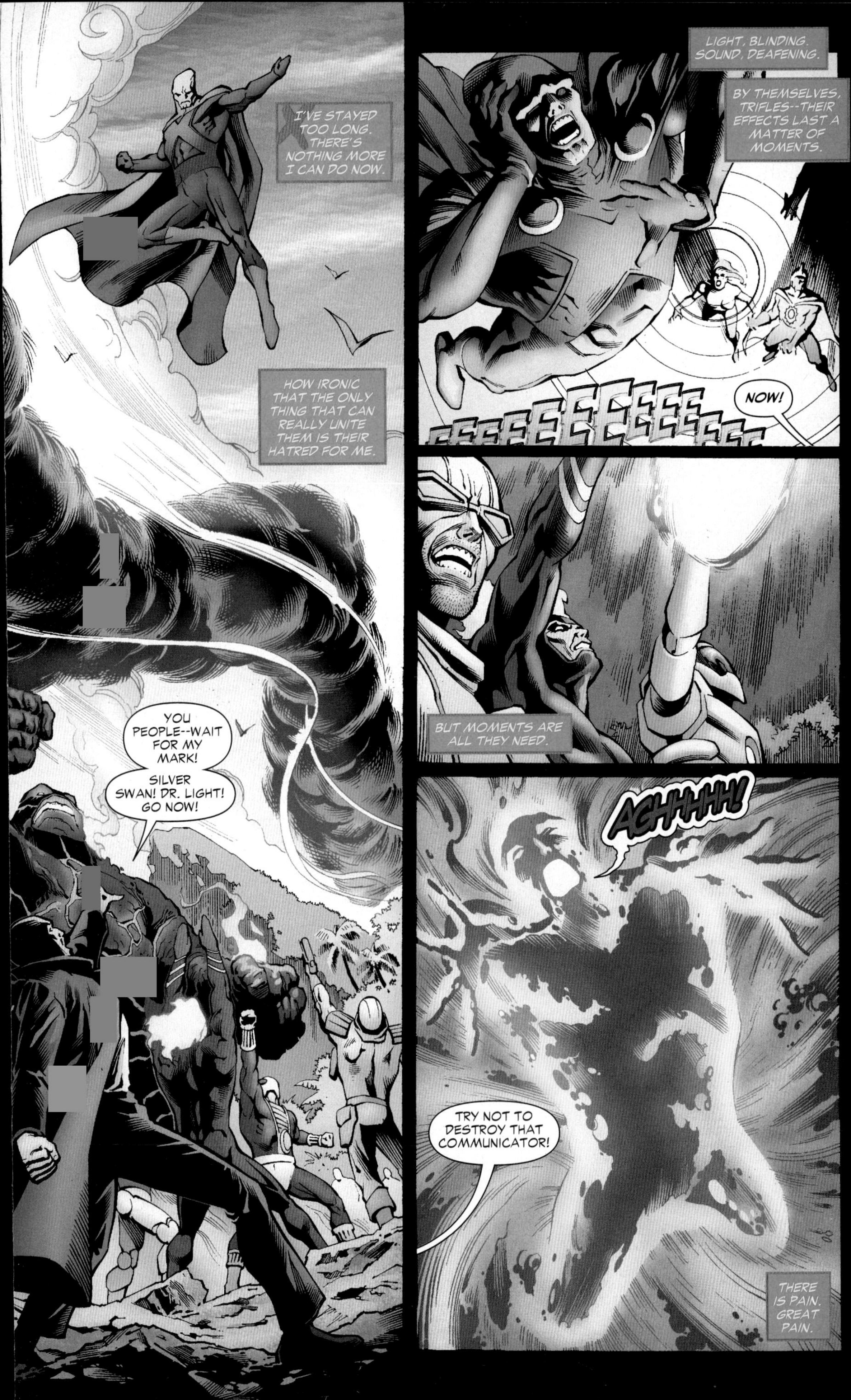
I'VE STAYED TOO LONG. THERE'S NOTHING MORE I CAN DO NOW.
HOW IRONIC THAT THE ONLY THING THAT CAN REALLY UNITE THEM IS THEIR HATRED FOR ME.
YOU PEOPLE--WAIT FOR MY MARK!
SILVER SWAN! DR. LIGHT! GO NOW!
LIGHT, BLINDING. SOUND, DEAFENING.
BY THEMSELVES, TRIFLES--THEIR EFFECTS LAST A MATTER OF MOMENTS.
NOW!
EEEEEEEEEEEEEEEEEEEE
BUT MOMENTS ARE ALL THEY NEED.
AGHHHHH!
TRY NOT TO DESTROY THAT COMMUNICATOR!
THERE IS PAIN. GREAT PAIN.

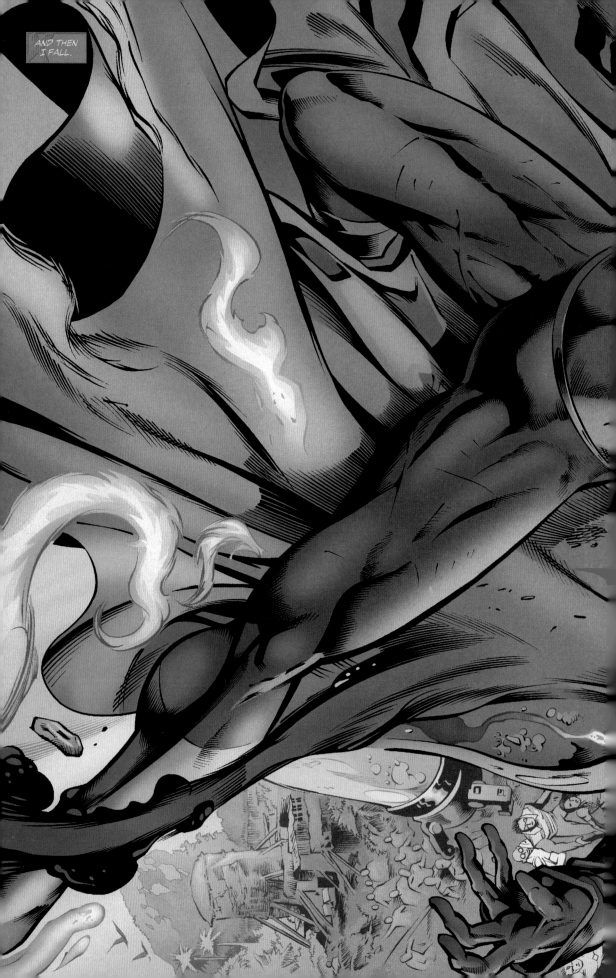

AND THEN
I FALL.

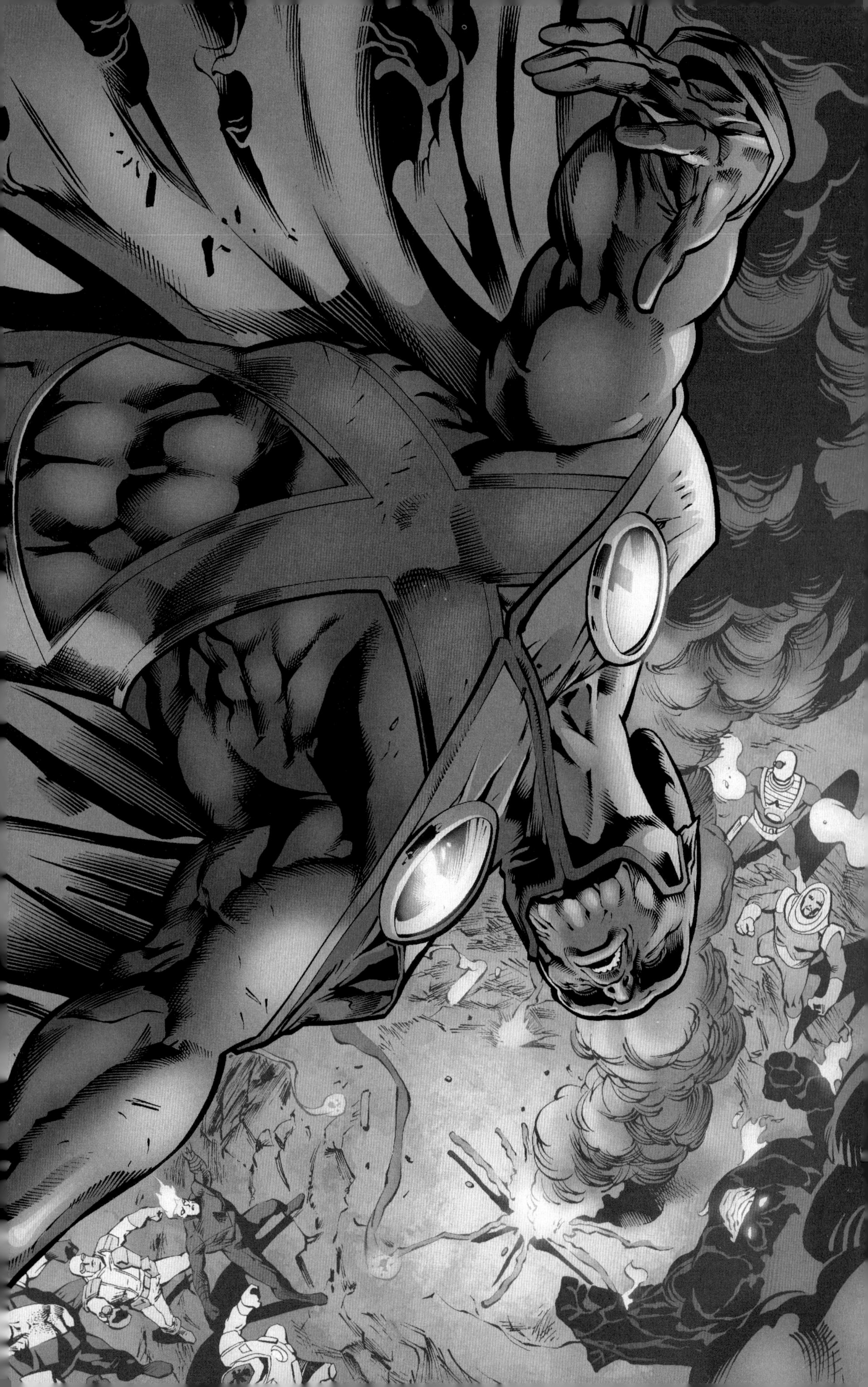

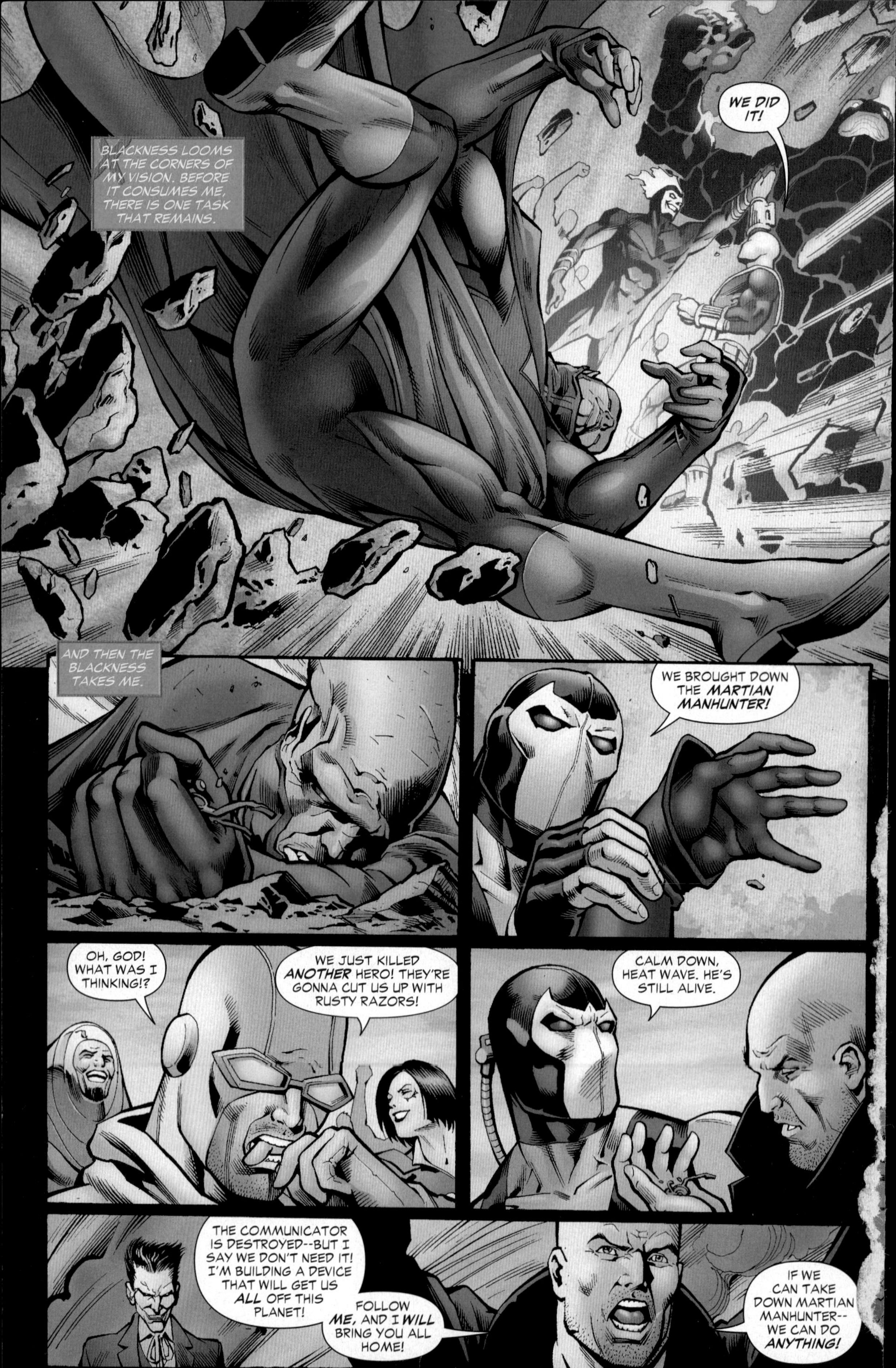
BLACKNESS LOOMS AT THE CORNERS OF MY VISION. BEFORE IT CONSUMES ME, THERE IS ONE TASK THAT REMAINS.
WE DID IT!
AND THEN THE BLACKNESS TAKES ME.
WE BROUGHT DOWN THE MARTIAN MANHUNTER!
OH, GOD! WHAT WAS I THINKING!?
WE JUST KILLED ANOTHER HERO! THEY'RE GONNA CUT US UP WITH RUSTY RAZORS!
CALM DOWN, HEAT WAVE. HE'S STILL ALIVE.
THE COMMUNICATOR IS DESTROYED--BUT I SAY WE DON'T NEED IT! I'M BUILDING A DEVICE THAT WILL GET US ALL OFF THIS PLANET!
FOLLOW ME, AND I WILL BRING YOU ALL HOME!
IF WE CAN TAKE DOWN MARTIAN MANHUNTER-- WE CAN DO ANYTHING!

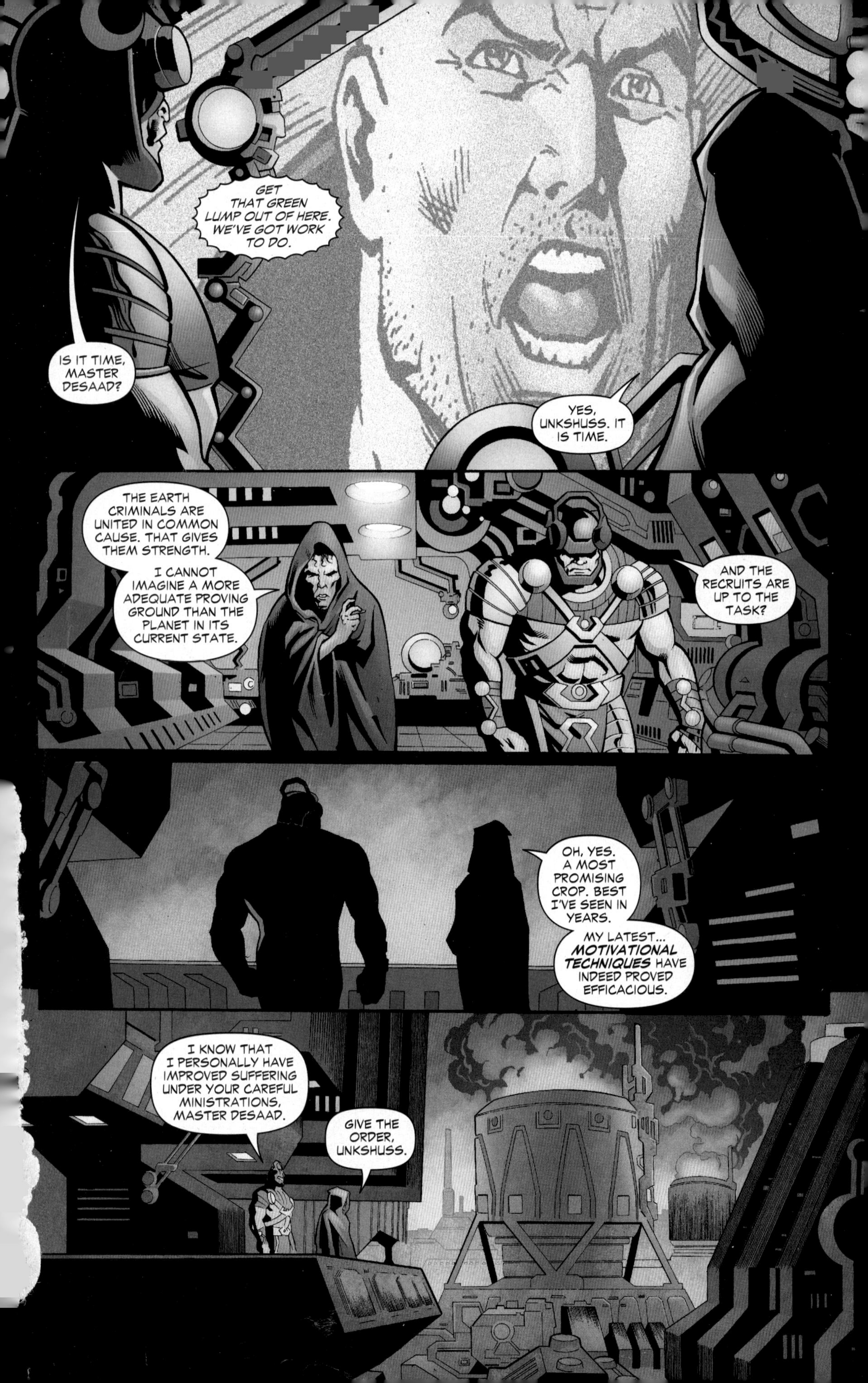
GET THAT GREEN LUMP OUT OF HERE. WE'VE GOT WORK TO DO.
IS IT TIME, MASTER DESAAD?
YES, UNKSHUSS. IT IS TIME.
THE EARTH CRIMINALS ARE UNITED IN COMMON CAUSE. THAT GIVES THEM STRENGTH.
I CANNOT IMAGINE A MORE ADEQUATE PROVING GROUND THAN THE PLANET IN ITS CURRENT STATE.
AND THE RECRUITS ARE UP TO THE TASK?
OH, YES. A MOST PROMISING CROP. BEST I'VE SEEN IN YEARS.
MY LATEST... MOTIVATIONAL TECHNIQUES HAVE INDEED PROVED EFFICACIOUS.
I KNOW THAT I PERSONALLY HAVE IMPROVED SUFFERING UNDER YOUR CAREFUL MINISTRATIONS, MASTER DESAAD.
GIVE THE ORDER, UNKSHUSS.

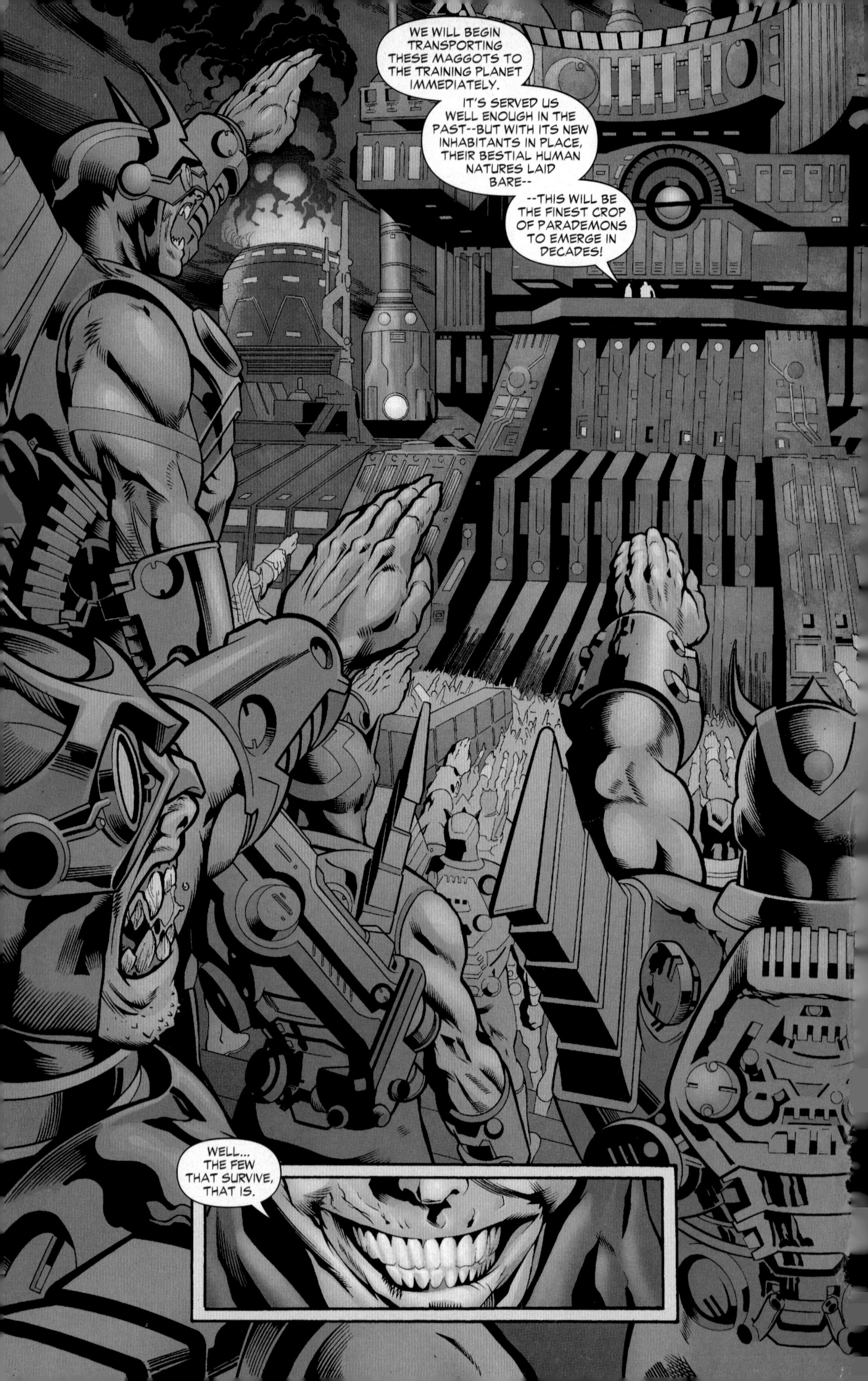
WE WILL BEGIN TRANSPORTING THESE MAGGOTS TO THE TRAINING PLANET IMMEDIATELY.
IT'S SERVED US WELL ENOUGH IN THE PAST--BUT WITH ITS NEW INHABITANTS IN PLACE, THEIR BESTIAL HUMAN NATURES LAID BARE--
--THIS WILL BE THE FINEST CROP OF PARADEMONS TO EMERGE IN DECADES!
WELL... THE FEW THAT SURVIVE, THAT IS.

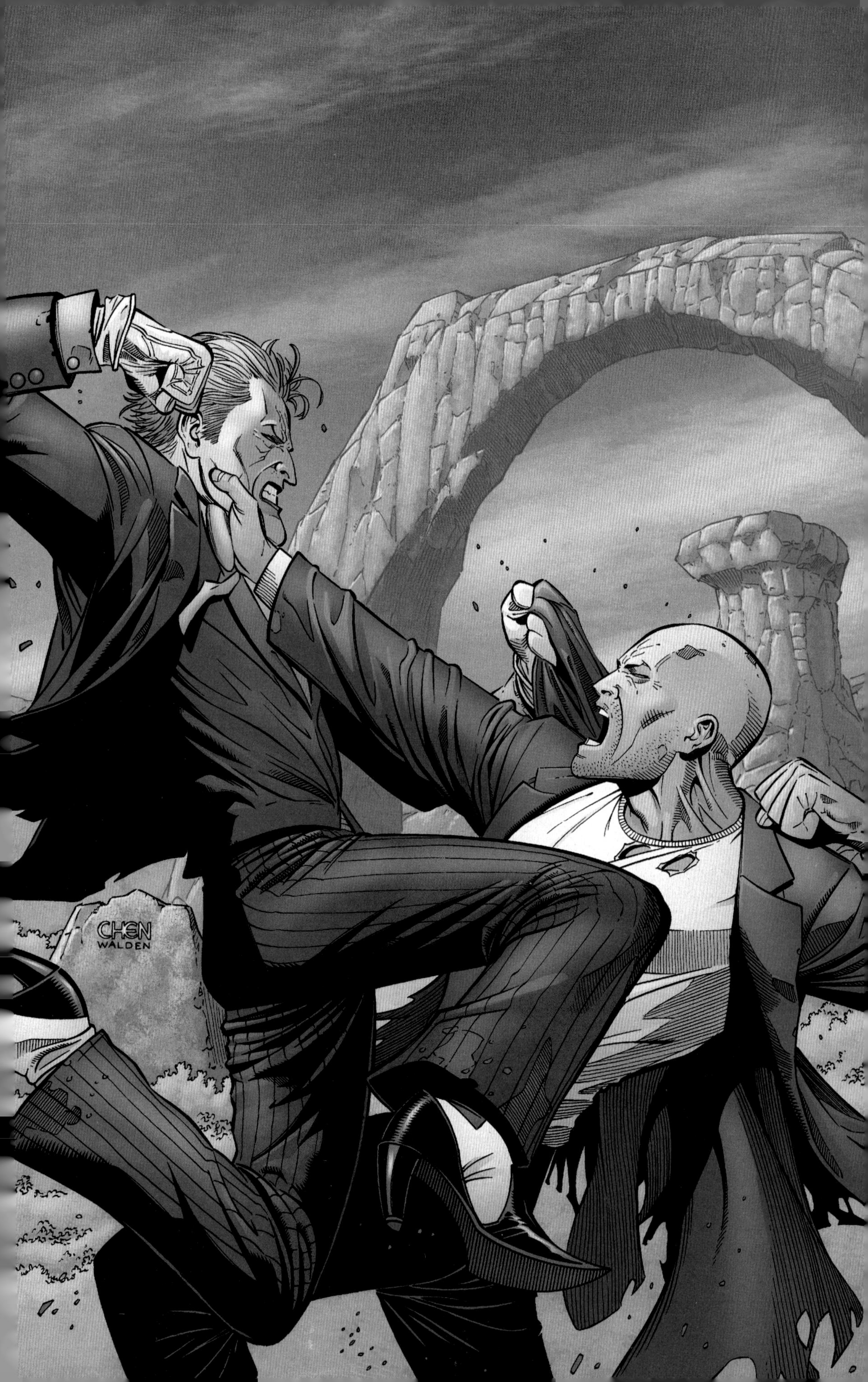
CHEN
WALDEN

Matthew Sturges
Writer

Sean Chen
Penciller

Walden Wong
Inker

John Kalisz
Colorist

Steve Wands
Letterer

CHAPTER SIX

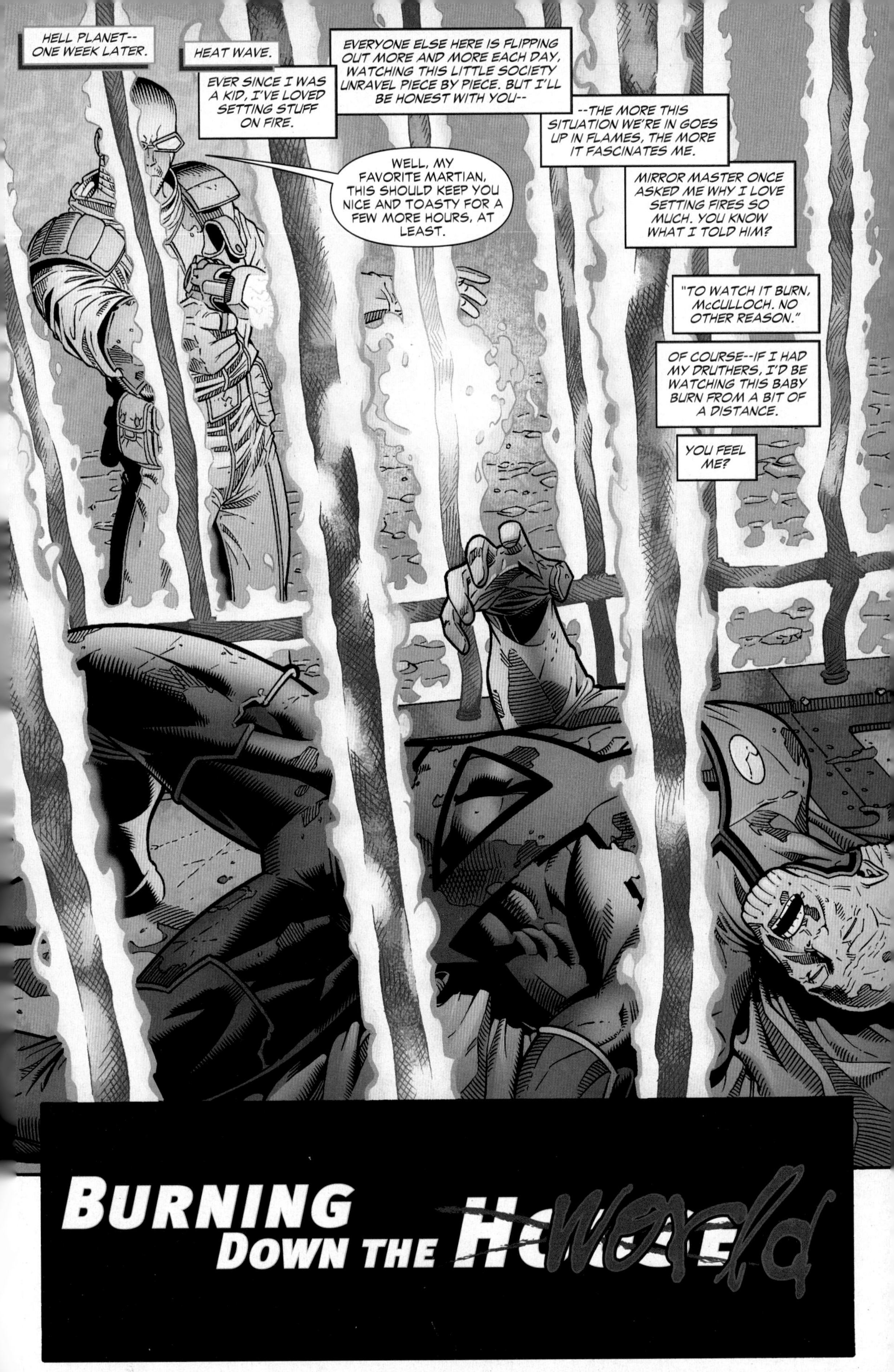
HELL PLANET--
ONE WEEK LATER.
HEAT WAVE.
EVER SINCE I WAS A KID, I'VE LOVED SETTING STUFF ON FIRE.
EVERYONE ELSE HERE IS FLIPPING OUT MORE AND MORE EACH DAY, WATCHING THIS LITTLE SOCIETY UNRAVEL PIECE BY PIECE. BUT I'LL BE HONEST WITH YOU--
--THE MORE THIS SITUATION WE'RE IN GOES UP IN FLAMES, THE MORE IT FASCINATES ME.
WELL, MY FAVORITE MARTIAN, THIS SHOULD KEEP YOU NICE AND TOASTY FOR A FEW MORE HOURS, AT LEAST.
MIRROR MASTER ONCE ASKED ME WHY I LOVE SETTING FIRES SO MUCH. YOU KNOW WHAT I TOLD HIM?
"TO WATCH IT BURN, McCULLOCH. NO OTHER REASON."
OF COURSE--IF I HAD MY DRUTHERS, I'D BE WATCHING THIS BABY BURN FROM A BIT OF A DISTANCE.
YOU FEEL ME?
BURNING DOWN THE HOUSE WORLD

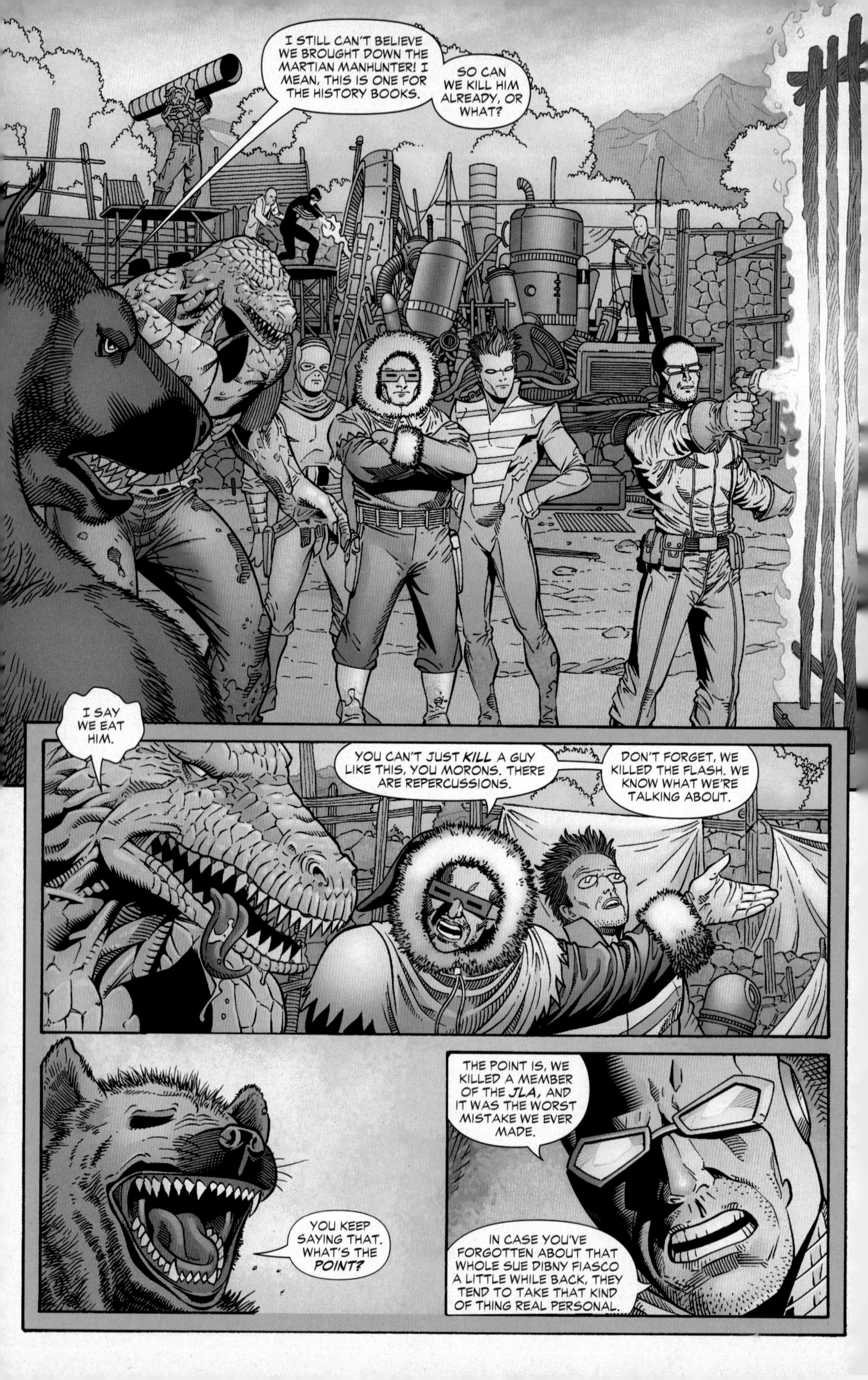
I STILL CAN'T BELIEVE WE BROUGHT DOWN THE MARTIAN MANHUNTER! I MEAN, THIS IS ONE FOR THE HISTORY BOOKS.
SO CAN WE KILL HIM ALREADY, OR WHAT?
I SAY WE EAT HIM.
YOU CAN'T JUST KILL A GUY LIKE THIS, YOU MORONS. THERE ARE REPERCUSSIONS.
DON'T FORGET, WE KILLED THE FLASH. WE KNOW WHAT WE'RE TALKING ABOUT.
YOU KEEP SAYING THAT. WHAT'S THE POINT?
THE POINT IS, WE KILLED A MEMBER OF THE JLA, AND IT WAS THE WORST MISTAKE WE EVER MADE.
IN CASE YOU'VE FORGOTTEN ABOUT THAT WHOLE SUE DIBNY FIASCO A LITTLE WHILE BACK, THEY TEND TO TAKE THAT KIND OF THING REAL PERSONAL.

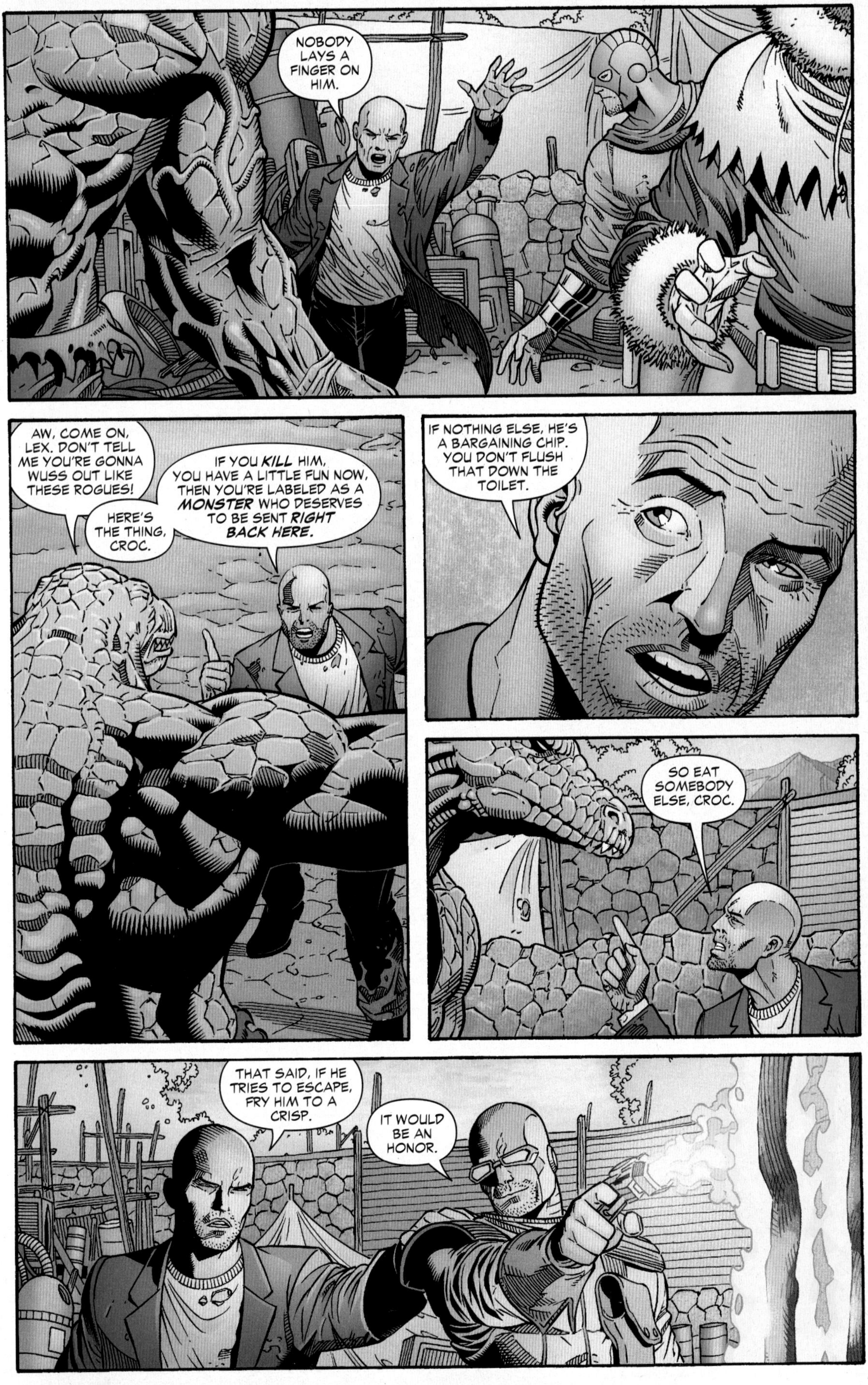
NOBODY LAYS A FINGER ON HIM.
AW, COME ON, LEX. DON'T TELL ME YOU'RE GONNA WUSS OUT LIKE THESE ROGUES!
HERE'S THE THING, CROC.
IF YOU *KILL* HIM, YOU HAVE A LITTLE FUN NOW, THEN YOU'RE LABELED AS A *MONSTER* WHO DESERVES TO BE SENT *RIGHT BACK HERE.*
IF NOTHING ELSE, HE'S A BARGAINING CHIP. YOU DON'T FLUSH THAT DOWN THE TOILET.
SO EAT SOMEBODY ELSE, CROC.
THAT SAID, IF HE TRIES TO ESCAPE, FRY HIM TO A CRISP.
IT WOULD BE AN HONOR.

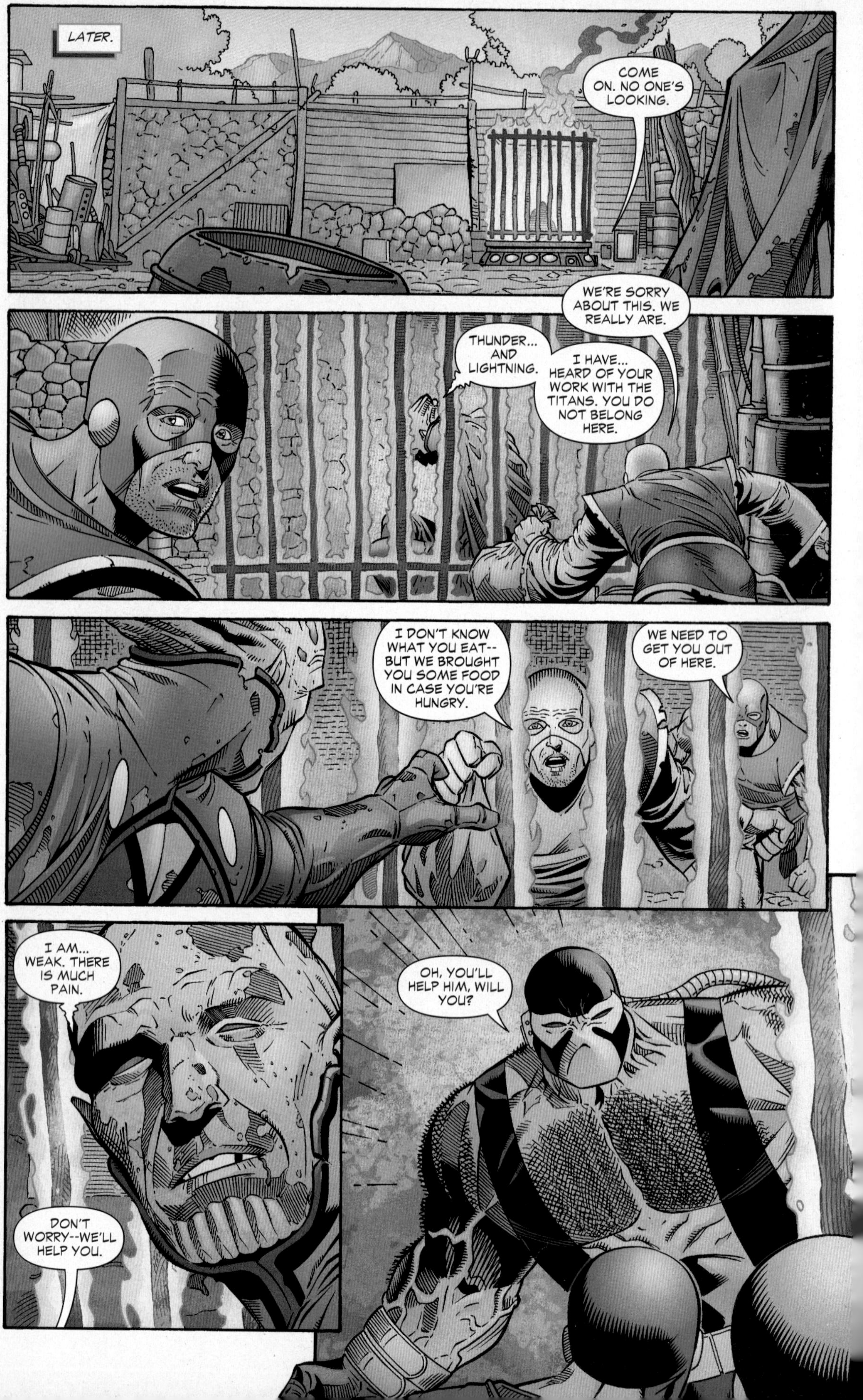
LATER.
COME ON. NO ONE'S LOOKING.
WE'RE SORRY ABOUT THIS. WE REALLY ARE.
THUNDER... AND LIGHTNING.
I HAVE... HEARD OF YOUR WORK WITH THE TITANS. YOU DO NOT BELONG HERE.
I DON'T KNOW WHAT YOU EAT-- BUT WE BROUGHT YOU SOME FOOD IN CASE YOU'RE HUNGRY.
WE NEED TO GET YOU OUT OF HERE.
I AM... WEAK. THERE IS MUCH PAIN.
DON'T WORRY--WE'LL HELP YOU.
OH, YOU'LL HELP HIM, WILL YOU?

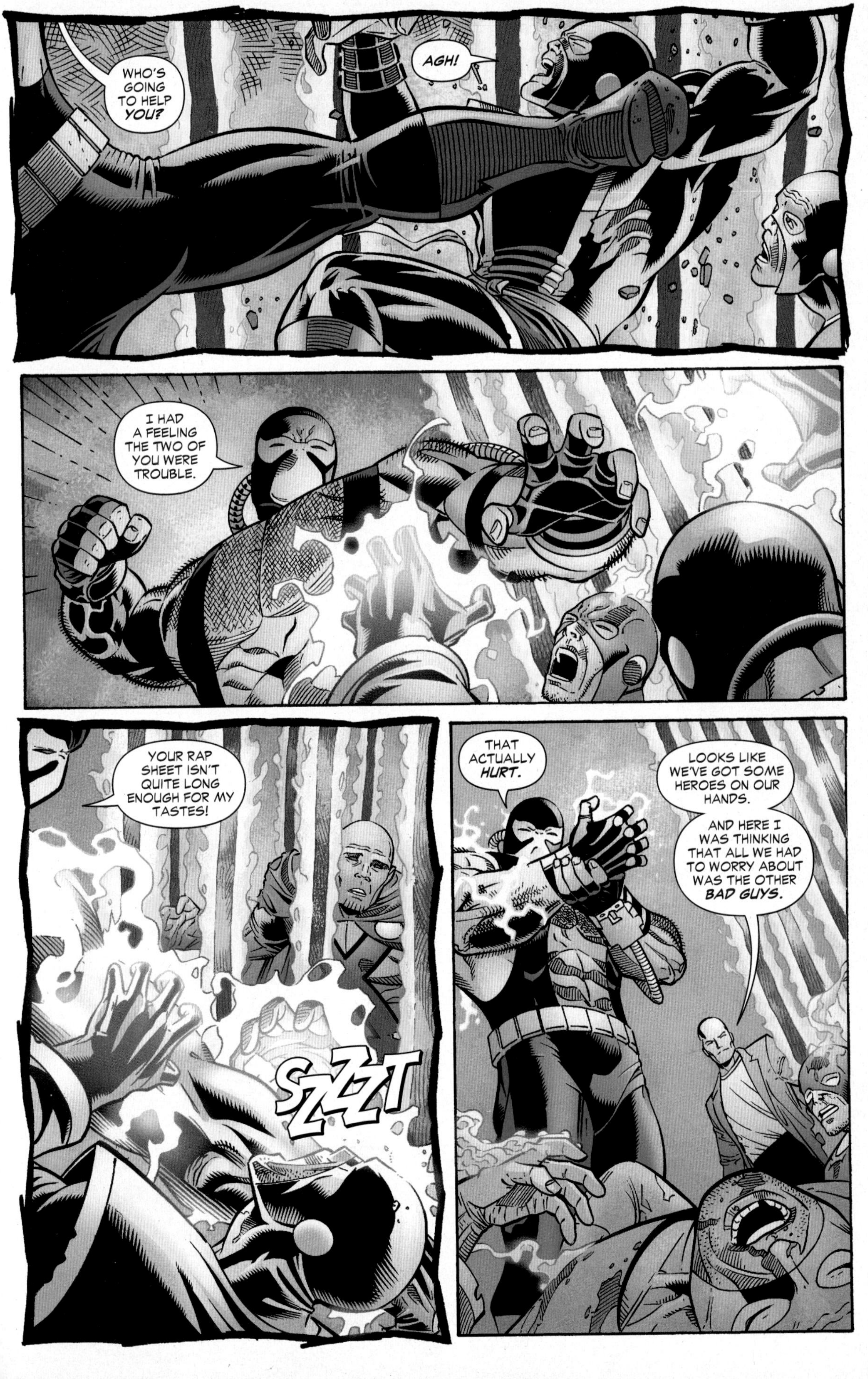
WHO'S GOING TO HELP *YOU?*
AGH!
I HAD A FEELING THE TWO OF YOU WERE TROUBLE.
YOUR RAP SHEET ISN'T QUITE LONG ENOUGH FOR MY TASTES!
SZZZT
THAT ACTUALLY *HURT.*
LOOKS LIKE WE'VE GOT SOME HEROES ON OUR HANDS.
AND HERE I WAS THINKING THAT ALL WE HAD TO WORRY ABOUT WAS THE OTHER *BAD GUYS.*

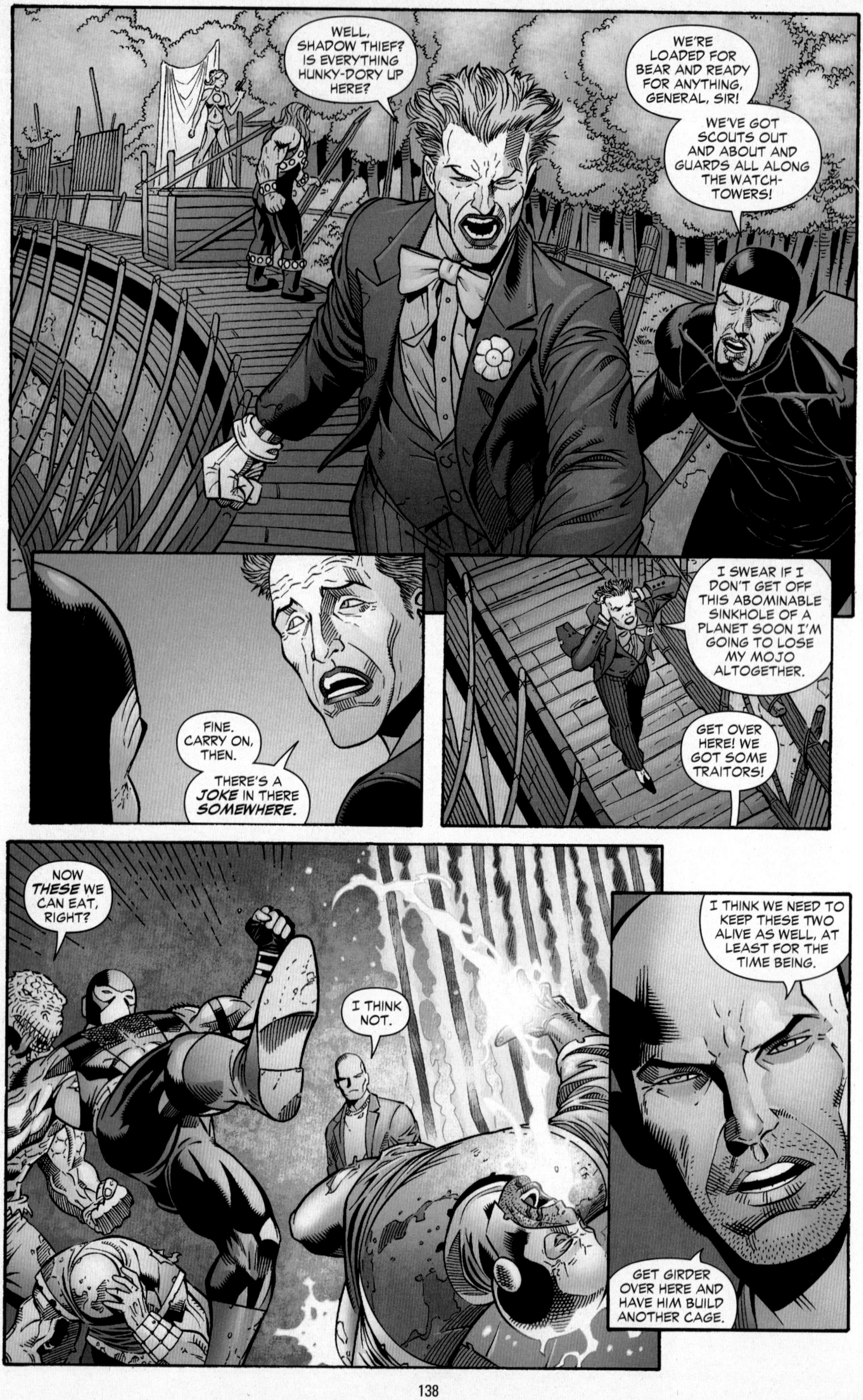
WELL, SHADOW THIEF? IS EVERYTHING HUNKY-DORY UP HERE?
WE'RE LOADED FOR BEAR AND READY FOR ANYTHING, GENERAL, SIR!
WE'VE GOT SCOUTS OUT AND ABOUT AND GUARDS ALL ALONG THE WATCH-TOWERS!
FINE. CARRY ON, THEN.
THERE'S A JOKE IN THERE SOMEWHERE.
I SWEAR IF I DON'T GET OFF THIS ABOMINABLE SINKHOLE OF A PLANET SOON I'M GOING TO LOSE MY MOJO ALTOGETHER.
GET OVER HERE! WE GOT SOME TRAITORS!
NOW THESE WE CAN EAT, RIGHT?
I THINK NOT.
I THINK WE NEED TO KEEP THESE TWO ALIVE AS WELL, AT LEAST FOR THE TIME BEING.
GET GIRDER OVER HERE AND HAVE HIM BUILD ANOTHER CAGE.

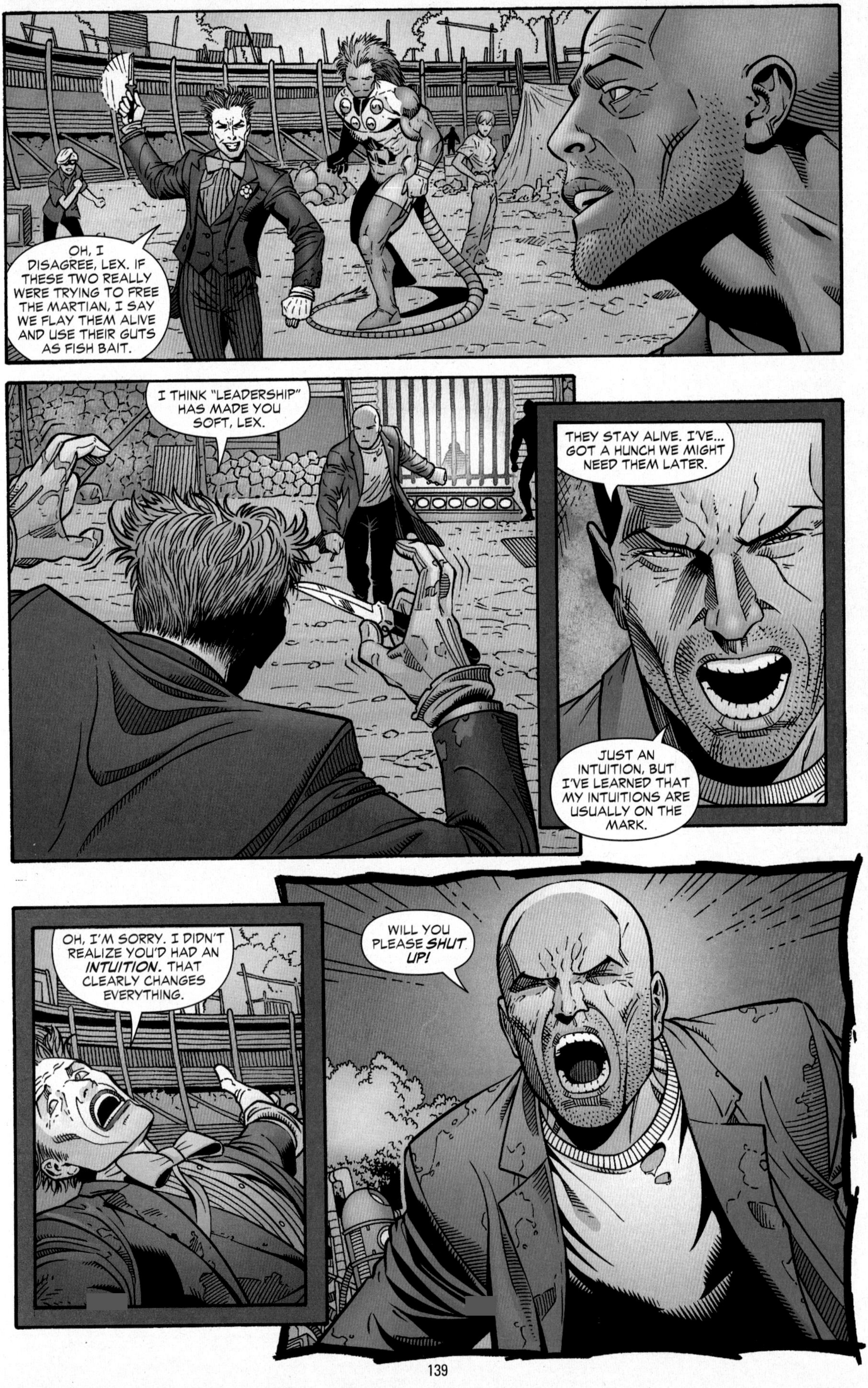
OH, I DISAGREE, LEX. IF THESE TWO REALLY WERE TRYING TO FREE THE MARTIAN, I SAY WE FLAY THEM ALIVE AND USE THEIR GUTS AS FISH BAIT.
I THINK "LEADERSHIP" HAS MADE YOU SOFT, LEX.
THEY STAY ALIVE. I'VE... GOT A HUNCH WE MIGHT NEED THEM LATER.
JUST AN INTUITION, BUT I'VE LEARNED THAT MY INTUITIONS ARE USUALLY ON THE MARK.
OH, I'M SORRY. I DIDN'T REALIZE YOU'D HAD AN *INTUITION.* THAT CLEARLY CHANGES EVERYTHING.
WILL YOU PLEASE ***SHUT UP!***

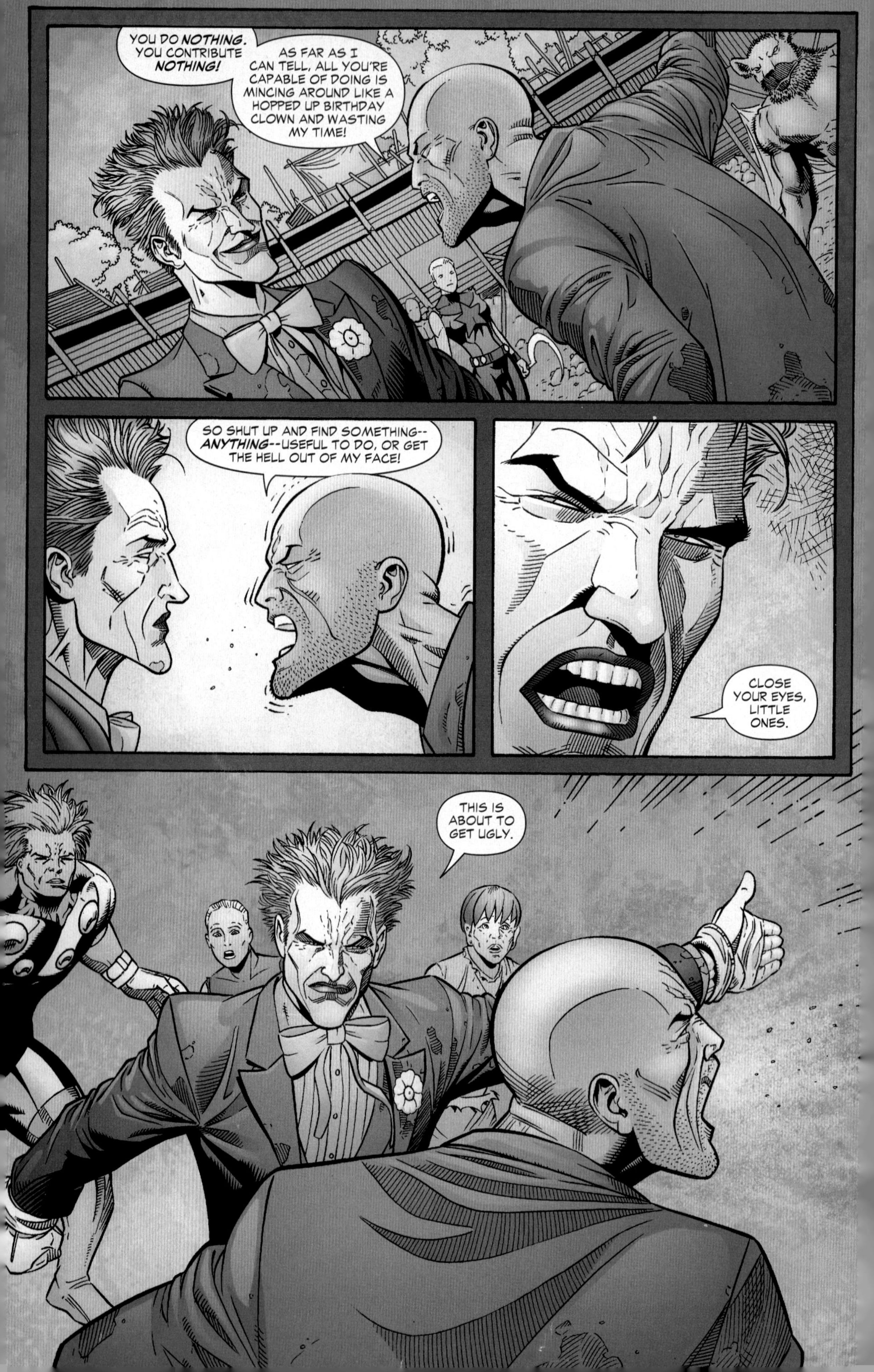
YOU DO NOTHING. YOU CONTRIBUTE NOTHING!
AS FAR AS I CAN TELL, ALL YOU'RE CAPABLE OF DOING IS MINCING AROUND LIKE A HOPPED UP BIRTHDAY CLOWN AND WASTING MY TIME!
SO SHUT UP AND FIND SOMETHING--ANYTHING--USEFUL TO DO, OR GET THE HELL OUT OF MY FACE!
CLOSE YOUR EYES, LITTLE ONES.
THIS IS ABOUT TO GET UGLY.

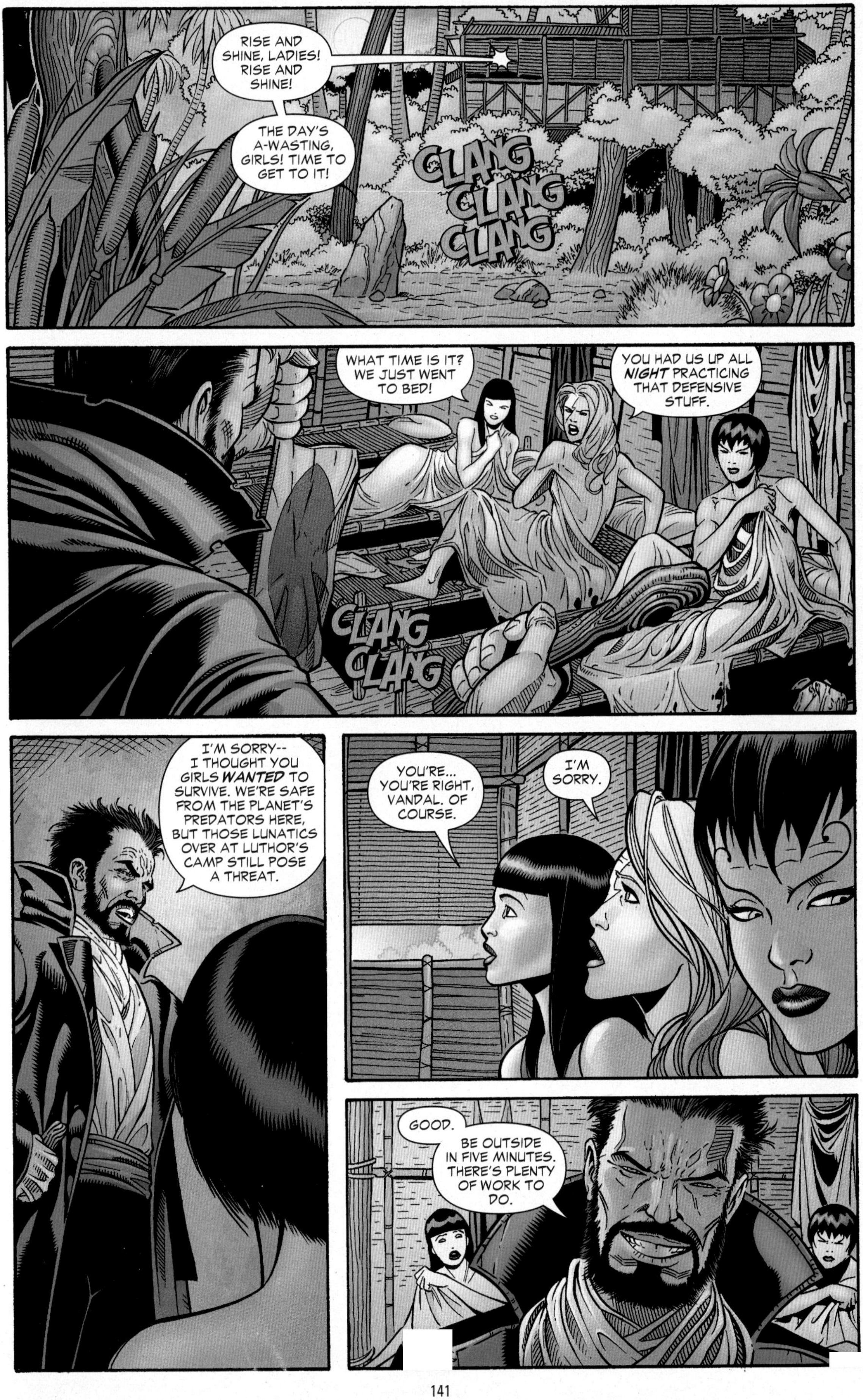
RISE AND SHINE, LADIES! RISE AND SHINE!
THE DAY'S A-WASTING, GIRLS! TIME TO GET TO IT!
CLANG CLANG CLANG
WHAT TIME IS IT? WE JUST WENT TO BED!
YOU HAD US UP ALL NIGHT PRACTICING THAT DEFENSIVE STUFF.
CLANG CLANG
I'M SORRY-- I THOUGHT YOU GIRLS WANTED TO SURVIVE. WE'RE SAFE FROM THE PLANET'S PREDATORS HERE, BUT THOSE LUNATICS OVER AT LUTHOR'S CAMP STILL POSE A THREAT.
YOU'RE... YOU'RE RIGHT, VANDAL. OF COURSE.
I'M SORRY.
GOOD.
BE OUTSIDE IN FIVE MINUTES. THERE'S PLENTY OF WORK TO DO.

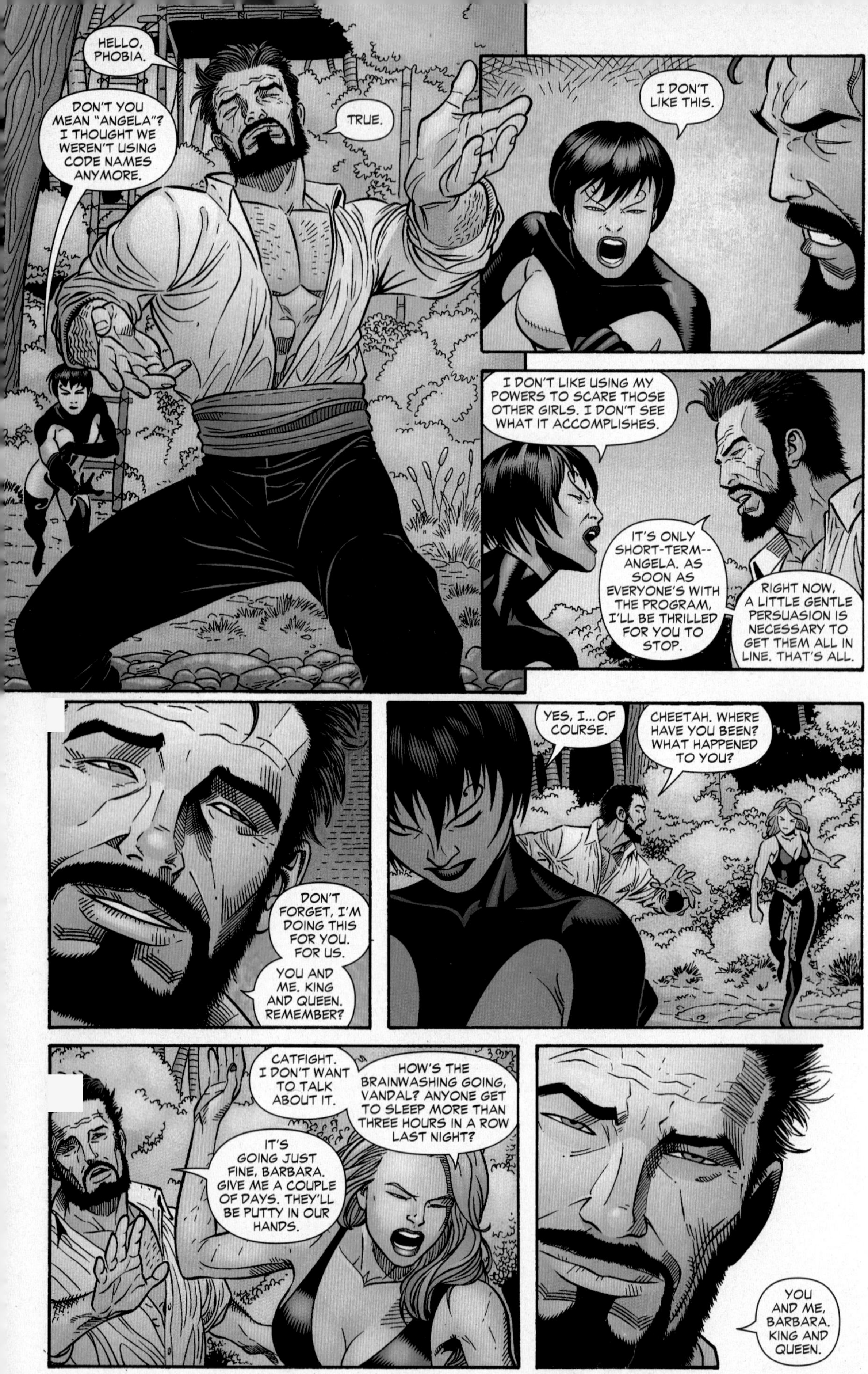
HELLO, PHOBIA.
DON'T YOU MEAN "ANGELA"? I THOUGHT WE WEREN'T USING CODE NAMES ANYMORE.
TRUE.
I DON'T LIKE THIS.
I DON'T LIKE USING MY POWERS TO SCARE THOSE OTHER GIRLS. I DON'T SEE WHAT IT ACCOMPLISHES.
IT'S ONLY SHORT-TERM-- ANGELA. AS SOON AS EVERYONE'S WITH THE PROGRAM, I'LL BE THRILLED FOR YOU TO STOP.
RIGHT NOW, A LITTLE GENTLE PERSUASION IS NECESSARY TO GET THEM ALL IN LINE. THAT'S ALL.
DON'T FORGET, I'M DOING THIS FOR YOU. FOR US.
YOU AND ME. KING AND QUEEN. REMEMBER?
YES, I...OF COURSE.
CHEETAH. WHERE HAVE YOU BEEN? WHAT HAPPENED TO YOU?
CATFIGHT. I DON'T WANT TO TALK ABOUT IT.
HOW'S THE BRAINWASHING GOING, VANDAL? ANYONE GET TO SLEEP MORE THAN THREE HOURS IN A ROW LAST NIGHT?
IT'S GOING JUST FINE, BARBARA. GIVE ME A COUPLE OF DAYS. THEY'LL BE PUTTY IN OUR HANDS.
YOU AND ME, BARBARA. KING AND QUEEN.

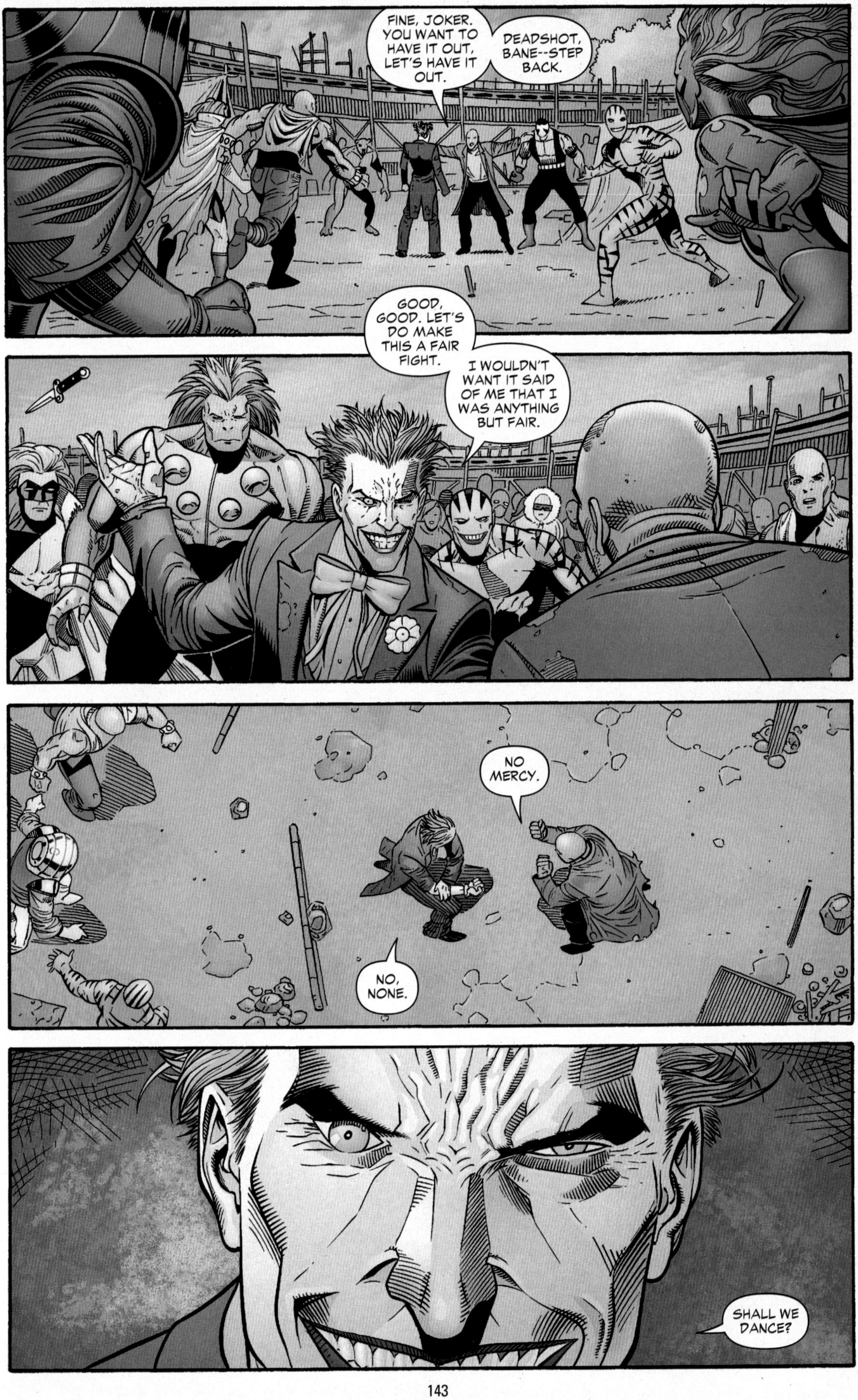
FINE, JOKER. YOU WANT TO HAVE IT OUT, LET'S HAVE IT OUT.
DEADSHOT, BANE--STEP BACK.
GOOD, GOOD. LET'S DO MAKE THIS A FAIR FIGHT.
I WOULDN'T WANT IT SAID OF ME THAT I WAS ANYTHING BUT FAIR.
NO MERCY.
NO, NONE.
SHALL WE DANCE?

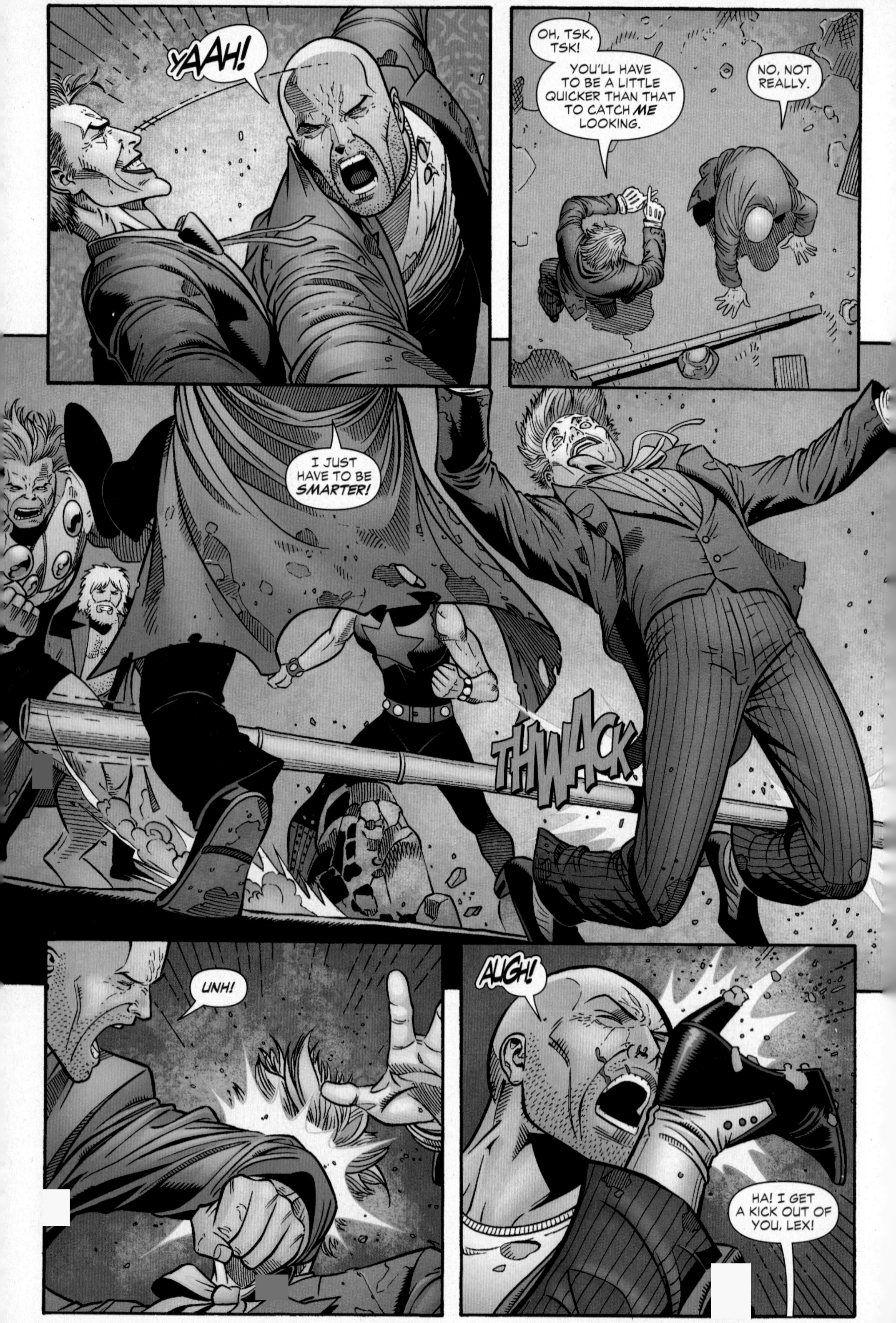
YAAH!
OH, TSK, TSK!
YOU'LL HAVE TO BE A LITTLE QUICKER THAN THAT TO CATCH ME LOOKING.
NO, NOT REALLY.
I JUST HAVE TO BE SMARTER!
THWACK
UNH!
AUGH!
HA! I GET A KICK OUT OF YOU, LEX!

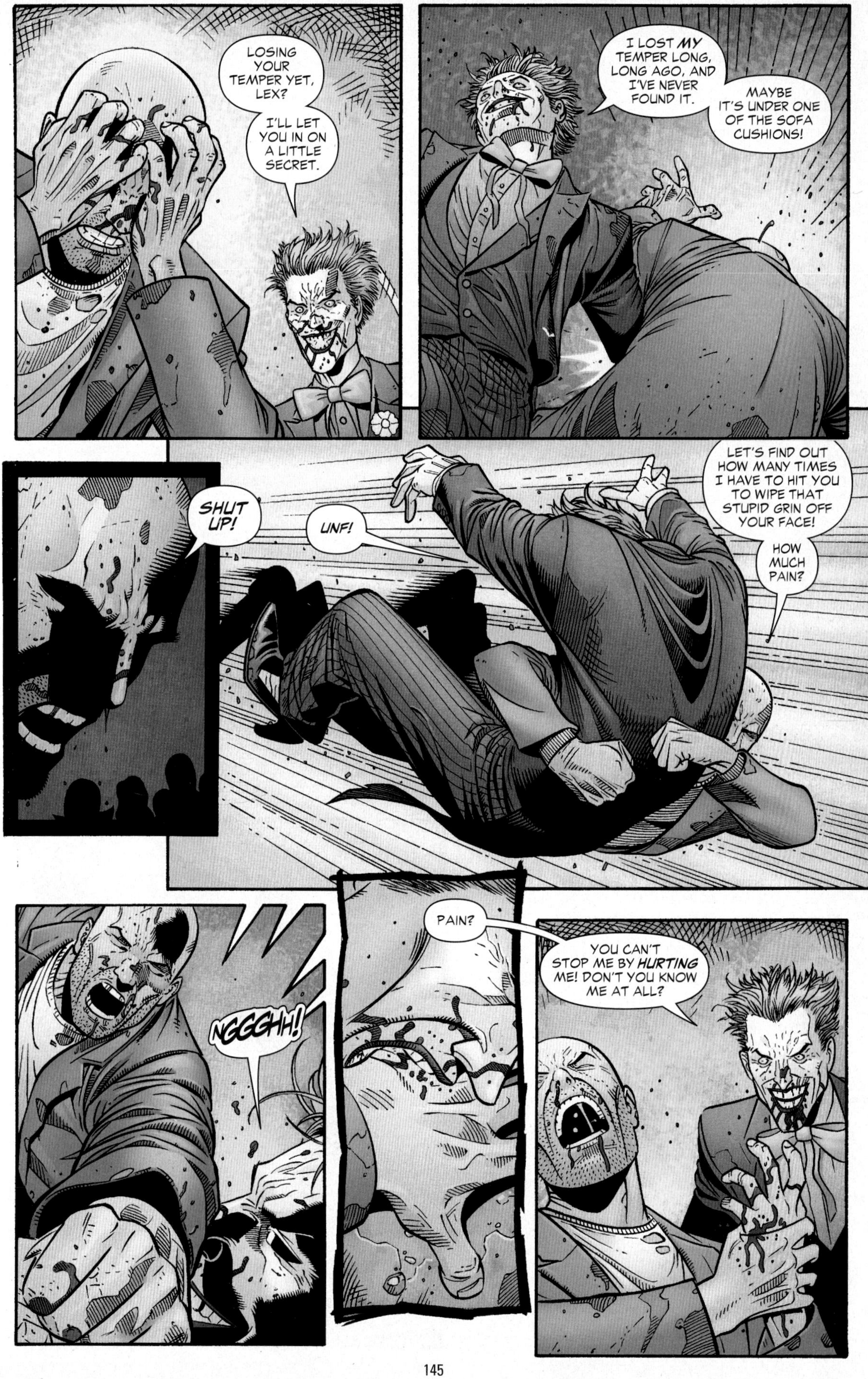

LOSING YOUR TEMPER YET, LEX?
I'LL LET YOU IN ON A LITTLE SECRET.
I LOST MY TEMPER LONG, LONG AGO, AND I'VE NEVER FOUND IT.
MAYBE IT'S UNDER ONE OF THE SOFA CUSHIONS!
SHUT UP!
UNF!
LET'S FIND OUT HOW MANY TIMES I HAVE TO HIT YOU TO WIPE THAT STUPID GRIN OFF YOUR FACE!
HOW MUCH PAIN?
NGGGHH!
PAIN?
YOU CAN'T STOP ME BY HURTING ME! DON'T YOU KNOW ME AT ALL?

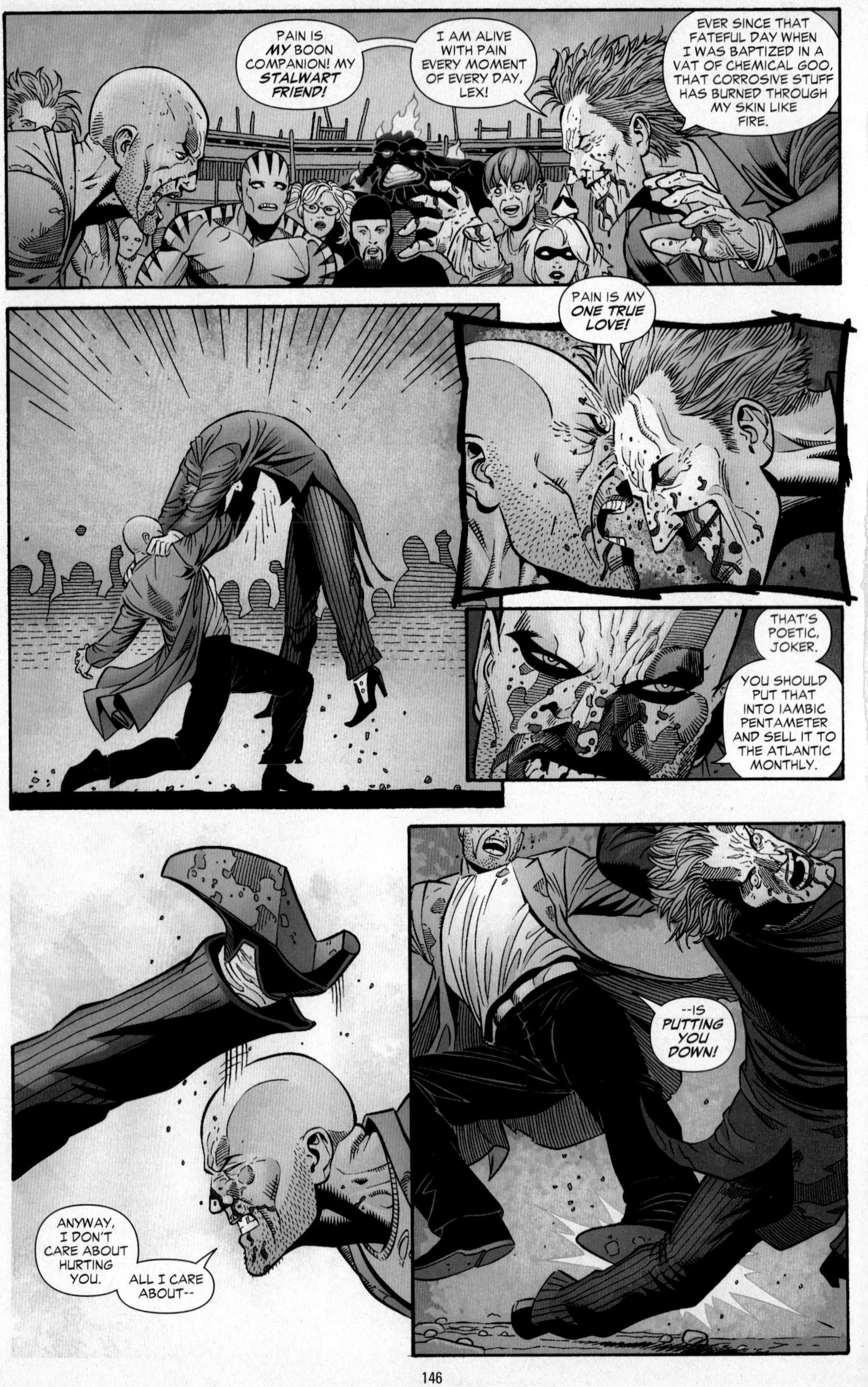
PAIN IS *MY* BOON COMPANION! MY *STALWART FRIEND!*
I AM ALIVE WITH PAIN EVERY MOMENT OF EVERY DAY, LEX!
EVER SINCE THAT FATEFUL DAY WHEN I WAS BAPTIZED IN A VAT OF CHEMICAL GOO, THAT CORROSIVE STUFF HAS BURNED THROUGH MY SKIN LIKE FIRE.
PAIN IS MY *ONE TRUE LOVE!*
THAT'S POETIC, JOKER.
YOU SHOULD PUT THAT INTO IAMBIC PENTAMETER AND SELL IT TO THE ATLANTIC MONTHLY.
ANYWAY, I DON'T CARE ABOUT HURTING YOU.
ALL I CARE ABOUT--
--IS *PUTTING YOU DOWN!*

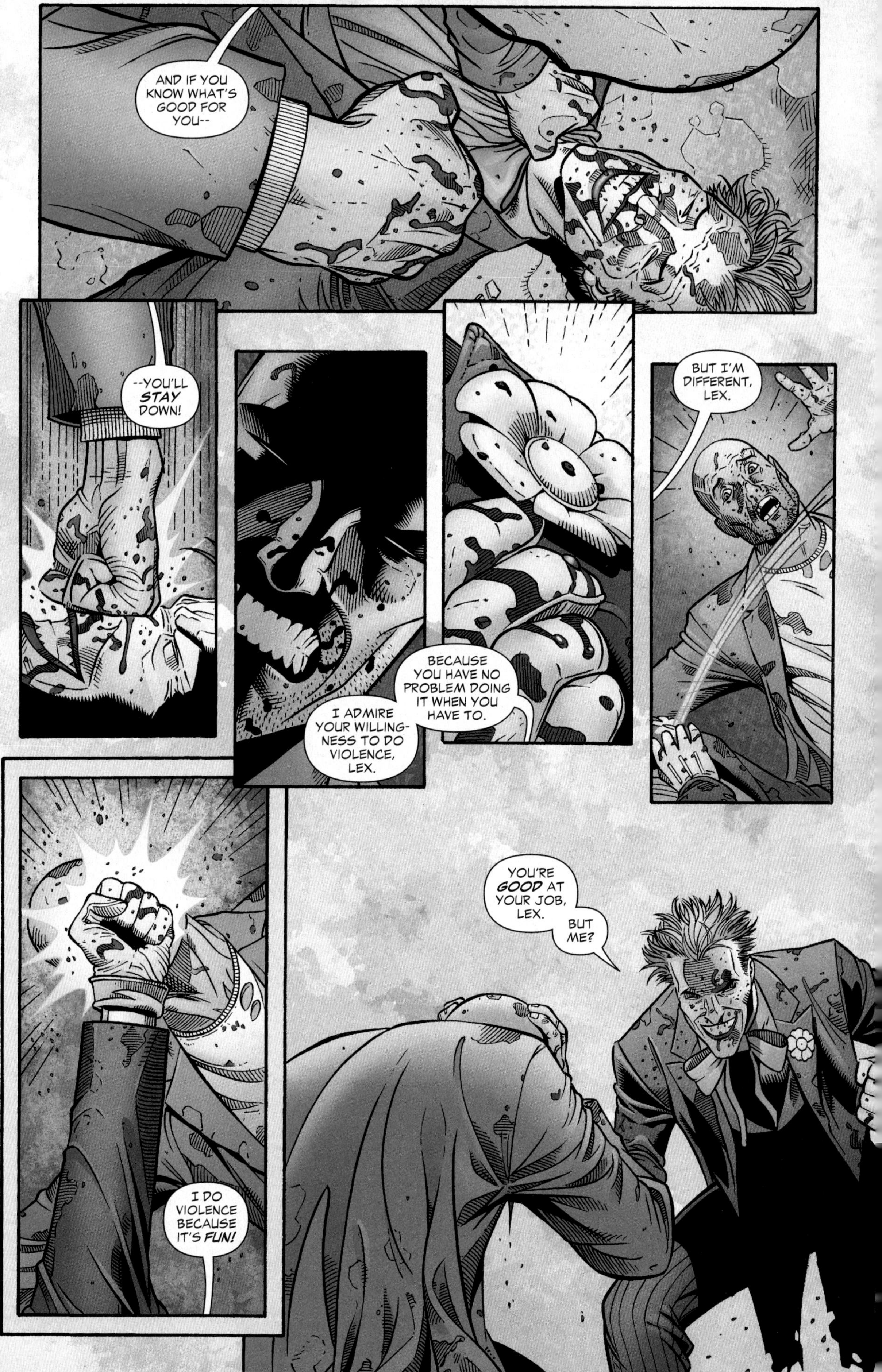
AND IF YOU KNOW WHAT'S GOOD FOR YOU--
--YOU'LL STAY DOWN!
I ADMIRE YOUR WILLING-NESS TO DO VIOLENCE, LEX.
BECAUSE YOU HAVE NO PROBLEM DOING IT WHEN YOU HAVE TO.
BUT I'M DIFFERENT, LEX.
I DO VIOLENCE BECAUSE IT'S FUN!
YOU'RE GOOD AT YOUR JOB, LEX.
BUT ME?

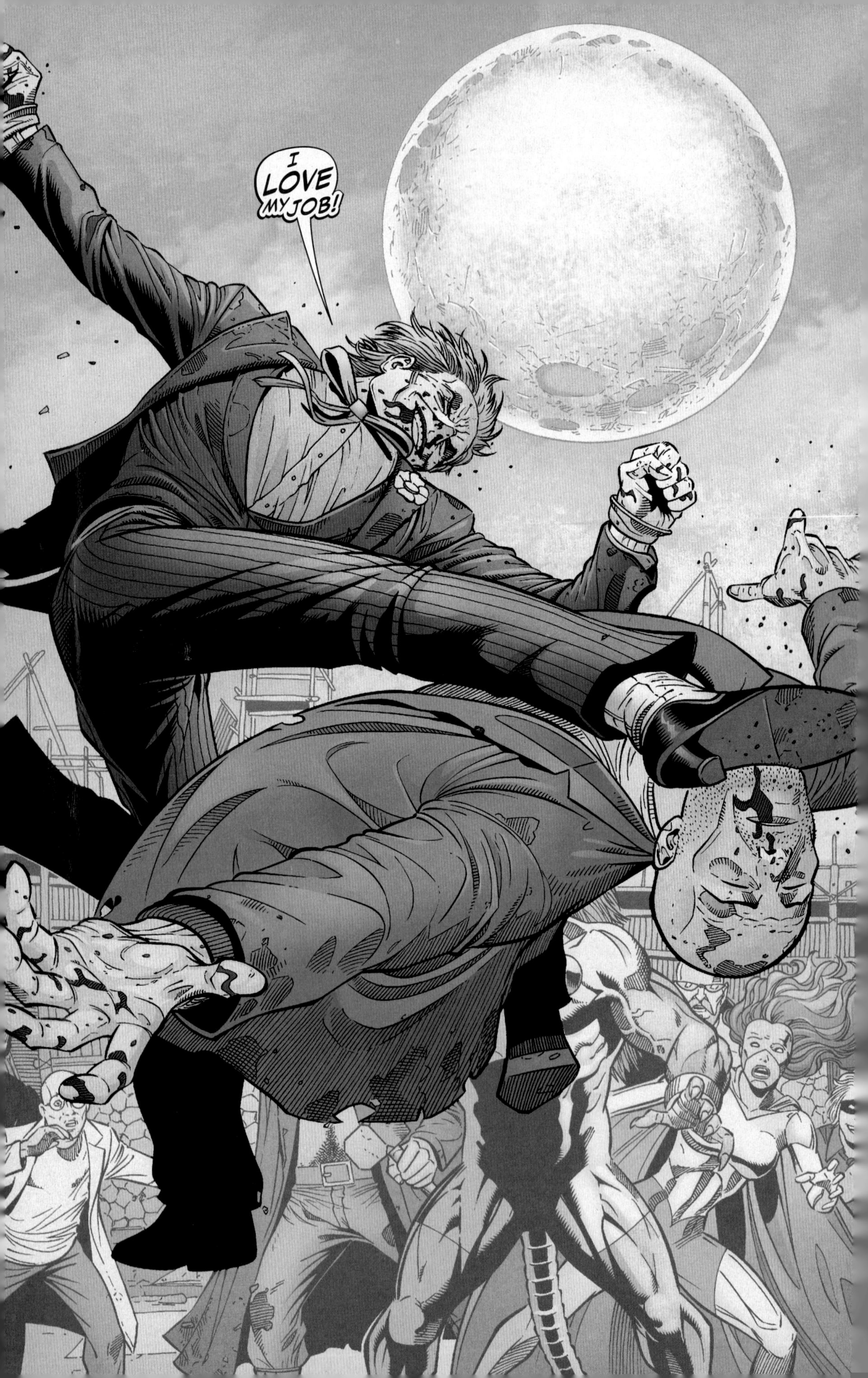
I LOVE MY JOB!

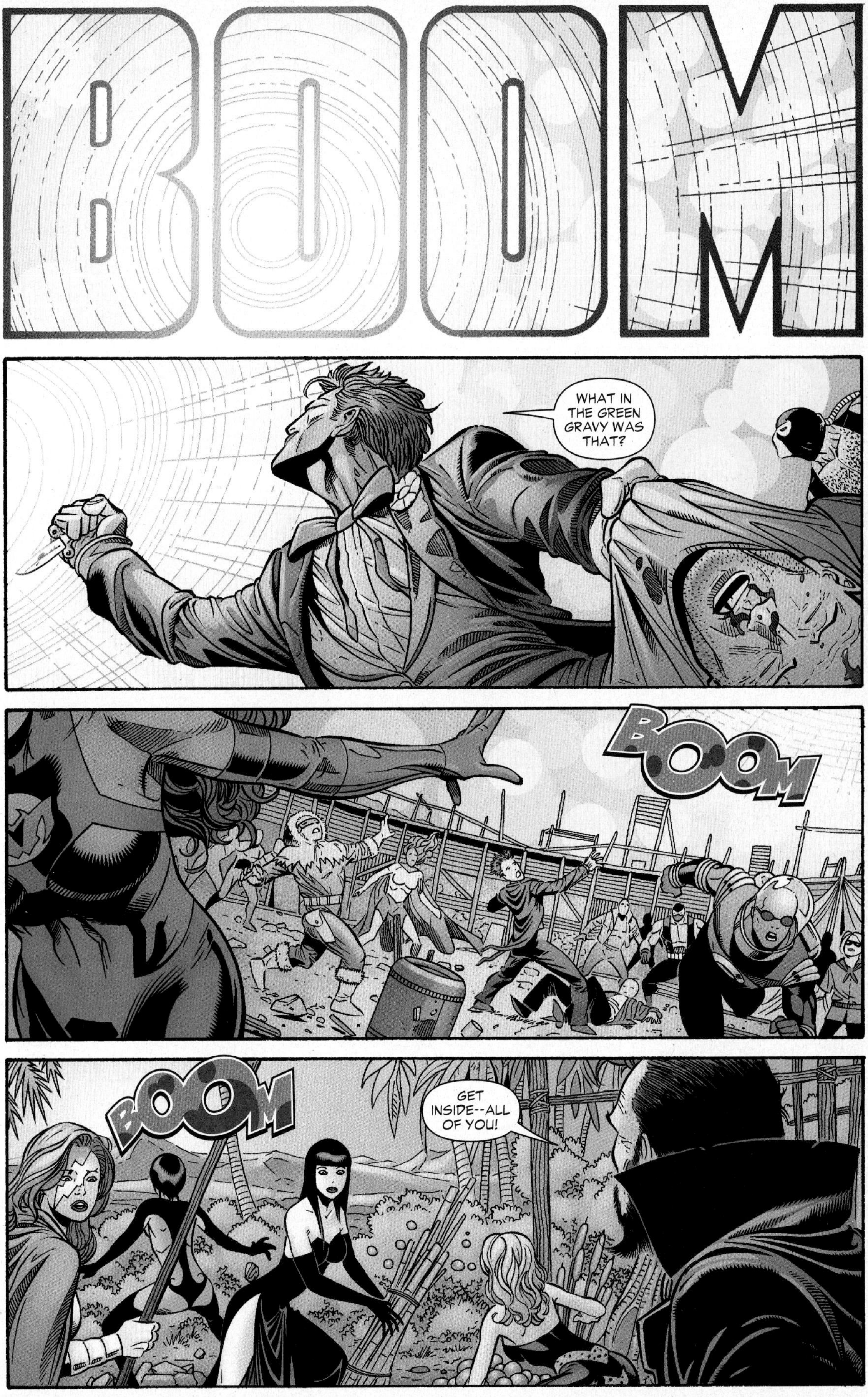
BOOM
WHAT IN THE GREEN GRAVY WAS THAT?
BOOM
BOOM
GET INSIDE--ALL OF YOU!

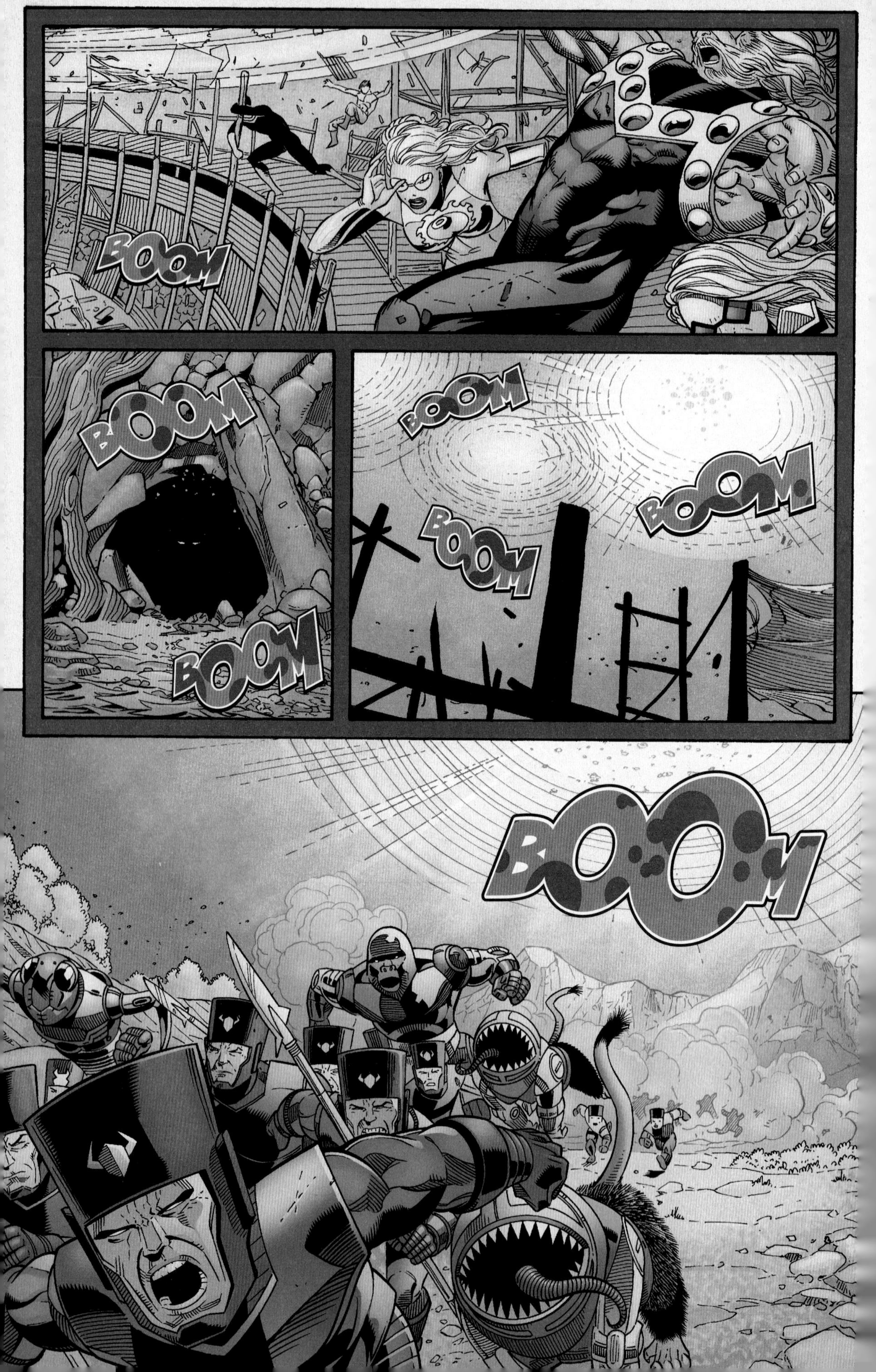
BOOM
BOOM
BOOM
BOOM
BOOM
BOOM
BOOM

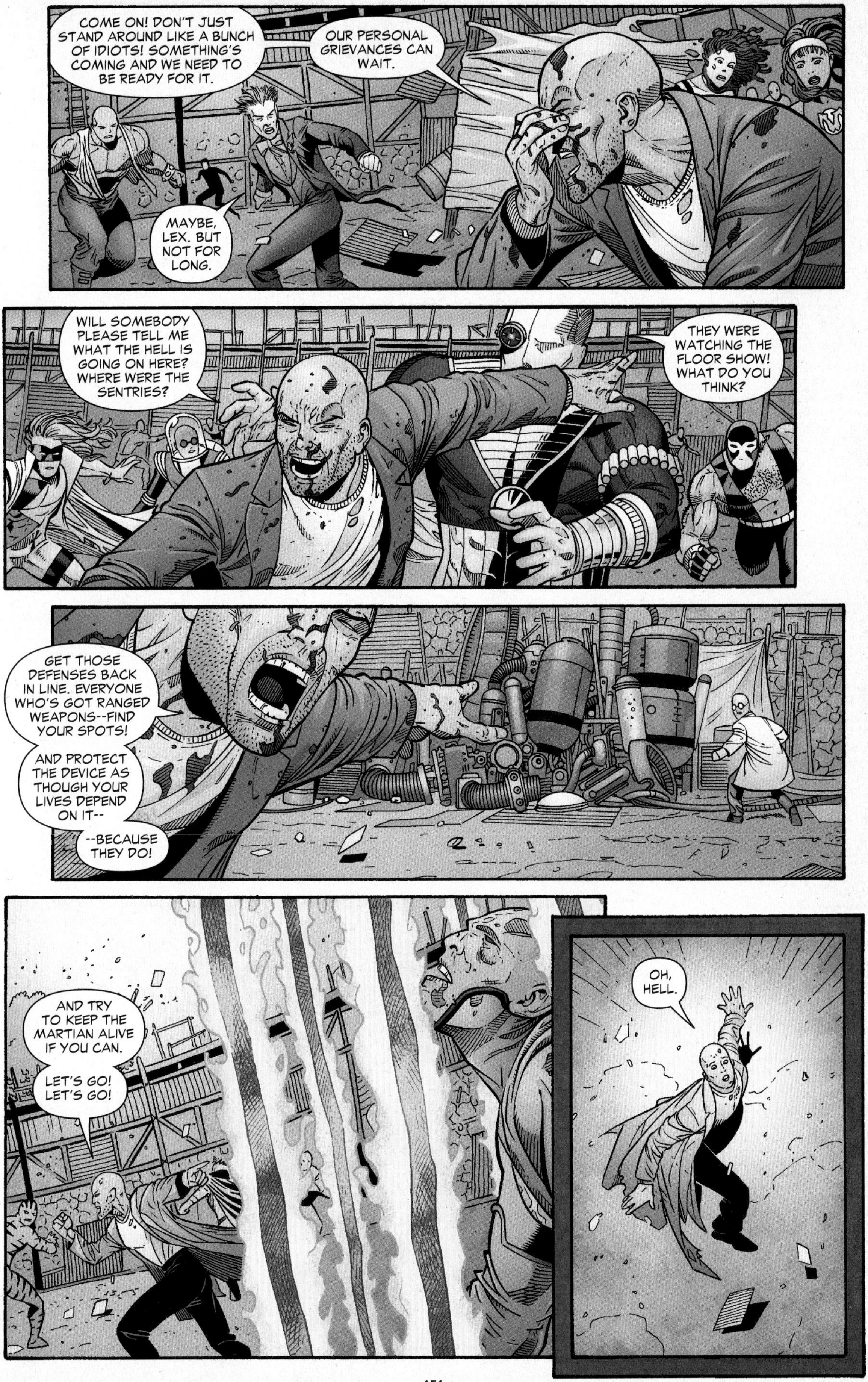
COME ON! DON'T JUST STAND AROUND LIKE A BUNCH OF IDIOTS! SOMETHING'S COMING AND WE NEED TO BE READY FOR IT.
OUR PERSONAL GRIEVANCES CAN WAIT.
MAYBE, LEX. BUT NOT FOR LONG.
WILL SOMEBODY PLEASE TELL ME WHAT THE HELL IS GOING ON HERE? WHERE WERE THE SENTRIES?
THEY WERE WATCHING THE FLOOR SHOW! WHAT DO YOU THINK?
GET THOSE DEFENSES BACK IN LINE. EVERYONE WHO'S GOT RANGED WEAPONS--FIND YOUR SPOTS!
AND PROTECT THE DEVICE AS THOUGH YOUR LIVES DEPEND ON IT--
--BECAUSE THEY DO!
AND TRY TO KEEP THE MARTIAN ALIVE IF YOU CAN.
LET'S GO! LET'S GO!
OH, HELL.

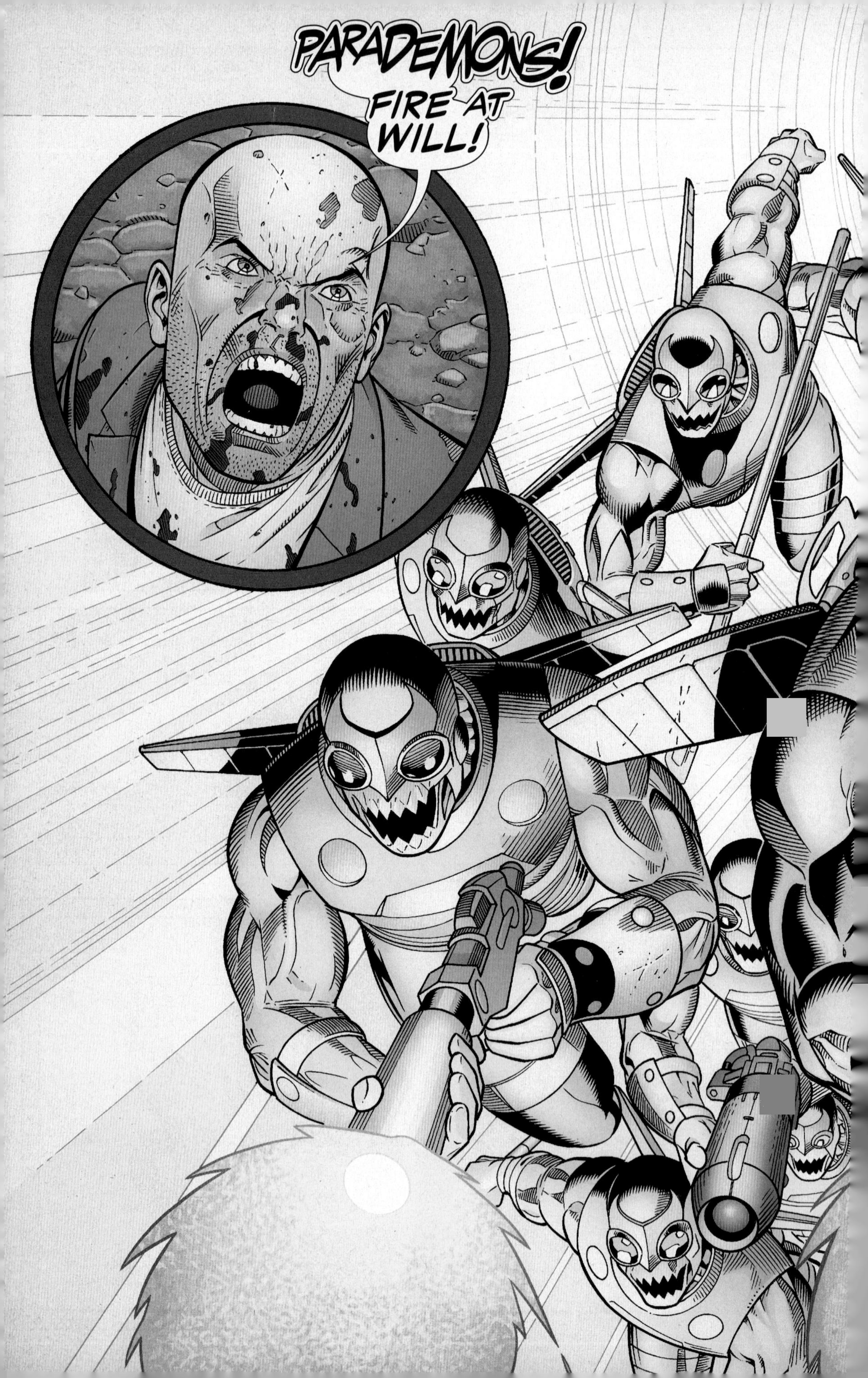
PARADEMONS!
FIRE AT WILL!

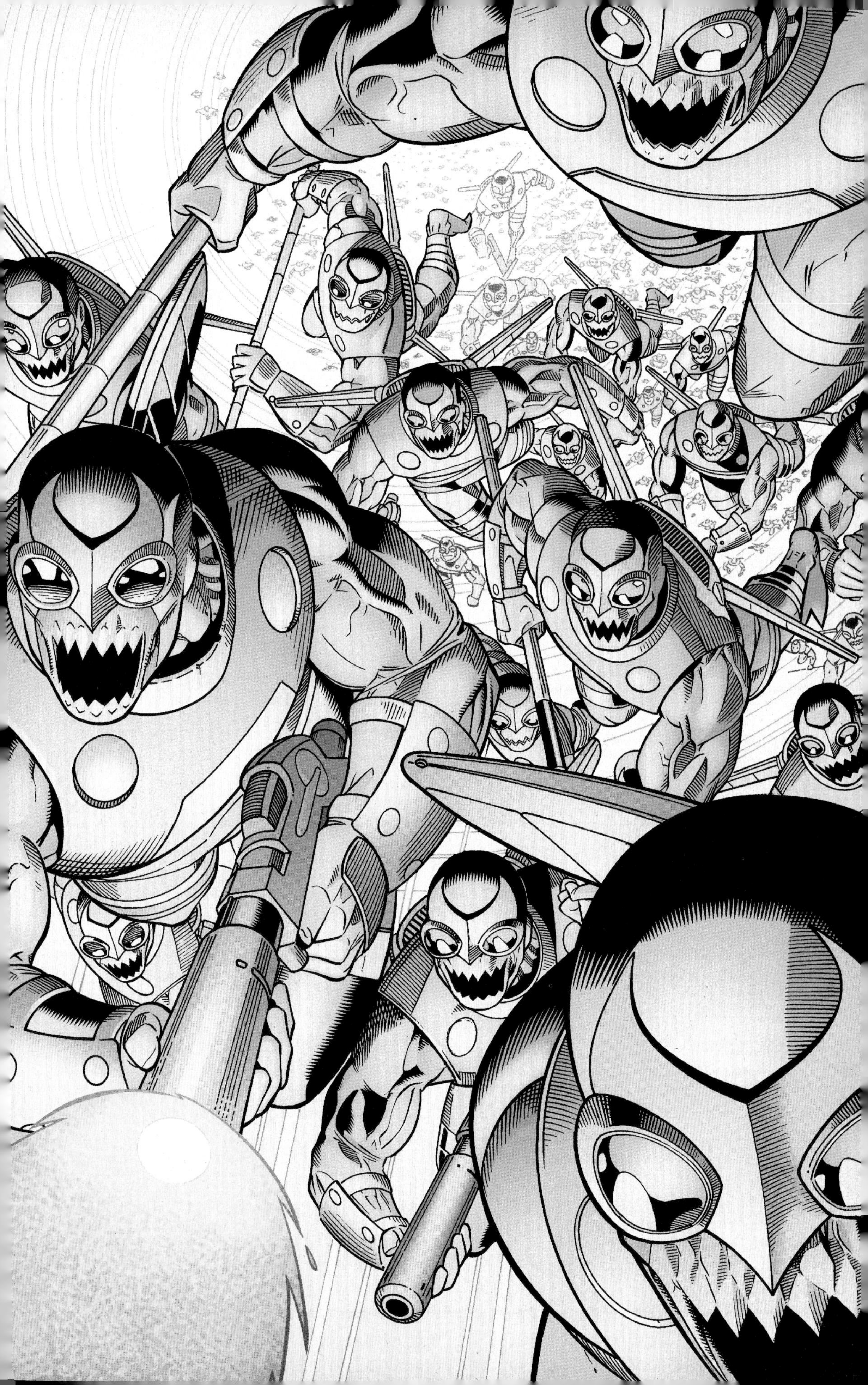

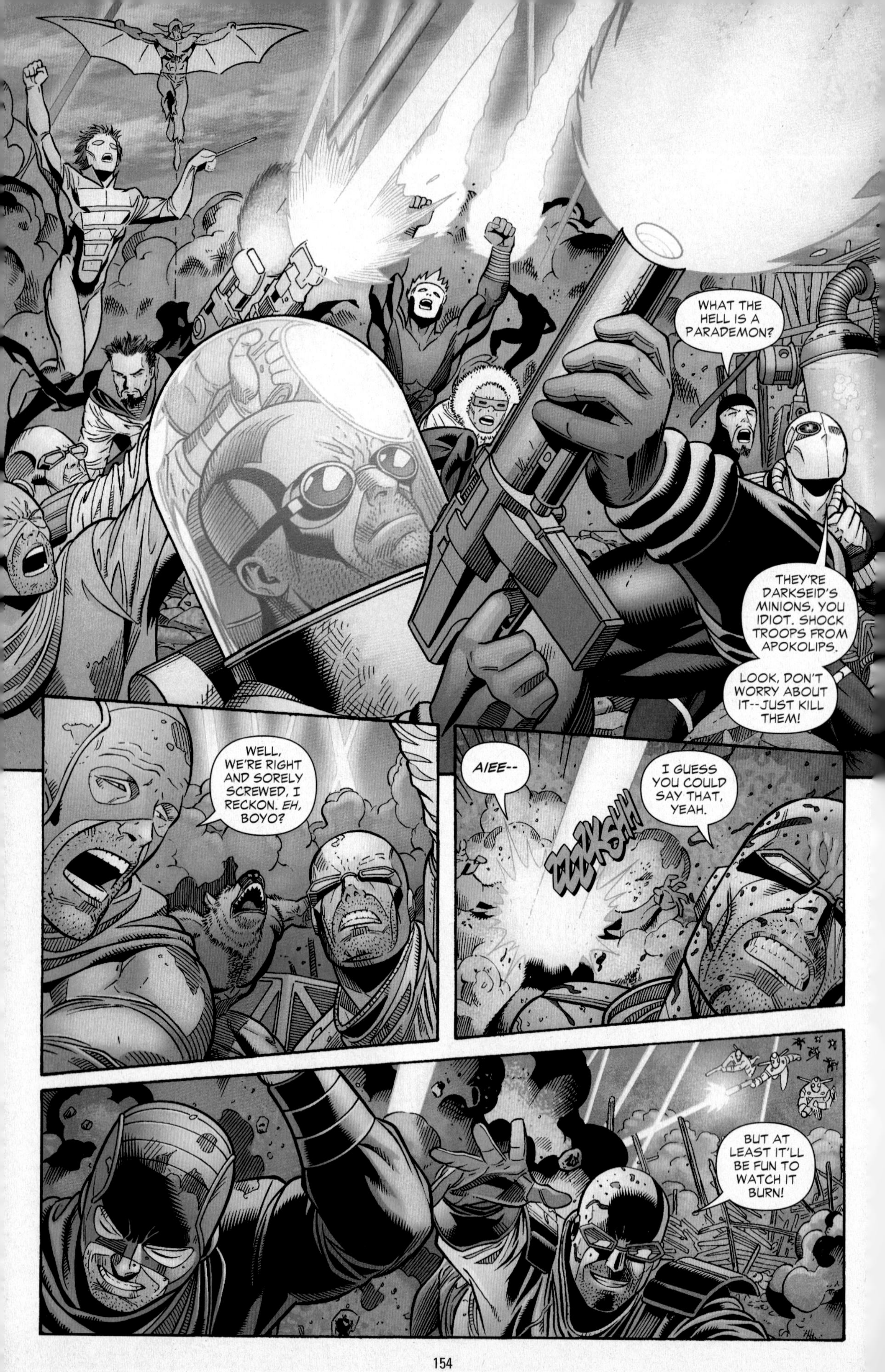
WHAT THE HELL IS A PARADEMON?
THEY'RE DARKSEID'S MINIONS, YOU IDIOT. SHOCK TROOPS FROM APOKOLIPS.
LOOK, DON'T WORRY ABOUT IT--JUST KILL THEM!
WELL, WE'RE RIGHT AND SORELY SCREWED, I RECKON. EH, BOYO?
AIEE--
I GUESS YOU COULD SAY THAT, YEAH.
DZZZKSHH
BUT AT LEAST IT'LL BE FUN TO WATCH IT BURN!

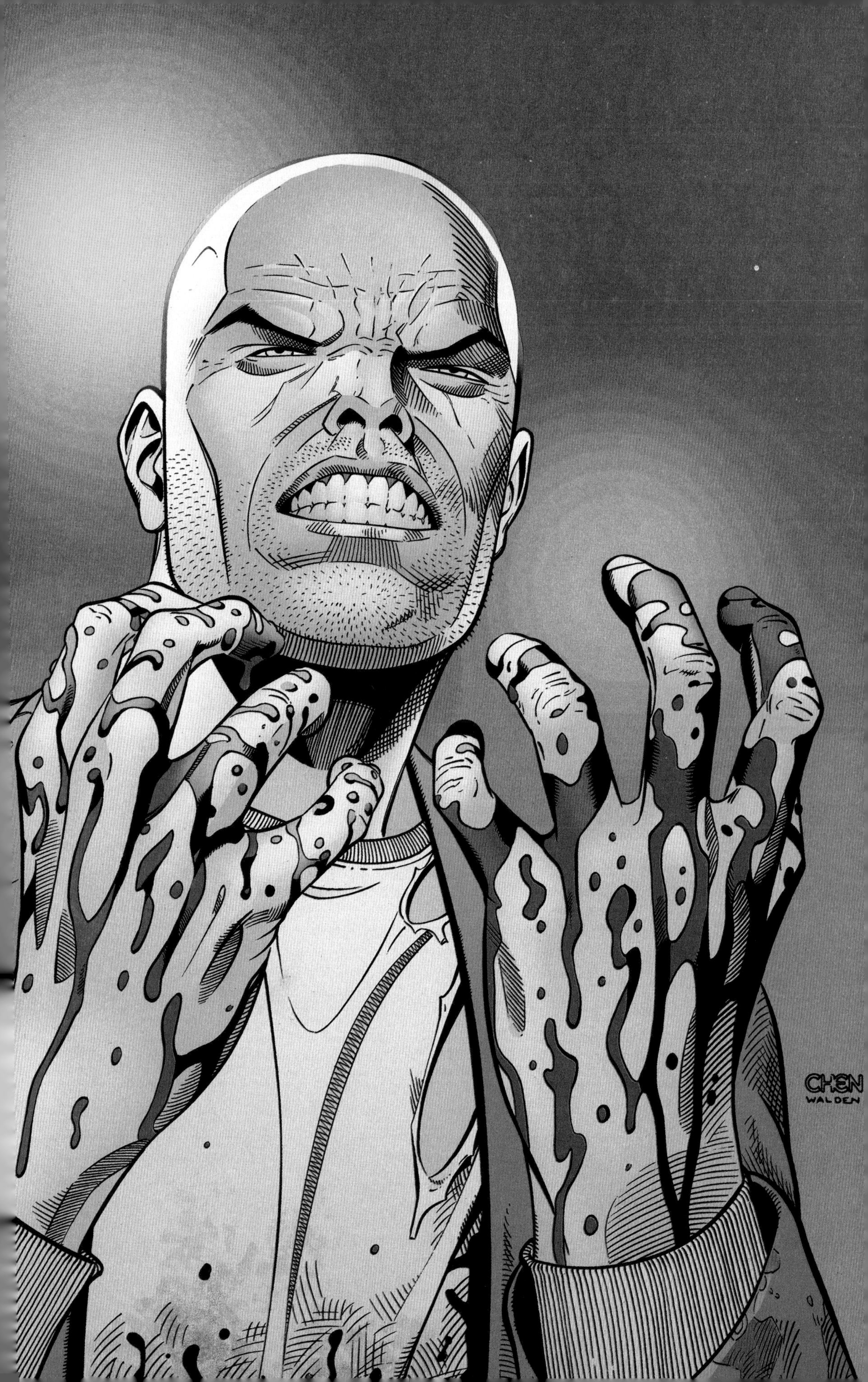
CHEN
WALDEN

Matthew Sturges
Writer

Sean Chen
Penciller

Walden Wong (pages 157-175)
Wayne Faucher (pages 176-186)
Inkers

John Kalisz
Tom Chu
Colorists

Steve Wands
Letterer

CHAPTER SEVEN

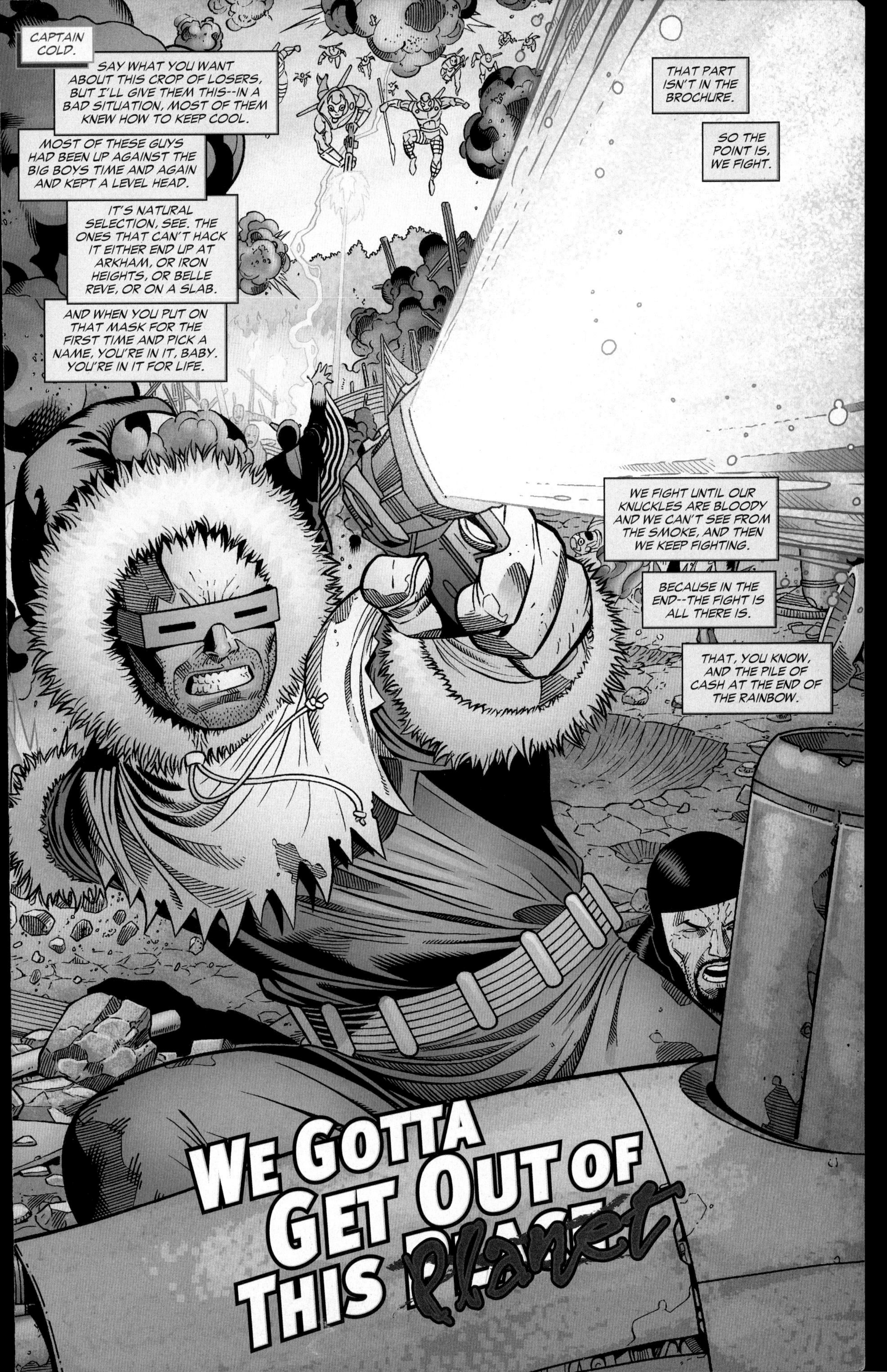
CAPTAIN COLD.
SAY WHAT YOU WANT ABOUT THIS CROP OF LOSERS, BUT I'LL GIVE THEM THIS--IN A BAD SITUATION, MOST OF THEM KNEW HOW TO KEEP COOL.
MOST OF THESE GUYS HAD BEEN UP AGAINST THE BIG BOYS TIME AND AGAIN AND KEPT A LEVEL HEAD.
IT'S NATURAL SELECTION, SEE. THE ONES THAT CAN'T HACK IT EITHER END UP AT ARKHAM, OR IRON HEIGHTS, OR BELLE REVE, OR ON A SLAB.
AND WHEN YOU PUT ON THAT MASK FOR THE FIRST TIME AND PICK A NAME, YOU'RE IN IT, BABY. YOU'RE IN IT FOR LIFE.
THAT PART ISN'T IN THE BROCHURE.
SO THE POINT IS, WE FIGHT.
WE FIGHT UNTIL OUR KNUCKLES ARE BLOODY AND WE CAN'T SEE FROM THE SMOKE, AND THEN WE KEEP FIGHTING.
BECAUSE IN THE END--THE FIGHT IS ALL THERE IS.
THAT, YOU KNOW, AND THE PILE OF CASH AT THE END OF THE RAINBOW.
WE GOTTA GET OUT OF THIS ~~PLACE~~ PLANET

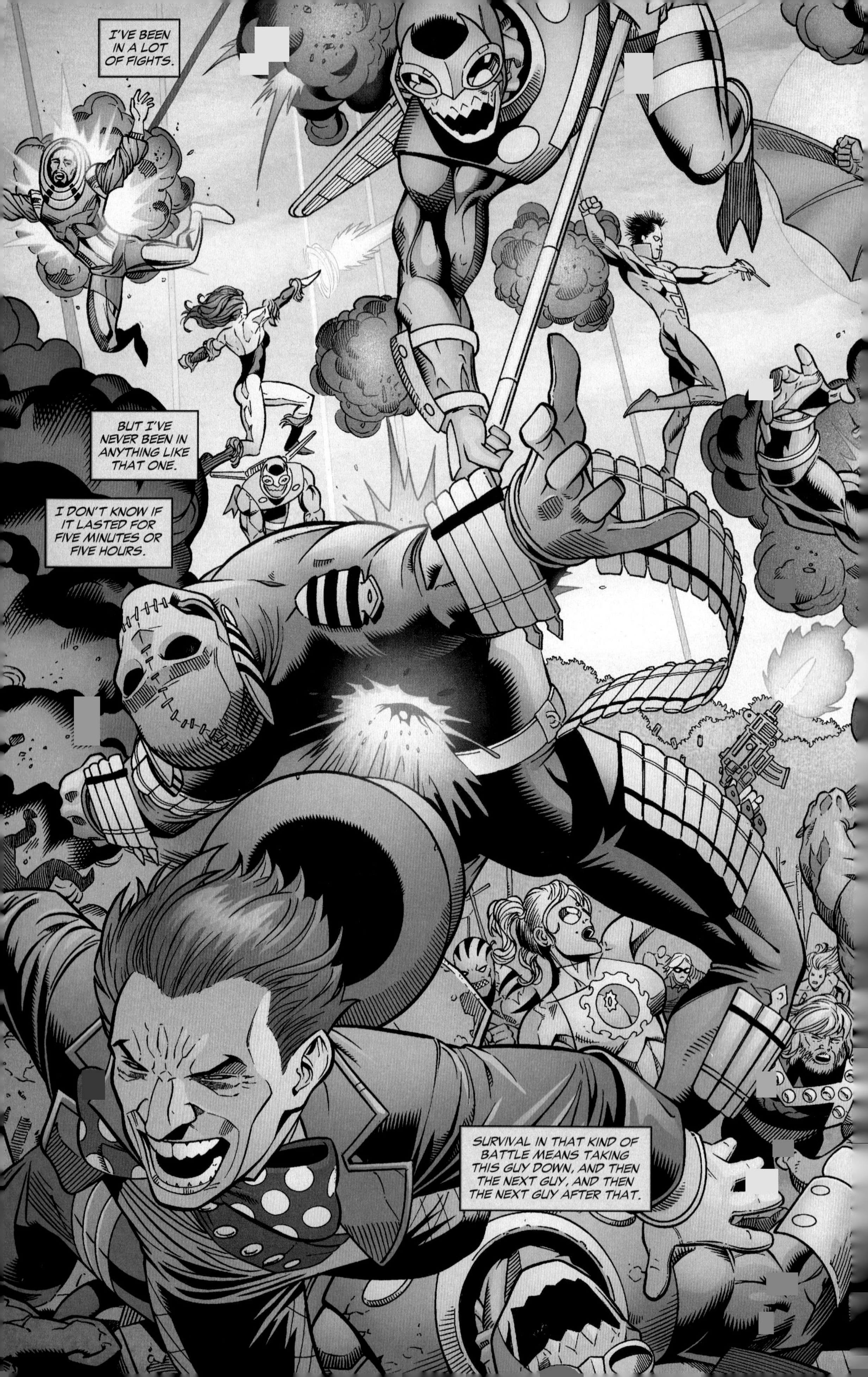
I'VE BEEN IN A LOT OF FIGHTS.
BUT I'VE NEVER BEEN IN ANYTHING LIKE THAT ONE.
I DON'T KNOW IF IT LASTED FOR FIVE MINUTES OR FIVE HOURS.
SURVIVAL IN THAT KIND OF BATTLE MEANS TAKING THIS GUY DOWN, AND THEN THE NEXT GUY, AND THEN THE NEXT GUY AFTER THAT.

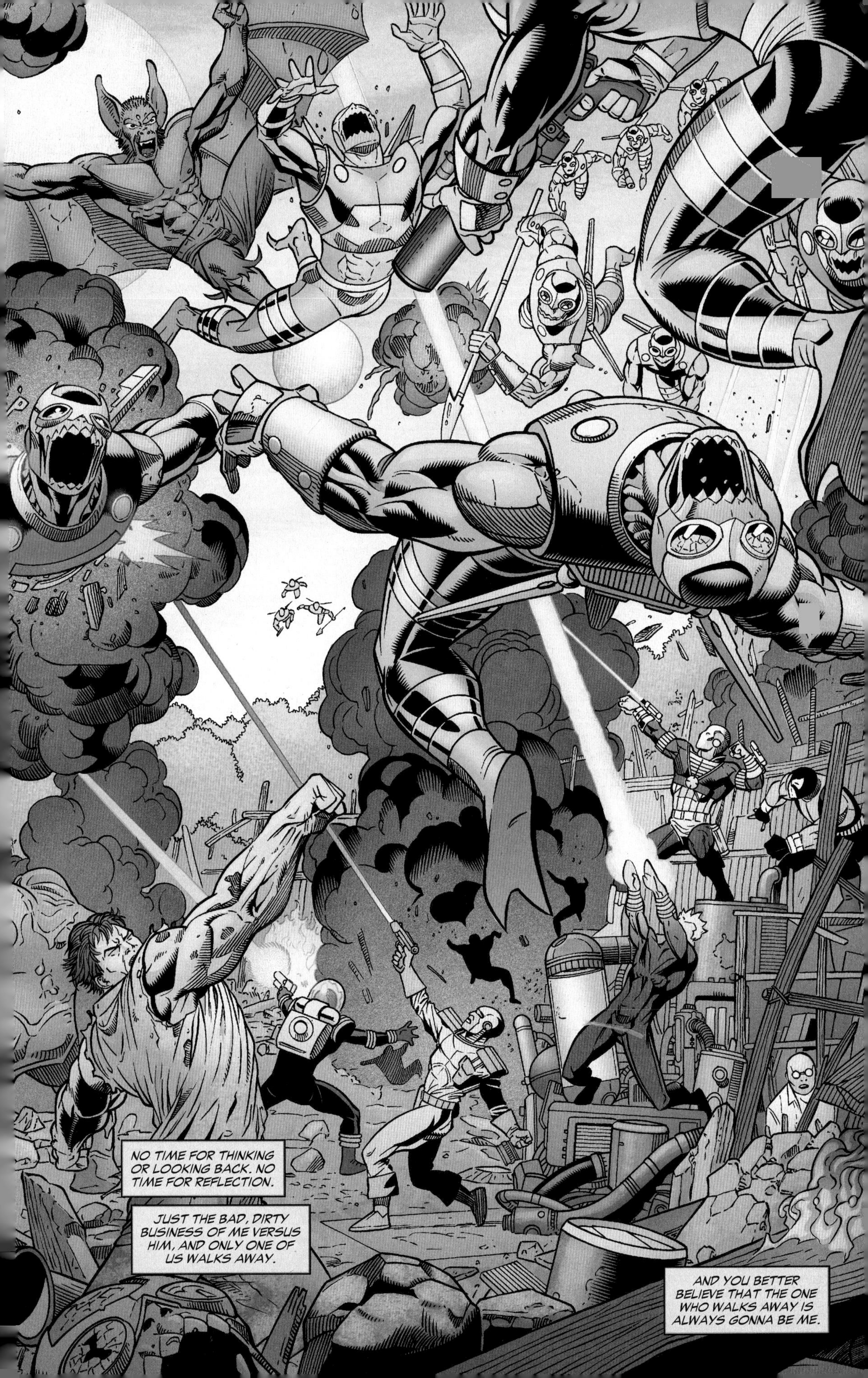
NO TIME FOR THINKING OR LOOKING BACK. NO TIME FOR REFLECTION.
JUST THE BAD, DIRTY BUSINESS OF ME VERSUS HIM, AND ONLY ONE OF US WALKS AWAY.
AND YOU BETTER BELIEVE THAT THE ONE WHO WALKS AWAY IS ALWAYS GONNA BE ME.

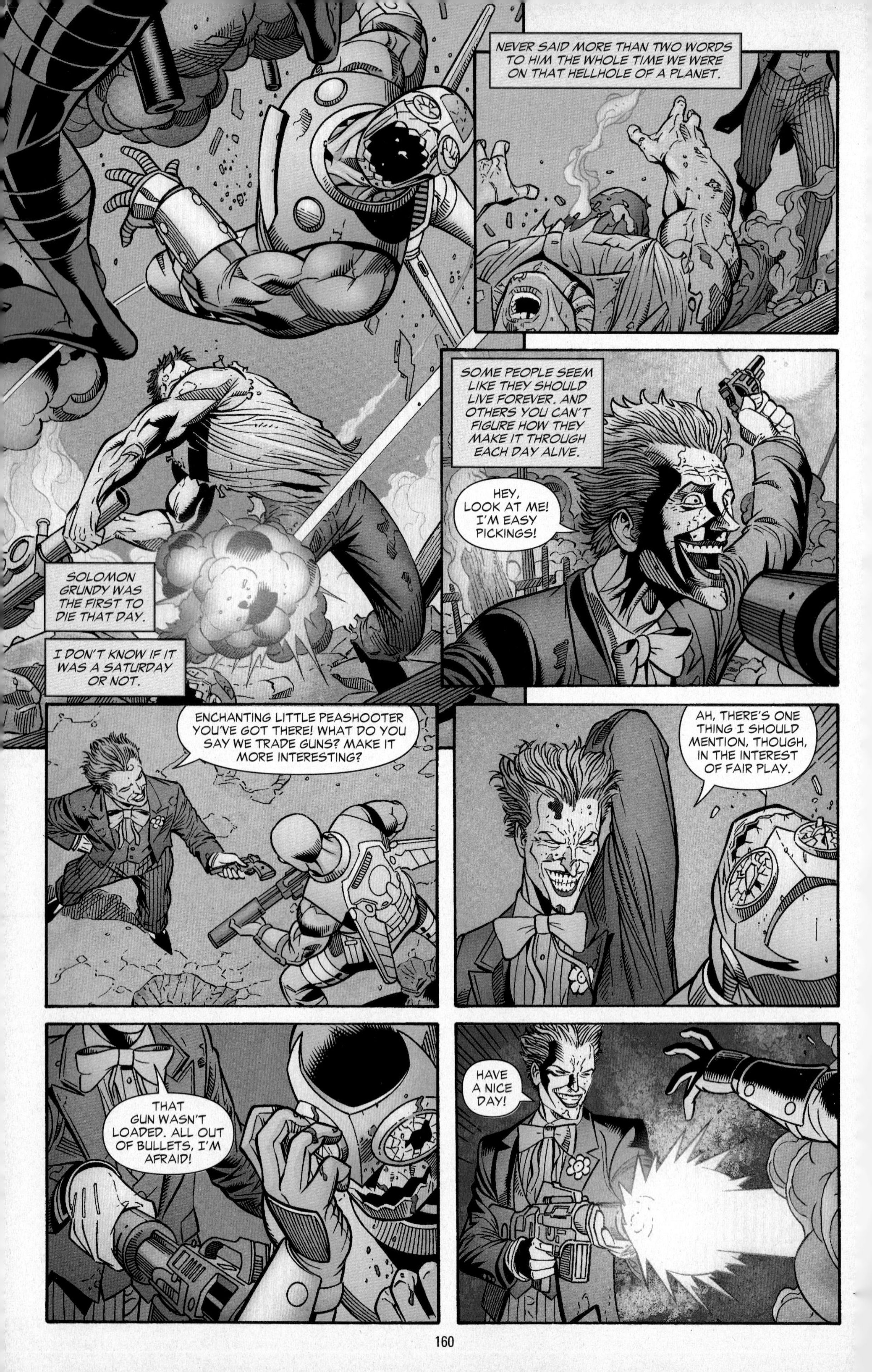

SOLOMON GRUNDY WAS THE FIRST TO DIE THAT DAY.
I DON'T KNOW IF IT WAS A SATURDAY OR NOT.
NEVER SAID MORE THAN TWO WORDS TO HIM THE WHOLE TIME WE WERE ON THAT HELLHOLE OF A PLANET.
SOME PEOPLE SEEM LIKE THEY SHOULD LIVE FOREVER. AND OTHERS YOU CAN'T FIGURE HOW THEY MAKE IT THROUGH EACH DAY ALIVE.
HEY, LOOK AT ME! I'M EASY PICKINGS!
ENCHANTING LITTLE PEASHOOTER YOU'VE GOT THERE! WHAT DO YOU SAY WE TRADE GUNS? MAKE IT MORE INTERESTING?
AH, THERE'S ONE THING I SHOULD MENTION, THOUGH, IN THE INTEREST OF FAIR PLAY.
THAT GUN WASN'T LOADED. ALL OUT OF BULLETS, I'M AFRAID!
HAVE A NICE DAY!

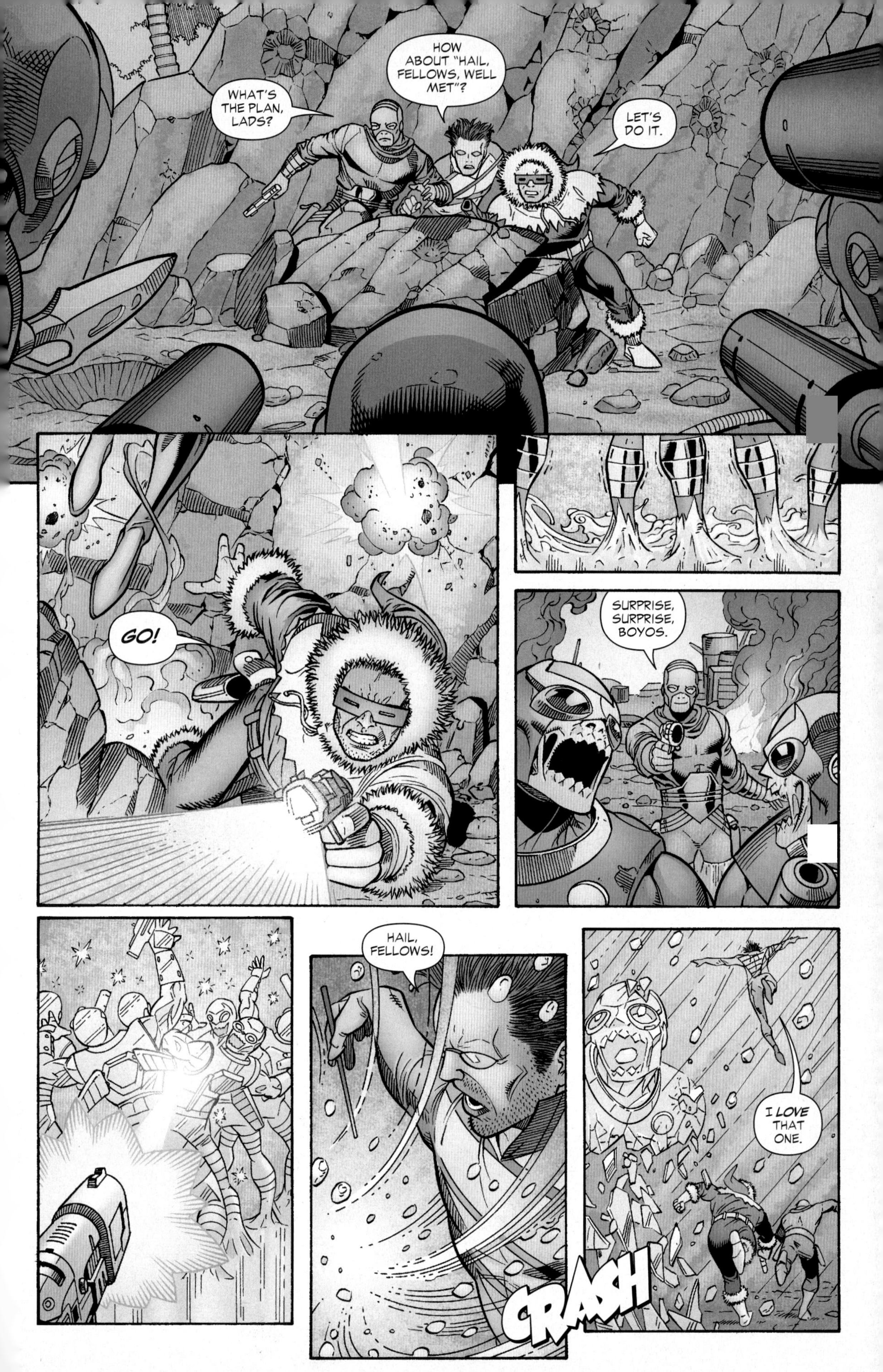
WHAT'S THE PLAN, LADS?
HOW ABOUT "HAIL, FELLOWS, WELL MET"?
LET'S DO IT.
GO!
SURPRISE, SURPRISE, BOYOS.
HAIL, FELLOWS!
I LOVE THAT ONE.
CRASH

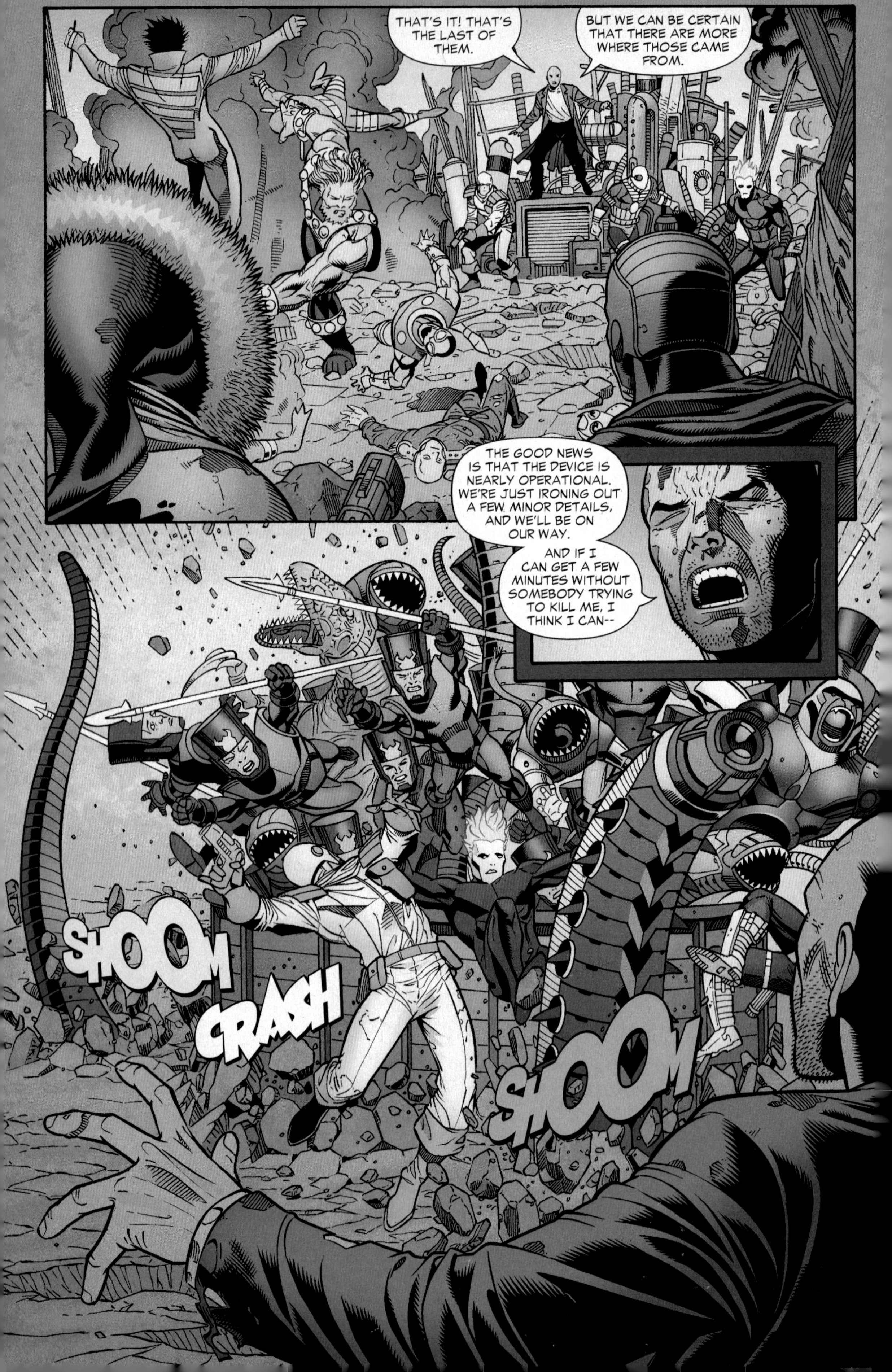
THAT'S IT! THAT'S THE LAST OF THEM.
BUT WE CAN BE CERTAIN THAT THERE ARE MORE WHERE THOSE CAME FROM.
THE GOOD NEWS IS THAT THE DEVICE IS NEARLY OPERATIONAL. WE'RE JUST IRONING OUT A FEW MINOR DETAILS, AND WE'LL BE ON OUR WAY.
AND IF I CAN GET A FEW MINUTES WITHOUT SOMEBODY TRYING TO KILL ME, I THINK I CAN--
SHOOM
CRASH
SHOOM

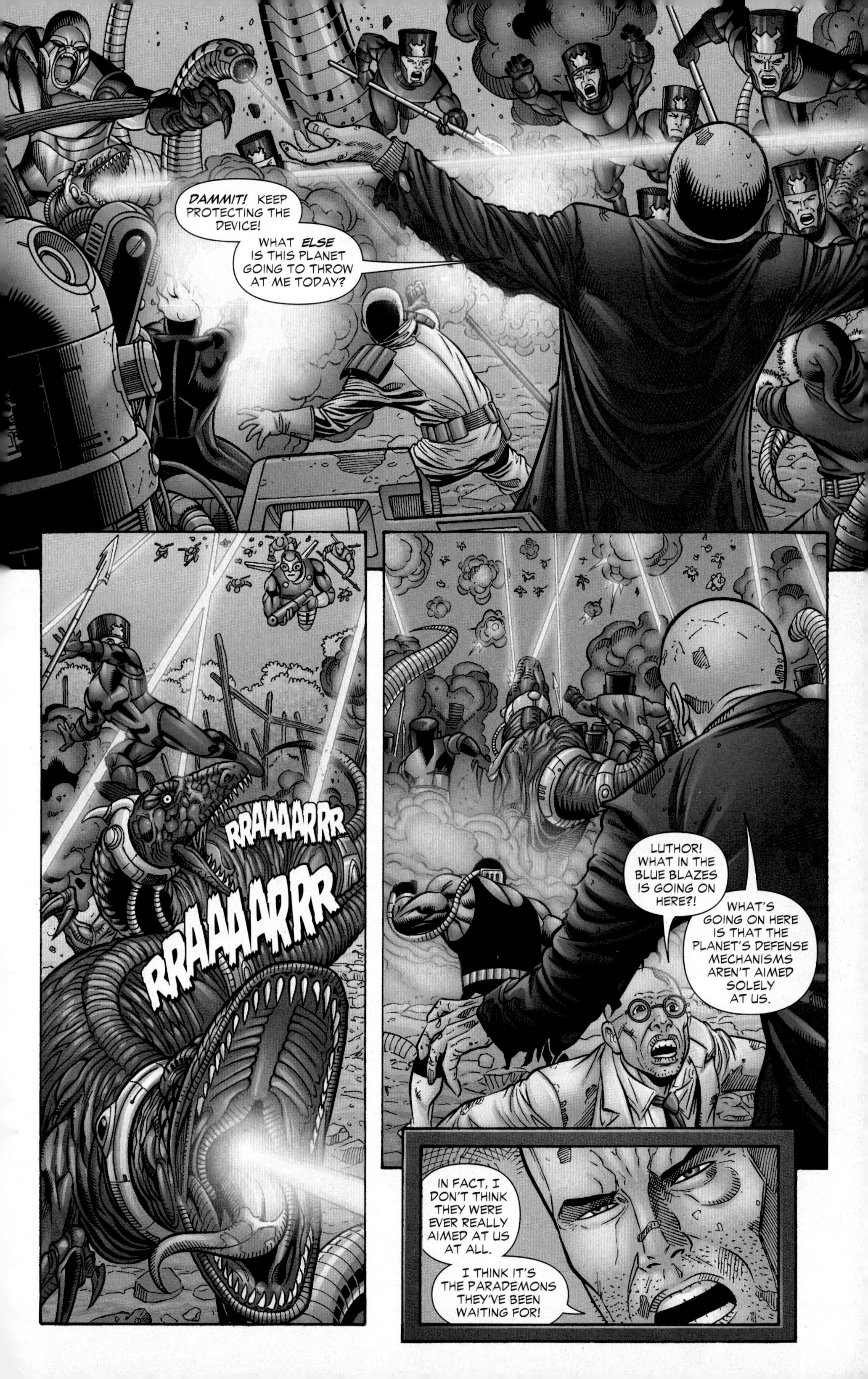

DAMMIT! KEEP PROTECTING THE DEVICE!
WHAT ELSE IS THIS PLANET GOING TO THROW AT ME TODAY?
RRAAAARRR
RRAAAARRR
LUTHOR! WHAT IN THE BLUE BLAZES IS GOING ON HERE?!
WHAT'S GOING ON HERE IS THAT THE PLANET'S DEFENSE MECHANISMS AREN'T AIMED SOLELY AT US.
IN FACT, I DON'T THINK THEY WERE EVER REALLY AIMED AT US AT ALL.
I THINK IT'S THE PARADEMONS THEY'VE BEEN WAITING FOR!

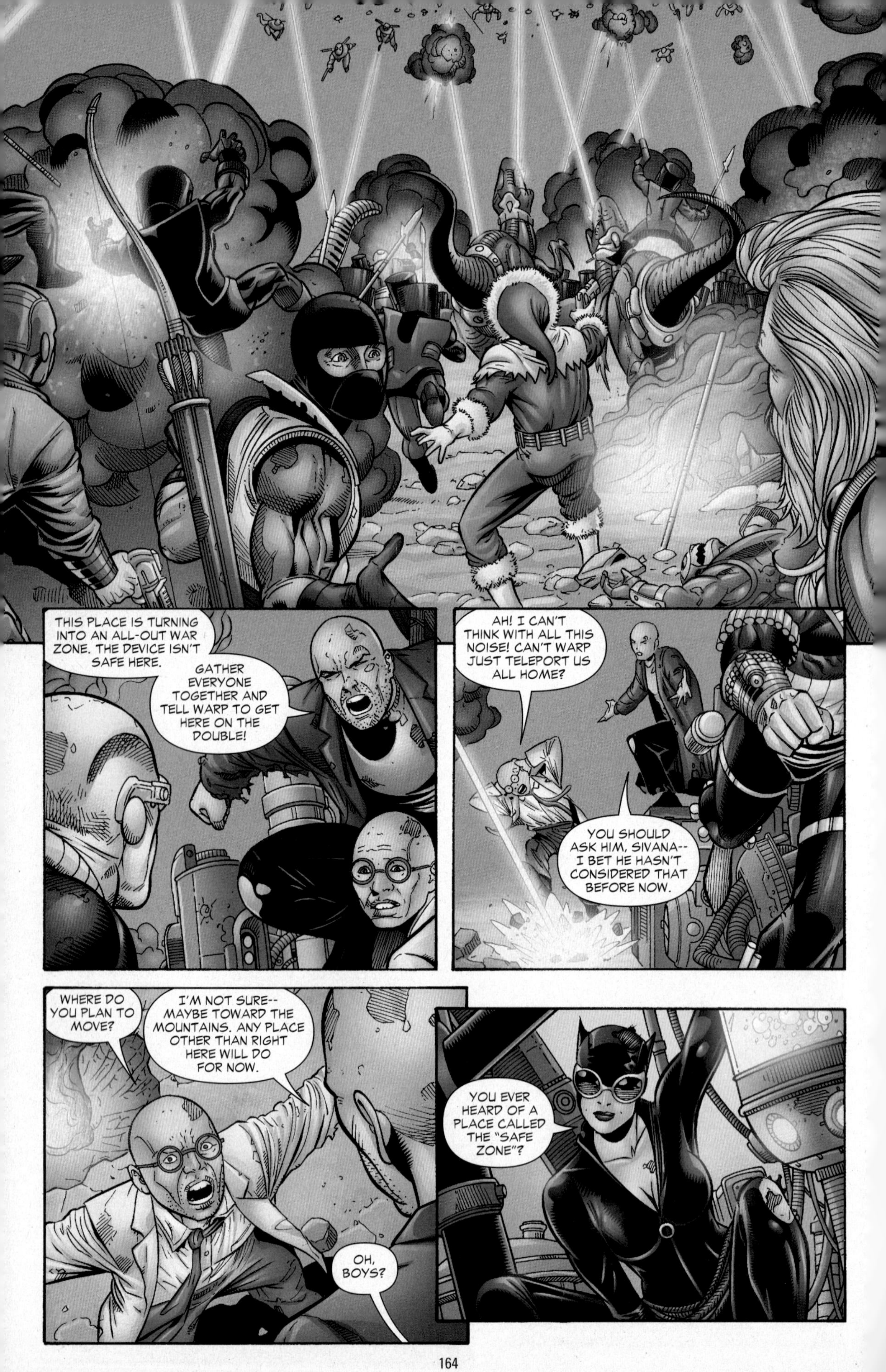
THIS PLACE IS TURNING INTO AN ALL-OUT WAR ZONE. THE DEVICE ISN'T SAFE HERE.
GATHER EVERYONE TOGETHER AND TELL WARP TO GET HERE ON THE DOUBLE!
AH! I CAN'T THINK WITH ALL THIS NOISE! CAN'T WARP JUST TELEPORT US ALL HOME?
YOU SHOULD ASK HIM, SIVANA-- I BET HE HASN'T CONSIDERED THAT BEFORE NOW.
WHERE DO YOU PLAN TO MOVE?
I'M NOT SURE-- MAYBE TOWARD THE MOUNTAINS. ANY PLACE OTHER THAN RIGHT HERE WILL DO FOR NOW.
OH, BOYS?
YOU EVER HEARD OF A PLACE CALLED THE "SAFE ZONE"?

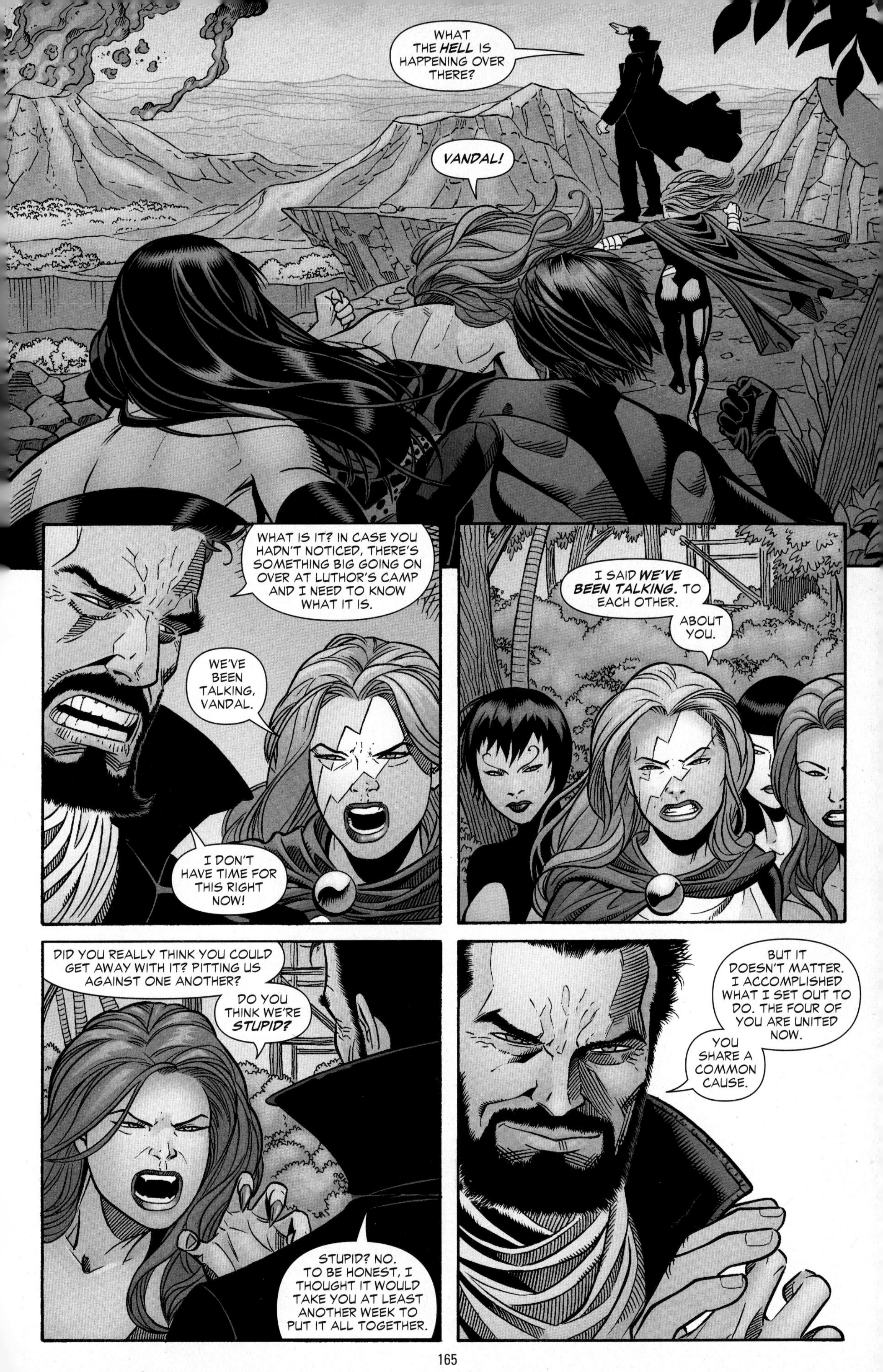

WHAT THE *HELL* IS HAPPENING OVER THERE?
VANDAL!
WHAT IS IT? IN CASE YOU HADN'T NOTICED, THERE'S SOMETHING BIG GOING ON OVER AT LUTHOR'S CAMP AND I NEED TO KNOW WHAT IT IS.
WE'VE BEEN TALKING, VANDAL.
I DON'T HAVE TIME FOR THIS RIGHT NOW!
I SAID *WE'VE BEEN TALKING.* TO EACH OTHER.
ABOUT YOU.
DID YOU REALLY THINK YOU COULD GET AWAY WITH IT? PITTING US AGAINST ONE ANOTHER?
DO YOU THINK WE'RE *STUPID?*
STUPID? NO. TO BE HONEST, I THOUGHT IT WOULD TAKE YOU AT LEAST ANOTHER WEEK TO PUT IT ALL TOGETHER.
BUT IT DOESN'T MATTER. I ACCOMPLISHED WHAT I SET OUT TO DO. THE FOUR OF YOU ARE UNITED NOW.
YOU SHARE A COMMON CAUSE.

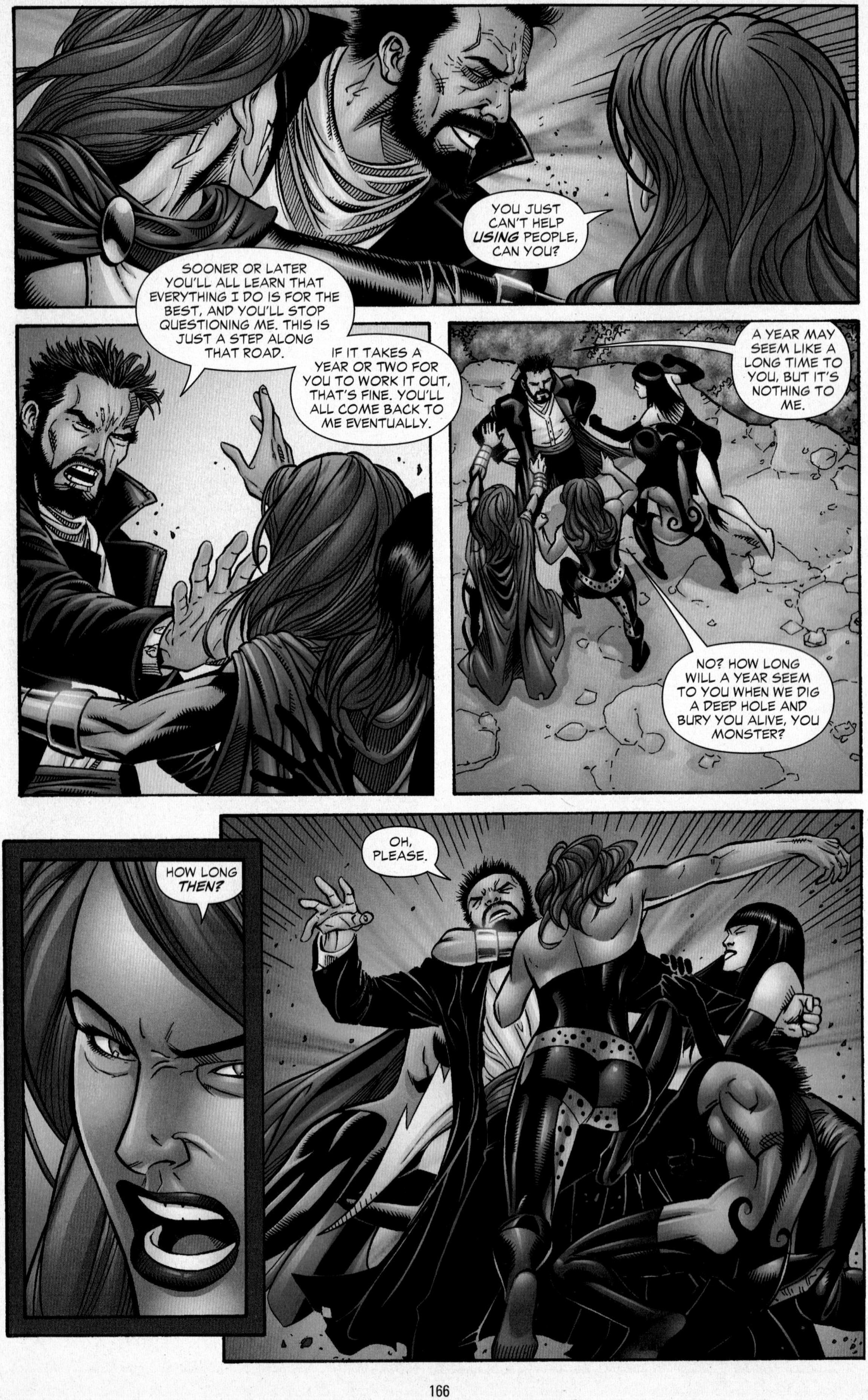
YOU JUST CAN'T HELP USING PEOPLE, CAN YOU?
SOONER OR LATER YOU'LL ALL LEARN THAT EVERYTHING I DO IS FOR THE BEST, AND YOU'LL STOP QUESTIONING ME. THIS IS JUST A STEP ALONG THAT ROAD.
IF IT TAKES A YEAR OR TWO FOR YOU TO WORK IT OUT, THAT'S FINE. YOU'LL ALL COME BACK TO ME EVENTUALLY.
A YEAR MAY SEEM LIKE A LONG TIME TO YOU, BUT IT'S NOTHING TO ME.
NO? HOW LONG WILL A YEAR SEEM TO YOU WHEN WE DIG A DEEP HOLE AND BURY YOU ALIVE, YOU MONSTER?
HOW LONG THEN?
OH, PLEASE.

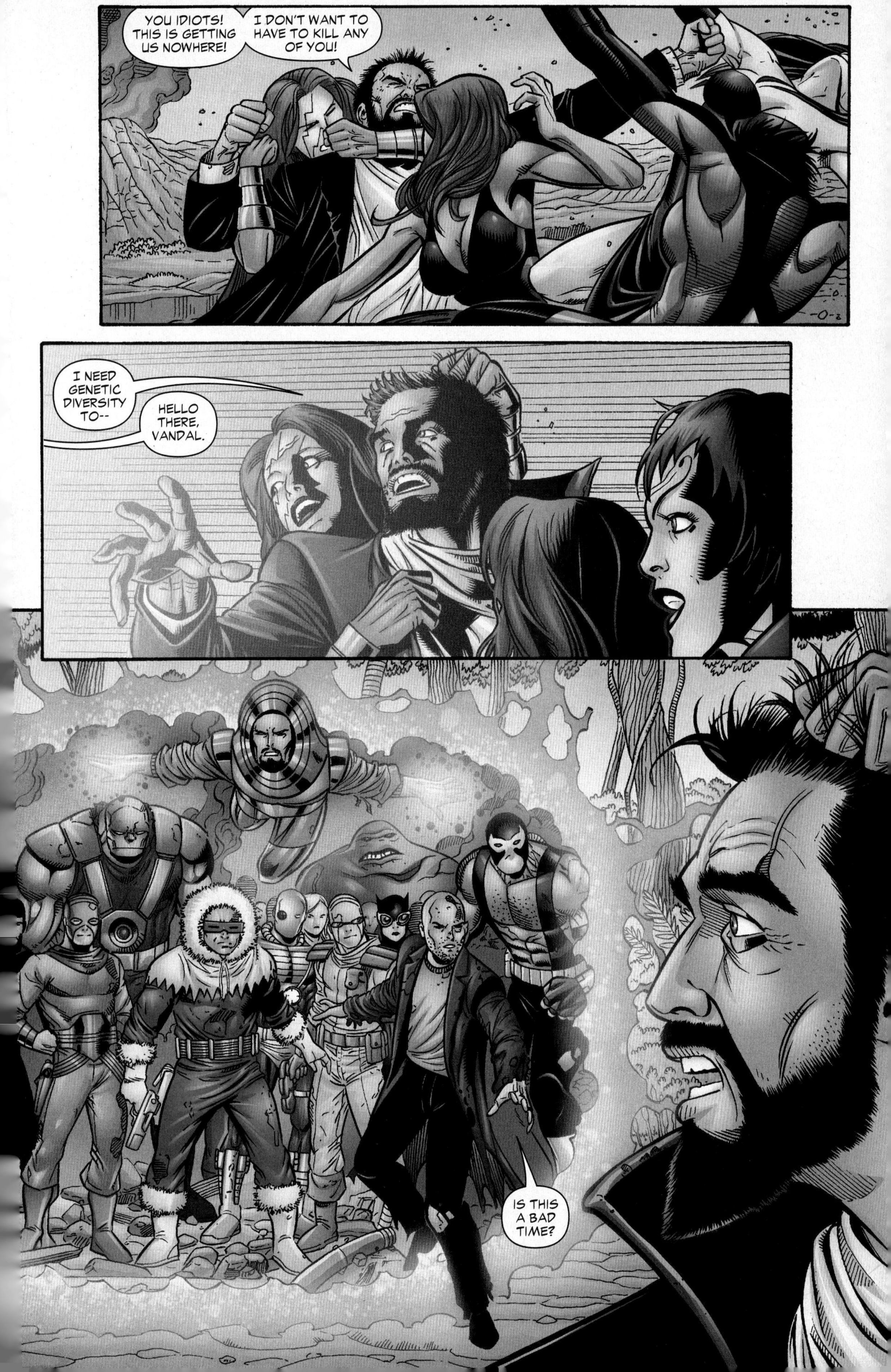
YOU IDIOTS! THIS IS GETTING US NOWHERE!
I DON'T WANT TO HAVE TO KILL ANY OF YOU!
I NEED GENETIC DIVERSITY TO--
HELLO THERE, VANDAL.
IS THIS A BAD TIME?

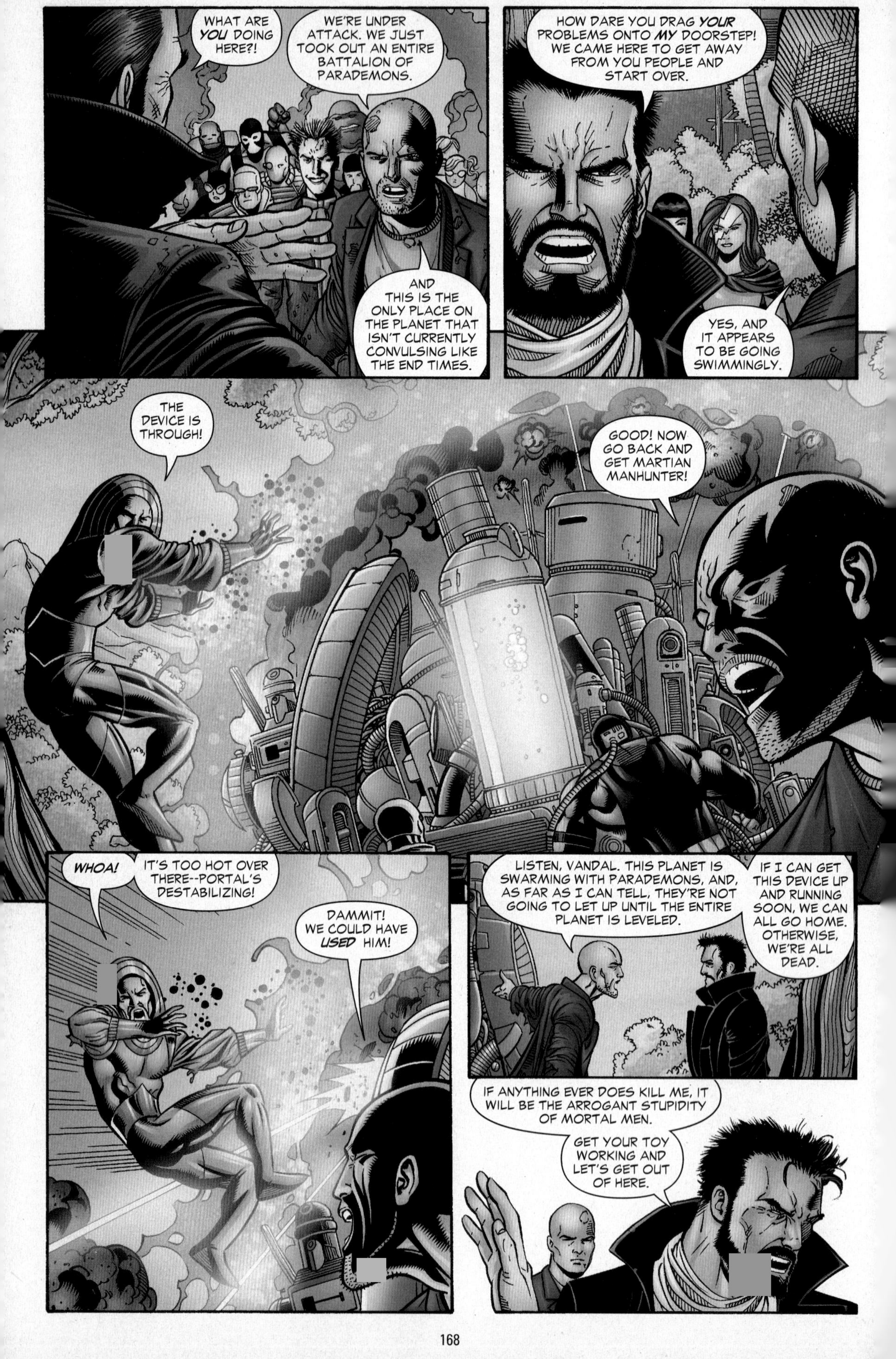
WHAT ARE *YOU* DOING HERE?!
WE'RE UNDER ATTACK. WE JUST TOOK OUT AN ENTIRE BATTALION OF PARADEMONS.
AND THIS IS THE ONLY PLACE ON THE PLANET THAT ISN'T CURRENTLY CONVULSING LIKE THE END TIMES.
HOW DARE YOU DRAG *YOUR* PROBLEMS ONTO *MY* DOORSTEP! WE CAME HERE TO GET AWAY FROM YOU PEOPLE AND START OVER.
YES, AND IT APPEARS TO BE GOING SWIMMINGLY.
THE DEVICE IS THROUGH!
GOOD! NOW GO BACK AND GET MARTIAN MANHUNTER!
WHOA!
IT'S TOO HOT OVER THERE--PORTAL'S DESTABILIZING!
DAMMIT! WE COULD HAVE *USED* HIM!
LISTEN, VANDAL. THIS PLANET IS SWARMING WITH PARADEMONS, AND, AS FAR AS I CAN TELL, THEY'RE NOT GOING TO LET UP UNTIL THE ENTIRE PLANET IS LEVELED.
IF I CAN GET THIS DEVICE UP AND RUNNING SOON, WE CAN ALL GO HOME. OTHERWISE, WE'RE ALL DEAD.
IF ANYTHING EVER DOES KILL ME, IT WILL BE THE ARROGANT STUPIDITY OF MORTAL MEN.
GET YOUR TOY WORKING AND LET'S GET OUT OF HERE.

"THEY'RE GOING TO COME LOOKING FOR YOU."

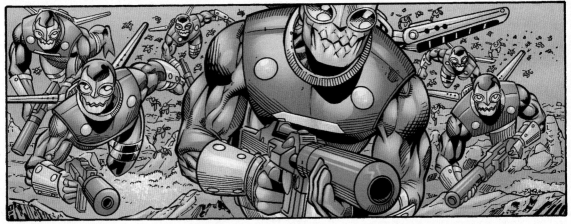

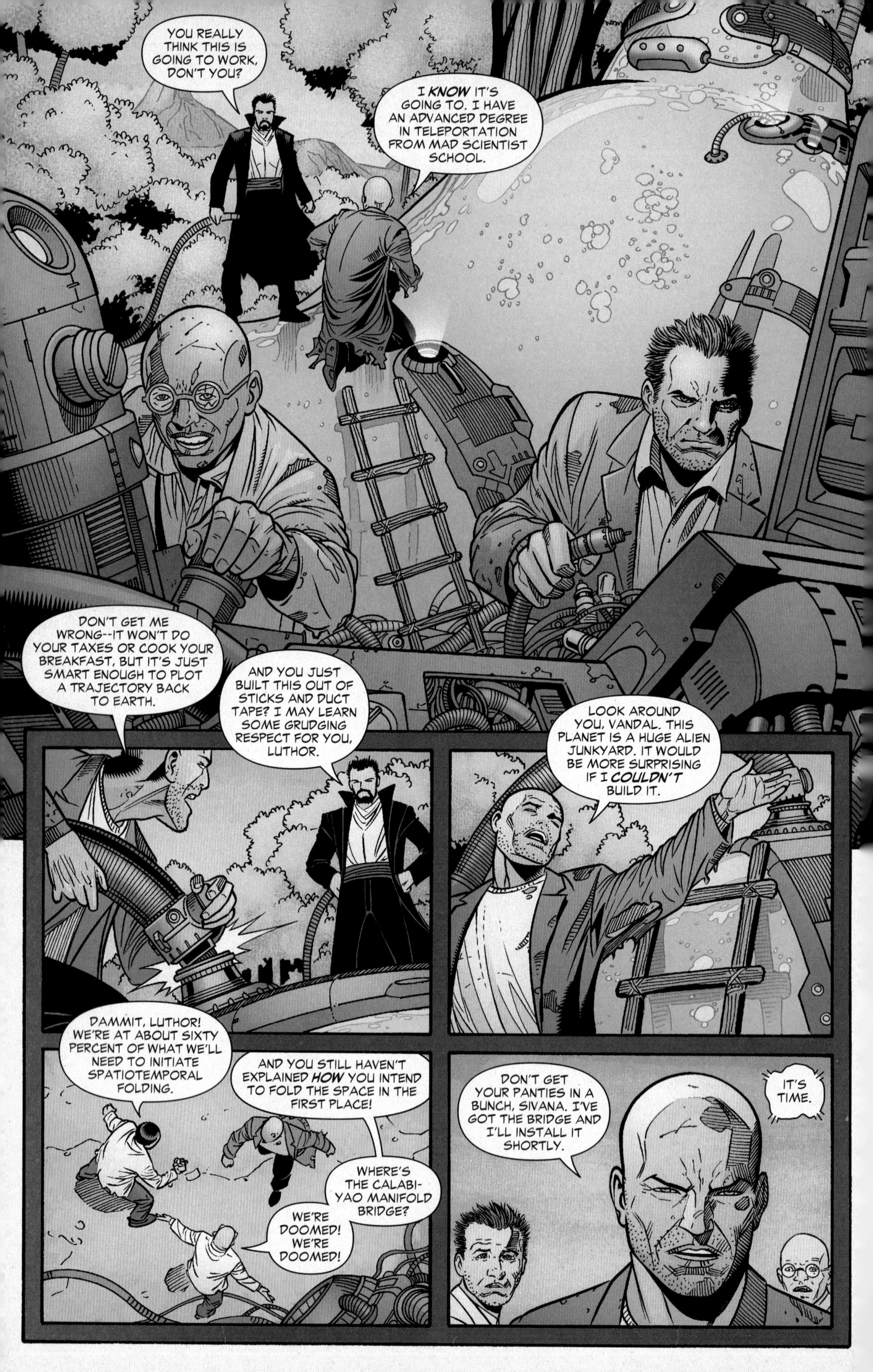
YOU REALLY THINK THIS IS GOING TO WORK, DON'T YOU?
I KNOW IT'S GOING TO. I HAVE AN ADVANCED DEGREE IN TELEPORTATION FROM MAD SCIENTIST SCHOOL.
DON'T GET ME WRONG--IT WON'T DO YOUR TAXES OR COOK YOUR BREAKFAST, BUT IT'S JUST SMART ENOUGH TO PLOT A TRAJECTORY BACK TO EARTH.
AND YOU JUST BUILT THIS OUT OF STICKS AND DUCT TAPE? I MAY LEARN SOME GRUDGING RESPECT FOR YOU, LUTHOR.
LOOK AROUND YOU, VANDAL. THIS PLANET IS A HUGE ALIEN JUNKYARD. IT WOULD BE MORE SURPRISING IF I COULDN'T BUILD IT.
DAMMIT, LUTHOR! WE'RE AT ABOUT SIXTY PERCENT OF WHAT WE'LL NEED TO INITIATE SPATIOTEMPORAL FOLDING.
AND YOU STILL HAVEN'T EXPLAINED HOW YOU INTEND TO FOLD THE SPACE IN THE FIRST PLACE!
WHERE'S THE CALABI-YAO MANIFOLD BRIDGE?
WE'RE DOOMED! WE'RE DOOMED!
DON'T GET YOUR PANTIES IN A BUNCH, SIVANA. I'VE GOT THE BRIDGE AND I'LL INSTALL IT SHORTLY.
IT'S TIME.

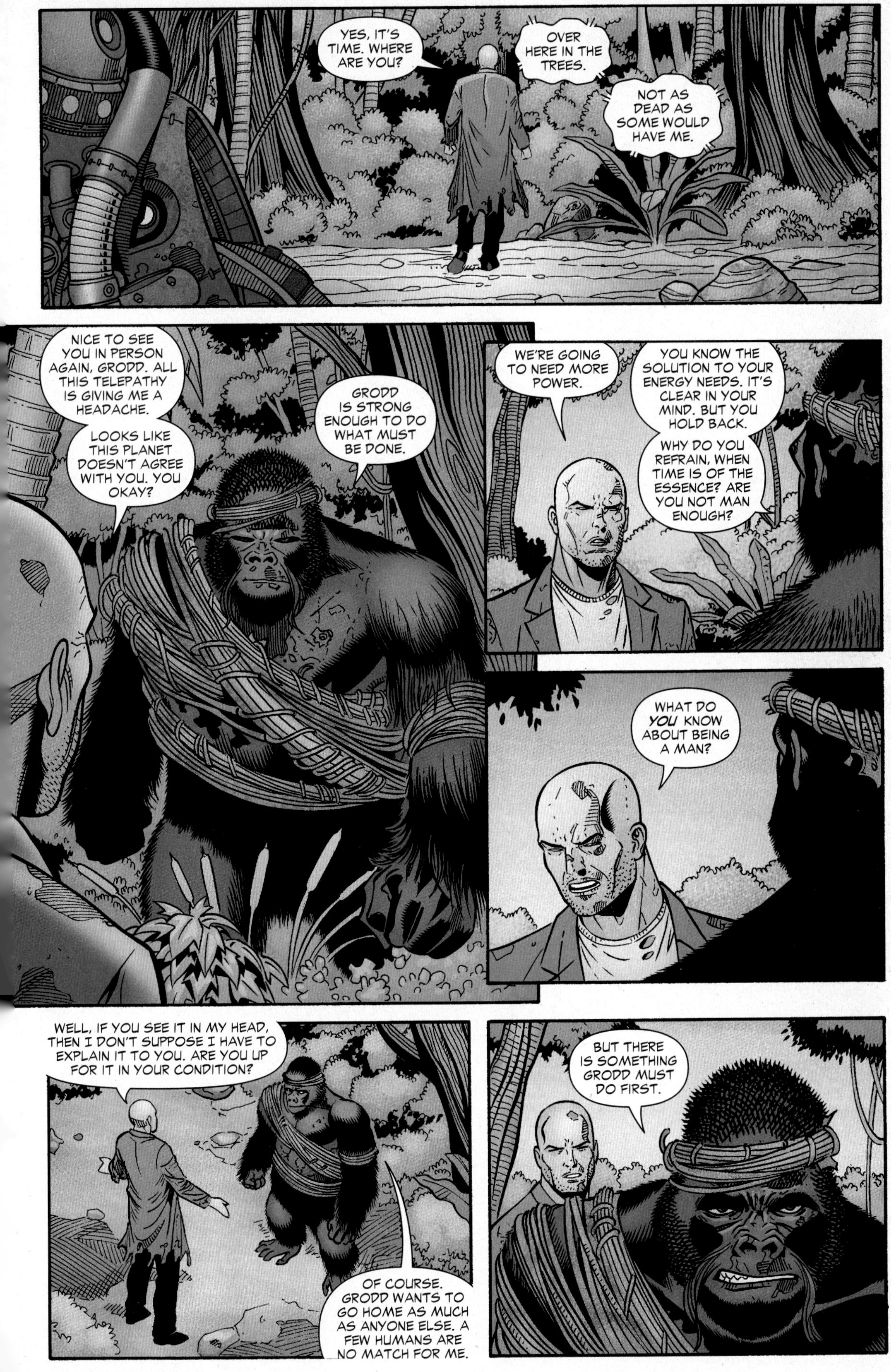
YES, IT'S TIME. WHERE ARE YOU?
OVER HERE IN THE TREES.
NOT AS DEAD AS SOME WOULD HAVE ME.
NICE TO SEE YOU IN PERSON AGAIN, GRODD. ALL THIS TELEPATHY IS GIVING ME A HEADACHE.
LOOKS LIKE THIS PLANET DOESN'T AGREE WITH YOU. YOU OKAY?
GRODD IS STRONG ENOUGH TO DO WHAT MUST BE DONE.
WE'RE GOING TO NEED MORE POWER.
YOU KNOW THE SOLUTION TO YOUR ENERGY NEEDS. IT'S CLEAR IN YOUR MIND. BUT YOU HOLD BACK.
WHY DO YOU REFRAIN, WHEN TIME IS OF THE ESSENCE? ARE YOU NOT MAN ENOUGH?
WHAT DO YOU KNOW ABOUT BEING A MAN?
WELL, IF YOU SEE IT IN MY HEAD, THEN I DON'T SUPPOSE I HAVE TO EXPLAIN IT TO YOU. ARE YOU UP FOR IT IN YOUR CONDITION?
OF COURSE. GRODD WANTS TO GO HOME AS MUCH AS ANYONE ELSE. A FEW HUMANS ARE NO MATCH FOR ME.
BUT THERE IS SOMETHING GRODD MUST DO FIRST.

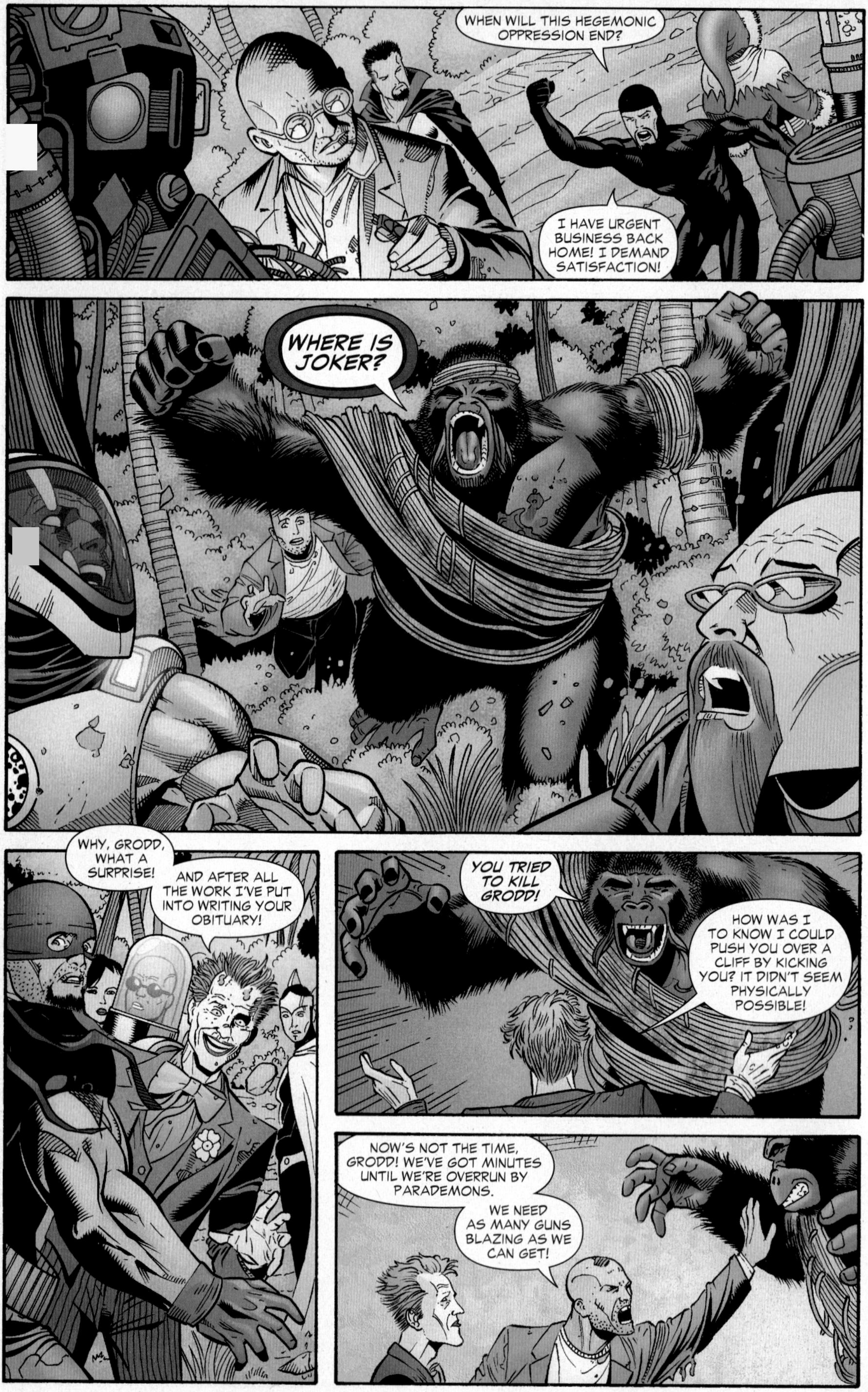
WHEN WILL THIS HEGEMONIC OPPRESSION END?
I HAVE URGENT BUSINESS BACK HOME! I DEMAND SATISFACTION!
WHERE IS JOKER?
WHY, GRODD, WHAT A SURPRISE!
AND AFTER ALL THE WORK I'VE PUT INTO WRITING YOUR OBITUARY!
YOU TRIED TO KILL GRODD!
HOW WAS I TO KNOW I COULD PUSH YOU OVER A CLIFF BY KICKING YOU? IT DIDN'T SEEM PHYSICALLY POSSIBLE!
NOW'S NOT THE TIME, GRODD! WE'VE GOT MINUTES UNTIL WE'RE OVERRUN BY PARADEMONS.
WE NEED AS MANY GUNS BLAZING AS WE CAN GET!

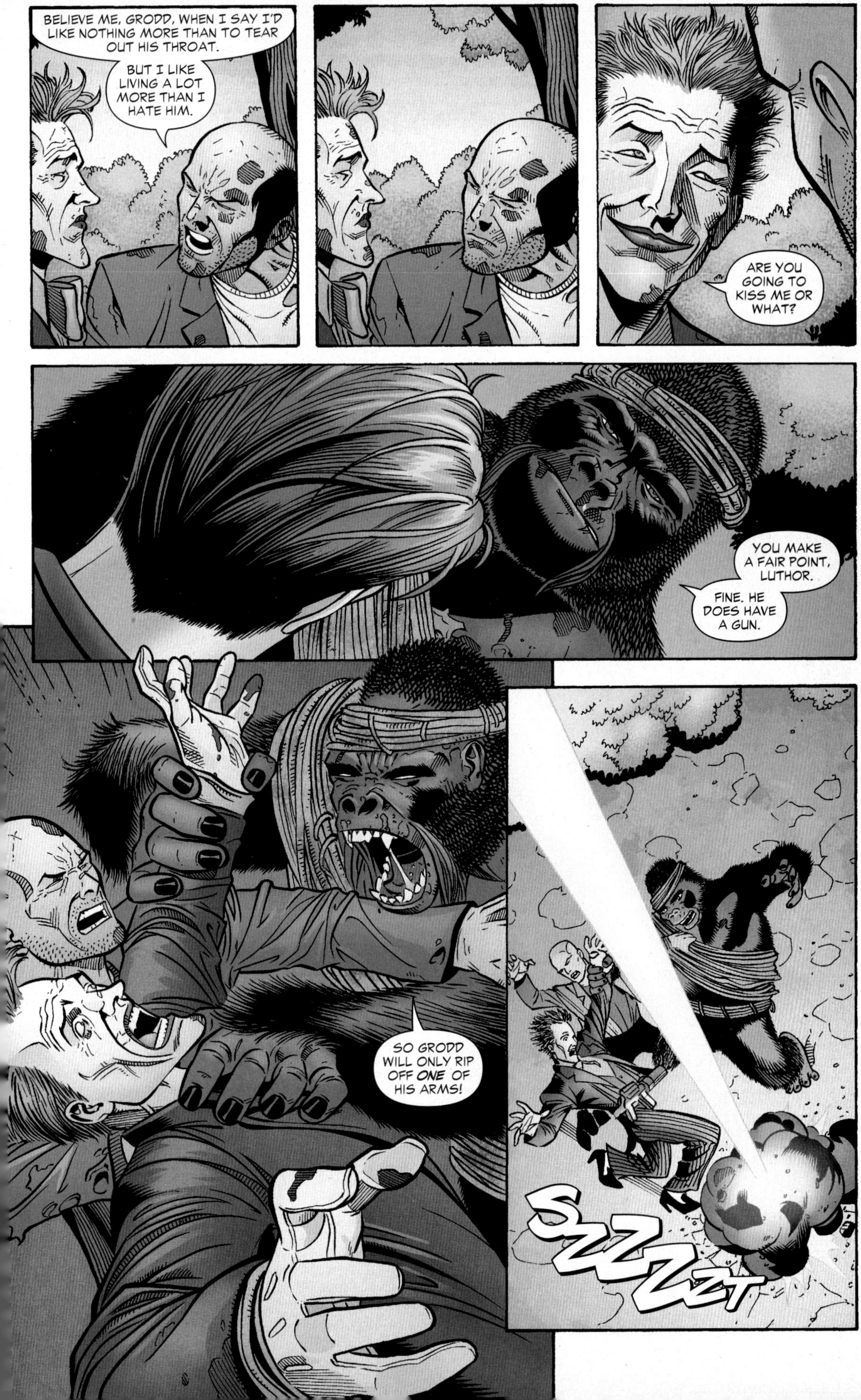
BELIEVE ME, GRODD, WHEN I SAY I'D LIKE NOTHING MORE THAN TO TEAR OUT HIS THROAT.
BUT I LIKE LIVING A LOT MORE THAN I HATE HIM.
ARE YOU GOING TO KISS ME OR WHAT?
YOU MAKE A FAIR POINT, LUTHOR.
FINE. HE DOES HAVE A GUN.
SO GRODD WILL ONLY RIP OFF ONE OF HIS ARMS!
SZZZZT

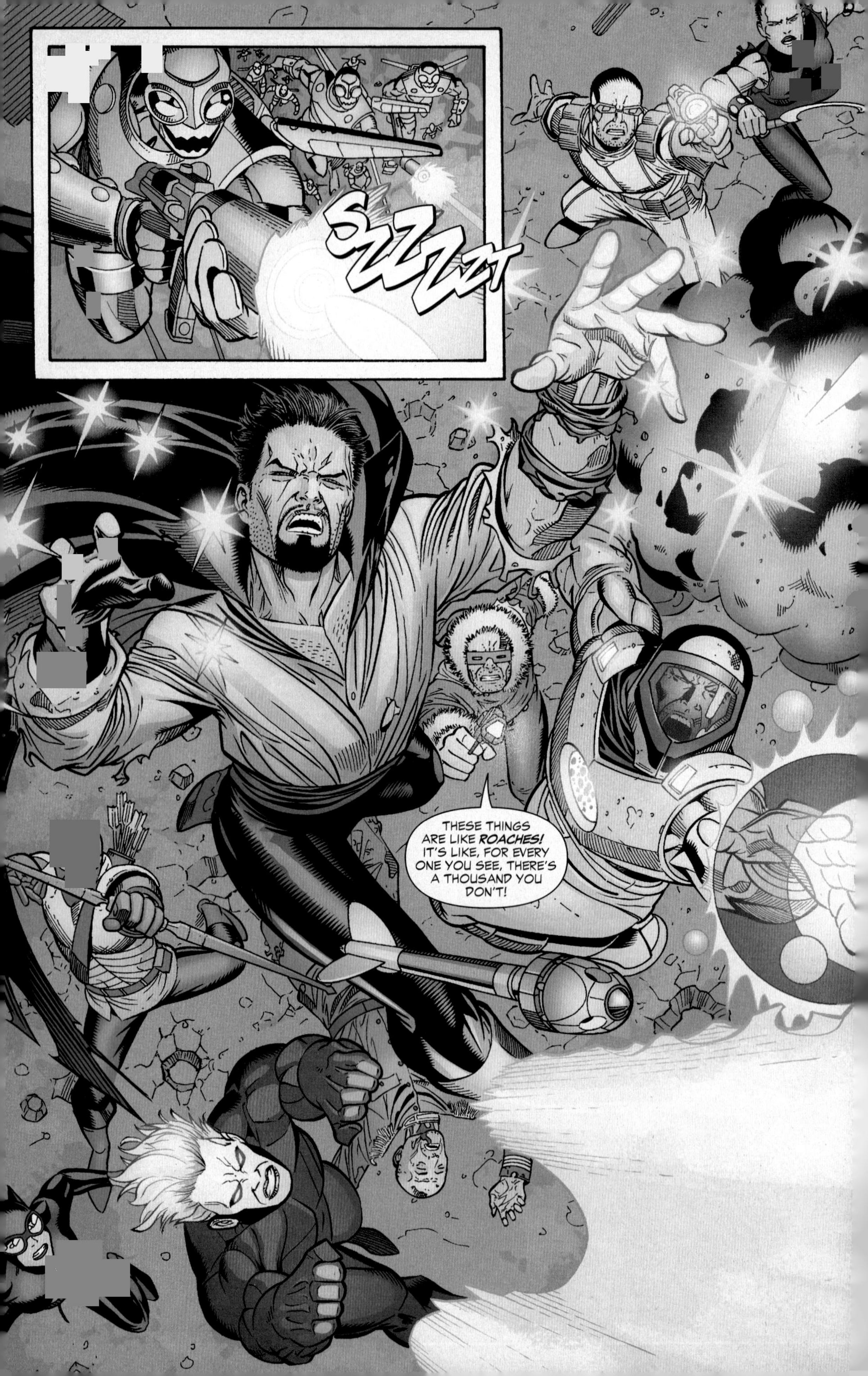
SZZZZT
THESE THINGS ARE LIKE ROACHES! IT'S LIKE, FOR EVERY ONE YOU SEE, THERE'S A THOUSAND YOU DON'T!

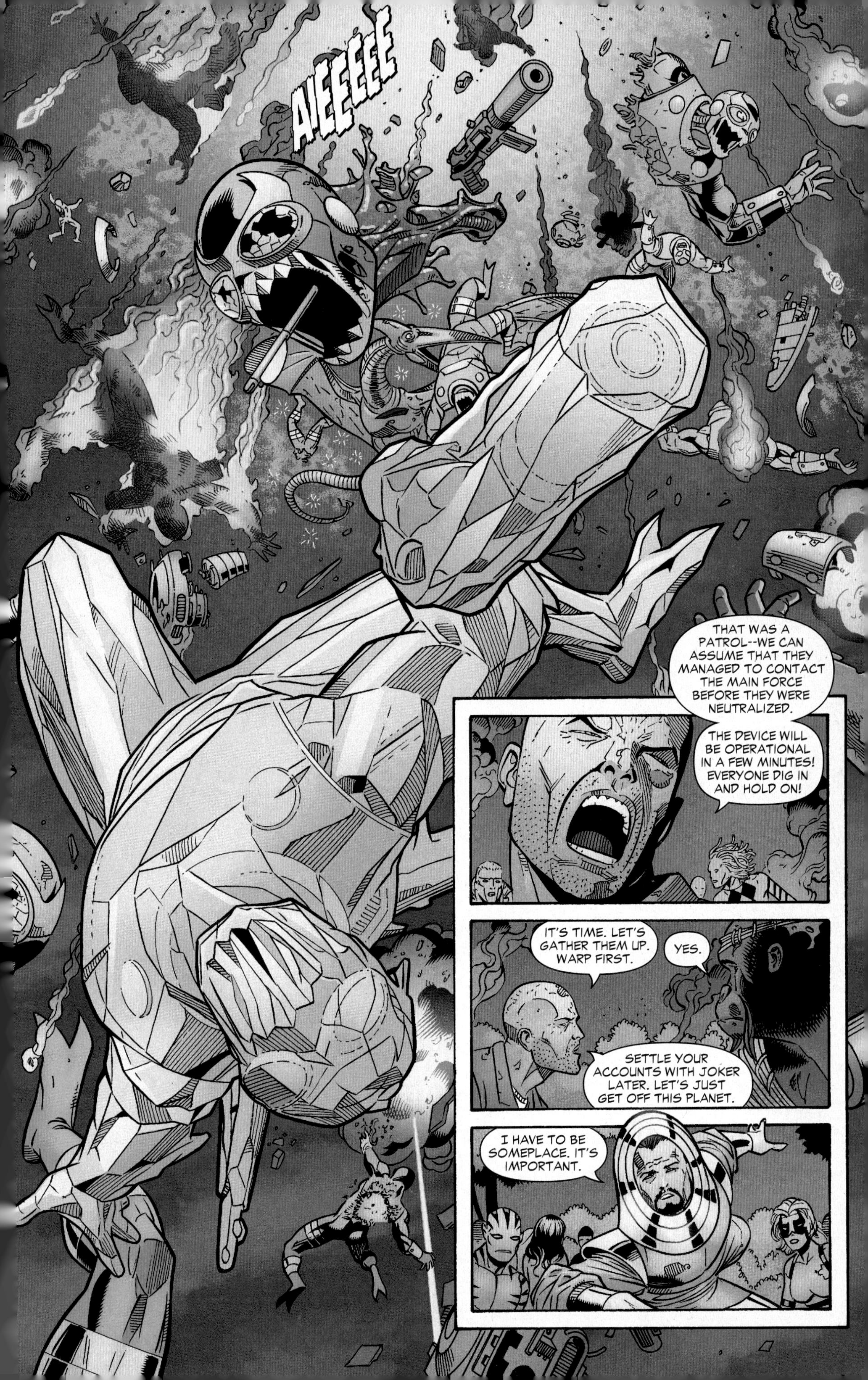
AIEEEEE
THAT WAS A PATROL--WE CAN ASSUME THAT THEY MANAGED TO CONTACT THE MAIN FORCE BEFORE THEY WERE NEUTRALIZED.
THE DEVICE WILL BE OPERATIONAL IN A FEW MINUTES! EVERYONE DIG IN AND HOLD ON!
IT'S TIME. LET'S GATHER THEM UP. WARP FIRST.
YES.
SETTLE YOUR ACCOUNTS WITH JOKER LATER. LET'S JUST GET OFF THIS PLANET.
I HAVE TO BE SOMEPLACE. IT'S IMPORTANT.

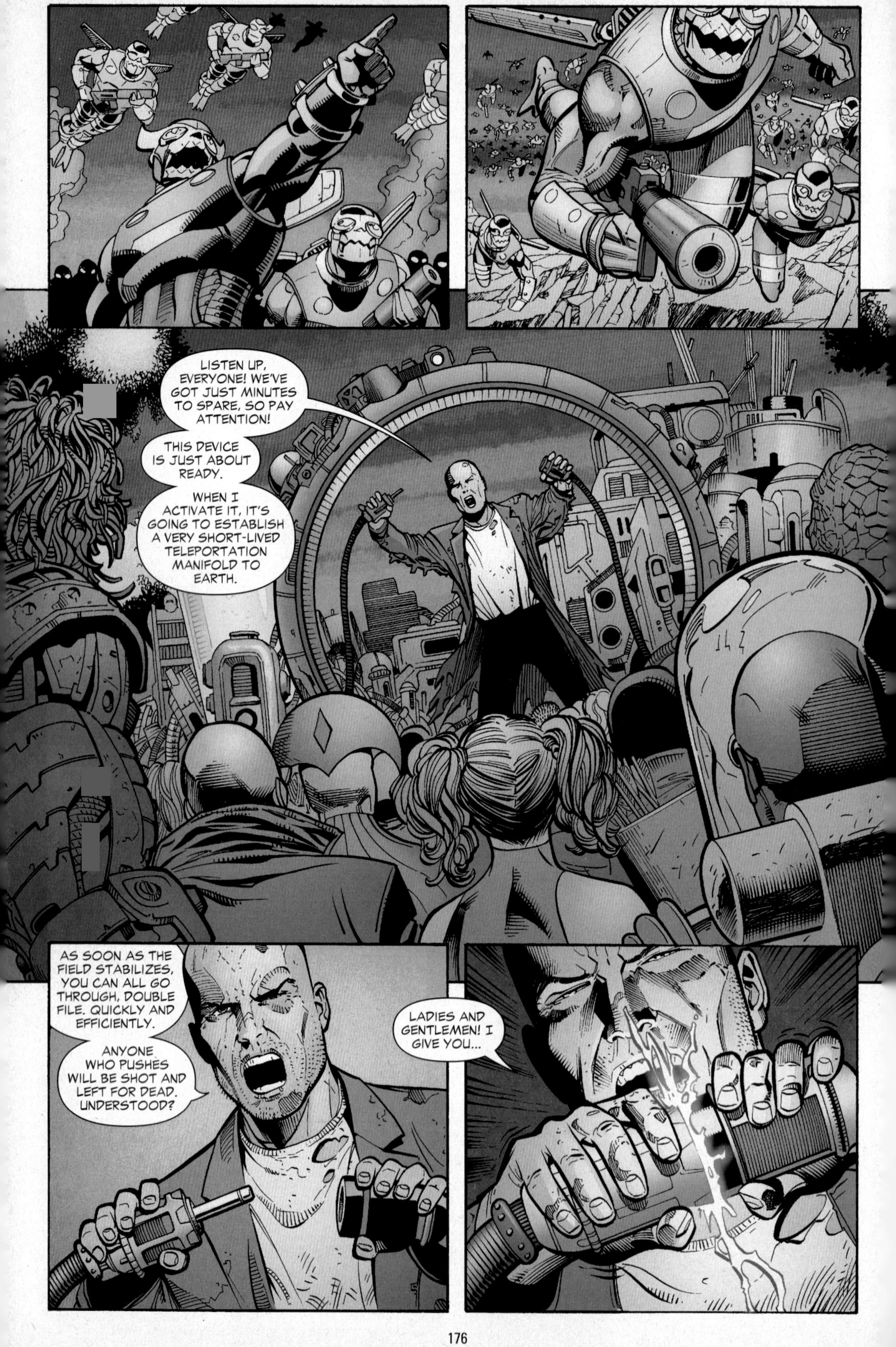
LISTEN UP, EVERYONE! WE'VE GOT JUST MINUTES TO SPARE, SO PAY ATTENTION!
THIS DEVICE IS JUST ABOUT READY.
WHEN I ACTIVATE IT, IT'S GOING TO ESTABLISH A VERY SHORT-LIVED TELEPORTATION MANIFOLD TO EARTH.
AS SOON AS THE FIELD STABILIZES, YOU CAN ALL GO THROUGH, DOUBLE FILE. QUICKLY AND EFFICIENTLY.
ANYONE WHO PUSHES WILL BE SHOT AND LEFT FOR DEAD. UNDERSTOOD?
LADIES AND GENTLEMEN! I GIVE YOU...

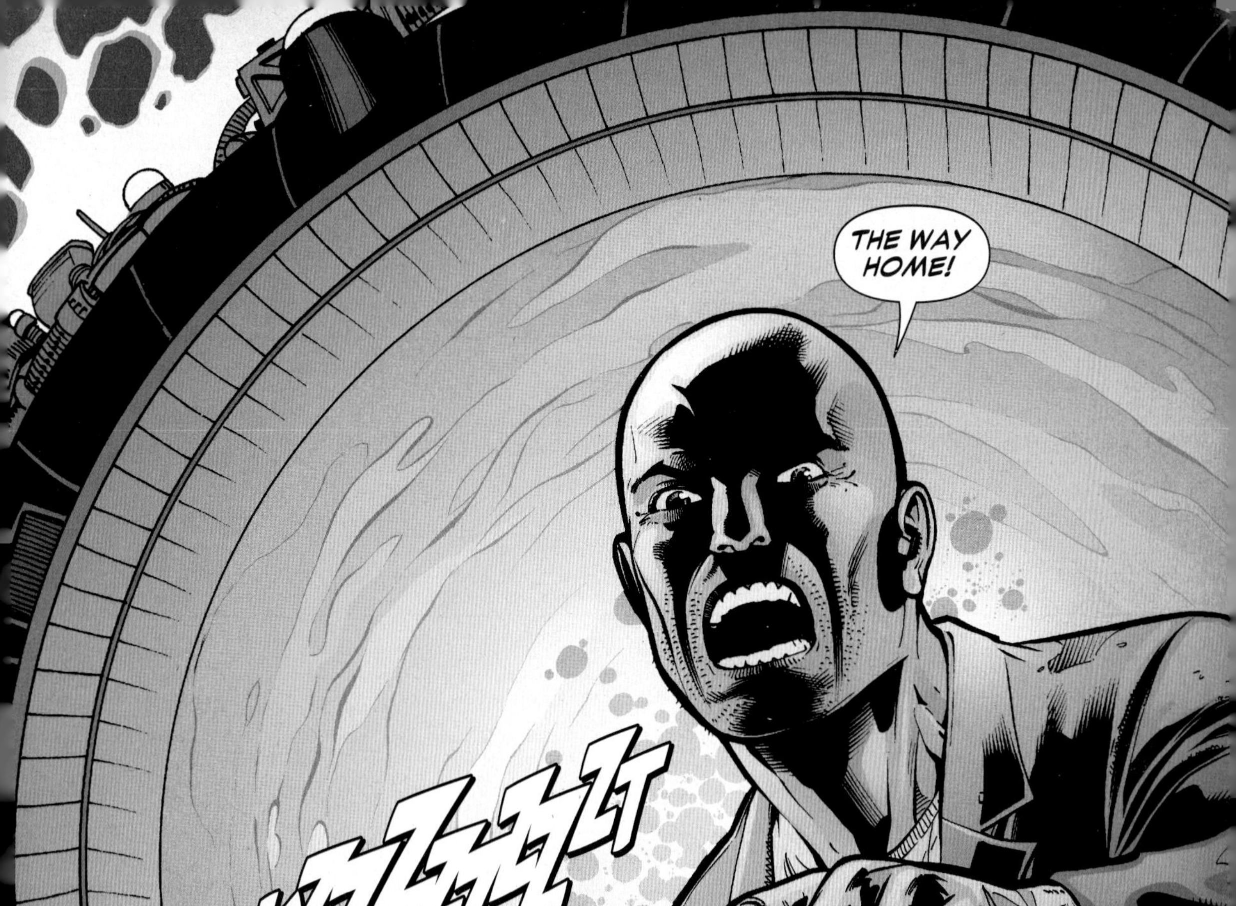
THE WAY HOME!
KZZZZZZZT

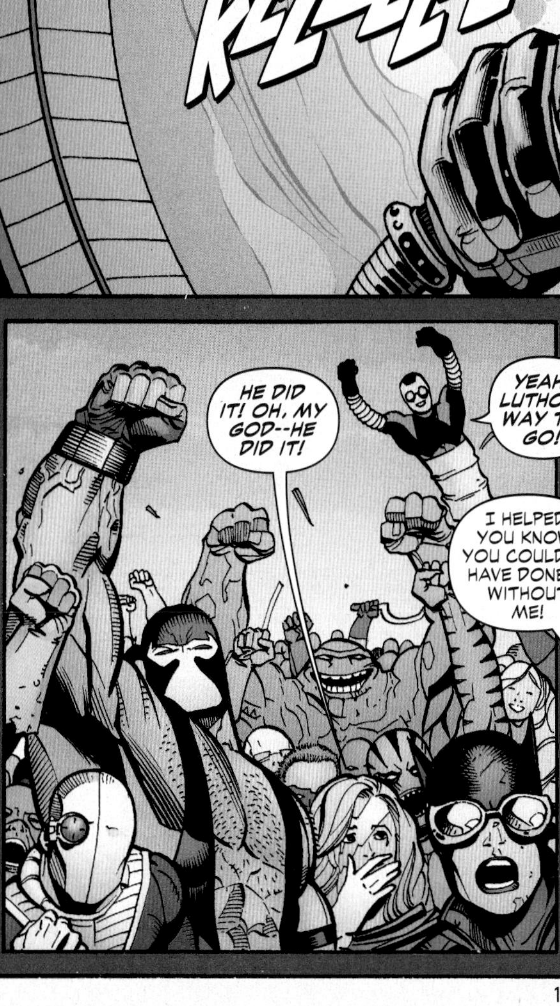
HE DID IT! OH, MY GOD--HE DID IT!
YEAH, LUTHOR! WAY TO GO!
I HELPED, YOU KNOW! YOU COULDN'T HAVE DONE IT WITHOUT ME!

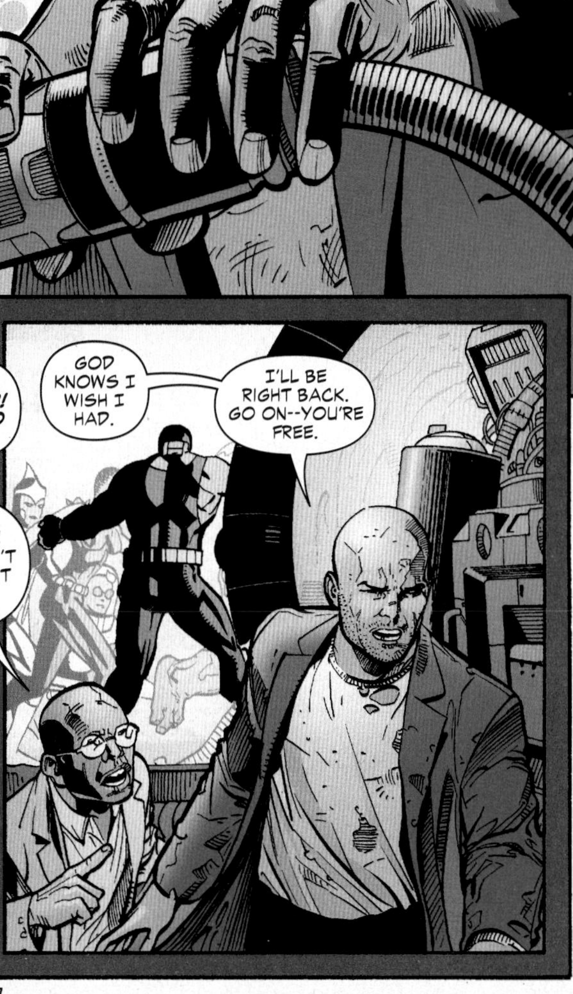
GOD KNOWS I WISH I HAD.
I'LL BE RIGHT BACK. GO ON--YOU'RE FREE.

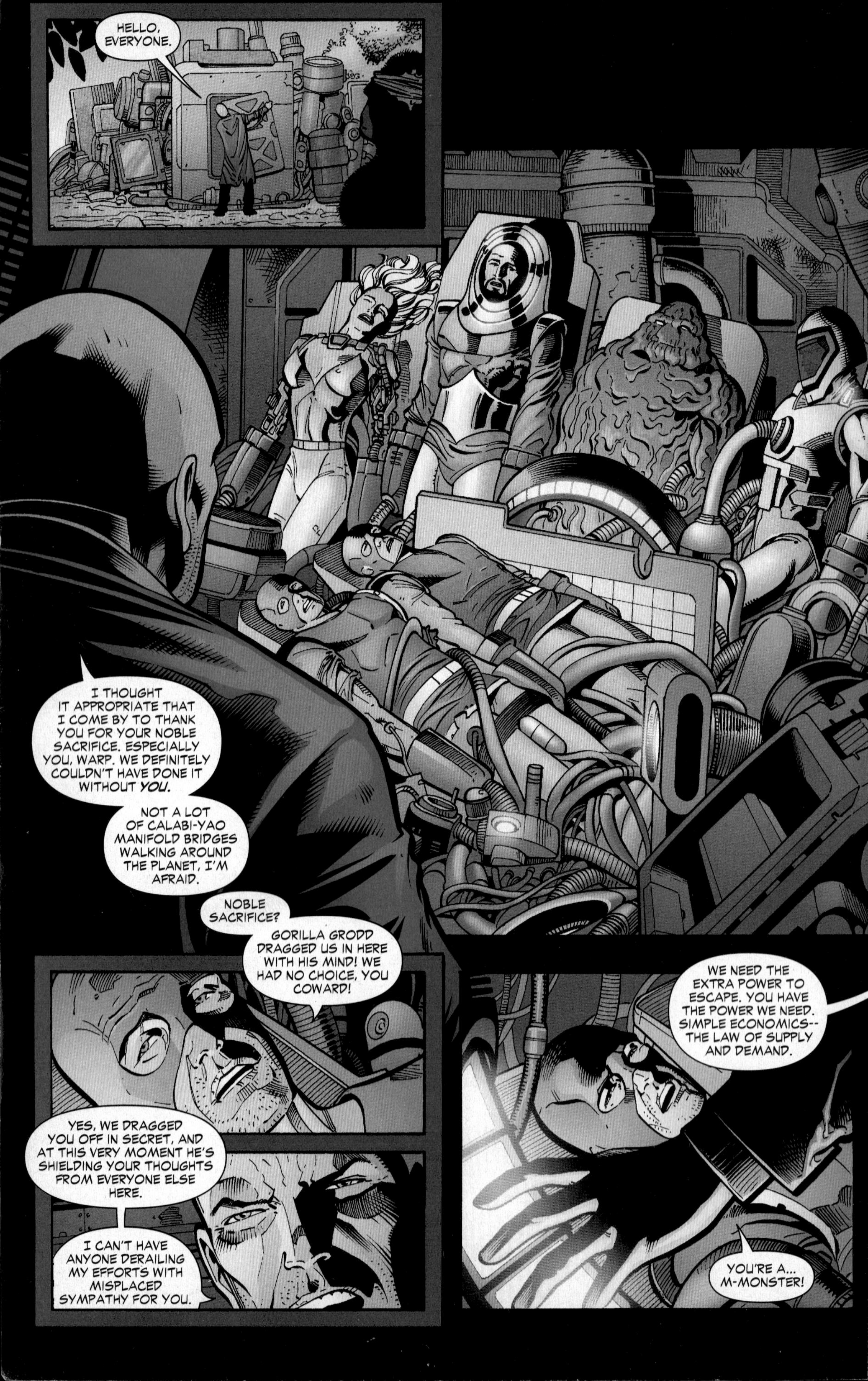
HELLO, EVERYONE.
I THOUGHT IT APPROPRIATE THAT I COME BY TO THANK YOU FOR YOUR NOBLE SACRIFICE. ESPECIALLY YOU, WARP. WE DEFINITELY COULDN'T HAVE DONE IT WITHOUT *YOU*.
NOT A LOT OF CALABI-YAO MANIFOLD BRIDGES WALKING AROUND THE PLANET, I'M AFRAID.
NOBLE SACRIFICE?
GORILLA GRODD DRAGGED US IN HERE WITH HIS MIND! WE HAD NO CHOICE, YOU COWARD!
YES, WE DRAGGED YOU OFF IN SECRET, AND AT THIS VERY MOMENT HE'S SHIELDING YOUR THOUGHTS FROM EVERYONE ELSE HERE.
I CAN'T HAVE ANYONE DERAILING MY EFFORTS WITH MISPLACED SYMPATHY FOR YOU.
WE NEED THE EXTRA POWER TO ESCAPE. YOU HAVE THE POWER WE NEED. SIMPLE ECONOMICS-- THE LAW OF SUPPLY AND DEMAND.
YOU'RE A... M-MONSTER!

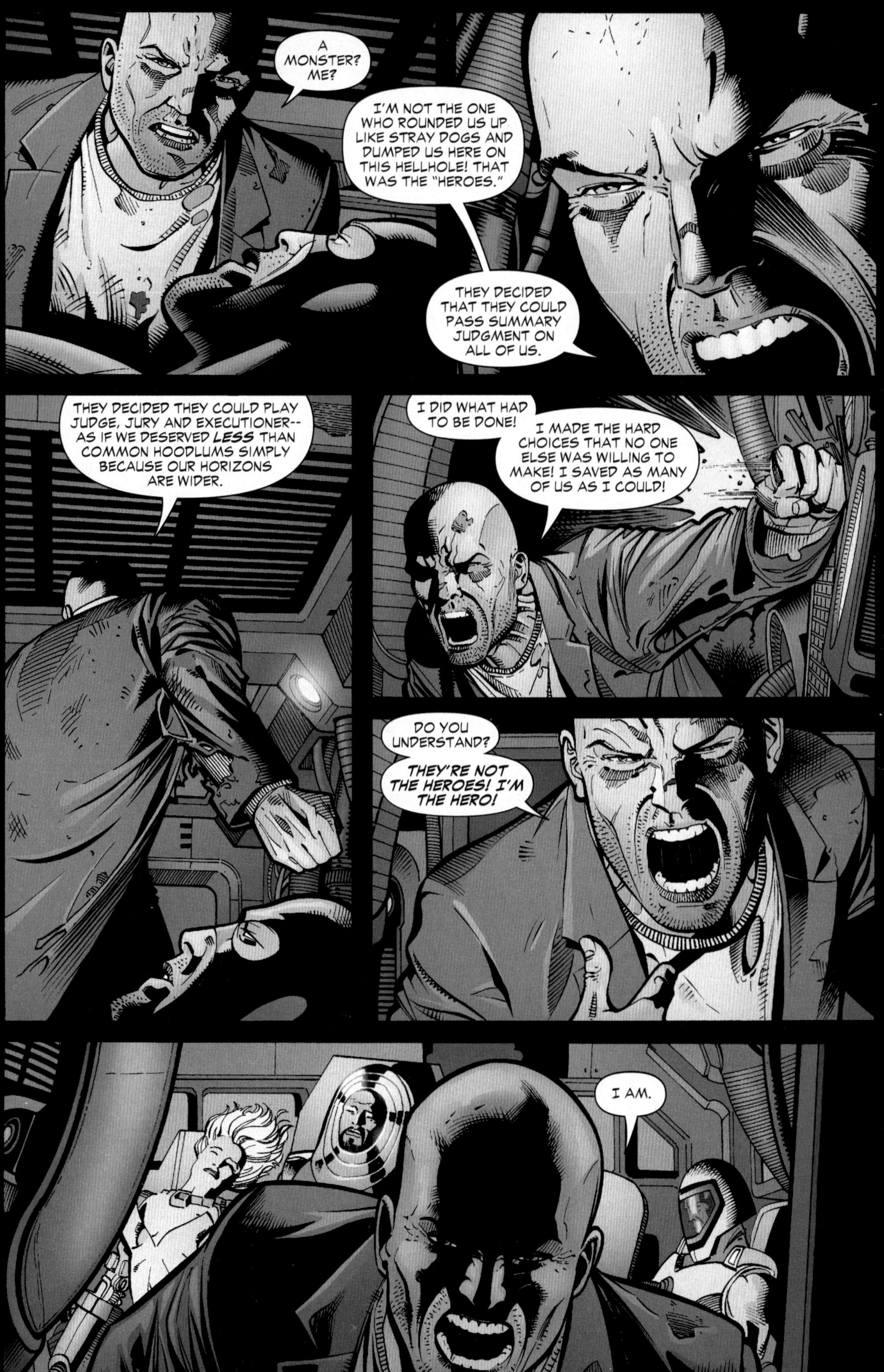
A MONSTER? ME?
I'M NOT THE ONE WHO ROUNDED US UP LIKE STRAY DOGS AND DUMPED US HERE ON THIS HELLHOLE! THAT WAS THE "HEROES."
THEY DECIDED THAT THEY COULD PASS SUMMARY JUDGMENT ON ALL OF US.
THEY DECIDED THEY COULD PLAY JUDGE, JURY AND EXECUTIONER-- AS IF WE DESERVED LESS THAN COMMON HOODLUMS SIMPLY BECAUSE OUR HORIZONS ARE WIDER.
I DID WHAT HAD TO BE DONE!
I MADE THE HARD CHOICES THAT NO ONE ELSE WAS WILLING TO MAKE! I SAVED AS MANY OF US AS I COULD!
DO YOU UNDERSTAND?
THEY'RE NOT THE HEROES! I'M THE HERO!
I AM.

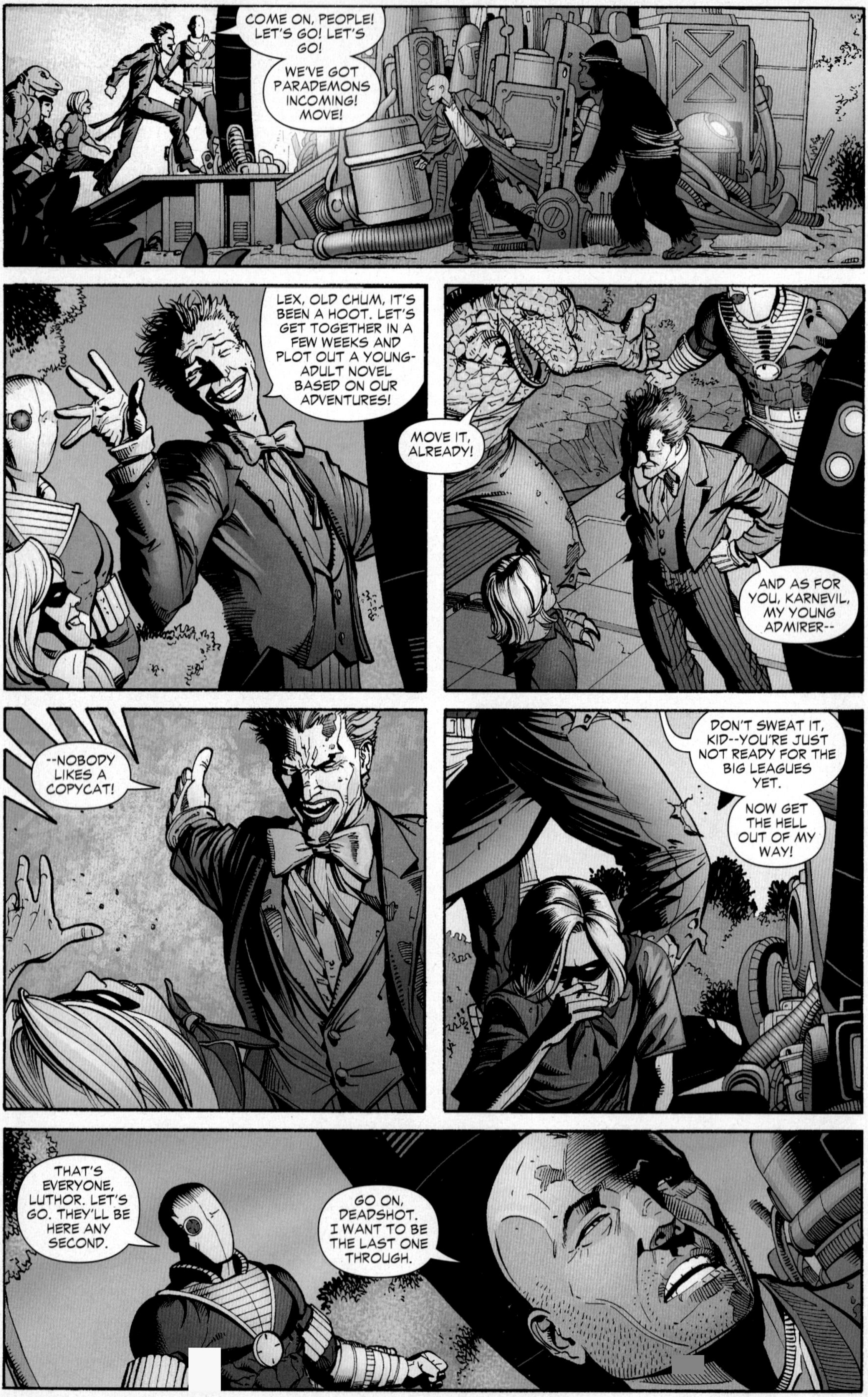
COME ON, PEOPLE! LET'S GO! LET'S GO!
WE'VE GOT PARADEMONS INCOMING! MOVE!
LEX, OLD CHUM, IT'S BEEN A HOOT. LET'S GET TOGETHER IN A FEW WEEKS AND PLOT OUT A YOUNG-ADULT NOVEL BASED ON OUR ADVENTURES!
MOVE IT, ALREADY!
AND AS FOR YOU, KARNEVIL, MY YOUNG ADMIRER--
--NOBODY LIKES A COPYCAT!
DON'T SWEAT IT, KID--YOU'RE JUST NOT READY FOR THE BIG LEAGUES YET.
NOW GET THE HELL OUT OF MY WAY!
THAT'S EVERYONE, LUTHOR. LET'S GO. THEY'LL BE HERE ANY SECOND.
GO ON, DEADSHOT. I WANT TO BE THE LAST ONE THROUGH.

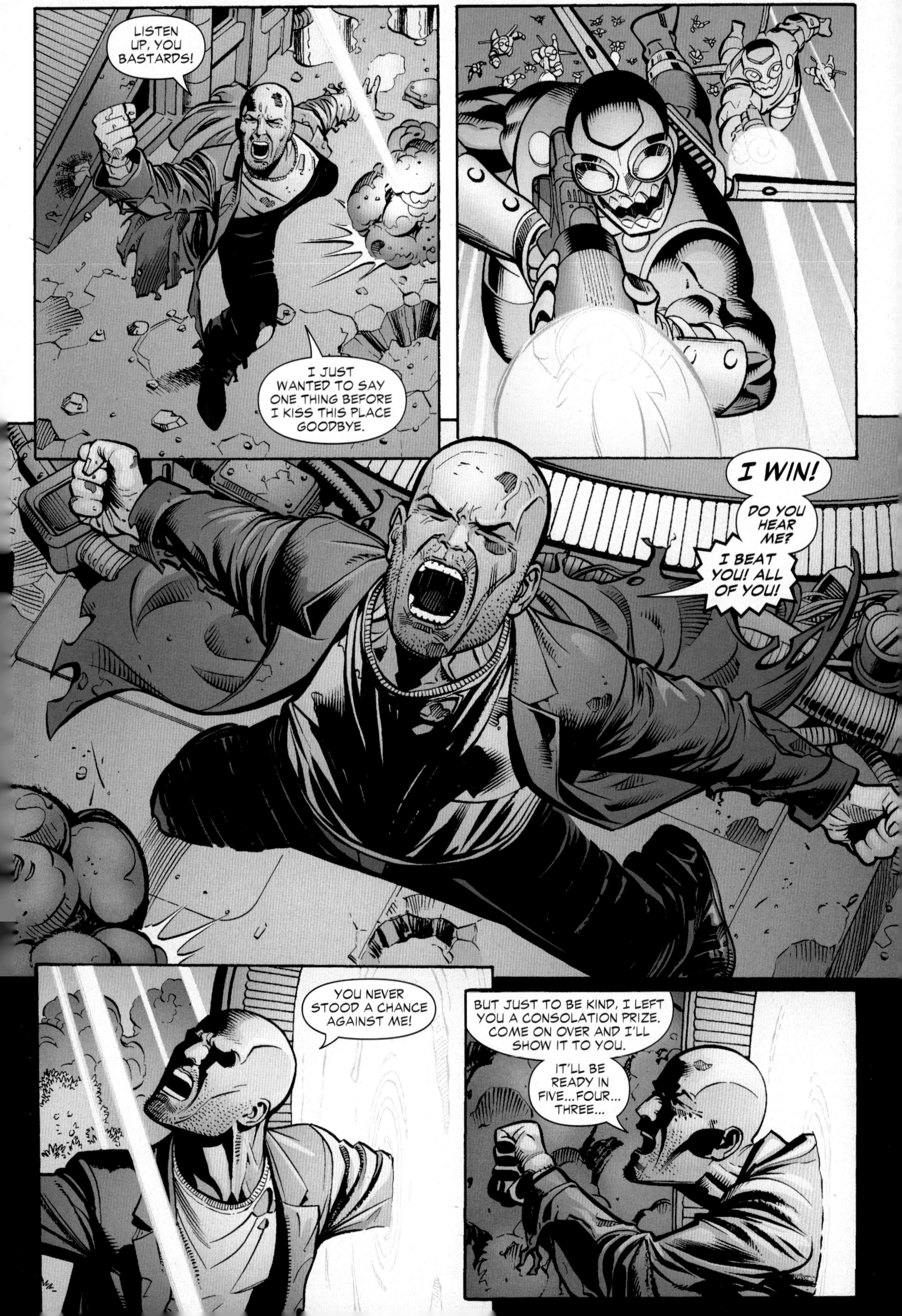
LISTEN UP, YOU BASTARDS!
I JUST WANTED TO SAY ONE THING BEFORE I KISS THIS PLACE GOODBYE.
I WIN!
DO YOU HEAR ME?
I BEAT YOU! ALL OF YOU!
YOU NEVER STOOD A CHANCE AGAINST ME!
BUT JUST TO BE KIND, I LEFT YOU A CONSOLATION PRIZE. COME ON OVER AND I'LL SHOW IT TO YOU.
IT'LL BE READY IN FIVE...FOUR... THREE...

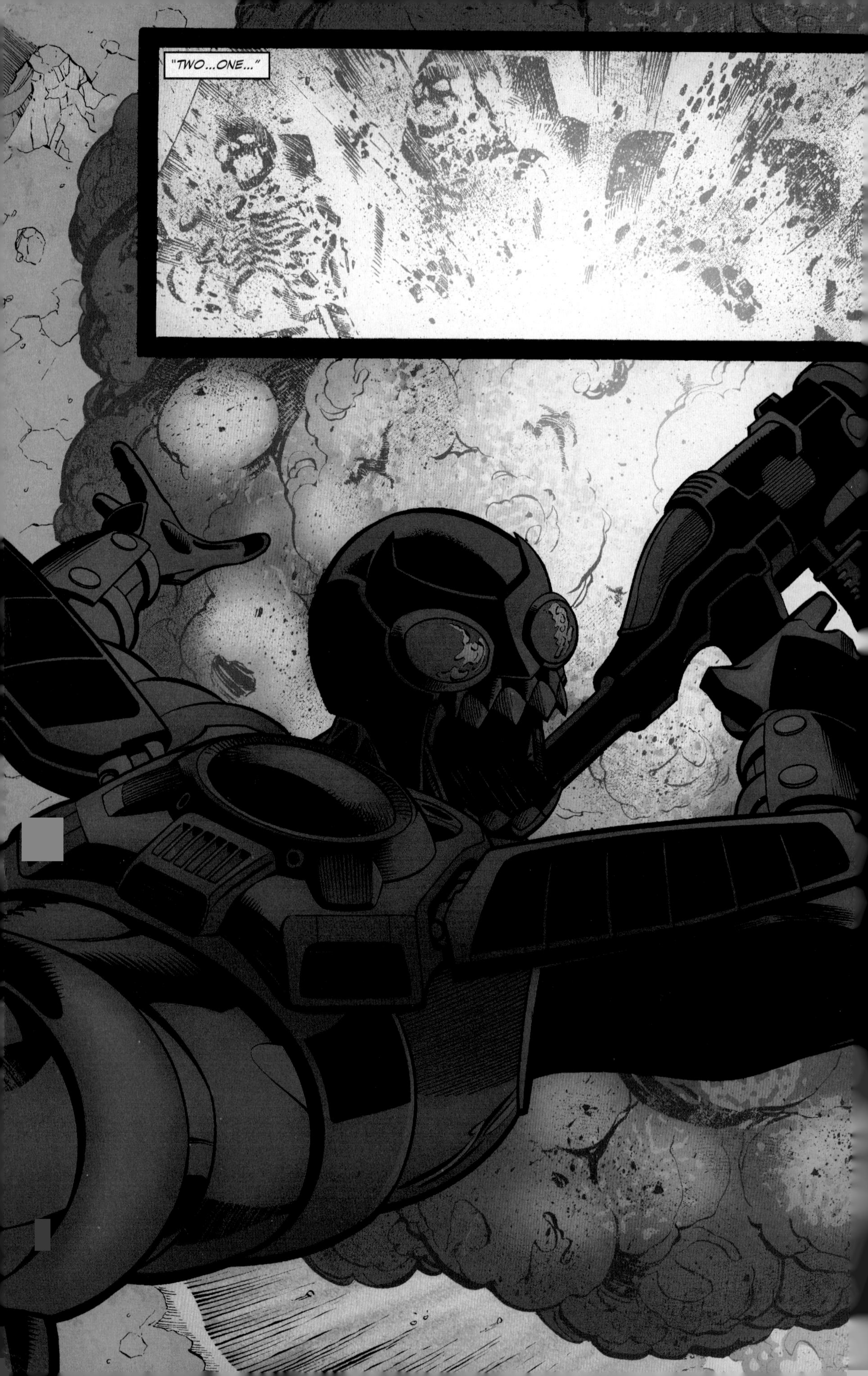
"TWO...ONE..."

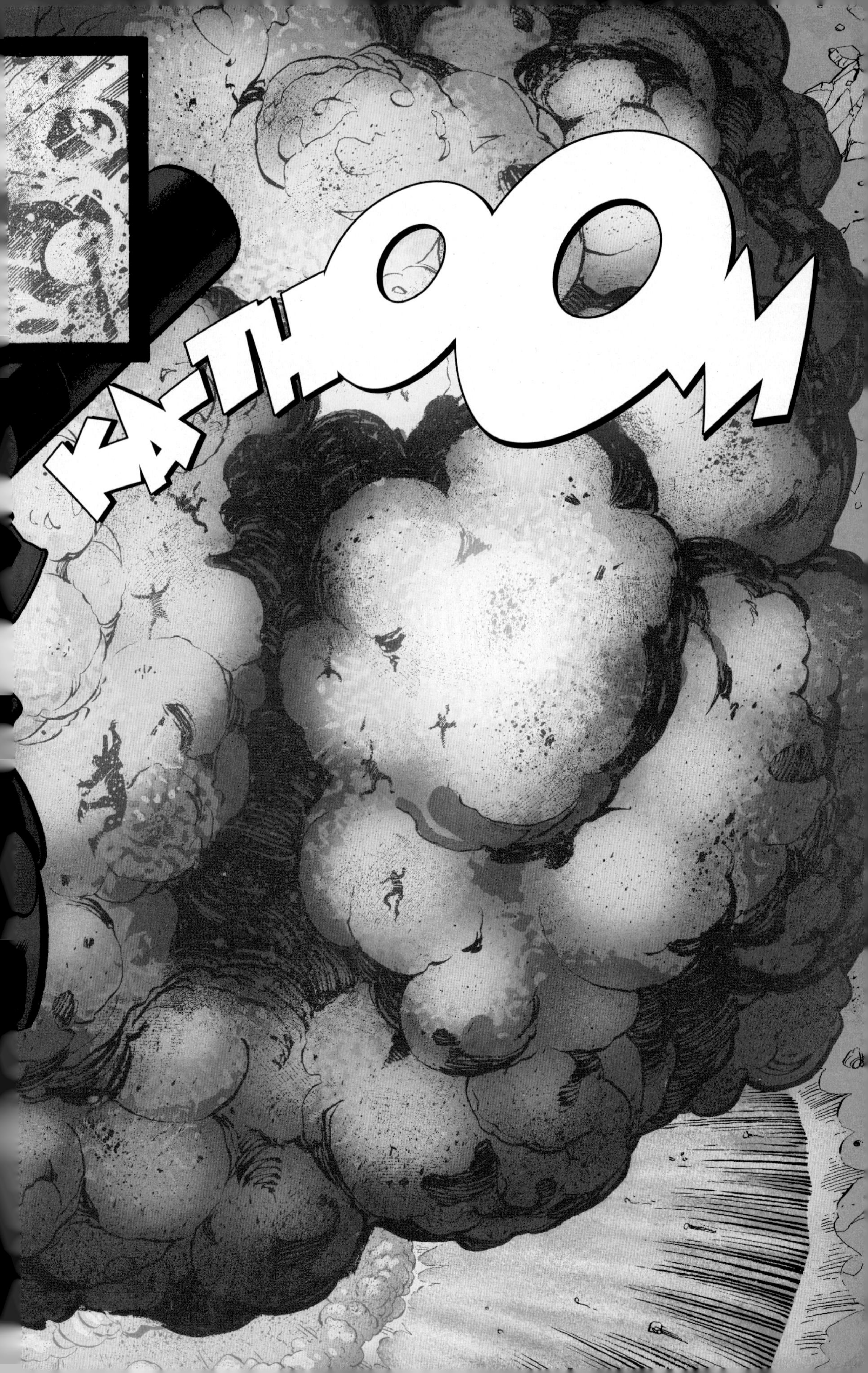
KA-THOOM

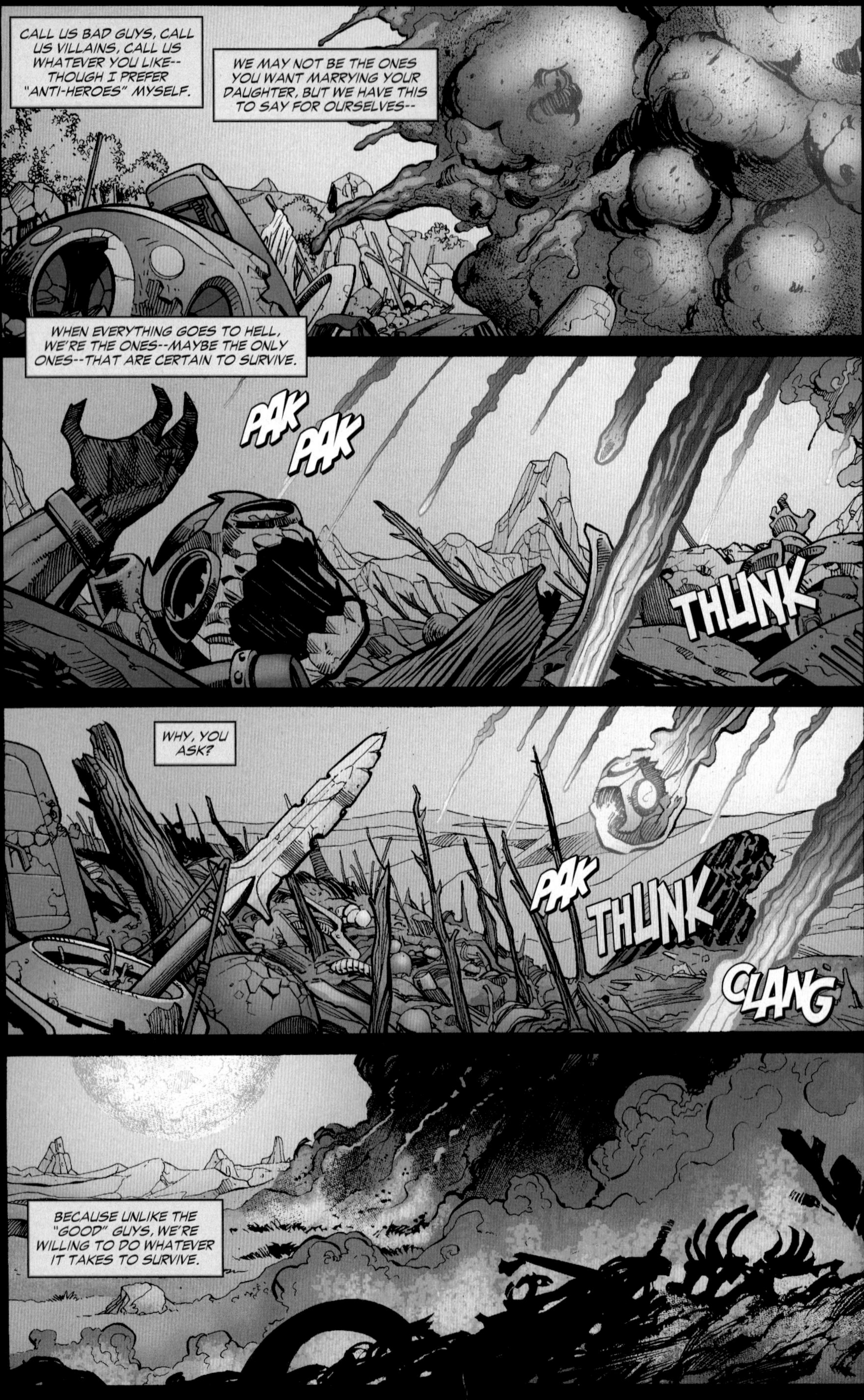
CALL US BAD GUYS, CALL US VILLAINS, CALL US WHATEVER YOU LIKE-- THOUGH I PREFER "ANTI-HEROES" MYSELF.
WE MAY NOT BE THE ONES YOU WANT MARRYING YOUR DAUGHTER, BUT WE HAVE THIS TO SAY FOR OURSELVES--
WHEN EVERYTHING GOES TO HELL, WE'RE THE ONES--MAYBE THE ONLY ONES--THAT ARE CERTAIN TO SURVIVE.
PAK
PAK
THUNK
WHY, YOU ASK?
PAK
THUNK
CLANG
BECAUSE UNLIKE THE "GOOD" GUYS, WE'RE WILLING TO DO WHATEVER IT TAKES TO SURVIVE.

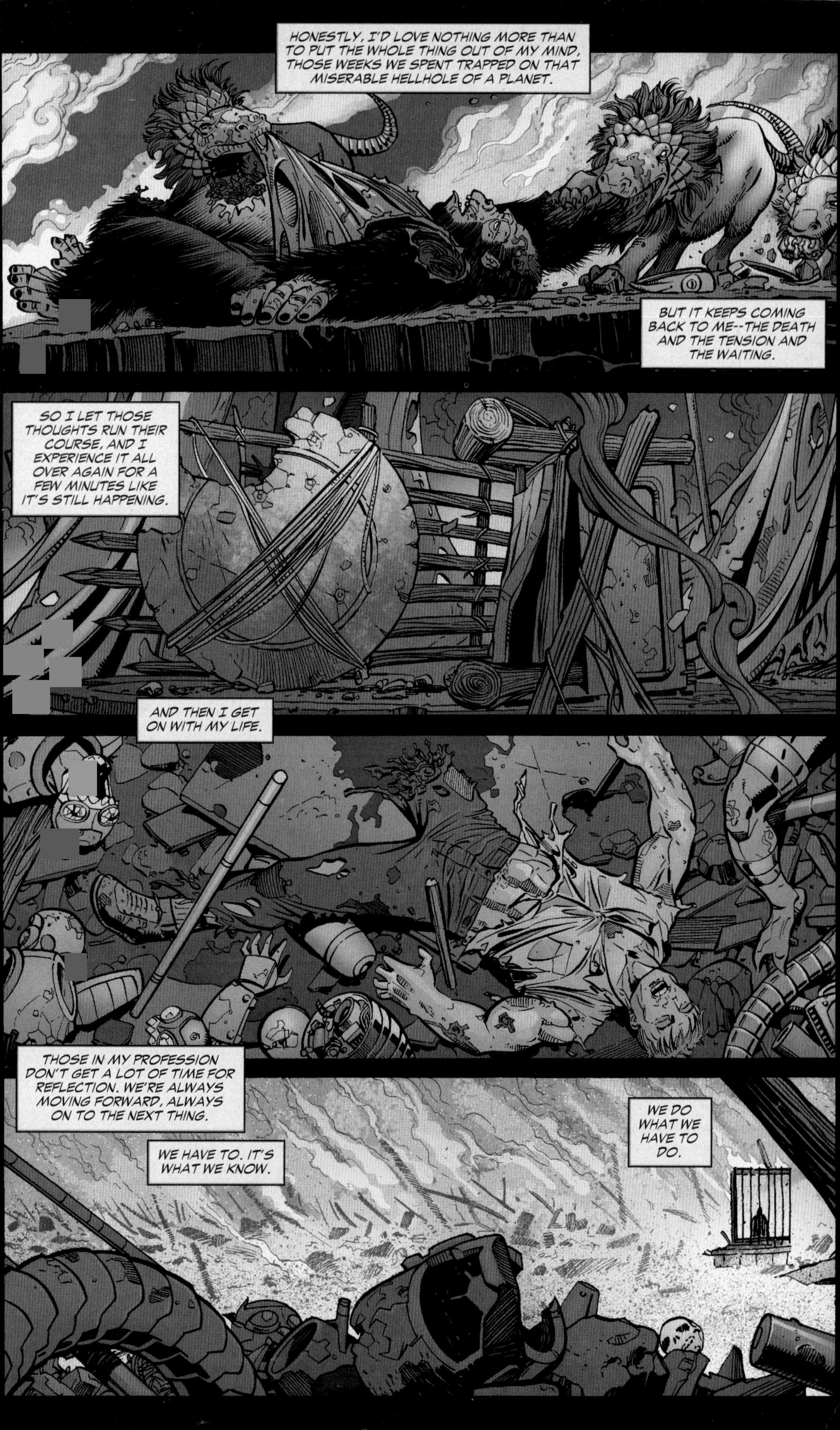
HONESTLY, I'D LOVE NOTHING MORE THAN TO PUT THE WHOLE THING OUT OF MY MIND, THOSE WEEKS WE SPENT TRAPPED ON THAT MISERABLE HELLHOLE OF A PLANET.
BUT IT KEEPS COMING BACK TO ME--THE DEATH AND THE TENSION AND THE WAITING.
SO I LET THOSE THOUGHTS RUN THEIR COURSE, AND I EXPERIENCE IT ALL OVER AGAIN FOR A FEW MINUTES LIKE IT'S STILL HAPPENING.
AND THEN I GET ON WITH MY LIFE.
THOSE IN MY PROFESSION DON'T GET A LOT OF TIME FOR REFLECTION. WE'RE ALWAYS MOVING FORWARD, ALWAYS ON TO THE NEXT THING.
WE HAVE TO. IT'S WHAT WE KNOW.
WE DO WHAT WE HAVE TO DO.

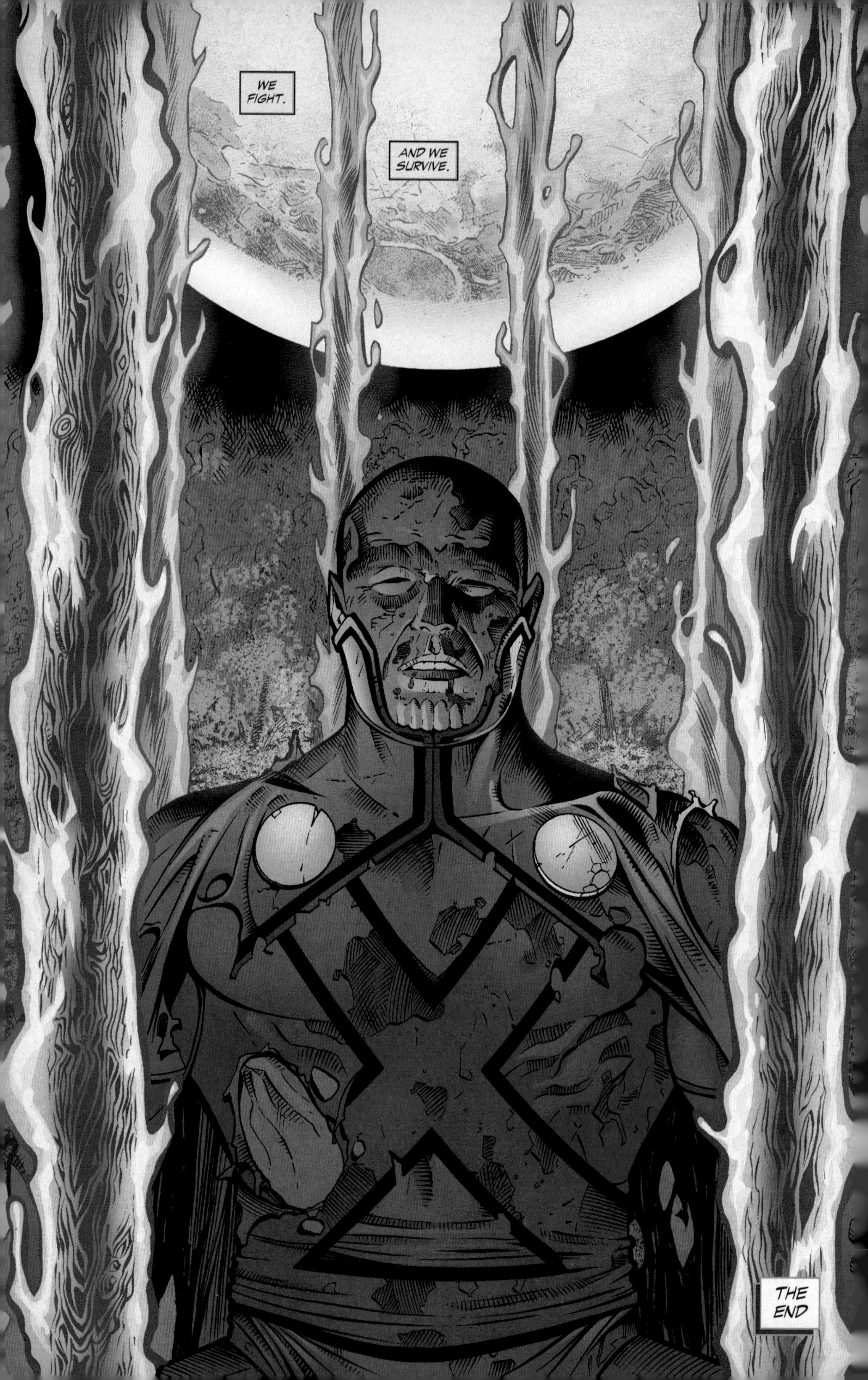
WE FIGHT.
AND WE SURVIVE.
THE END

SALVATION RUN #1 VARIANT COVER ART BY JOE CORRONEY

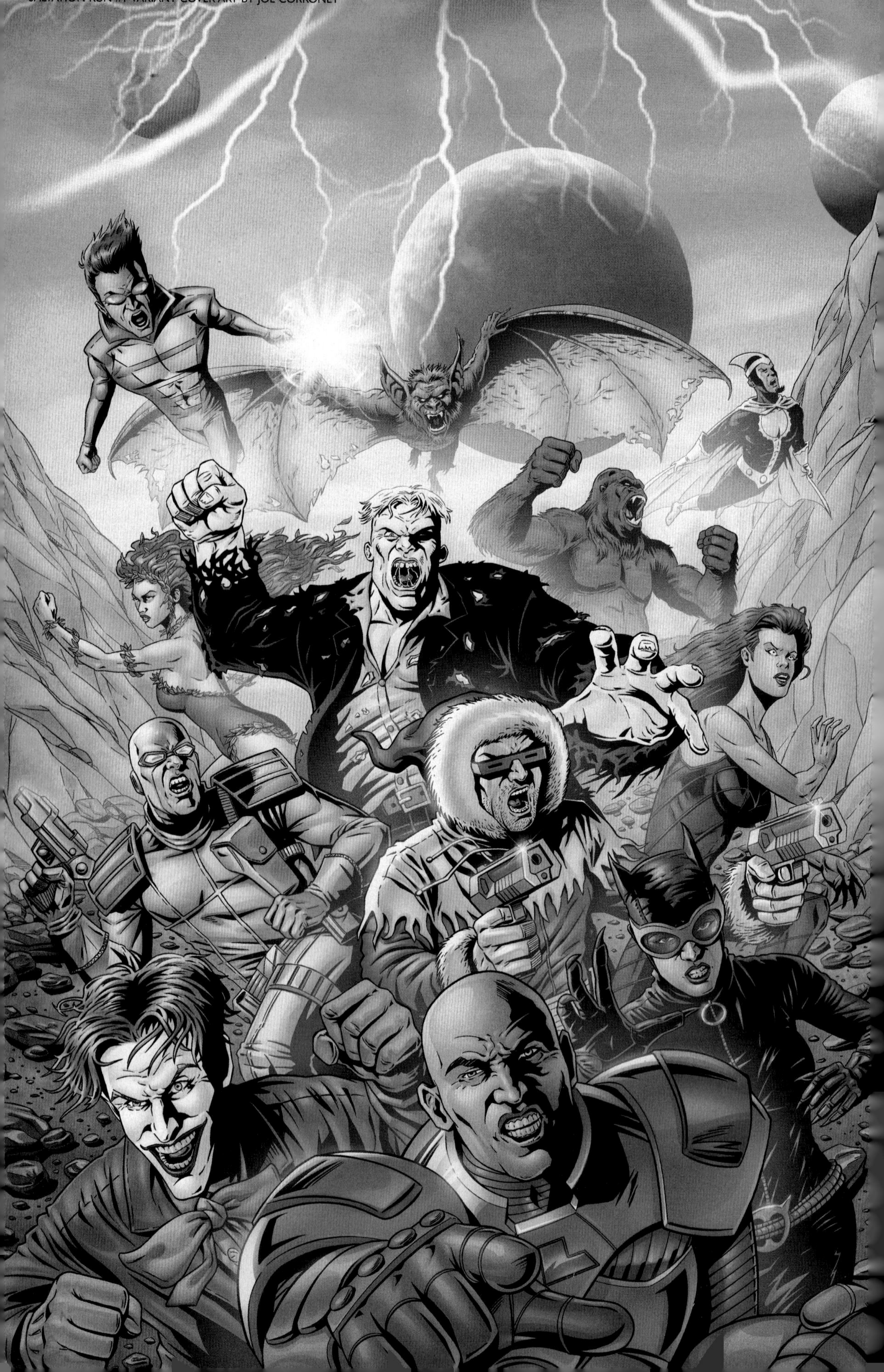

SALVATION RUN #3 UNUSED COVER ART BY SEAN CHEN & WALDEN WONG, WITH JOHN KALISZ

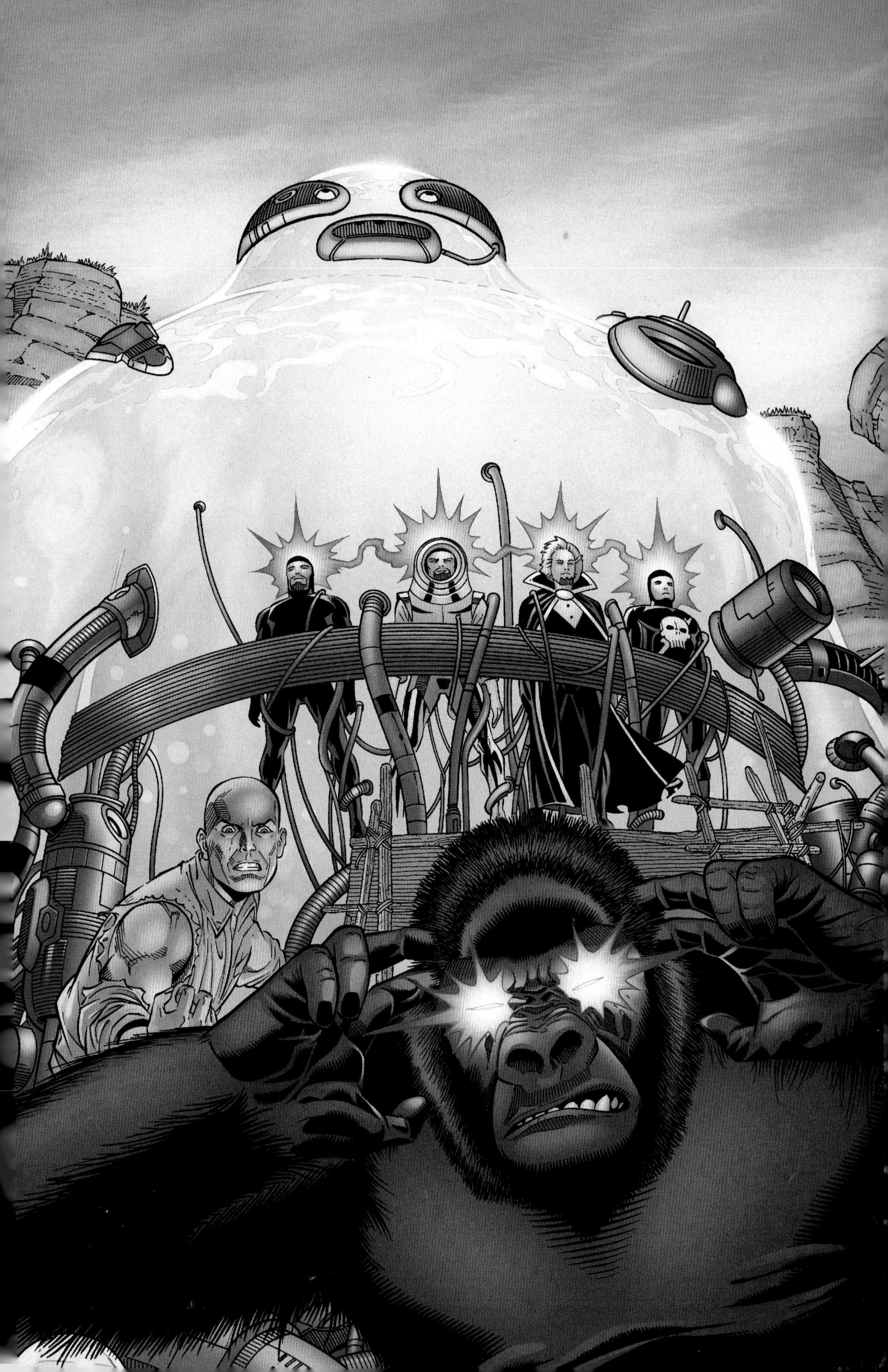

SALVATION RUN #7 VARIANT COVER ART BY NEAL ADAMS, WITH MOOSE BAUMAN

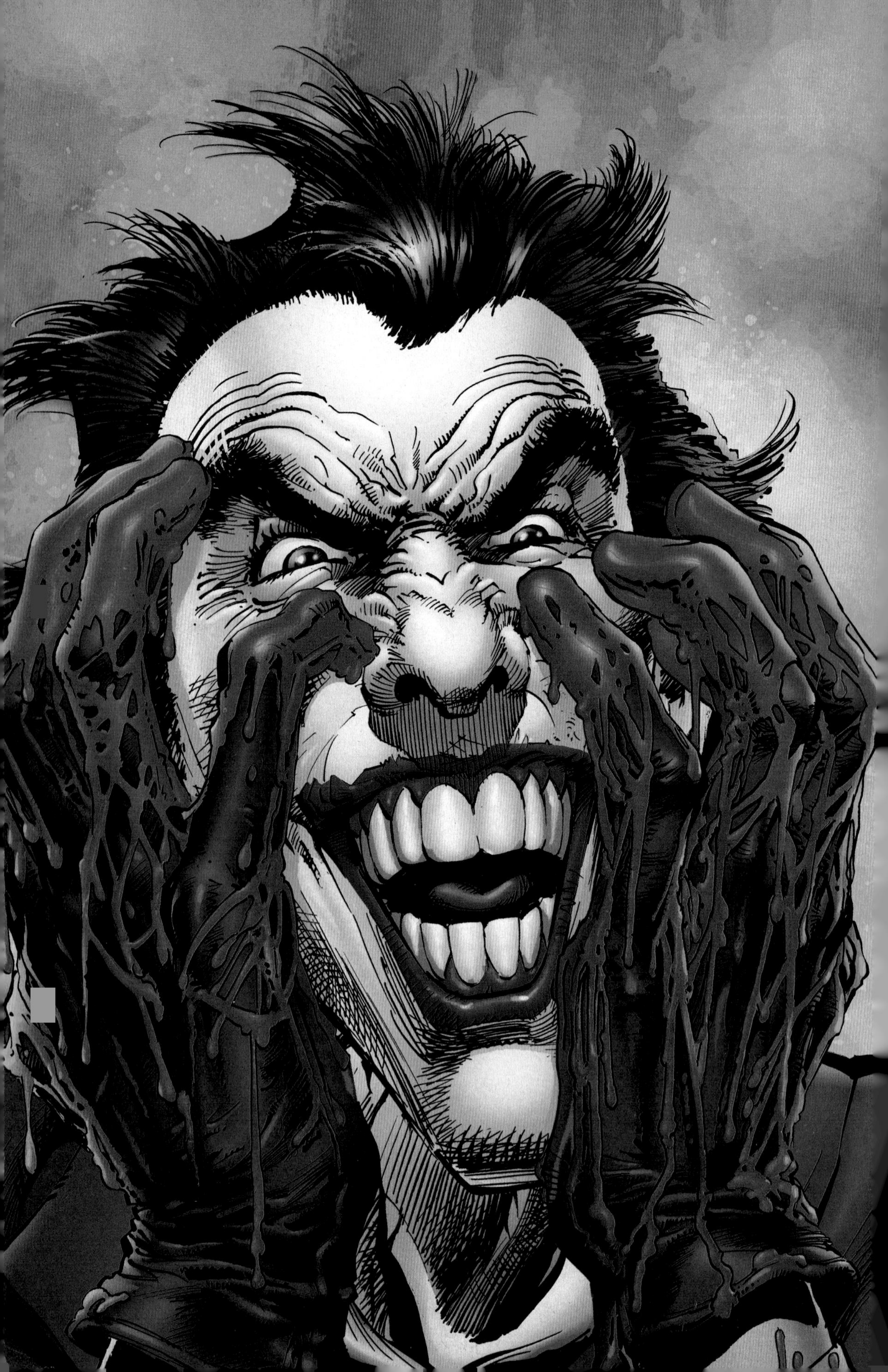